Beginning XNA 2.0 Game Programming
From Novice to Professional

Alexandre Lobão, Bruno Evangelista, and
José Antonio Leal de Farias

Apress®

Beginning XNA 2.0 Game Programming: From Novice to Professional

Copyright © 2008 by Alexandre Lobão, Bruno Evangelista, José Antonio Leal de Farias

ISBN-13 (pbk): 978-1-59059-924-2

ISBN-10 (pbk): 1-59059-924-1

ISBN-13 (electronic): 978-1-4302-0512-8

ISBN-10 (electronic): 1-4302-0512-1

Printed and bound in the United States of America 9 8 7 6 5 4 3 2 1

Trademarked names may appear in this book. Rather than use a trademark symbol with every occurrence of a trademarked name, we use the names only in an editorial fashion and to the benefit of the trademark owner, with no intention of infringement of the trademark.

Lead Editor: Ewan Buckingham
Technical Reviewer: Fabio Claudio Ferracchiati
Editorial Board: Clay Andres, Steve Anglin, Ewan Buckingham, Tony Campbell, Gary Cornell,
    Jonathan Gennick, Matthew Moodie, Joseph Ottinger, Jeffrey Pepper, Frank Pohlmann,
    Ben Renow-Clarke, Dominic Shakeshaft, Matt Wade, Tom Welsh
Senior Project Manager: Kylie Johnston
Copy Editor: Susannah Davidson Pfalzer
Associate Production Director: Kari Brooks-Copony
Senior Production Editor: Laura Cheu
Compositor: Dina Quan
Proofreader: April Eddy
Indexer: Becky Hornyak
Artist: April Milne
Cover Designer: Kurt Krames
Manufacturing Director: Tom Debolski

Distributed to the book trade worldwide by Springer-Verlag New York, Inc., 233 Spring Street, 6th Floor, New York, NY 10013. Phone 1-800-SPRINGER, fax 201-348-4505, e-mail orders-ny@springer-sbm.com, or visit http://www.springeronline.com.

For information on translations, please contact Apress directly at 2855 Telegraph Avenue, Suite 600, Berkeley, CA 94705. Phone 510-549-5930, fax 510-549-5939, e-mail info@apress.com, or visit http://www.apress.com.

Apress and friends of ED books may be purchased in bulk for academic, corporate, or promotional use. eBook versions and licenses are also available for most titles. For more information, reference our Special Bulk Sales–eBook Licensing web page at http://www.apress.com/info/bulksales.

The source code for this book is available to readers at http://www.apress.com.

Contents at a Glance

Contents

■CHAPTER 8   Rendering Pipeline, Shaders, and Effects

■CHAPTER 9   Lights, Camera, Transformations!

Foreword

It's hard to believe the runaway popularity XNA has achieved in the short period of time since it was released in late 2006. At that time, I got together with a couple friends to check out (with some trepidation, I must confess) whether games really could be written in managed code. We were very excited, and everyone wanted to know if you could get the same benefits from writing games using managed code as you do when creating standard Windows programs. We knew people in the game programming community were worried about managed code's execution speed, and many people simply didn't believe a "real" game could be created using XNA. As time passed, though, more and more people began to realize the truth: there are a great number of benefits to using managed code, and the performance concerns are exaggerated.

You haven't experienced the full potential of the Xbox 360 or, indeed, Windows until you've created your own homegrown games for these innovative systems—and with the XNA Framework, the only limit is your imagination! From an educational perspective, due to its simplicity, XNA is also a great choice for anyone wanting to learn or teach the C# programming language. Game development offers an excellent common ground for collaboration between computer science students and their counterparts in other disciplines such music, the arts, and design. In fact, XNA has become such an important technology for Microsoft that the company has decided to create a new game development category in 2008 for the famous Imagine Cup (http://www.imaginecup.com), Microsoft's largest student contest.

With the release of the XNA Framework 2.0, I have again become excited about the future of game development. And when I see a book like this, which explains the basics of game programming and XNA in a clear and simple style, I get even more excited, and I hope you will be as well. Whether you've never tried to write a game before, or you are simply looking for advice on the best way to do things in XNA, I think you'll be happy with what you find: after reading this book you'll be able to apply your newfound knowledge to write your own XNA cross-platform games.

I'm waiting to see what the ever-growing community of XNA game developers will create next. It's exciting to think that we'll probably see games that break all the rules of the current gaming genres, because with a vibrant community comes innovation, and with innovation comes truly unique ideas.

I look forward to the games of the future—I hope you'll be the person writing them!

Amintas Lopes Neto
Academic Relations Manager, Microsoft Brazil

About the Authors

 **ALEXANDRE LOBÃO** is a passionate man. His first passion was reading, starting with large books—Mark Twain, Érico Veríssimo, Jules Verne, Monteiro Lobato, Alexandre Dumas, and others—when he was seven. When he was twelve, he discovered his two next passions: playing and creating games (by that time on his first Apple computer), and writing.

Many years later—he's about forty now—these passions flourish. Now he is a teacher of academic game development courses, has written four books on the topic, and has participated in some Brazilian game development contests both as a contestant and as a judge. He has also written short stories, children's books, and young adult books, and in 2008 he released his first romance, *The Name of the Eagle*, currently only available in Portuguese. And, of course, he still loves to read, from Ken Follett to Paulo Coelho.

His ultimate passions—starting in 1995 and still burning now—are his wife, Waléria, and his kids, Natália and Rafael.

Alexandre believes that lives need passion to be lived entirely, and hopes that this book helps light this passion in readers' hearts. You can find his work at http:// www.AlexandreLobao.com.

 **BRUNO EVANGELISTA** is a game developer with a passion for computer graphics. Bruno started programming when he was ten—his father taught him how to write programs in BASIC—and he always dreamed of creating games instead of just playing them.

Bruno was a graphics programmer at VirsaT, where he worked on the Peixis game, (winner of the JogosBR 2006—the Brazilian national contest of complete games); having previously worked as a software engineer at Olympya. He has also worked on some projects and game demos developed with C++, C#, and Java using DirectX, OpenGL, and XNA.

Besides his professional experience, Bruno has hosted courses and tutorials about XNA, OpenGL, and shader development at conferences and universities, such as the Brazilian Symposium on Computer Graphics and Image Processing (SIBGRAPI), Brazilian Symposia on Games and Digital Entertainment (SBGAMES), Gamefest Brazil, Federal University of Minas Gerais (UFMG), and others.

Today, 22-year-old Bruno is an avid XNA developer who has taken second and third place, respectively, in the 2006 and 2007 XNA Challenge Brazil competitions.

Bruno received his Bachelor of Science degree in computer science from PUC-MG in 2006 and is currently a Master of Science student in computer science at UFMG. He lives in Belo Horizonte, Brazil. You can find his work at http://www.BrunoEvangelista.com.

 ◼**JOSÉ ANTONIO LEAL DE FARIAS** has been a game programmer since he acquired his first computer in 1985, when he tried to draw aliens on an 80×25 pixel screen. After obtaining a degree in Computer Science, he established one of the first game companies in Brazil in 1997, called Hardcode Entertainment. He has worked on many diverse gaming projects in Europe and the US. In 2004 he received the Most Valuable Professional award from Microsoft for his contributions to the Brazilian coding community. In 2006 he established the Sharp Games community, devoted to studying and spreading advice about the XNA platform. You can find the portal for Sharp Games at http://www.sharpgames.net.

About the Technical Reviewer

FABIO CLAUDIO FERRACCHIATI is a senior consultant and a senior analyst/developer using Microsoft technologies. He works for Brain Force (http://www.brainforce.com) in its Italian branch (http://www.brainforce.it). He is a Microsoft Certified Solution Developer for .NET, a Microsoft Certified Application Developer for .NET, a Microsoft Certified Professional, and a prolific author and technical reviewer. Over the past ten years he's written articles for Italian and international magazines and coauthored more than ten books on a variety of computer topics. You can read his LINQ blog at http://www.ferracchiati.com.

Acknowledgments

I would like to thank David Weller—although he could not help with this book—for being a great buddy and a source of inspiration for me and for many guys from the academic and indie game development communities. And a special thanks to Amintas Neto, from Microsoft Brazil, for his great work fostering XNA development at Brazilian universities.

Alexandre Lobão

I would like to thank God for his countless blessings and for giving me the opportunity to work on this great book; my parents Kathia and Gledson, who always motivated me to do my best; my stepfather Claudio, my stepmother Celida, and my brothers for all their support; and a special thanks to my girlfriend Helenice for all these great years together.

Also a special thanks to Alessandro Silva, a great friend and game developer who studied with me during my university years; Carlos Augusto, who contributed some assets for the XNA TPS game; and Francisco Ardisson, who helped translate some parts of the book.

In this long journey I had a few mentors and guides who helped me to get here and who I cannot forget to mention: Theldo Franqueira, Marcelo Nery, Fabio Policarpo, Rosilane Mota, Luiz Chaimowicz, Renato Ferreira, Esteban Clua, Fabio Tirelo, and Harlen Batagelo. Thank you for all I have learned from you!

Bruno Evangelista

First, I'd like to thank all the Sharp Games community for the encouragement and suggestions they provided me, and especially my friends Shinji and Amintas Neto for everything they've done for XNA in Brazil.

I also need to say thanks to Microsoft; to its MVP program; to Leonardo Tolomelli, my MVP lead; and to all other MVPs in Brazil who always are a source of inspiration for me.

Also a special thanks to my wife Cecir for having enormous love and patience with me when this book was being planned and written; to my four-year-old son Leonardo for his critical sense of what is a good game; and to my parents for continuing to love a son who read books on assembly language when the other boys read *Spiderman* comics.

José Antonio Leal de Farias

Introduction

According to the point-of-sale information compiled by NPD Group (http://www.NPD. com), a leading US marketing information provider, computer and video game sales totaled more than seven billion dollars in each of the last three years.

The video game software industry is accountable for more than six billion dollars of this total. If we include portable and console hardware, software, and accessory sales, in 2006 the video game industry generated revenue of close to twelve and a half billion dollars, exceeding the previous record of around two billion dollars. By the time we completed this book—early 2008—no statistics were available yet for 2007, but there's no expectation of lower figures.

With Microsoft XNA, for the first time ever a nonprofessional game developer can create single and multiplayer games that can run on both PCs and the Xbox 360 console.

These figures alone might be reason enough to interest someone in learning XNA and becoming a game developer, trying to get a share of a market that's more profitable than the Hollywood movie-making one.

Although, let's be fair and not hide the facts. Unfortunately, there are few openings in this area: about one game programming job per every thousand "real life" programming jobs. Worse than that, on average, the game industry pays its programmers less than other industries do.

After digesting these facts, if you still think that working as a game developer might be cool and rewarding, then this book is for you! We also have some good news: with Microsoft's promise to open its LIVE market, allowing anyone to sell its games to other LIVE members, there may be a potential ten-million-user market (January 2008 figures) for your homemade games soon!

This book has the goal of introducing you to XNA, the new cross-platform game programming framework from Microsoft, and also presenting you with basic concepts from the game programming industry, showing how these concepts map to the XNA world. The samples in this book, which include some complete games, will give you the knowledge you need to create your own simple games.

That said, this book won't present you with hardcore math and physics or dig into advanced programming concepts, which are indeed needed if you really want to become a professional hardcore game developer. Instead, this book is a first step into this industry, presenting an overview of most of the things you have to know, giving you the ability to create a roadmap for further studies in this area.

More than that, this book intends to be fun! One of the most interesting things you'll see in the game programming industry is the unmatched passion of the people who work in it. If there's one goal for this book, it's to light this passion in novices' hearts with simple explanations and, especially, with cool game examples, so this fire can keep burning in the years to come.

After all, this is a book written with such passion!

What Is XNA?

XNA is a play on words. It stands for "It's Not an Acronym." Microsoft's world is so full of acronyms that it decided to create a name that looks like an acronym, but isn't, just for fun.

But XNA is much more than that. The innovative concept of bringing to the average Joe the power to create his own games for the Xbox 360 is a great technological innovation, which comes with many efforts from Microsoft to establish an active community for game creators (joining both the Windows and Xbox 360 game programming communities) and also to establish programs in the academic area to support institutions that wish to create courses using retail Xbox 360 consoles.

These efforts become obvious when we notice that Microsoft XNA Game Studio 2.0 can be downloaded at no charge from Microsoft's site, at http://www.microsoft.com/XNA. Microsoft also offers free game content, including video tutorials, starter kits (ready-made games, which can be freely customized), samples, and other support content at the XNA Creator's Club: http://creators.XNA.com.

The last step in making Microsoft LIVE known as the "YouTube for games" is the ability to upload the games you created to Xbox LIVE and distribute (or even sell) your games to anyone in the world with a LIVE connection. No wonder the nonprofessional game programmer community is so excited, with XNA Game Studio launching and the frequent updates with new content on the XNA Creator's Club site!

The greatest secret behind XNA's success is that it's easy—much easier than any console programming application programming interface (API), and also easier than any Windows game programming API, because of the abstraction it provides for details that you need to worry about in other APIs. XNA uses the same integrated development environment (IDE)—XNA Game Studio Express—and the same framework for developing games both for Windows and Xbox 360 platforms, which ensures a high degree of compatibility. However, there are differences in the lower layer. The Xbox 360 console runs a compact version of the .NET Framework, so you must be careful: not all functions available in Windows will run on the Xbox 360.

We'll address all this in more detail as we progress through the book, but you can always find the latest information about XNA architecture at Microsoft's XNA site and at the XNA Creator's Club site.

Who This Book Is For

This book is targeted to anyone who wants to start developing games, both for the Windows and Xbox 360 platforms. It can be used as a first step on a long road toward a game development career, or can simply be used by those who have a great idea for a simple game—the next Tetris—and always wanted to have the basic knowledge, straight and simple, of how to create games.

Briefly, this book is targeted to those who want to have fun by creating or modifying simple games, sharing them with friends, and playing them on Windows, Xbox 360, or both.

How This Book Is Structured

This book is organized so you can start learning generic game programming concepts, such as common gaming terminology and math, see how these concepts are implemented in XNA, and then apply these concepts to real, simple games. We believe that this organization improves your learning, so you'll be ready to create your own XNA games after finishing the book.

Chapter 1, "Game Planning and Programming Basics"

In this chapter, you'll learn important game planning concepts that will help you create great games, and also some general game programming concepts and how these concepts map to XNA. You'll also create your first XNA program.

Chapter 2, "2-D Graphics, Audio, and Input Basics"

In this chapter you'll familiarize yourself with some fundamental concepts related to 2-D game programming, along with some samples that will make you easily understand how the XNA Framework implements these concepts. You'll also discover how to use sound and the Xbox 360 controller in your applications.

Chapter 3, "Creating Your First 2-D Game"

This chapter is where the real fun begins! You'll find out how to put together the ideas you saw in the last chapters to create a complete game, Rock Rain. Besides tips on how to improve this simple but addictive game, you'll learn details you need to pay attention to when moving games to the Xbox 360.

Chapter 4, "Improving Your First 2-D Game"

You're still in the 2-D programming world; in this chapter you'll explore other concepts such as creating menus, moving through game screens, managing players' scores, and more.

Chapter 5, "Basics of Game Networking"

In this chapter you'll learn about one of the most exciting features of XNA 2.0: the ability to create network-enabled games, allowing you to connect different machines, directly or through LIVE.

Chapter 6, "Rock Rain Live!"

Getting back to your 2-D game, you'll now learn how to create a multiplayer version, including a new opening scene that allows players to create or join a match on other machines.

Chapter 7, "3-D Game Programming Basics"

Expanding the concepts you learned in the previous chapters, this chapter will introduce you to the fundamentals of 3-D game programming. You'll learn how to create a 3-D scene, load and manipulate 3-D objects, move the camera, and everything else you need to know to start digging into virtual 3-D worlds.

Chapter 8, "Rendering Pipeline, Shaders, and Effects"

Getting deeper into the 3-D world, you'll learn more details about the Content Pipeline and the use of effects and shaders in XNA, paving the way to create your first 3-D game.

Chapter 9, "Lights, Camera, Transformations!"

In this chapter, you'll create the base objects used in any 3-D game, which will help you manage lights and cameras, and apply transformations to your 3-D objects.

Chapter 10, "Generating a Terrain"

Every 3-D game that uses a landscape needs a terrain, and in this chapter we'll present the steps for creating, adjusting, and drawing the terrain, and also how to calculate object collisions with the terrain.

Chapter 11, "Skeletal Animation"

XNA 2.0 doesn't offer default support to read and play animations created by the modelers along with the 3-D models. In this chapter you'll learn how to create a custom model processor to read and play animation data.

Chapter 12, "Creating a Third-Person Shooter Game"

In this chapter you put it all together, using the knowledge from the last few chapters to create a simple 3-D third-person shooter.

Chapter 13, "Closing Words"

As we said, this book is fun, and includes a lot of information about game programming, but it's only a first step. In these last few pages, the authors present the advice they always give to their students when finishing a game programming course.

Prerequisites

Before you continue to the first chapter, be sure to download and install the latest version of XNA, which is easy to find in the Downloads section at `http://www.microsoft.com/XNA`. We also recommend that you download the DirectX Software Development Kit (SDK), which comes with some content you can use when learning XNA. Don't forget, also, to download and install the XNA Starter Kits and samples at `http://creators.XNA.com`. All these tools and samples are free to download and use.

If you don't have a copy of Microsoft Visual Studio, you must also download a free copy of Microsoft Visual C# Express, whose download link can also be found at `http://www.microsoft.com/XNA`.

Book Code and Errata

Although you can maximize your learning by typing the book code while you're reading, sometimes you simply can't wait to see the code running. If you're in a hurry, look for the book name at the Apress site, `http://www.apress.com`: all the book code is available for downloading.

Please note that, especially in the later chapters, some repetitive parts of the code were omitted to help you focus on the most relevant parts. The complete code listings are available at `http://www.apress.com`.

Although Apress and the authors make their best efforts to ensure that there are no errors in the book code or text, sometimes a bug appears. You can always find the most recent code and any text or code errata at the Apress site, http://www.apress.com. All you have to do is to look for the book name.

Contacting the Authors

Alexandre Lobão is available from his personal web site, at http://www.AlexandreLobao.com, which includes all his works as an author, comics writer, and movie script writer.

Bruno Evangelista also maintains a personal web site, with his game programming projects, including downloadable content, at http://www.BrunoEvangelista.com.

José Leal is the head of a top Brazilian C# programming community, Sharp Games, available at http://www.sharpgames.net.

■ ■ ■

CHAPTER 1

Game Planning and Programming Basics

In this chapter we present some fundamental concepts of planning and programming games that you must keep in mind when creating games. We won't discuss everything about planning a game, or present all general concepts regarding game programming. However, after reading this chapter you'll understand the basic ideas behind creating a game and how XNA makes game development easy for you.

Planning the Game

The effort involved in creating a good game starts way before the coding phase. Somewhat undervalued by nonprofessional game programmers, the planning is the most important phase of your game development project. That's because in this phase you define the guidelines for all the next stages.

Before thinking about which game you'll create, you have to choose your *target market*, because this choice will define the direction for your entire game development effort.

NPD Group, in its research, divides the market into six categories: heavy gamers (who constantly play games and are responsible for most of the market sales), avid console gamers (who buy mainly console games, and might play console games many hours a day), mass market gamers (who usually only buy "blockbuster" games), prefer portable gamers (as the category name says, they prefer playing games using portable devices), secondary gamers (who usually don't buy games, and play games bought by other people), and infrequent gamers (who play games every so often).

We won't provide an extensive study of these segments, but let's highlight some significant points about the two "edge" categories:

- *Infrequent gamers*: These gamers are also called "casual players." Games for this player category must be easy to play, with no complex storyline, and must provide challenging but brief levels, to give the player a feeling of accomplishment in short matches. Games for such a market usually don't rely on highly detailed 3-D graphics or extraordinary sound effects, and include card games (poker, hearts, solitaire, and so on), puzzles (Tetris, Sudoku, crosswords, and so on), board games (mah-jongg, chess, checkers, and so on), and similar. Don't be fooled about such games: although they might be easier to develop, they rely on balanced levels and game play to sustain the appeal for the players, which can be hard to achieve.

- *Heavy gamers*: This group, also called "hardcore gamers," takes playing games seriously. They are usually moved by difficult challenges and a good storyline that helps the players immerse themselves in the game world. Games for such players usually include extremely detailed 3-D environments, engaging background music and sound effects, and a long game play with many challenges.

Once you choose the target market, the next logical step is to define the game genre. There are many divisions of game genres, but sticking with NPD Group's research approach, the best-selling game genres are presented in Table 1-1.

Table 1-1. *Best-Selling Computer and Video Games by Units Sold*

Computer Game	Console Game	Genre
30.8%		Strategy
19.8%	9.3%	Children & Family Entertainment
14.4%	8.7%	Shooter
12.4%	7.8%	Role-Playing
5.8%		Adventure
4.7%	30.1%	Action
3.7%	17.3%	Sports
	11.1%	Racing
	4.7%	Fighting
8.4%	11%	Others

Copyright NPD Group, 2005

■**Note** A detail worth noting in Table 1-1 is that the best-selling game genres are fairly different from computer and console games. For instance, the best-selling genre in computer games—strategy—is accountable for almost one-third of sales in this segment, but it's not even among the seven top-selling genres in console games. Fortunately, with XNA you aren't forced to choose one platform: you can create a game that will run with minimal adjustments on both Xbox 360 and computers.

Choosing the target market and the game genre for your game will help you to narrow down your choices about which game to develop. And, if you already have a game in mind, thinking about these points will help you to refine your ideas to the next step: defining the team involved in the game development project, and choosing your place in such a team. This leads us to a second important game development concept: *the game team.*

Smaller teams, or even a single multiskilled person, might create games for casual players, while creating games for hardcore players might involve a team with dozens of people skilled in different areas.

Although you might be able to develop games on your own, developing a game is always more than simply coding. You'll need nice graphics and sound effects, and you'll need to design the game levels, just to name a few different activities in the game project. In a big game development project, you'll need skills such as the following:

- *Project management*: Someone must be in charge of controlling time, scope, resources needed, communications, coordination between team members, and so on. Even if you're developing a game with a few friends of yours, it's crucial to define "who's in charge" to solve problems and define the project direction.

- *Script writers*: The script writers are responsible for writing the game storyline, ultimately defining the challenges to face and the mysteries to solve. They usually help define the whole game background, such as the game characters, the dialogue, and the level division.

- *Level designers*: Level designers usually create and use tools to define each of the game levels, according to the programming premises given by the coding team and the story written by the script writers.

- *Artists*: "Artists" is a broad category, encompassing concept art creators, computer art creators, the people responsible for texturing (creating textures for the 3-D models), computer colorists, and so on. These folks create the "splash" or opening game screen and the game menus and static images, and might also create the art for the marketing team.

- *Modelers*: These people are responsible for creating the 3-D models for the game, following the concept and computer art.

- *Animators*: Creating a 3-D model is not the same thing as animating it, so some teams include specialists in creating the model animations for the game. This team also creates the *cut-scenes*—the video sequences presented in the beginning of the game and at special points in the game, such as when a player wins a challenge, or at the beginning or ending of each level.

- *Musicians*: This is also a broad category, which ranges from the responsibility for writing (and playing) the game background and ambience music to the people who create voices and sound effects for the game.

- *Programmers*: Someone must be in charge of writing the game code, including all math and physics calculations needed to meet the desired game effects. This book is intended as the first step into this category.

- *Testers*: It's not advisable that the same person who writes the code be accountable for testing it. The goal for the testers is to find as many bugs as they can, trying to do unexpected things inside the game so the bugs surface in the game development process instead of during the player's game.

This list goes on, including people who are responsible for preparing and conducting the marketing efforts for the game, people who deal with publishing channels, and people who take care of the needed hardware and software infrastructure for the game development and, sometimes, for the game publishing (if the project includes Internet game servers, for example).

Enhancing Your Plan for a Great Game

Choosing the game's target market and genre and selecting the right people for the game project aren't the only key points you need to think about when planning your game.

A lot of information is available in books and on the Internet about planning games. Here we'll provide you with an overview of some points you simply can't afford to live without when planning your game.

- *Game goal*: Everything starts with a clearly defined game goal: to win the World Cup, to defeat the evil mage and avoid the world's destruction, to save as many lemmings as you can in each level. This goal ultimately guides the creation of the game storyline and defines whether it's an innovative game or just another clone of a best-selling title.

- *Ending criteria*: Besides the game goal, it's also important to define the game-end criteria: when to end the game, which includes the player's winning criteria (usually the game goal or some goal related to it) and the nonwinning criteria (when the number of lives reaches zero, when the time is up, and so on). When defining the nonwinning game-end criteria, it's also important to define how the player will return to a new game. Providing a saving or autosaving feature is crucial for long games, but might diminish the challenge for a short game such as chess or solitaire.

- *Storyline*: Closely related to the game goal, the storyline provides a background that explains and justifies the game goal, and is crucial to keep the player immersed in the game. When there's a storyline to be followed (not all games have one), everything in the game must contribute to it. The wrong music or a small out-of-place detail in a game would break the illusion as much as seeing someone using a wristwatch in a movie such as *Gladiator*. Creating nonlinear storylines makes the players feel like their decisions make a difference in the game flow, which, although hard to achieve, greatly improves the gaming experience.

- *Playability*: The playability refers to how easy and fun the game is to play. The first 15 playing minutes are vital for players to decide if they'll keep playing, so the game should provide a balance of easy-to-control movements for beginners, and complex (and harder to use) movements for advanced players.

- *Replayability*: This term refers to the desire players have, after finishing a game, to go back and play again. For simple games such as Tetris, the appeal of playing again is obvious, but for more complex games you must plan this appeal in the form of built-in features (such as extra levels unlocked every time the player finishes the game), or as game extensions the player can download or buy.

- *Forgiveness*: Entering in the details of game play, this concept refers to the programmer's ability to provide the correct balance between mathematical accuracy and playability. For example, in a shooter game, if the player shoots a bullet that passes close to an enemy without touching the enemy, it's better to count it as an accurate shot. On the other hand, the programmer might choose to decrement the player's energy only for enemy shots that hit the player's character's torso, ignoring bullets on head, arms, and legs, to make the game easier.

- *Challenge*: You might say that challenge is the opposite of forgiveness: it's the game's ability to provide difficult but not impossible challenges to beat. If the game is too easy—or too hard—the player will simply exchange it for a better-balanced one. The game can provide different skill levels to choose from, and must offer levels with increasingly difficult challenges to keep the player interested.

- *Reward*: Rewarding players when they win is as important as offering good challenges for them to beat. These rewards—which might be special items, money, energy, lives, unlocking new levels, and so on—include prize in-level challenges (such as an amount of gold and extra experience gained for every monster defeated), end-of-level awards (such as presenting a cut-scene and giving bonus points), and a big show at the game ending. Remember: nothing is more frustrating for a player than spending dozens of hours to win a game only to see a puny "congratulations" screen in the end!

- *Saving and registering*: How the game will save the players' evolution and the means it provides to the players to register their experience are important parts of the game playability and reward system. In long games, providing a way for players to start easily from where they left off, a way to register their high scores and compare to other people, and even the ability to "take pictures" from the game to present later to their friends might make the difference needed to provide the right appeal.

- *Game "ecosystem"*: Nowadays, the game team must remember that a game isn't only a game. It includes communities of players on the Internet, homemade extensions created by fans, and so on. These thoughts must guide all game development, from planning a long-term game franchise, coding a game that allows expansions, and establishing marketing approaches to increment the participation of fans in online communities, among other initiatives.

- *Polishing*: A great game is only great if every detail is planned and developed to contribute to player immersion, and especially if such details are tested to work as planned. If a game appears to offer some freedom of choice to the player, but presents a "you can't do this" message—or, even worse, an error message—every time the player tries something imaginative, it's halfway to a total failure. Always remember to include test time in every game project, even for the simpler ones!

Enough planning for now. In the next section, you'll get to create your first XNA program and explore the game programming concepts behind it.

XNA Game Programming Concepts

In this section you'll create an empty XNA game solution, and dig into the solution details to understand the basic concepts behind the program.

If you haven't done so, be sure to download and install the latest version of XNA Game Studio and Visual C# Express Edition from http://www.microsoft.com/XNA. If you already have Visual Studio 2005, XNA Game Studio will work just fine. The samples in this book work in either programming environment.

Once everything is in place, run Visual C# now and choose File ➤ New Project. You'll see the dialog box in Figure 1-1.

In this dialog, click the Windows Game (2.0) project type and click OK to create a new game project named WindowsGame1. Notice that version 2.0 includes extra project types in the New Project dialog, so be sure you always select the 2.0 version of the project templates.

You'll probably want to pay attention to the Location field in this dialog, because it shows the location in which your project will be created. You're free to change this location to your directory of choice.

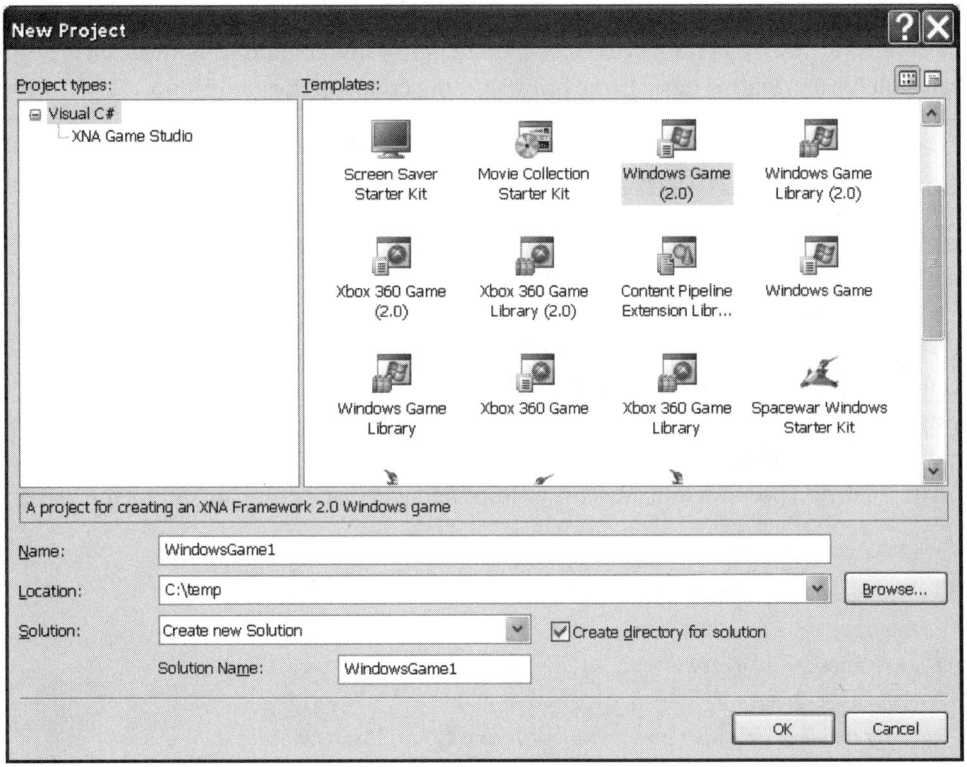

Figure 1-1. *Creating a new Windows Game (2.0) project in Visual C# Express Edition*

Once the project is created, choose the Start Debug icon in the toolbar, or press the F5 key to run the newly created game. Although it's not impressive right now—just a blue screen—as you'll see, this program has all the basics needed to start coding a game.

Close the game window, and analyze the files that were created for you. The Solution Explorer shows the newly created files (see Figure 1-2).

Figure 1-2. *The Solution Explorer for a Windows Game project*

Along with an icon and a thumbnail file, in Figure 1-2 you can see that two code files were created for you: `Program.cs` and `Game1.cs`. To better understand what these files mean, you have to learn a basic game programming concept: the game loop.

General Game Structure

The central logic for every game includes preparing the environment where the game will run, running the game in a loop until the game ending criteria is met, and cleaning up the environment.

The idea of having the main program logic running in a loop is crucial for a game, because the game needs to keep running whether or not it has user interaction. This doesn't happen with some commercial applications, which only do something in response to user input.

The following pseudocode presents a simplified game structure, including the game loop:

```
Initialize graphics, input and sound
Load resources
Start game loop.  In every step:
    Gather user input
    Perform needed calculations  (AI, movements, collision detection, etc.)
    Test for game ending criteria - if met, stop looping
    Draw (render) screen, generate sounds and game controller feedback
Finalize graphics, input, and sound
Free resources
```

It's a simplified view—for instance, you can load resources inside the game loop when beginning each game level—but it still provides a good idea about a game's internal details.

Before XNA, this game structure had to be coded from scratch, so you had to contend with many details that weren't directly related to your game. XNA hides most of this complexity from you. When you create a new Windows Game project, the two files created encompass creating an object of the `Microsoft.Xna.Framework.Game` class (`Game1` object), presenting the code with the meaningful methods of this class you need to override, and calling the `Run` method, which starts the game loop.

The next pseudocode fragment presents `Game1` methods organized as the generic game loop presented before, so you can understand the general structure of the code before entering its details.

```
Game1() - General initialization (Game1.cs)
Initialize() - Game initialization (Game1.cs)
LoadContent() - Load Graphics resources (Game1.cs)
Run() - Start game loop (Program.cs).  In every step:
```

```
   Update() - Read user input, do calculations, and test for game ending (Game1.cs)
   Draw() - Renderization code (Game1.cs)
UnloadContent() - Free graphics resources (Game1.cs)
```

Comparing the two preceding pseudocode excerpts, you can see that the Windows Game project type provides you with a ready-made basic game structure, so you can start by including your game-specific code.

Let's see the details for each of the project files.

Opening the Program.cs file, you can see that there are only ten code lines (not counting the using statements), as presented in the following code snippet:

```
static class Program
{
    static void Main(string[] args)
    {
        using (Game1 game = new Game1())
        {
            game.Run();
        }
    }
}
```

This code fragment includes the Program class, where you have the XNA application entry point—the Main function. This function has only two lines: one for creating the game object from the Game1 class, and another for calling the Run method of this object, which, as you already know, starts the game loop.

Note that by creating the object in a using statement, it is automatically freed when the statement ends. Another point to remember is that the args argument on the Main function receives the command-line parameters used when calling the game. If you wish to include command-line arguments in your game—such as special cheat codes for helping you test the game—this is where you need to deal with them.

The Game1 class is implemented in the Game1.cs file. A quick look at the Game1 class in this file shows you that it's derived from the Microsoft.Xna.Framework.Game class, the base class offered by XNA that encapsulates window creation, graphics, audio and input initialization, and the basic game logic we already talked about.

Let's open it to explore its details in the next sections.

Game Initialization

The Game1 class starts by defining and creating objects that will reference the graphics device manager, most commonly referred to in the gaming world as *device*, and a SpriteBatch object, used to draw text and 2-D images. The Game1 class constructor also configures the root directory for the content manager, which is the entry point for the XNA Content Pipeline, so the XNA Framework is informed of where to find the game content (graphics, sounds, 3-D models, fonts, and so on). The following code bit presents the device and content manager initialization:

```
public class Game1 : Microsoft.Xna.Framework.Game
    {
        GraphicsDeviceManager graphics;
        SpriteBatch spriteBatch;


        public Game1()
        {
            graphics = new GraphicsDeviceManager(this);
            Content.RootDirectory = "Content";
        }
```

You don't need to change these first lines, nor include code here—you can simply use them as is. In the next sections we'll see some details about the device and the Content Pipeline, so you can get an overall idea of what's happening behind the scenes.

The Graphics Device Manager

The graphics device manager, or simply device, is your entry point to the graphics handling layer, and includes methods, properties, and events that allow you to query and change this layer. In other words, the device represents the way to manage the access to the graphic card feature.

For now, all you need to know is that by creating the graphics object of the GraphicsDeviceManager class, a game window is created for you, and you'll use the graphics object when performing any graphics operation. All the complexities about querying the features and initializing the 3-D graphics layer are hidden from you.

The Content Pipeline Manager

The Content Pipeline is one of the most interesting features XNA brings you, because it simplifies how your game deals with content generated by different content generation tools.

In a non-XNA game, you have to worry about how to load game content as audio, graphics, and 3-D models: Where is the content located? How will your program read this content? Do you have the right libraries to read the content in the format it was created in, by the commercial 3-D tool you're using to create it?

The Content Pipeline streamlines the processing of all game content so you can deal with it easily. It comprises a number of steps, which include importers to read the content and generate a well-known format, a processor that reads this format, a content compiler that generates the ready-to-use content, and finally the content manager. Figure 1-3 presents a high-level view of the Content Pipeline.

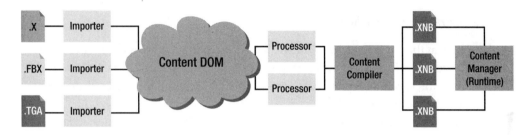

Figure 1-3. *The XNA Content Pipeline*

One interesting thing about the Content Pipeline is that it is based on content you effectively include in your C# project. That means that when the project is built, the content is transformed into a recogizable format and moved to a known directory, so the program will always know where to find the content and how to read it.

When including content in your XNA program, you use one of the content importers provided as part of the framework. These importers normalize the content data, putting it in a format that can be easily processed later. The importers support the following file formats:

- *3-D file formats*: X (used by DirectX), FBX (transport file format, originally created by Autodesk and supported by most commercial and many freeware tools).

- *Material file formats*: FX (effect files, which can be used to describe 3-D model rendering details or add effects to the 3-D scene).

- *2-D file formats*: BMP, DDS, DIB, HDR, JPG, PFM, PNG, PPM, and TGA (the most commonly used image file formats).

- *Font description*: SPRITEFONT (XML files used by XNA, which describe how to generate a texture map from a specific font type size. The game then uses the images on the texture map to write text onscreen).

- *Audio file formats*: .XAP (generated by the XACT tool, which imports most of the audio file formats).

After the importers process the content, the processors will read this content and generate an object the game can handle at runtime.

Finally, the game uses the content manager to read such objects so they can be easily used.

You can extend the content compiler to include new processors, and you can also extend the Content Pipeline with new importers, so you don't have to stick to the predefined formats.

Game Initialization Methods in an XNA Game

Looking back at the game logic pseudocode, you can see that before entering the game loop you have to do the needed initialization and load the game resources. Besides the class constructor, seen in the previous sections, in XNA such initialization is done in the Initialize and LoadContent methods.

For now, all you need to know is why there are two initialization routines; in later chapters you'll see details and examples for each of these methods.

The Initialize method is called once when you execute the Run method (described in the beginning of this section), just before the game loop starts. This is the right place to include any nongraphical initialization routines, such as preparing the audio content.

This method also includes a call to its base method, which iterates through a GameComponents collection and calls the Initialize method for each of them. That means that you can create game components that the Game class will also call, when you're creating more sophisticated games. But don't worry about this detail right now: we'll get back to it when creating our games.

The graphics are loaded in a separate method because sometimes the game needs to reload the graphics. The graphics are loaded according to the current device settings to provide maximum performance. So, when these settings change (such as when you change the game resolution or when you go from windowed to full screen mode), you need to reload the graphics. The LoadContent method is called every time the game needs to load or reload the graphics.

Game Finalization

Before presenting the game loop–related methods, we'll give a quick overview of the game finalization routines.

Because XNA's internal closing routines and XNA's garbage collector do most of the finalization routines for you, the finalization is simplified.

The basic game project you created includes an overload for the UnloadContent method. Like its peer used to load graphics, this method is called every time the game needs to free any graphics resources you have loaded.

Advanced games might include specific routines in each game class to load and unload graphic resources, not requiring the use of these load and unload methods.

Game Loop

Most of the game processing occurs inside the game loop. It's here where the game checks if there is player input to process, the game characters' artificial intelligence is calculated, the game components' movements are executed, the collisions between them are considered, the game ending criteria is checked, and finally, where the controller vibration is activated, the sound is played, and the screen is drawn.

The Microsoft.Xna.Framework.Game class provides two overridable methods that the internal game loop calls: Update, where you must include the game calculations, and Draw, where you draw the game components. Let's take a closer look at these methods, presented in the next code snippet, to highlight some relevant details:

```
protected override void Update(GameTime gameTime)
{
    // Allows the game to exit
    if (GamePad.GetState(PlayerIndex.One).Buttons.Back ==
        ButtonState.Pressed)
            this.Exit();
    base.Update(gameTime);
}

protected override void Draw(GameTime gameTime)
{
    graphics.GraphicsDevice.Clear(Color.CornflowerBlue);
    base.Draw(gameTime);
}
```

The first important point to discuss is the gameTime parameter received by both methods. This parameter is crucial to all the game logic, because the game must know how much time has passed since the last step on the game loop to do the right calculations—for example, to calculate the correct position for the game components according to their speeds in the game. Let's take a closer look at the GameTime class properties:

- ElapsedGameTime: This property represents the amount of game time since the last time the game loop was called. Dealing with game time means that the game loop is called a fixed number of times per second, so the game logic can use game time as a basic unit of time to perform calculations. Creating games based on game time instead of real time is easier, because the game can define movements expressed in units per game update, simply incrementing the game components by the calculated rate in every update. When the IsFixedTimeStep property of the Game class is true, this class ensures that Update will be called the right number of times per second, dropping frames in a game slowdown if necessary.

- ElapsedRealTime: This property represents the amount of real time since the last time the game loop was called. By setting the IsFixedTimeStep property of the Game class to false, the game loop will run at maximum speed, being called as many times as possible per second. This might increase the code complexity, but also might allow for greater speed in the game.

- TotalGameTime *and* TotalRealTime: These properties represent the total amount of time since the game started, counted in game time (fixed units per second) or real time.

- IsRunningSlowly: If the Game class is calling the Update method less than defined in the Game.TargetElapsedTime property, this property is set to true, so the game has the information to do any needed adjustments.

Another detail worth mentioning about the Update method is that it comes with a predefined code for ending the game when the Back button is pressed in the Xbox 360 controller:

```
if (GamePad.GetState(PlayerIndex.One).Buttons.Back == ButtonState.Pressed)
    this.Exit();
```

The GamePad class allows access to the current state of the controller and enables the game to fire the controller vibration. The class doesn't buffer user input, so the information you gather is exactly synchronized with current user interaction. As you can infer by the previous code, you can check for buttons, triggers, thumbsticks, or directional pad status.

We'll talk about dealing with player input in the next chapter, including gamepad, mouse, and keyboard input.

The Draw method includes a line to clear the graphics device, filling the game window with a single color—CornflowerBlue:

```
graphics.GraphicsDevice.Clear(Color.CornflowerBlue);
```

As we stated before, the device (represented here by the graphics variable) is your interface to the graphics layer and will be used in every graphics operation. In this case, the code shows a use of the GraphicsDevice property, which exposes properties and methods that allow reading and configuring many details about game rendering. We won't get into further details about this class now; you'll learn more about it in the next chapters, when seeing the basics of 2-D and 3-D game programming and when creating your games.

Summary

This chapter showed basic game programming concepts presented in a Windows Game XNA project type. These general concepts are present in any game, so make sure you understand the idea behind the general game structure, especially the idea of the game loop:

```
Initialize graphics, input and sound
Load resources
Start game loop.  In every step:
    Gather user input
    Perform needed calculations  (AI, movements, collision detection, etc.)
    Test for game ending criteria - if met, stop looping
    Draw (render) screen, generate sounds and game controller feedback
Finalize graphics, input, and sound
Free resources
```

It's also important to review the mapping of this general structure for games to the XNA Game class overridable methods:

```
Game1() - General initialization (already written for us)
Initialize() - Include nongraphics initialization here
LoadContent() - Include graphics initialization here
Run() - Start game loop.  In every step:
    Update() - Include code here to read and process user input, do calculations
               for AI, movements, and collisions, and test for game ending
    Draw() - Include the drawing (renderization) code here
UnloadContent() - Free graphics resources
```

In the next chapter, you'll write some simple examples that explore 2-D game programming concepts, so you'll be ready to start creating 2-D games with XNA.

CHAPTER 2

■ ■ ■

2-D Graphics, Audio, and Input Basics

In this chapter you'll create a simple program that manipulates simple 2-D graphics. By doing so, you'll explore some relevant concepts used when creating 2-D games, such as use of sprites and basic collision detection algorithms.

You'll also explore basic concepts about how to use audio, and you'll deal with user input in XNA through simple examples, so you'll be ready to create 2-D games.

2-D Graphics

If you followed the directions presented in the last chapter, by now you know how to create a simple, empty Windows Game project using XNA Game Studio. In this section you'll create a basic project that displays two simple 2-D images onscreen. You'll learn how to move them and make them collide with the window borders and against each other.

Commonly Used Gaming Terms

Many terms used in game programming jargon describe specific uses of 2-D graphics in a game. Let's see some of the most common ones:

- *Sprite*: A sprite is a 2-D image that can be manipulated independently from the rest of a game scene. This term is used often to describe the image displayed or the class used by the game to display the image (which includes properties such as velocity, position, width and height, and so on). Because the computer always draws the 2-D image as a rectangle, usually a sprite encompasses transparent areas so it provides the illusion of a nonrectangular drawing. The term "animated sprite" also refers to a sprite whose images change at predetermined time intervals, to generate the illusion of movement (such as a walking man or a spinning wheel).

- *Textures*: This term means a 2-D image loaded over a 3-D model, which can be seen from any point of view, depending on the position of the model and the position of the camera used to render the scene. You can use textures to help create the illusion of a highly detailed model when a detailed image is mapped over a simple 3-D model.

- *Billboard*: This is also a term used in the 3-D world to represent a texture that is mapped into a special plane that is always perpendicular to the camera axis. Using 3-D–like images in billboarding is an effective technique to create game components such as trees, a road sign, or a torch in the wall without the need to create highly detailed models. This allows more detailed scenes with the same rendering processing power.

- *Background*: A 2-D game scene is usually composed of a background image with many sprites displayed over it. When this background is a moving image, you have a *scrolling background*, which is the main characteristic in games called *scrollers*. It's also worth mentioning *parallax scrolling*, a special scrolling technique in which the 2-D game has more than one scrolling background with different scrolling speeds, which provides the illusion of a 3-D environment. For example, while the player character moves to the left, trees and bushes behind it move at the player's speed, mountains "far away" from the character move slowly, and clouds in the sky move very slowly.

- *Tiles*: These small images are used as—well—tiles to compose a bigger image, usually a level background. For example, platform games typically use tiles to create different platform levels based on the same basic images. The term *tiled map* is often used to describe game levels created with tiles, and sometimes to describe files with the needed information to create such levels based on tiles. A classic example of the use of tiles is for building a terrain. Role Playing Games (RPG) usually provide a level-editor application where the user can build the level, picking different tiles from the application and joining them together.

2-D and Screen Coordinate Systems

Although a 2-D game uses many math concepts, in this section we'll explore only the most basic ones. However, if you understand the ideas expressed in this chapter, you'll be able to build upon this knowledge when creating your 2-D games, and easily learn other related concepts.

You'll create a simple XNA program to present the concepts of drawing sprites, moving them onscreen, and colliding sprites with one another and the game window border. However, before you start coding, let's talk about 2-D coordinate systems and screen coordinates.

You probably heard about *2-D coordinate systems* in school, when creating simple graphics in geometry. Just to remind you, Figure 2-1 represents a triangle, expressed by each of its vertices, in a 2-D coordinate system. Analyze the vertices' coordinates to make sure you understand the concept.

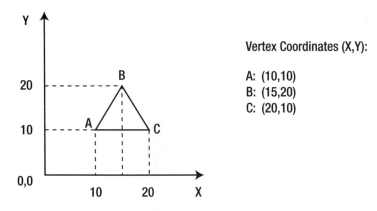

Figure 2-1. *A triangle in a 2-D coordinate system*

The main difference between the coordinate system presented in Figure 2-1 and the coordinates used when creating a 2-D game—called "screen coordinates"—is that the axis origin is not in the bottom left, but in the top left position, as depicted in Figure 2-2. Compare the two figures to understand how this difference impacts the vertices' definition: the higher a vertex appears onscreen, the lower its Y coordinate.

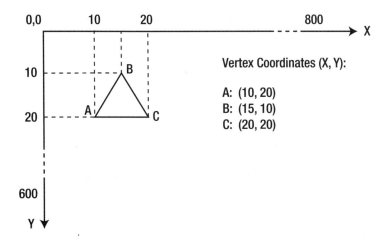

Figure 2-2. *The same triangle, in screen coordinates*

Another detail is that the screen coordinates are directly related to the screen resolution. So, if you configure your monitor to an 800 × 600 resolution, that means that the X axis will have 800 pixels (each pixel is an independent point onscreen) and the Y axis will have 600 pixels, as suggested in Figure 2-2.

Drawing a Sprite Using XNA

Let's now create a simple example in XNA to display a sprite in a given position on the screen.

Start by creating a new project, or opening the empty project you created in the previous chapter.

To group the sprite image and some associated properties (such as position, size, and velocity), you'll create a simple class, which will be extended later in this chapter when we explore new concepts. The following code listing presents a simple sprite class, including the following properties:

- texture: Stores the sprite image using XNA's Texture2D class. This class has many properties and methods to help deal with textures; you'll see some of them in Chapters 3 and 4. The texture is stored in this class as a 2-D grid of *texels*. Similar to pixels, which are the smallest unit that can be drawn on the screen, texels are the smallest unit that can be stored by the graphics board, and include color and transparency values.

- size: Stores the sprite's size using XNA's Vector2 class. This class has two properties, X and Y, which are used to store the image width and height.

- position: Stores the position of the sprite using XNA's Vector2 class. The X and Y properties of the class store the screen coordinates for the sprite.

```
class clsSprite
{
    public Texture2D texture;      //  sprite texture
    public Vector2 position;       //  sprite position onscreen
    public Vector2 size;           //  sprite size in pixels

    public clsSprite (Texture2D newTexture, Vector2 newPosition, Vector2 newSize)
    {
        texture = newTexture;
        position = newPosition;
        size = newSize;
    }
}
```

For now, this class only stores the sprite properties, and does not include any method. Because your goal here is to keep the code simple, you won't create properties using the get/set structure, although it's advisable to do so when creating properties in your games. The next code sample presents an example of how to use such a structure, in case you want to improve the code by yourself.

```
int _gameLevel;  // Stores the current game level
public static int GameLevel
{
   get
   {
      return _gameLevel;
   }
   set
   {
      _gameLevel = value;
   }
}
```

The first step in creating a sprite is to include a new image in your game, so you can use it through the Content Pipeline. Go to the XNA Creator's Club site (http://creators.xna.com) and save the XNA thumbnail image that appears on the site home page (or download the image directly from http://creators.xna.com/themes/default/images/common/xna_thumbnail.png). Once you have this image in your hard drive, include it in your project by pressing the left mouse button over the Solution Explorer window, as shown in Figure 2-3, selecting Add ➤ Existing Item, and choosing the image you just downloaded.

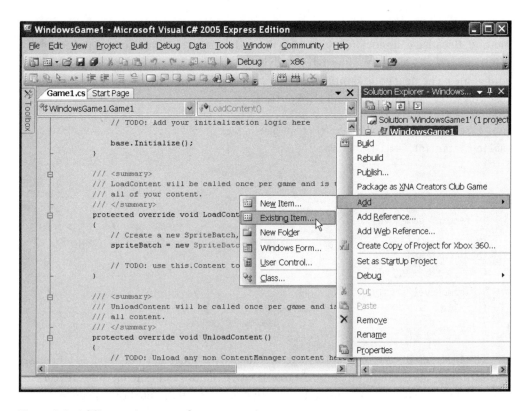

Figure 2-3. *Adding an image to the game project*

After including the image in the game solution, select the image name in the Solution Explorer window and press F4. This brings up (if it's not already visible) the Properties window for the recently included image, as presented in Figure 2-4.

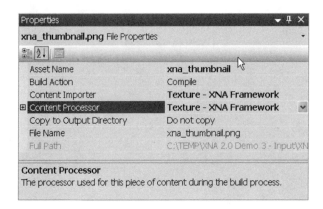

Figure 2-4. *The image properties*

The Properties window presents information such as the content importer and the content processor used for this content (also called *asset*). If you don't remember these concepts, refer to the previous chapter for a refresh! In this window you also can see the Asset Name property, which defines how your code will refer to this content.

Once you have this image, the next step is including the code for drawing it on the screen. To do this, you'll need a SpriteBatch (an XNA class that draws sprites onscreen) and the texture that will be used as the sprite image (in this case, you'll load this texture into your clsSprite class).

A new Windows Game project already creates a SpriteBatch object for you, so you'll start by creating a ClsSprite object in the Game1 class. Include this definition in the beginning of the class, just after the device and sprite batch objects that were automatically created for you. You'll see something like the next code fragment:

```
public class Game1 : Microsoft.Xna.Framework.Game
{
    GraphicsDeviceManager graphics;  // The Device
SpriteBatch spriteBatch;     // The Sprite renderer

    clsSprite mySprite;              // My Sprite Class
```

Obviously, you need to create these objects with valid values before using them. You do so in the LoadContent method because, as you saw in the previous chapter, this is the right place to include graphics initialization. Because the project already creates the SpriteBatch object, all you need to do is create the clsSprite object:

```
protected override void LoadContent()
{

    // Load a 2D texture sprite
    mySprite = new clsSprite(Content.Load<Texture2D>("xna_thumbnail"),
                        new Vector2(0f, 0f), new Vector2(64f, 64f));

    // Create a SpriteBatch to render the sprite
    spriteBatch = new SpriteBatch(graphics.GraphicsDevice);

}
```

■Note Although the previous code sample uses Vector2(0f, 0f) to define a zeroed 2-D vector, you could use the Vector2.Zero static property as well. The XNA Framework offers such properties to improve the code's readability.

Even though you only included a single code line, a lot of things are going on. Let's see: you created your sprite class by using the content manager to load the Texture2D based on the image asset name, xna_thumbnail. You also defined the sprite position as (0, 0) and decided on the sprite size: 64 pixels wide and 64 pixels tall.

As for the SpriteBatch creation, it's worth noticing that you're passing the graphics device as a parameter. In the previous chapter, we mentioned that the device (represented here by the graphics variable) is your entry point to the graphics handling layer, and through it you would do any graphical operations. Here, you are informing the SpriteBatch which device it should use when drawing the sprites; later in this chapter you'll also use the device to change the program's window size.

It's always a good programming practice to destroy everything you created when the program ends. To do this, you need to dispose the clsSprite and the SpriteBatch you created in the LoadContent method. As you probably guessed, you do this in the UnloadContent method. The code for disposing the objects follows:

```
protected override void UnloadContent()
{

    //  Free the previously allocated resources
    mySprite.texture.Dispose();
    spriteBatch.Dispose();

}
```

Finally, you need to include code to draw the sprite using the SpriteBatch object you created. You use the SpriteBatch, as its name suggests, to draw a batch of sprites, grouping one or more calls to its Draw method inside a block started by a call to Begin and closed by a call to the End method, as follows:

```
protected override void Draw(GameTime gameTime)
{
    graphics.GraphicsDevice.Clear(Color.CornflowerBlue);

    spriteBatch.Begin();
    spriteBatch.Draw(mySprite.texture, mySprite.position, Color.White);
    spriteBatch.End();

    base.Draw(gameTime);
}
```

There are many overloads for the Draw method, which allow you to draw only part of the original texture, to scale or rotate the image, and so on. You are using the simplest one, which receives only three arguments: the texture to draw, the position in screen coordinates (both from your clsSprite object), and a color channel modulation used to tint the image. Using any color other than white in this last parameter draws the image with a composition of its original colors and the color tone used.

Another detail worth mentioning is that the Begin method can also receive parameters that will be used when rendering every sprite in the block. For instance, if the texture has transparency information, you can tell the SpriteBatch to take this into account when drawing, by changing the Begin code line to the following:

```
spriteBatch.Begin(SpriteBlendMode.AlphaBlend);
```

Running the program now results in a window with the sprite sitting in the upper left corner—the (0,0) position of the program window—as shown in Figure 2-5.

Figure 2-5. *The sprite rendered in the (0,0) position of the program window*

If you want to change the size of the window (for example, to a 400 × 400 window), you can inform the device about the new dimensions (through the graphics object) in the LoadContent method, by including the following code lines:

```
graphics.PreferredBackBufferWidth = 400;
graphics.PreferredBackBufferHeight = 400;
graphics.ApplyChanges();
```

In fact, in these lines you're changing the *back buffer* width and height, which reflects in the window size, because you're working in windowed mode. This back buffer is part of the technique used to draw the game scene without image flickering, called *double buffering*. In double buffering, you use two places, or buffers, to draw and display the game scene: while the first one is presented to the player, the second, invisible one (the "back buffer") is being drawn. After the drawing is finished, the back buffer content is moved to the screen, so the player doesn't see only part of the scene if it takes too long to be drawn (the bad visual effect known as "flickering").

Fortunately, you don't need to care about such details, because XNA hides this complexity from you. But it's always good to understand why the property is called `PreferredBackBufferWidth` instead of something like `PreferredWindowsWidth`!

Moving the Sprite on the Screen

Because you work directly with screen coordinates when creating 2-D games, moving a sprite is simple: all you need to do is draw the sprite in a different position. By increment-ing the X coordinate of the sprite position, the sprite moves to the right; by decrementing, you move the sprite to the left. If you want to move the sprite down onscreen, you need to increment the Y coordinate, and you move the sprite up by decrementing the Y coordi-nate. Keep in mind that the (0,0) point in screen coordinates is the upper left corner of the window.

The XNA Framework basic game project provides a specific place to do the game cal-culations: the `Update` overridable method.

You can move the sprite by simply adding one line in the code, incrementing the X position of the sprite, according to the following line of code:

```
mySprite1.position.X += 1;
```

Because you use the sprite's `position` property when rendering the sprite in the `Draw` method, by including this line you'll be able to see the sprite moving across the window, to the right, until it disappears from the screen.

To create a more game-like sprite, let's do something a little more sophisticated. First, create a new property in the `clsSprite` class, `velocity`, that defines the sprite velocity on both the X and Y axis. Then, modify the class constructor to receive and store the screen coordinates, so you can include a method that moves the sprite according to the given velocity, which doesn't let the sprite move off the screen. So, delete the code line that changes the X position of the sprite, and perform the three following simple steps:

1. Modify the sprite class constructor, and change the sprite creation code in the Game1 class. In the clsSprite.cs file, make the following adjustment to the class constructor:

```
private Vector2 screenSize;
public clsSprite (Texture2D newTexture, Vector2 newPosition, Vector2 newSize,
                  int ScreenWidth, int ScreenHeight)
{
    texture = newTexture;
    position = newPosition;
    size = newSize;
    screenSize = new Vector2(ScreenWidth, ScreenHeight);
}
```

Now, change the sprite creation code accordingly in the Game1.cs file, at the LoadContent method:

```
mySprite1 = new clsSprite(Content.Load<Texture2D>("xna_thumbnail"),
                  new Vector2(0f, 0f), new Vector2(64f, 64f),
                  graphics.PreferredBackBufferWidth,
                  graphics.PreferredBackBufferHeight);
```

2. Create a new property in the sprite class, velocity:

```
public Vector2 velocity;
```

You can set this velocity to (1,1) in the LoadContent method, after the sprite creation code, so you'll inform the sprite that it should move one pixel per update on both the X and Y axes. That way the sprite will move diagonally onscreen.

```
mySprite1.velocity = new Vector2(1, 1);
```

3. You have the screen bounds; you have the speed. Now you need to create a method—let's call it Move—in the sprite class that moves the sprite according to the sprite velocity, respecting the screen boundaries. The code for this method follows:

```
public void Move()
{
    // if we'll move out of the screen, invert velocity

    // checking right boundary
    if(position.X + size.X + velocity.X > screenSize.X)
        velocity.X = -velocity.X;
```

```
        // checking bottom boundary
        if (position.Y + size.Y + velocity.Y > screenSize.Y)
            velocity.Y = -velocity.Y;
        // checking left boundary
        if (position.X + velocity.X < 0)
            velocity.X = -velocity.X;
        // checking bottom boundary
        if (position.Y + velocity.Y < 0)
            velocity.Y = -velocity.Y;

        // since we adjusted the velocity, just add it to the current position
        position += velocity;
    }
```

Because Vector2 classes represent both the sprite position and velocity, you could simply add the vectors to change the sprite position. However, because you don't want to add the velocity if it will take the sprite off the screen, you include code to invert the velocity in this situation.

Check the previous code: testing for left and top screen boundaries is a direct test, because the sprite position is given by its upper left corner. However, when checking if the sprite will leave the screen on the right, you have to sum the sprite width to the sprite's X position. When checking if the sprite is leaving through the bottom of the screen, you must sum the sprite height to its Y position. Read the code carefully to be sure you understand the tests, and then run the code. The sprite will move through the screen and bounce on the window borders!

Coding for Collision Detection

Making the sprite bounce on the window borders is already a simple collision detection test, but in 2-D games you usually want to test for collisions between sprites.

If you look for "collision detection algorithm" in a search engine on the Internet, you'll find thousands of pages presenting many different algorithms for detecting collisions on 2-D and 3-D systems. We won't enter in much detail here; we'll just present a simple example to help you understand the concept. Later, you'll see some algorithms in action in Chapter 3.

When testing for collisions, it's usually not reasonable to test every single pixel of a sprite against every single pixel of another sprite, so the collision algorithms are based on approximating the object shape with some easily calculated formula. The most common collision detection algorithm is known as *bounding boxes*, which approximate the object shape with one or more "boxes." Figure 2-6 represents a plane sprite, whose form is approximated by two boxes.

Figure 2-6. *Two boxes may be used to calculate collisions for a plane sprite.*

An easy way to implement the bounding box test is simply to check if the X,Y position of the upper bound corner in the first box (which wraps the first sprite you want to test) is inside the second box (which wraps the second object to test). In other words, check whether the X and Y of the box being tested are less than or equal to the corresponding X and Y of the other box, plus the width of the other box.

In your clsSprite class, implement a method (named Collides) that will receive a sprite as a parameter, and test the received sprite against the current sprite. If there's a collision, the method will return true.

```
public bool Collides(clsSprite otherSprite)
{
    // check if two sprites collide
    if (this.position.X + this.size.X > otherSprite.position.X &&
        this.position.X < otherSprite.position.X + otherSprite.size.X &&
        this.position.Y + this.size.Y > otherSprite.position.Y &&
        this.position.Y < otherSprite.position.Y + otherSprite.size.Y)
        return true;
    else
        return false;
}
```

Check the code against the graphic example from Figure 2-7 to be sure you understand the algorithm.

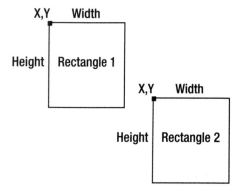

Figure 2-7. *Two nonoverlapping boxes*

According to the code sample, the two boxes will only overlap if both X and Y coordinates of rectangle 2 are within range (X to X + width, Y to Y + height) of rectangle 1. Looking at the diagram, you see that the Y coordinate for rectangle 2 is *not* greater than the Y coordinate plus the height of rectangle 1. This means that your boxes *might* be colliding. But when checking the X coordinate of rectangle 2, you see that it's greater than the X coordinate plus the width of rectangle 1, which means that no collision is possible.

In Figure 2-8, you do have a collision.

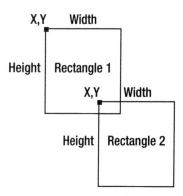

Figure 2-8. *Two overlapping boxes*

In this case, you can check that both X and Y positions of rectangle 2 are within the range of rectangle 1. In the code sample you also do the opposite test, checking if the X,Y coordinates of rectangle 1 are within the range of rectangle 2. Because you're checking just one point, it's possible for rectangle 2's top left corner to be outside rectangle 1, but the top left of rectangle 1 to be inside rectangle 2.

To test your method, you'll create a second, standing sprite in the middle of the window. To do this, you need to replicate the sprite creation code and include the code for testing collisions in the Update method of the Game1 class.

At first, include the sprite's variable definition at the beginning of the Game1 class, along with the previous sprite definition.

```
clsSprite mySprite2;
```

Now, in the LoadContent method, include the code for the sprite creation:

```
mySprite2 = new clsSprite(Content.Load<Texture2D>("xna_thumbnail"),
                    new Vector2(200f, 200f), new Vector2(64f, 64f),
                    graphics.PreferredBackBufferWidth,
                    graphics.PreferredBackBufferHeight);
```

And, in the UnloadContent method, include the code for disposing it:

```
mySprite2.texture.Dispose();
```

Finally, in the Draw method, include the code for drawing the new sprite. The code for drawing the two sprites follows:

```
spriteBatch.Begin(SpriteBlendMode.AlphaBlend);
spriteBatch.Draw(mySprite1.texture, mySprite1.position, Color.White);
spriteBatch.Draw(mySprite2.texture, mySprite2.position, Color.White);
spriteBatch.End();
```

If you run the program now, you'll see both sprites, but they aren't bouncing yet. You can make them bounce by including the call to the Collides method in the Update method, as follows:

```
// Move the sprite
mySprite1.Move();
//  Test the collision
if (mySprite1.Collides(mySprite2))
    mySprite1.velocity *= -1;
```

In this code, you invert the velocity of mySprite1 by multiplying it by –1. This inverts the sign of (X,Y) members of the Vector2 velocity property.

Running the code now, you'll see the sprites moving and bouncing against each other and against the window borders, as presented in Figure 2-9.

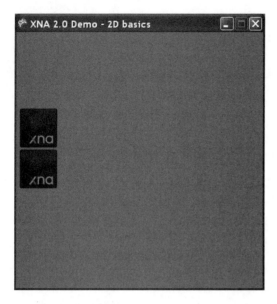

Figure 2-9. *The sprites now move and collide.*

Game Input

In this section we'll explore basic concepts of dealing with user input in XNA. You'll create an improved version of your sample, in which you'll move the second sprite you created using the Xbox 360 gamepad.

Using the Xbox 360 Gamepad

When you create a new XNA Windows Game project type, the Update method of the Game1 class already includes code for dealing with user input:

```
// Allows the game to exit
if (GamePad.GetState(PlayerIndex.One).Buttons.Back == ButtonState.Pressed)
    this.Exit();
```

This code presents the GamePad class: the basic entry point to get user input from the Xbox 360 gamepad. If you explore the GamePad properties and methods using Visual C# Express IntelliSense, you'll easily understand how to use the GetState method to get the current state of buttons (Buttons structure), the thumbsticks (ThumbSticks structure), Directional Pad (DPad structure), and the controller triggers (Triggers structure). There is also a property to inform you if the gamepad is connected (IsConnected).

Another interesting detail worth mentioning is that you can vibrate the gamepad by calling the SetVibration method of the GamePad class.

Let's see how you can use this information to improve your example.

To make the second sprite move according to the gamepad, all you need to do is include two new code lines in the Update method of the Game1 class:

```
// Change the sprite 2 position using the left thumbstick
mySprite2.position.X += GamePad.GetState(PlayerIndex.One).ThumbSticks.Left.X;
mySprite2.position.Y -= GamePad.GetState(PlayerIndex.One).ThumbSticks.Left.Y;
```

Check the operations you're doing in the previous code: you're adding the X property of the left thumbstick to the X position of the sprite, and subtracting the Y property to the corresponding sprite position. If you think it's weird, look back at the section "2-D and Screen Coordinate Systems" in this chapter: the X position increments from left to right, and the Y position increments from top to bottom of the screen. The X and Y properties of the thumbsticks range from –1 to 1, according to how much the thumbstick is pushed to the right or the bottom (positive values) or left and up (negative values).

To make the gamepad vibrate when sprite1 collides with sprite2 is just as easy: simply change the collision detection code in the Update method of the Game1 class to reflect the next code fragment:

```
if (mySprite1.Collides(mySprite2))
{
    mySprite1.velocity *= -1;
    GamePad.SetVibration(PlayerIndex.One, 1.0f, 1.0f);
}
else
    GamePad.SetVibration(PlayerIndex.One, 0f, 0f);
```

Run the program now and move the sprite with the gamepad. When the sprites overlap, the gamepad vibrates.

■Tip The second and third arguments of the SetVibration method range from 0 to 1, and define the speed for the left (low frequency) and right (high frequency) motors. You can include code in your program to generate different types of vibrations depending on the game conditions—for example, if the game collision is on the left or on the right of the player character.

Using the Keyboard

If, instead of the gamepad, you want to use the keyboard to control the sprite position, you can use KeyBoard.GetState to get the current state of any key:

```
KeyboardState keyboardState = Keyboard.GetState();
if (keyboardState.IsKeyDown(Keys.Up))
    mySprite2.position.Y -= 1;
if (keyboardState.IsKeyDown(Keys.Down))
    mySprite2.position.Y += 1;
if (keyboardState.IsKeyDown(Keys.Left))
    mySprite2.position.X -= 1;
if (keyboardState.IsKeyDown(Keys.Right))
    mySprite2.position.X += 1;
```

Using the Mouse

If, on the other hand, you want to use the mouse to control the sprite, you could use Mouse.GetState to get the current position of the mouse, and include code to make the sprite head to the current mouse position with the following code:

```
if (mySprite2.position.X < Mouse.GetState().X)
    mySprite2.position.X += 1;
if (mySprite2.position.X > Mouse.GetState().X)
    mySprite2.position.X -= 1;
if (mySprite2.position.Y < Mouse.GetState().Y)
    mySprite2.position.Y += 1;
if (mySprite2.position.Y > Mouse.GetState().Y)
    mySprite2.position.Y -= 1;
```

Game Audio

In this section you'll improve your example by including background sound and a bouncing sound effect, thus exploring basic audio concepts in XNA.

XNA deals with sound using the same structure it uses to manage graphics: the Content Pipeline. To XNA, sound is just another type of game content.

But there is a difference, in fact: although you can directly add graphics content in a XNA game project, the sound content to be added must be in a specific file format, generated by the Microsoft Cross-Platform Audio Creation Tool, known as XACT.

Creating Audio Content with XACT

You use XACT to create sound banks and wave banks, compiled into an XAP file, which the game can then use through the content manager.

In this section you'll learn the basics of how to create audio content with XACT and use it in a program, so you'll be ready to include audio content in your games. In the following chapters you'll see how to do this when creating real games!

The first step is to run XACT. Look for it in Start ➤ Programs ➤ XNA Game Studio Express ➤ Tools ➤ Cross-Platform Audio Creation Tool (XACT). The XACT main window displays, and a new XACT project is automatically created for you.

In the left side of the window, you can see a tree with New Project as a root and many types of child nodes below it. Right-click Wave Bank and select New Wave Bank in the presented pop-up menu, as shown in Figure 2-10.

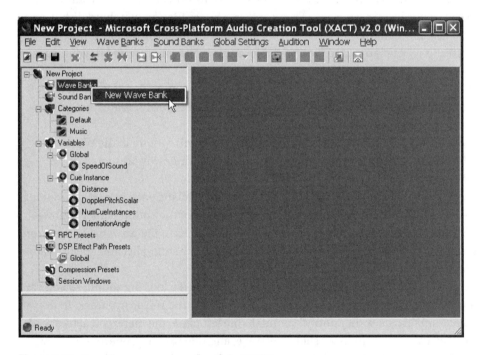

Figure 2-10. *Creating a new wave bank in XACT*

A new, blank window with the new wave bank is created in the right side of the window. Right-click this window now, and a new pop-up menu is presented (see Figure 2-11).

Figure 2-11. *Operations available for wave banks*

In the operations available for wave banks, choose Insert Wave File(s). To stick with easily found wave files, search for chord.wav and notify.wav files on your hard disk. These files are installed by default in Windows, as system event sounds. If you don't find these files, feel free to pick up any wave files available. The two files are inserted in your wave bank.

You'll also need to create a sound bank. Right-click the Sound Banks item, in the left menu, and insert a new sound bank. A new window, with the newly created sound bank, is created in the right side of the main window.

To better see the windows, let's take a moment to organize them: in the Windows menu, choose the Tile Horizontally option. The resulting window is presented in Figure 2-12.

Select both the file names in the wave bank now (by clicking each one while pressing the Ctrl key) and drag them to the second panel in the left of the Sound Bank window—the panel with Cue Name and Notes columns. The file names in the wave bank turn from red to green, and the file names are added as contents in the sound list and cue list in the Sound Bank window.

One last step before saving your audio project: you need a looping sound, so you can learn how to play, pause, and stop sound to use as background music in games. To do this, in the sound list, click the "notify" sound. In the left pane, the hierarchical tree reads Track 1 ➤ Play Wave ➤ notify. Now click Play Wave, and refer to the properties window that is displayed in the bottom right of the main window. You'll see a check box named Infinite in the Looping properties group. Mark this check box, as seen in Figure 2-13.

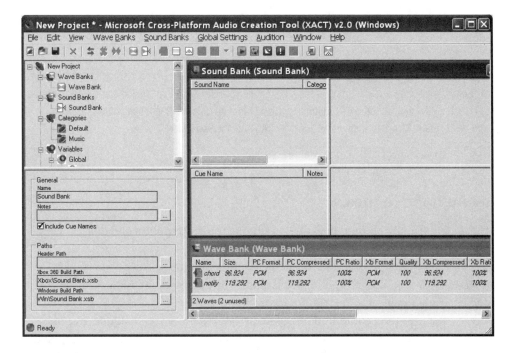

Figure 2-12. *The XACT tool, after organizing its windows*

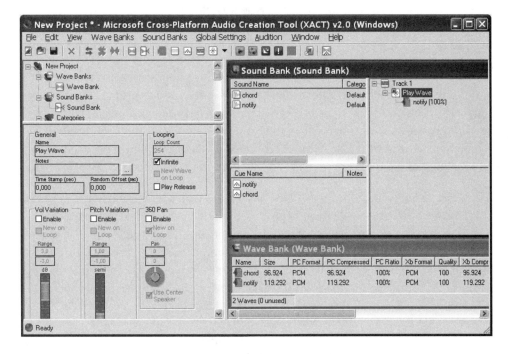

Figure 2-13. *Setting Play Wave properties in the XACT tool*

Now, save the project as MySounds.xap. You're ready to use the sounds in your program!

■**Note** To hear the sound samples from the sound bank or from the wave bank inside XACT by pressing the Play button on the toolbar, the XACT Auditioning Utility must be running. Run it by choosing Start ➤ Programs ➤ Microsoft XNA Game Studio ➤ Tools ➤ XACT Auditioning Utility.

Using Audio in Games

XNA makes using audio content in games as simple as using graphics and dealing with player input.

As a first step, you need to include the audio content in the solution, so you can use it through the Content Pipeline. Then, you'll define the audio-related objects, initialize these objects, and finally, use the content in the game code.

You include the audio content in the game in the same way you included graphics content earlier in this chapter: by right-clicking the Solution Explorer and choosing Add New Item from the pop-up menu. Remember, when the Add Existing Item dialog box is open, you need to choose Content Pipeline Files in the "Files of type" drop-down list, so you can see the MySounds.XAP file, generated in the first part of this section.

After including the XAP file in the solution, you need to create the objects to manage the file contents. You need three objects: the AudioEngine, the WaveBank, and the SoundBank.

The AudioEngine object is the program reference to the audio services in the computer, and is used mainly to adjust a few general settings and as a parameter to create the wave and sound banks. When creating an AudioEngine object in your program, you need to notify the name of the global settings file for the XACT content as a parameter. This settings file name is generated when the XAP file is compiled, and as a default has the same name as the XAP file, with the XGS extension.

The WaveBank is a collection of wave files (sound files with a WAV extension). To create this bank in your code, you'll need to pass as parameters the audio engine object (which must be previously created) and the compiled wave bank file, which is generated when you compile your project with the default name Wave Bank.xwb. Although the wave bank is not explicitly used in your program, you need to create this object because the sound cues in the sound bank depend on the wave files in this bank.

The SoundBank is a collection of sound cues. You can define cues as references to the wave files stored in the wave bank, along with properties that establish details on how to play these wave files, and methods that let you manage their playback.

The next code sample shows how to extend the previous example by including code to create and initialize the audio components:

```
// Audio objects
AudioEngine audioEngine;
WaveBank waveBank;
SoundBank soundBank;

protected override void Initialize()
{
    audioEngine = new AudioEngine("MySounds.xgs");
    //  Assume the default names for the wave and sound bank.
    //    To change these names, change properties in XACT.
    waveBank = new WaveBank(audioEngine, "Wave Bank.xwb");
    soundBank = new SoundBank(audioEngine, "Sound Bank.xsb");

    base.Initialize();
}
```

There are two ways to play a sound: a simple playback or in a playback loop. Once you initialize the audio objects, doing a playback is a matter of calling a simple method: PlayCue. You can improve on the previous example by playing a sound cue every time the sprites collide. Find the collision detection test in the Update method of the Game1 class, and adjust it to play the "chord" sound sample, as follows:

```
if (mySprite1.Collides(mySprite2))
{
    mySprite1.velocity *= -1;
    GamePad.SetVibration(PlayerIndex.One,1.0f, 1.0f);
    soundBank.PlayCue("chord");
}
else
    GamePad.SetVibration(PlayerIndex.One, 0f, 0f);
}
```

You can also extend the sample by including the infinite looping sound you defined in the XACT project; however, to do this, you need more control over the sound than simply starting to play it from the sound bank. You need a way to start it, then stop, pause, or resume it when needed, and even some way to know the current state of the sound (playing, paused, stopped, and so on).

The Cue object provides the methods and properties you need to accomplish this. Let's extend our example by creating a new Cue object, named MyLoopingSound, in Game1:

```
Cue myLoopingSound;
```

In the `Initialize` method, read the sound cue and play it by including the following code fragment:

```
myLoopingSound = soundBank.GetCue("notify");
myLoopingSound.Play();
```

In this code fragment you use the `Play` method to start the playback of the "notify" sound, which was included in the XACT project earlier in this section. Because you set the Looping property in the XACT interface (Figure 2-13) of this sound to Infinite, the sound will continuously play when you start your program. Run the program now and check for yourself.

The `Cue` object offers a series of methods and properties that give you better control over the playback. The next code sample presents an example of how to pause and resume the cue when the "B" button is pressed in the Xbox 360 gamepad. If you don't have a gamepad plugged into your computer, you can change this to a keyboard key or a mouse button, using what you learned earlier in this chapter.

```
// Play or stop an infinite looping sound when pressing the "B" button
if (GamePad.GetState(PlayerIndex.One).Buttons.B == ButtonState.Pressed)
{
    if (myLoopingSound.IsPaused)
        myLoopingSound.Resume();
    else
        myLoopingSound.Pause();
}
```

Note The `Stop` method for the cue object lets you stop the sound immediately or "as authored," which means that the audio engine will wait for the end of the current sound phase or the next transition to stop the sound gracefully. But remember: if you stop a sound, you can't play it again, unless you call the `GetCue` method once again.

Summary

In this chapter you learned the basic 2-D graphics vocabulary, and how to create a simple XNA program that enables you to load, display, and move images.

It's important to remember how to load a `Texture2D` from the Content Pipeline:

```
Texture2D MyTexture = Content.Load<Texture2D>("xna_thumbnail")
```

and how to display this texture using a SpriteBatch object:

```
spriteBatch.Begin();
spriteBatch.Draw(MyTexture, new Vector2(0f, 0f), Color.White);
spriteBatch.End();
```

You also saw that with a few lines of code, you can not only create sprites that collide in XNA, but also deal with player input and playing sounds.

When reading player input, remember the basic objects: GamePad, Keyboard, and Mouse. These three objects provide a GetState method that allows you to get the player input, returning, respectively, a GamePadState, a KeyboardState, and a MouseState object, each one with the information from the corresponding input device.

As for the audio, you need to remember that before using any sound in your game, you need to create a project in XACT, which generates the XAP content file that can be included in your game solution. Once the content is in place and the proper audio object's initialization is done, you can play sounds directly from the sound bank using the Play method, or get a Cue from the sound bank and use its properties and methods to play, pause, resume, or stop playing a sound.

With this knowledge, you're now prepared to put it all together in a real game. That's exactly what you'll do in the next chapter. Get your umbrella and prepare for the Rock Rain—the complete game you'll create in the next chapter!

■ ■ ■

CHAPTER 3

Creating Your First 2-D Game

Now let's start the fun. In this chapter you're going to create your first game and explore some of the techniques seen in the previous chapter. Your first game will be both simple and fun. By the end you will have exercised many principles of 2-D games, not only acquiring answers, but more importantly, discovering the questions that must be answered before starting a game project. Let's go.

Designing an XNA Game

Before anything, as trivial as the game might seem, it must be well planned. Many projects fail because of too little effort in this phase, which leads to projects without a defined end, or even projects that are finished but with a completely different result from the initial project. This book intends to teach making games the right way, so let's start right.

Design for the First Game: Rock Rain

"You're an intergalactic explorer and you're stuck in an endless asteroid field! How long will you resist this rock rain?" This is the main "theme" of your game, a frenetic challenge where you need to dodge a lot of asteroids that pass rapidly across the screen. It's like an Asteroids clone (a popular classic game).

This is a simple and old game concept, where players need to dodge a group of obstacles on the screen, and the longer they remain without a collision, the more points they get. Additionally, the quantity of meteors increases as time goes by, making the challenge harder and harder. To satisfy your curiosity, Figure 3-1 shows the screen of your first game.

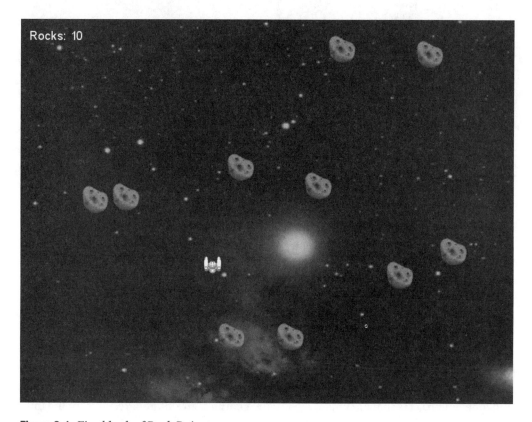

Rocks: 10

Figure 3-1. *Final look of Rock Rain*

Right now, you'll clarify the game *constraints and rules* before you program anything. In the case of Rock Rain they're simple:

- The player is able to move freely around the screen and cannot leave the screen border.

- The meteors appear at the top of the screen and move down with a random angle and speed. After some time a new meteor is added to this "rain."

- The score is given per the number of meteors on the screen.

- If the player collides with a meteor, the player's score will be zeroed and the game will restart with the initial quantity of meteors.

Looks clear, doesn't it? Values such as the starting quantity of meteors and how long it should take before another meteor is added to the screen were not specified because they're game parameters. We'll talk about them next.

Talking like a game programmer, things like spaceships, meteors, and score are *objects* in your game. You should also detail these objects before you start programming anything. Note that each object in the game has its own characteristics and *behavior*: the rocks fall, the player controls the spaceship, the score grows with the meteor count, and so on. The correct definition of the behavior and the state control of the game's objects is the most challenging task in game programming. That's why it should be well thought out before you start to build anything else.

You'll have only three sound effects: music that plays while the game is active, a sound that plays when a new meteor is added to the game, and an explosion sound that plays when the player collides with a meteor. Also on this collision you'll make the player's Xbox 360 gamepad shake, to give an impact effect.

Let's Get to It

Well, as you might have guessed, start by creating a Windows Game project called RockRain. The Solution Explorer in your Visual Studio looks like Figure 3-2.

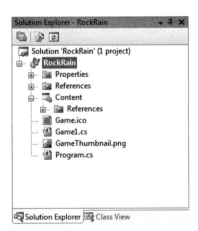

Figure 3-2. *XNA Game Solution window with the Rock Rain project created*

The Content folder is a special item in XNA Games projects. In this project, you'll put all the game's assets, such as images, sounds, and so on—that is, everything that should be loaded through the Content Pipeline.

Drawing the Background

Start by putting a background in your game. For a space game, nothing is better than an image of a galaxy! Add the file SpaceBackground.dds to the Content folder. You can find this file in the Source Code/Download area of the Apress web site at http://www.apress.com.

Now you should load this texture so that it fits the whole screen of the game. First define the texture in your code. Add this attribute to your Game1 class:

```
// Background texture
private Texture2D backgroundTexture;
```

Now, as you saw in the previous chapter, you'll load this texture and initialize the spriteBatch object in the LoadContent method:

```
// Create a new SpriteBatch, which can be used to draw textures.
spriteBatch = new SpriteBatch(GraphicsDevice);
// Load all textures
backgroundTexture = content.Load<Texture2D>(" SpaceBackground");
}
```

You have to load the texture using the spriteBatch object, like you saw in the previous chapter. First declare it in the Game1 class:

```
private SpriteBatch spriteBatch = null;
```

Finally, you can draw the background. Add the following code in the Draw() method of the Game1 class:

```
// Draw background texture in a separate pass.
spriteBatch.Begin();
spriteBatch.Draw(backgroundTexture,new Rectangle(0, 0,
          graphics.GraphicsDevice.DisplayMode.Width,
          graphics.GraphicsDevice.DisplayMode.Height),
          Color.LightGray);
spriteBatch.End();
```

Now you can run the game by pressing F5. If everything is correct, the result will be like Figure 3-3.

Figure 3-3. *Rock Rain background*

Creating the Player's GameComponent

The player is represented in the game as a small spaceship that can be controlled using an Xbox 360 gamepad or a PC keyboard. The image of this spaceship is in the RockRain. png file. Add it to the project inside the Content folder. This texture contains the image of the player's spaceship and also the meteors that the player must avoid (see Figure 3-4).

Figure 3-4. *Player and meteor texture*

Like you did with the background, first declare the texture in the Game1 class:

```
private Texture2D meteorTexture;
```

Then load it in the LoadContent method right after loading the background texture:

```
meteorTexture = content.Load<Texture2D>(" RockRain");
```

■Note The graphics in this chapter and the next were built using SpriteLIB GPL. SpriteLib GPL is a collection of static and animated graphic objects (also commonly known as sprites) and can be found at http://www.flyingyogi.com/fun/spritelib.html.

Now you'll create a class that represents the player in the game. Add a new GameComponent to the project, name the file Ship.cs (as in Figure 3-5), and click OK. A new file is added to the project that contains a class that derives from GameComponent. This GameComponent will be visible in the game; therefore it must be drawn. Derive from DrawableGameComponent so that you have a Draw() method you can use to draw it in the game.

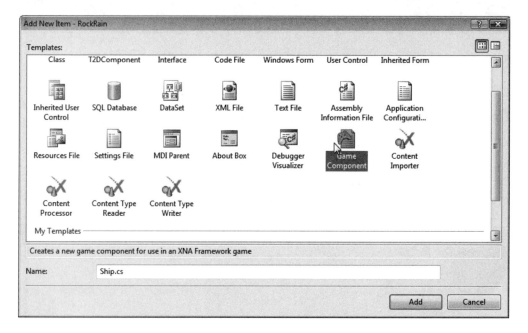

Figure 3-5. *Adding a new GameComponent*

This component copies the texture region that contains the picture of the spaceship in the specified position. To accomplish that, it needs the texture where this picture is, the coordinates of the picture in this texture, and the coordinates on the screen where the picture must be rendered.

Regarding the component's behavior, it only needs to move according to the Xbox 360 gamepad movement or the keyboard, and verify if the picture is still "in" the screen. That is, the spaceship cannot disappear by leaving the defined margins of the game's window.

See that you have two steps of a DrawableGameComponent well defined. In the Draw() method you'll copy the spaceship picture to the screen and in the Update() method you'll update the screen according to the Xbox 360 gamepad or keyboard state. This class code follows:

```
#region Using Statements
using System;
using System.Collections.Generic;
using Microsoft.Xna.Framework;
using Microsoft.Xna.Framework.Graphics;
using Microsoft.Xna.Framework.Input;
#endregion

namespace RockRain
{
    /// <summary>
    /// This is a game component that implements the player ship.
    /// </summary>
    public class Ship : Microsoft.Xna.Framework.DrawableGameComponent
    {
        protected Texture2D texture;
        protected Rectangle spriteRectangle;
        protected Vector2 position;

        // Width and height of sprite in texture
        protected const int SHIPWIDTH = 30;
        protected const int SHIPHEIGHT = 30;

        // Screen Area
        protected Rectangle screenBounds;

        public Ship(Game game, ref Texture2D theTexture)
            : base(game)
        {
```

```
            texture = theTexture;
            position = new Vector2();

            // Create the source rectangle.
            // This represents where the sprite picture is in the surface
            spriteRectangle = new Rectangle(31, 83, SHIPWIDTH, SHIPHEIGHT);

#if XBOX360
            // On the 360, we need to be careful about the TV's "safe" area.
            screenBounds = new Rectangle(
                    (int)(Game.Window.ClientBounds.Width * 0.03f),
                    (int)(Game.Window.ClientBounds.Height * 0.03f),
                    Game.Window.ClientBounds.Width -
                    (int)(Game.Window.ClientBounds.Width * 0.03f),
                    Game.Window.ClientBounds.Height -
                    (int)(Game.Window.ClientBounds.Height * 0.03f));#else
            screenBounds = new Rectangle(0,0,
                Game.Window.ClientBounds.Width,
                Game.Window.ClientBounds.Height);
#endif
        }


        /// <summary>
        /// Put the ship in your start position in the screen
        /// </summary>
        public void PutinStartPosition()
        {
            position.X = screenBounds.Width / 2;
            position.Y = screenBounds.Height - SHIPHEIGHT;
        }


        /// <summary>
        /// Update the ship position
        /// </summary>
        public override void Update(GameTime gameTime)
        {
            // Move the ship with the Xbox controller
            GamePadState gamepadstatus = GamePad.GetState(PlayerIndex.One);
            position.Y += (int)((gamepadstatus.ThumbSticks.Left.Y * 3) * -2);
            position.X += (int)((gamepadstatus.ThumbSticks.Left.X * 3) * 2);
```

```csharp
    // Move the ship with the keyboard
    KeyboardState keyboard = Keyboard.GetState();
    if (keyboard.IsKeyDown(Keys.Up))
    {
        position.Y -= 3;
    }
    if (keyboard.IsKeyDown(Keys.Down))
    {
        position.Y += 3;
    }
    if (keyboard.IsKeyDown(Keys.Left))
    {
        position.X -= 3;
    }
    if (keyboard.IsKeyDown(Keys.Right))
    {
        position.X += 3;
    }

    // Keep the ship inside the screen
    if (position.X < screenBounds.Left)
    {
        position.X = screenBounds.Left;
    }
    if (position.X > screenBounds.Width - SHIPWIDTH)
    {
        position.X = screenBounds.Width - SHIPWIDTH;
    }
    if (position.Y < screenBounds.Top)
    {
        position.Y = screenBounds.Top;
    }
    if (position.Y > screenBounds.Height - SHIPHEIGHT)
    {
        position.Y = screenBounds.Height - SHIPHEIGHT;
    }

    base.Update(gameTime);
}

/// <summary>
/// Draw the ship sprite
```

```
///  </summary>
public override void Draw(GameTime gameTime)
{
    // Get the current spritebatch
    SpriteBatch sBatch =
        (SpriteBatch)Game.Services.GetService(typeof(SpriteBatch));

    // Draw the ship
    sBatch.Draw(texture, position, spriteRectangle, Color.White);

    base.Draw(gameTime);
}

///  <summary>
///  Get the bound rectangle of ship position in screen
///  </summary>
public Rectangle GetBounds()
{
    return new Rectangle((int)position.X, (int)position.Y,
        SHIPWIDTH, SHIPHEIGHT);
}
    }
}
```

Note that the Draw() method does not create a SpriteBatch, like you did when you rendered the background texture. Ideally (following the "batch" concept), you should not keep creating and destroying SpriteBatch objects because this jeopardizes the application's performance. You could create a "global" SpriteBatch and use it in your classes. However, this would create a coupling between your GameComponents with a global attribute of a specific game (which is not desirable). XNA has an excellent solution to supply this "global" object and still allow you to reuse the component's code easily: the Game Services.

You can think of a Game Service as a service that is available to anyone who has a reference to a Game. The idea behind it is that a component should be able to depend on certain types, or services, for its functionality. If that service isn't available, then the component can't operate correctly.

In this case, the Draw() method will look for an active SpriteBatch directly in the GameServices and use it to draw itself on the screen. Of course, someone has to add this SpriteBatch to the GameServices. So, add the following code right after creating the SpriteBatch in the LoadContent method of the Game1 class:

```
// Add the SpriteBatch service
Services.AddService(typeof(SpriteBatch), spriteBatch);
```

All the GameComponents of your game will use this SpriteBatch.

Let's talk a little about this class. The Update() method checks the keyboard and Xbox 360 gamepad to update the Position attribute and change the position of the ship on the screen. In this method you also check if the ship is inside the screen bounds. If not, the code keeps the ship inside the visible area of the screen.

The GetBound() method just returns the rectangle that has the ship boundaries in the screen. You'll use this rectangle later to do collision tests with meteors. Finally, the PutinStartPosition() puts the ship in your initial position, centered horizontally in the bottom area of the screen. This method is called when you need to put the ship in your initial position; for example, when a new round starts.

Now let's test this GameComponent. Create a Start() method that will be used to initialize the game objects (only the player for the moment), as in the following code:

```
/// <summary>
/// Initialize the game round
/// </summary>
private void Start()
{
    // Create (if necessary) and put the player in start position
    if (player == null)
    {
        // Add the player component
        player = new Ship(this, ref meteorTexture);
        Components.Add(player);
    }
    player.PutinStartPosition();
}
```

Observe that the player attribute contains a reference to the player's GameComponent. You also need to add this component to the components list of the Game itself to be able to have XNA call the Draw() and Update() methods of this object in the game, as you saw in the previous chapter.

Finally, declare the player attribute in the Game1 class:

```
private Ship player;
```

Now let's go back a little in the game's logic as a whole. The game's logic is normally implemented inside the Update() method of the Game class. In your case you can start with the following code:

```
/// <summary>
/// Allows the game to run logic such as updating the world,
/// checking for collisions, gathering input, and playing audio.
```

```
/// </summary>
/// <param name="gameTime">Provides a snapshot of timing values.</param>
protected override void Update(GameTime gameTime)
{
    // Allows the game to exit
    gamepadstatus = GamePad.GetState(PlayerIndex.One);
    keyboard = Keyboard.GetState();
    if ((gamepadstatus.Buttons.Back == ButtonState.Pressed) ||
        (keyboard.IsKeyDown(Keys.Escape)))
    {
        Exit();
    }

    // Start if not started yet
    if (player == null)
    {
        Start();
    }

    // Update all other components
    base.Update(gameTime);
}
```

Initially this code checks if the user pressed the Esc key or the Back button of the Xbox 360 gamepad, which ends the game. Then, if necessary, the code starts the game through the Start() method.

One detail is still missing. The Draw() method of your game only draws the background. You also have to make it draw all the other GameComponents of the game, so add the following code right after the code that draws the background:

```
// Start rendering sprites
spriteBatch.Begin(SpriteBlendMode.AlphaBlend);
// Draw the game components (sprites included)
base.Draw(gameTime);
// End rendering sprites
spriteBatch.End();
```

Save and execute the code. Now you can move the spaceship around the screen with the Xbox 360 gamepad or the PC arrow keys. Observe that all the movement logic of the spaceship is being done by its own component that you created, though XNA automatically calls its Update() method through the base.Update() call of the Game1 class. You'll create meteors following the same principle. The difference is that the player won't move the meteors.

Creating the Meteors

The concepts you used to create a component for the player are the same that you'll use to create the meteors. The only difference is that the meteors' initial position and movement depend on a random factor. The meteors' code follows:

```
#region Using Statements
using System;
using System.Collections.Generic;
using Microsoft.Xna.Framework;
using Microsoft.Xna.Framework.Content;
using Microsoft.Xna.Framework.Graphics;
#endregion

namespace FirstGame
{
    /// <summary>
    /// This is a game component that implements the rocks the player must avoid.
    /// </summary>
    public class Meteor : Microsoft.Xna.Framework.DrawableGameComponent
    {
        protected Texture2D texture;
        protected Rectangle spriteRectangle;
        protected Vector2 position;
        protected int Yspeed;
        protected int Xspeed;
        protected Random random;

        // Width and height of sprite in texture
        protected const int METEORWIDTH = 45;
        protected const int METEORHEIGHT = 45;

        public Meteor(Game game, ref Texture2D theTexture)
            : base(game)
        {
            texture = theTexture;
            position = new Vector2();

            // Create the source rectangle.
            // This represents where the sprite picture is in the surface
            spriteRectangle = new Rectangle(20, 16, METEORWIDTH, METEORHEIGHT);
```

```
        // Initialize the random number generator and put the meteor in
        // your start position
        random = new Random(this.GetHashCode());
        PutinStartPosition();
    }

    /// <summary>
    /// Initialize Meteor Position and Velocity
    /// </summary>
    protected void PutinStartPosition()
    {
        position.X = random.Next(Game.Window.ClientBounds.Width - METEORWIDTH);
        position.Y = 0;
        Yspeed = 1 + random.Next(9);
        Xspeed = random.Next(3) - 1;
    }

    /// <summary>
    /// Allows the game component to draw your content in the game screen
    /// </summary>
    public override void Draw(GameTime gameTime)
    {
        // Get the current spritebatch
        SpriteBatch sBatch =
                    (SpriteBatch) Game.Services.GetService(typeof(SpriteBatch));

        // Draw the meteor
        sBatch.Draw(texture, position, spriteRectangle, Color.White);

        base.Draw(gameTime);
    }

    /// <summary>
    /// Allows the game component to update itself.
    /// </summary>
    /// <param name="gameTime">Provides a snapshot of timing values.</param>
    public override void Update(GameTime gameTime)
    {
        // Check if the meteor is still visible
        if ((position.Y >= Game.Window.ClientBounds.Height) ||
            (position.X >= Game.Window.ClientBounds.Width) || (position.X <= 0))
        {
```

```
            PutinStartPosition();
        }

        // Move meteor
        position.Y += Yspeed;
        position.X += Xspeed;

        base.Update(gameTime);
    }

    /// <summary>
    /// Check if the meteor intersects with the specified rectangle
    /// </summary>
    /// <param name="rect">test rectangle</param>
    /// <returns>true, if has a collision</returns>
    public bool CheckCollision(Rectangle rect)
    {
        Rectangle spriterect = new Rectangle((int)position.X, (int)position.Y,
                 METEORWIDTH, METEORHEIGHT);
        return spriterect.Intersects(rect);
    }
  }
}
```

Note that the `PutinStartPosition()` method puts the meteor in a random horizontal position on the top of the screen and also obtains the vertical and horizontal displacement speed of the meteor, which each call of the class's `Update()` method refreshes.

Note that a `CheckCollision()` method verifies if the rectangle that delimits the meteor intersects with a rectangle passed as a parameter, and obviously, will be the rectangle that delimits the position of the player's spaceship on screen.

Now let's put the meteors on the screen. Add the following code in the `Start()` method of the `Game1` class:

```
// Add the meteors
for (int i = 0; i < STARTMETEORCOUNT; i++)
{
    Components.Add(new Meteor(this, ref meteorTexture));
}
```

The `STARTMETEORCOUNT` constant defines the initial number of meteors that will appear in the game. Declare it in the `Game1` class as follows:

```
private const int STARTMETEORCOUNT = 10;
```

Execute the program by pressing F5. Look at the beauty of the meteor rain. Note that each instance of the Meteor component behaves in an independent way, just like the Ship component does.

Creating the Game Logic

Your game components are practically ready. Now you have to make them work together. That is, when the player's spaceship collides with a meteor, the game will restart.

So, just as you have a Start() method that initializes the game components, create a method called DoGameLogic() that executes the game logic itself. Right now, this method only iterates the game component list, to check if a meteor collided with the player's spaceship. If there's any collision, the meteors should be taken out of the game so that they can be re-created in their initial position. This code follows:

```
/// <summary>
/// Run the game logic
/// </summary>
private void DoGameLogic()
{
    // Check collisions
    bool hasCollision = false;
    Rectangle shipRectangle = player.GetBounds();
    foreach (GameComponent gc in Components)
    {
        if (gc is Meteor)
        {
            hasCollision = ((Meteor)gc).CheckCollision(shipRectangle);
            if (hasCollision)
            {
                // Remove all previous meteors
                RemoveAllMeteors();
                // Let's start again
                Start();

                break;
            }
        }
    }
}
/// <summary>
/// Remove all meteors
/// </summary>
```

```
private void RemoveAllMeteors()
{
    for (int i = 0; i < Components.Count; i++)
    {
        if (Components[i] is Meteor)
        {
            Components.RemoveAt(i);
            i--;
        }
    }
}
```

Now call the DoGameLogic() method inside the Update() method of the Game1 class, right before the line that contains the base.Update(gameTime) call. This calls your game logic inside the game loop. Execute the program and see that when the spaceship collides with the meteor, the program puts all the objects in their initial position and keeps on this loop until the user leaves the application.

Now let's make the player's life a little harder. In your game, a new meteor will be added after some time is passed. As the meteors behave in an independent way, you only need to add a new Meteor component to the game and it does all the rest. This is done with the method in the following code. Call this method inside the doGameLoop() method, after the foreach loop.

```
/// <summary>
/// Check if it is time for a new rock!
/// </summary>
private void CheckforNewMeteor()
{
    // Add a rock each ADDMETEORTIME
    if ((System.Environment.TickCount - lastTickCount) > ADDMETEORTIME)
    {
        lastTickCount = System.Environment.TickCount;
        Components.Add(new Meteor(this, ref meteorTexture));
        rockCount++;
    }
}
```

See that there is a constant called ADDMETEORTIME that represents the interval, in milliseconds, that a new meteor should be added. Declare it in the Game1 class as follows:

```
private const int ADDMETEORTIME = 5000;
```

This 5 seconds (or 5,000 milliseconds) is a "magic number," and you can change it to alter the game difficulty later. Two new attributes store the number of meteors added (rockCount) and the time to calculate the desired interval (lastTickCount). Declare them as follows:

```
private const int ADDMETEORTIME = 5000;
private int lastTickCount;
private int rockCount;
```

You should initialize these attributes in the Start() method, so add the following code to this method:

```
// Initialize a counter
lastTickCount = System.Environment.TickCount;
// Reset rock count
rockCount = STARTMETEORCOUNT;
```

So, every five seconds a new meteor is added to the game. Run it again and see how long you can play without hitting a rock.

Adding Sounds

As you saw in Chapter 2, there's more to adding a sound to the game than adding the WAV files to your project. Due to format differences between the PC and the Xbox, XNA games can only use files created by the XACT tool.

For Rock Rain, you'll need three WAV files, which you can find in the Source Code/ Download area of the Apress web site at http://www.apress.com:

- Explosion.wav: An explosion sound that plays when the player collides with a meteor

- Backmusic.wav: The game's background music

- Newmeteor.wav: Plays when a new meteor is added to the game

Create a new XACT project, and add these WAV files to create a Wave Bank, a Sound Bank (to Backmusic.wav), and the Sound Cues. Save this project as audio.xap and add it to the project, inside the Content folder.

Before you add the code to play the sounds, create one more GameComponent to help you with this task. Add a new GameComponent and save it as AudioComponent.cs. Right after, add the following code:

```
#region Using Statements
using System;
using System.Collections.Generic;
using Microsoft.Xna.Framework;
using Microsoft.Xna.Framework.Audio;
#endregion

namespace RockRain
{
    /// <summary>
    /// Handle the audio in the game
    /// </summary>
    public class AudioComponent : Microsoft.Xna.Framework.GameComponent
    {
        private AudioEngine audioEngine;
        private WaveBank waveBank;
        private SoundBank soundBank;

        public AudioComponent(Game game)
            : base(game)
        {
        }

        /// <summary>
        /// Allows the game component to perform any initialization it needs to
        /// before starting to run.  This is where it can query for any required
        /// services and load content.
        /// </summary>
        public override void Initialize()
        {
            // Initialize sound engine
            audioEngine = new AudioEngine("Content\\audio.xgs");
            waveBank = new WaveBank(audioEngine, "Content\\Wave Bank.xwb");
            if (waveBank != null)
            {
                soundBank = new SoundBank(audioEngine, "Content\\Sound Bank.xsb");
            }

            base.Initialize();
        }
```

```
        /// <summary>
        /// Allows the game component to update itself.
        /// </summary>
        /// <param name="gameTime">Provides a snapshot of timing values.</param>
        public override void Update(GameTime gameTime)
        {
            audioEngine.Update();
            base.Update(gameTime);
        }

        /// <summary>
        /// Play a cue
        /// </summary>
        /// <param name="cue">cue to be played</param>
        public void PlayCue(string cue)
        {
            soundBank.PlayCue(cue);
        }
    }
}
```

It's a simple component, but it will help you with your sound effects. This class just encapsulates methods to load and play sounds that you saw in the previous chapter. Before you do anything else, declare an object of this class in the Game1 class so that you can use it:

```
// Audio Stuff
private AudioComponent audioComponent;
```

Initialize it in the Initialize() method of the Game1 class:

```
audioComponent = new AudioComponent(this);
Components.Add(audioComponent);
// Start the background music
audioComponent.PlayCue("backmusic");
```

Also, add the following code inside the DoGameLogic() method, so that the explosion sound is played before calling the Start() method again:

```
audioComponent.PlayCue("explosion");
```

Then, add the following code inside CheckforNewMeteor() so that a sound is heard when a new meteor is added to the game, right after the line that contains rockCount++:

```
audioComponent.PlayCue("newmeteor");
```

Execute the game and see how the sound effects make the game even more entertaining.

Adding a Scoreboard

The Rock Rain scoreboard only shows the current number of meteors on the screen. As you saw in the previous chapter, first you need to create the game source and draw it in the game. Note that the scoreboard is a typical GameComponent, but to show that you don't need to create a component for that, let's draw this scoreboard in the Draw() method of the Game1 class.

Then, add a new Sprite Font. Call it font and add the following code to declare an object for it:

```
private SpriteFont gameFont;
```

Initialize the object in the LoadGraphicsContent() method just as you did with the other contents—inside the if statement, as follows:

```
// Load game font
gameFont = content.Load<SpriteFont>("Content\\font");
```

Now you only have to draw it right after drawing the game sprites. So, add the following code in the Draw() method of the Game1 class:

```
// Draw Score
spriteBatch.Begin();
spriteBatch.DrawString(gameFont, "Rocks: " + rockCount.ToString(),
new Vector2(15, 15), Color.YellowGreen);
spriteBatch.End();
```

Note that you used a separate spriteBatch object, only to draw the scoreboard. That way, the steps to draw the background picture, the sprites, and the scoreboard are also separated in the video card, avoiding possible "confusion" that the card might experience.

■Note Be careful with the use of third-party fonts in your games. Some fonts such as TrueType and OpenType are not royalty-free and have legal restrictions regarding their use, especially fonts used by Windows. There's a great diversity of free fonts that can be obtained in web sites across the Internet.

Shake, Baby!

Your game is almost ready. Now let's add one more effect to the game: the vibration. When players collide with a meteor, in addition to the explosion sound, you'll make the Xbox 360 gamepad vibrate so they can feel the collision impact.

As you saw in the previous chapter, you can start and finish the Xbox 360 gamepad vibration through the SetVibration() method. You're going to create a nonvisual GameComponent that will help you with this effect. So, add a new GameComponent to the project as usual and add the following code:

```
#region Using Statements
using System;
using System.Collections.Generic;
using Microsoft.Xna.Framework;
using Microsoft.Xna.Framework.Input;
#endregion

namespace FirstGame
{
    /// <summary>
    /// This component helps shake your Xbox 360 gamepad
    /// </summary>
    public class SimpleRumblePad : Microsoft.Xna.Framework.GameComponent
    {
        private int time;
        private int lastTickCount;

        public SimpleRumblePad(Game game)
            : base(game)
        {
        }

        /// <summary>
        /// Allows the game component to update itself.
        /// </summary>
        /// <param name="gameTime">Provides a snapshot of timing values.</param>
        public override void Update(GameTime gameTime)
        {
            if (time > 0) {
                int elapsed = System.Environment.TickCount - lastTickCount;
                if (elapsed >= time)
                {
                    time = 0;
```

```
                GamePad.SetVibration(PlayerIndex.One, 0, 0);
            }
        }
        base.Update(gameTime);
    }

    /// <summary>
    /// Turn off the rumble
    /// </summary>
    protected override void Dispose(bool disposing)
    {
        GamePad.SetVibration(PlayerIndex.One, 0, 0);

        base.Dispose(disposing);
    }

    /// <summary>
    /// Set the vibration
    /// </summary>
    /// <param name="Time">Vibration time</param>
    /// <param name="LeftMotor">Left Motor Intensity</param>
    /// <param name="RightMotor">Right Motor Intensity</param>
    public void RumblePad(int Time, float LeftMotor, float RightMotor)
    {
        lastTickCount = System.Environment.TickCount;
        time = Time;
        GamePad.SetVibration(PlayerIndex.One, LeftMotor, RightMotor);
    }
    }
}
```

In this class, the RumblePad() method receives the amount of time that the controller should stay vibrating and the vibration motor's intensity as parameters. So, also as usual, declare it in the Game1 class, as follows:

```
// Rumble Effect
private SimpleRumblePad rumblePad;
```

Initialize it in the Initialize() method of the Game1 class:

```
rumblePad = new SimpleRumblePad(this);
Components.Add(rumblePad);
```

Make the controller vibrate right after executing the explosion sound, in the DoGameLogic() method:

```
// Shake!
rumblePad.RumblePad(500, 1.0f, 1.0f);
```

Congratulations—you've just finished your first game!

Modifying and Deploying to the Xbox 360

You know that XNA technology allows you to create games for the PC as well as the Xbox 360, so if you wish to make a console version of Rock Rain, all you have to do is create a copy of this project for Xbox 360. Just right-click your Windows Project for Rock Rain and choose Create Copy of Project for Xbox 360, as shown in Figure 3-6. Compile, and it's ready to go. You immediately have a game that works on the Xbox 360.

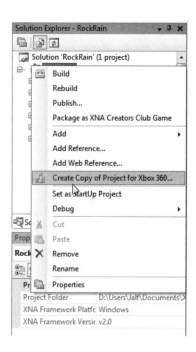

Figure 3-6. *Creating an Xbox 360 version of Rock Rain*

However, not everything is that simple. First, to deploy your game in the Xbox 360 you need a Creator's Club subscription, which enables your PC and the correctly registered console to communicate. This subscription is paid and can be renewed annually or every three months. Besides this, to deploy the game your console must be connected to the Xbox LIVE network.

Also note the difference between televisions (used by the consoles) and monitors (used by the PC). In an ordinary PC monitor you have access to all areas of the screen, whereas in a TV you're forced to use what is called the *safe area*. Briefly, safe area is a term used in television production to describe the areas of the television picture that can be seen on television screens.

In other words, not everything that you put on the screen is visible on an ordinary TV. Older TVs can display less of the space outside of the safe area than ones made more recently. Flat panel screens, plasma, and liquid crystal display (LCD) screens generally can show most of the "unsafe" area.

This leads you to a problem regarding the *margin* of the screen. As the player cannot leave the margin of the screen, knowing exactly where the visible margin of the screen is can be a problem. Normally, the game industry works with a 3 to 5 percent margin in relation to the physical margin of the screen.

So, in your Ship class, which represents the player's spaceship, add this code in the part where you calculated the size of the screen, in the class constructor:

```
#if XBOX360
      // On the 360, we need be careful about the TV's "safe" area.
      screenBounds = new Rectangle((int)(Game.Window.ClientBounds.Width * 0.03f),
                         (int)(Game.Window.ClientBounds.Height * 0.03f),
                         Game.Window.ClientBounds.Width -
      (int)(Game.Window.ClientBounds.Width * 0.03f),
      Game.Window.ClientBounds.Height -
        (int)(Game.Window.ClientBounds.Height * 0.03f));
#else
      screenBounds = new Rectangle(0,0,Game.Window.ClientBounds.Width,
                Game.Window.ClientBounds.Height);
#endif
```

All you do is this: if it's an Xbox 360 project, compile the code that creates the rectangle that defines the screen margin with a size 3 percent smaller than the rectangle of a PC project, which takes all the monitor space. It's that simple.

Summary

In this chapter you learned the basics about creating 2-D games, and you went through a small project phase, focusing on the items that the game programmer and designer should have in mind before starting to write any code.

You also learned how to model your game using GameComponents and create the game logic itself, modifying and testing the state of these components inside the game's loop. You saw that you can implement simple sprites using GameComponents and take advantage of all the classes that XNA already offers.

You also saw how you can add sounds and vibration effects to your game, as well as use a conditional compilation to solve the "safe area" issue of using TVs with video game consoles.

■ ■ ■

CHAPTER 4

Improving Your First 2-D Game

Let's face reality. Rock Rain is cool, fun, but—it's too simple, isn't it? In this chapter, you're going to add some more characteristics of a "real game" to it. We'll show you some more sophisticated techniques you can use to create an even more fun game. Let's go.

Planning Rock Rain's New Version

A striking feature of any game is missing in Rock Rain: the presentation screen! When the player runs the game, he's immediately thrown in the meteor field without warning. The ideal would be to show a screen—the game presentation—leading to another screen with instructions, the game help, and an option to start the game itself. That's much more elegant.

Let's also change some aspects of the playability. Now the game will have animated sprites and an energy meter, and will be able to be played by two players simultaneously. That's more interesting, isn't it?

So, start creating a new project and call it RockRainEnhanced, the same way you did in the previous chapter. Add a new folder called Core, and add to this folder the AudioComponent and the SimpleRumblePad that you created in the version of Rock Rain in the previous chapter, because you're also going to use these again in this new project. You can find more media content for this game, including new textures and sounds, in the Source Code/Download area of the Apress web site at http://www.apress.com, so add this stuff in your Content project folder.

Creating the Game Screens

All modern games have many *screens*: a screen for the opening, a screen for the instructions, a screen for the game itself, and so on. Because in each screen what is shown is a lot more than a simple image, in the game industry it's common to call these screens *scenes*.

A scene is composed (normally) of some background image, background music, and a group of "actors" that "act" in the scene to show to the user some information about the game.

For example, look at the opening screen of Rock Rain Enhanced in Figure 4-1.

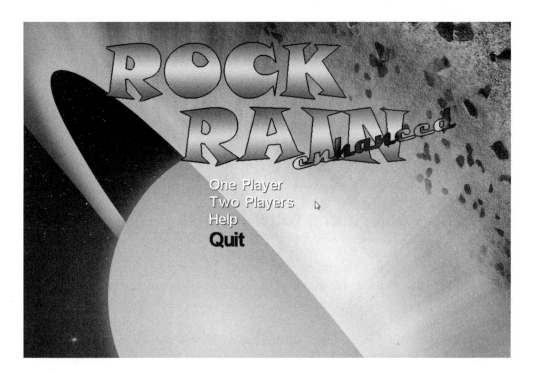

Figure 4-1. *Opening screen*

In this scene you have a nice background screen and two words that come up from the screen's margin to form the word "Rock Rain," as well as an options menu for the game, along with background music.

Note that you have some "actors" here in this scene. Besides the sprites that have moved to form the game's title, you have an animated menu that moves with the Xbox 360 gamepad or keyboard. This group of images, sounds, and actors forms this scene. The user can go to another scene according to the menu options. In this version of Rock Rain you have three scenes: the *start scene*, the *help scene*, and the *action scene*. Figure 4-2 shows the flow of these game scenes.

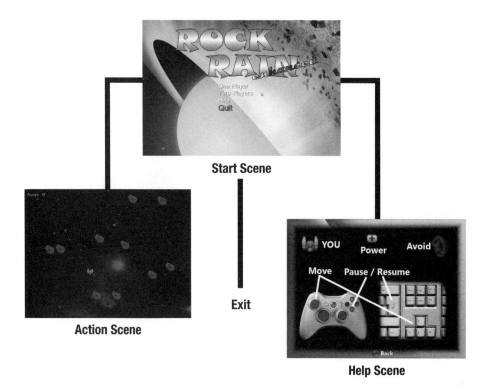

Figure 4-2. *Flow of the game scenes*

Now, using XNA terms, each game scene is a GameComponent that has other GameComponents representing the actors of the scene. Each scene has its own unique qualities, but also some things in common. For example, each scene contains its own collection of GameComponents that represents the actors in that scene. Also, in each scene a method shows it or closes it according to the flow of the scenes that the user chose (when you open the action scene you'll have to also close the start scene, for example).

You'll also be able to *pause* each scene. This is useful when you want to interrupt a game for a fast trip to the bathroom, for example. You do this by simply *not* executing the Update() method of the scene's GameComponents. Remember that XNA calls the Update() method to update the status of a GameComponent. If it isn't called, the GameComponent won't be updated and it will be "stopped" in the game scene.

In this architecture, the only GameComponents that will be added to the list of the game's components are the scenes, because the other GameComponents that build the scene itself will be added to the lists of components of the proper scene.

You'll initially create the class that implements the common functionality of the scenes, then add a new GameComponent called GameScene. For project organization purposes, put it inside the Core folder.

Start with the code. First, your scene is a visual component, so derive it from DrawableGameComponent instead of GameComponent. Next, as mentioned, each scene contains your own list of actors, meaning that it has your own list of GameComponents. Start declaring it in the class as follows:

```
/// <summary>
/// List of child GameComponents
/// </summary>
private readonly List<GameComponent> components;
```

Also add a property to expose the Components list, to be able to add to new actors to the scene from the derived classes:

```
/// <summary>
/// Components of Game Scene
/// </summary>
public List<GameComponent> Components
{
    get { return components; }
}
```

In the constructor of this class, you'll initialize this list and set that the component will not be visible or will have its status updated initially, using the attributes Visible and Enabled of the DrawableGameComponent class:

```
/// <summary>
/// Default Constructor
/// </summary>
public GameScene(Game game) : base(game){
    components = new List<GameComponent>();
    Visible = false;
    Enabled = false;
}
```

Then, to show or hide the scene, change the values of these attributes. You create two methods for this:

```
/// <summary>
/// Show the scene
/// </summary>
public virtual void Show()
{
    Visible = true;
    Enabled = true;
```

```
}
/// <summary>
/// Hide the scene
/// </summary>
public virtual void Hide()
{
    Visible = false;
    Enabled = false;
}
```

Now you have to handle the actors of the scene correctly. For each call to the Update() method of the scene, you have to call the respective method for each actor in the scene, to update your status. If the object of the scene is disabled (Enabled = false), then XNA won't call the Update() method, and none of the actors of the scene will be updated either, because its respective Update() methods won't have executed:

```
/// <summary>
/// Allows the GameComponent to update itself.
/// </summary>
/// <param name="gameTime">Provides a snapshot of timing values.</param>
public override void Update(GameTime gameTime)
{
    // Update the child GameComponents (if Enabled)
    for (int i = 0; i < components.Count; i++)
    {
        if (components[i].Enabled)
        {
            components[i].Update(gameTime);
        }
    }
    base.Update(gameTime);
}
```

The drawing code for the actors is similar. For each Draw() method executed in the scene, call the Draw() method for each DrawableGameComponent that is inserted in the list of components of the scene:

```
/// <summary>
/// Allows the GameComponent to draw your content in the game screen
/// </summary>
public override void Draw(GameTime gameTime)
{
    // Draw the child GameComponents (if drawable)
```

```
    for (int i = 0; i < components.Count; i++)
    {
        GameComponent gc = components[i];
        if ((gc is DrawableGameComponent) &&
            ((DrawableGameComponent) gc).Visible)
        {
            ((DrawableGameComponent) gc).Draw(gameTime);
        }
    }
    base.Draw(gameTime);
}
```

In short, all that this GameComponent does is correctly manipulate calling the Draw() and Update() methods of the game class, drawing and updating the other GameComponents that compose a scene. Also, note that the Show() and Hide() methods show and hide a game scene, avoiding the execution of the Draw() and Update() methods using the Visible and Enabled properties. Simple, isn't it?

Let's create three GameComponents derived from this class: one for the start scene of the game, another for the help scene, and another for the action scene itself. The game class will show the correct scene according to the game state. That is, you start in the opening scene, then players can go to the action scene, and go back to the opening after losing all their lives. Alternatively, players can choose to go to the help scene from the start scene, and so on, until they choose the option to leave the start scene.

So, add three GameComponents called StartScene, HelpScene, and ActionScene, respectively. As you start with the help scene, declare it in the Game1 class of your game, as follows:

```
// Game Scenes
protected HelpScene helpScene;
// Active Game Scene
protected GameScene activeScene;
```

Note that these three GameComponents will be derived from the GameScene class, seen before. However, you don't need to change them now—you'll go back to each of them shortly. The activeScene attribute contains the active scene in the game.

Creating the Help Screen

Let's start with the most simple scene in this game. In this scene, you'll show the game instructions, and the user will be able to click the A button on the Xbox 360 gamepad or the Enter key on the keyboard to go back to the initial scene.

This scene contains only the instructions of how to play the game, and you can create it just by showing a simple image with the game instructions. However, as the scene is composed of GameComponents, first you need one GameComponent to draw images.

Add a new GameComponent to the Core folder and name it ImageComponent.cs. Again, this component is a visual component, so derive it from DrawableGameComponent instead of GameComponent.

This GameComponent is able to draw a texture on the screen in centered mode or stretched mode, to fit the image on the screen. To do so, add the following enumeration, which the constructor will use to inform the component that the image has to be drawn:

```
public enum DrawMode
{
    Center = 1,
    Stretch,
};
```

You already know that you need a Texture2D object, a Rectangle object, and a SpriteBatch object to draw an image, besides the proper attribute that describes how the image will be drawn in this case. Declare these objects in the class:

```
// Texture to draw
protected readonly Texture2D texture;
// Draw Mode
protected readonly DrawMode drawMode;
// SpriteBatch
protected SpriteBatch spriteBatch = null;
// Image Rectangle
protected Rectangle imageRect;
```

In the class constructor, calculate the destination rectangle of the image on the screen, which depends on how the image will be drawn, in the DrawMode enumeration value:

```
/// <summary>
/// Default constructor
/// </summary>
/// <param name="game">The game object</param>
/// <param name="texture">Texture to Draw</param>
/// <param name="drawMode">Draw Mode</param>
public ImageComponent(Game game, Texture2D texture, DrawMode drawMode)
: base(game)
{
        this.texture = texture;
```

```
        this.drawMode = drawMode;
        // Get the current spritebatch
        spriteBatch = (SpriteBatch)
                Game.Services.GetService(typeof (SpriteBatch));

        // Create a rectangle with the size and position of the image
        switch (drawMode)
        {
            case DrawMode.Center:
            imageRect = new Rectangle((Game.Window.ClientBounds.Width -
                    texture.Width)/2,(Game.Window.ClientBounds.Height -
                    texture.Height)/2,texture.Width, texture.Height);
            break;
            case DrawMode.Stretch:
                    imageRect = new Rectangle(0, 0, Game.Window.ClientBounds.Width,
                            Game.Window.ClientBounds.Height);
            break;
        }
    }
```

In the `Draw()` method, you just use the `SpriteBatch` object to draw the image:

```
/// <summary>
/// Allows the GameComponent to draw itself.
/// </summary>
/// <param name="gameTime">Provides a snapshot of timing values.</param>
public override void Draw(GameTime gameTime)
{
    spriteBatch.Draw(texture, imageRect, Color.White);
    base.Draw(gameTime);
}
```

Observe that putting an image in a scene might not be as simple as previously thought. If this image is shown on a TV or on an ordinary monitor with a 4:3 aspect ratio, it will be displayed correctly. However, if it is drawn on a widescreen monitor or regular TV, it can be distorted and it will look weird on the screen.

So, you can create two images: one for the 4:3 monitors and TVs, and another for widescreen. You can choose the image to be drawn according to the screen type, although you'll always have to create two versions of each image that you want to show. Another often used alternative is to draw *two* overlapping images. One image is in the background, distorted to take up the whole screen (widescreen or not), and another is drawn centered on top, so it looks okay whether in widescreen or not. In your game, you'll use the textures in Figure 4-3.

Also note the treatment that was given to the input processing. You always compare the device's previous state with its current state to control if a user in fact pressed a button or key in the current scene.

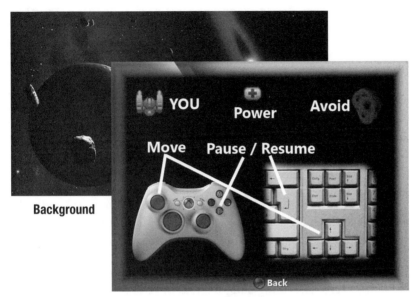

Figure 4-3. *Images that are part of the help scene*

That way, your help scene has only two GameComponents that draw images: one to draw the background image and another to draw the foreground image with the instructions. Add a new class called HelpScene and add the code from Listing 4-1.

Listing 4-1. *Help Scene GameComponent*

```
#region Using Statements

using Microsoft.Xna.Framework;
using Microsoft.Xna.Framework.Graphics;
using RockRainEnhanced.Core;

#endregion

namespace RockRainEnhanced
{
    /// <summary>
```

```
/// This is a GameComponent that represents the help scene
/// </summary>
public class HelpScene : GameScene
{
    public HelpScene(Game game, Texture2D textureBack, Texture2D textureFront)
        : base(game)
    {
        Components.Add(new ImageComponent(game, textureBack,
            ImageComponent.DrawMode.Stretch));
        Components.Add(new ImageComponent(game, textureFront,
            ImageComponent.DrawMode.Center));
    }
}
}
```

Also add the following code in the Game1 class and change the LoadContent() method to see this component in action. You just load the associated content, create an instance of HelpScene, and execute the Show() method of the HelpScene object:

```
// Textures
protected Texture2D helpBackgroundTexture, helpForegroundTexture;

/// <summary>
/// LoadContent will be called once per game and is the place to load
/// all your content.
/// </summary>
protected override void LoadContent()
{
    // Create a new SpriteBatch, which can be used to draw textures.
    spriteBatch = new SpriteBatch(graphics.GraphicsDevice);
    Services.AddService(typeof (SpriteBatch), spriteBatch);

    // Create the Credits / Instruction Scene
    helpBackgroundTexture = Content.Load<Texture2D>("helpbackground");
    helpForegroundTexture = Content.Load<Texture2D>("helpForeground");
    helpScene = new HelpScene(this, helpBackgroundTexture,
            helpForegroundTexture);
    Components.Add(helpScene);
    helpScene.Show();
    activeScene = helpScene;
}
```

Execute the code. The result appears in Figure 4-4. See how the scene is adequately shown both in normal format (4:3) and in widescreen (16:9).

Figure 4-4. *Help scene in normal and widescreen format*

Creating the Opening Screen

The opening screen of a game always gives a "taste" of the game itself. Normally it's something striking, which must show some of the game features and give the user a navigation menu between the game itself, options, help, and so on.

For Rock Rain, you'll create a scene with the game name in large letters coming from the screen borders and an option menu right beneath (1980s arcade style), with a background with some meteor theme. You'll use the textures in Figure 4-5 to do this.

Foreground

Background

Figure 4-5. *Textures of the opening screen*

Then, you'll have four actors in the opening screen. One is named "Rock," which comes into the scene from the left and goes to the center. The second one is named "Rain," and comes from the right also to the center of the screen. The third is named "enhanced," which keeps blinking right below the word "Rain."

The fourth actor shows after the preceding three, and is a menu with the game options. Because it's a little more sophisticated than just a sprite animation, you'll first create a GameComponent to handle menus.

Creating the Menu Component

Your menu for the game will be simple and functional at the same time. It will be drawn using two different fonts, where the bigger font will highlight the selected item.

Start adding a new GameComponent called TextMenuComponent in the Core folder. Again, this component is a visual component, so derive it from DrawableGameComponent instead of GameComponent.

In this component, you'll need two fonts to draw the text in normal and selected status, a string list with the items to be drawn, the color of the regular and selected items, the size and position of the menu and, as always, a SpriteBatch object to draw the text in the screen. So, add the following code to the class to declare these objects:

```
// SpriteBatch
protected SpriteBatch spriteBatch = null;
// Fonts
protected readonly SpriteFont regularFont, selectedFont;
// Colors
protected Color regularColor = Color.White, selectedColor = Color.Red;
// Menu Position
protected Vector2 position = new Vector2();
// Items
protected int selectedIndex = 0;
private readonly StringCollection menuItems;
// Size of menu in pixels
protected int width, height;
```

Also add a set of properties to handle these attributes:

```
/// <summary>
/// Set the Menu Options
/// </summary>
/// <param name="items"></param>
public void SetMenuItems(string[] items)
{
        menuItems.Clear();
        menuItems.AddRange(items);
        CalculateBounds();
}


/// <summary>
/// Width of menu in pixels
/// </summary>
public int Width
{
        get { return width; }
}
/// <summary>
/// Height of menu in pixels
/// </summary>
public int Height
{
        get { return height; }
```

```
}
/// <summary>
/// Selected menu item index
/// </summary>
public int SelectedIndex
{
        get { return selectedIndex; }
        set { selectedIndex = value; }
}
/// <summary>
/// Regular item color
/// </summary>
public Color RegularColor
{
        get { return regularColor; }
        set { regularColor = value; }
}
/// <summary>
/// Selected item color
/// </summary>
public Color SelectedColor
{
        get { return selectedColor; }
        set { selectedColor = value; }
}
/// <summary>
/// Position of component in screen
/// </summary>
public Vector2 Position
{
        get { return position; }
        set { position = value; }
}
```

Notice the CalculateBounds() in the SetMenuItems() method. The items on the menu are drawn centered horizontally. To do this, you need to calculate the width and the height of the menu—values that might vary in accordance with the items that have been added to the component and the font size. The CalculateBounds() method does this calculation using the MeasureString() method of the SpriteFont class, which gets the string size in pixels using this font:

```
/// <summary>
/// Get the menu bounds
/// </summary>
protected void CalculateBounds()
{
    width = 0;
    height = 0;
    foreach (string item in menuItems)
    {
        Vector2 size = selectedFont.MeasureString(item);
        if (size.X > width)
        {
            width = (int) size.X;
        }
        height += selectedFont.LineSpacing;
    }
}
```

The Draw() method that draws these elements is simple, because you need only a
loop drawing each item, below each other, using the correct font for the selected and regular entries. Each item is drawn with a little overlapped shadow, created by drawing the
same text twice, which gives a better look to the text. The code of this method follows:

```
/// <summary>
/// Allows the GameComponent to draw itself.
/// </summary>
/// <param name="gameTime">Provides a snapshot of timing values.</param>
public override void Draw(GameTime gameTime)
{
    float y = position.Y;
    for (int i = 0; i < menuItems.Count; i++)
    {
        SpriteFont font;
        Color theColor;
        if (i == SelectedIndex)
        {
            font = selectedFont;
            theColor = selectedColor;
        }
        else
        {
            font = regularFont;
```

```
            theColor = regularColor;
        }

        // Draw the text shadow
        spriteBatch.DrawString(font, menuItems[i],
            new Vector2(position.X + 1, y + 1), Color.Black);
        // Draw the text item
        spriteBatch.DrawString(font, menuItems[i],
            new Vector2(position.X, y), theColor);
        y += font.LineSpacing;
    }

    base.Draw(gameTime);
}
```

In fact, the drawn part of this class is the simplest part. This component must handle the user input as well, using the keyboard (up and down arrows) or the Xbox 360 gamepad. You want some sound effects to notify users when they change or select a menu item. In this case, add some new attributes to this class, to handle sound and user input:

```
// Used to handle input
protected KeyboardState oldKeyboardState;
protected GamePadState oldGamePadState;
// For audio effects
protected AudioComponent audioComponent;
```

As you did before, the Update() method is the right place to handle the user input. You just check the keyboard and the gamepad state, as you saw in the previous chapters, to change the attribute's selectedIndex value:

```
/// <summary>
/// Allows the GameComponent to update itself.
/// </summary>
/// <param name="gameTime">Provides a snapshot of timing values.</param>
public override void Update(GameTime gameTime)
{
    GamePadState gamepadState = GamePad.GetState(PlayerIndex.One);
    KeyboardState keyboardState = Keyboard.GetState();

    bool down, up;
    // Handle the keyboard
    down = (oldKeyboardState.IsKeyDown(Keys.Down) &&
```

```
        (keyboardState.IsKeyUp(Keys.Down)));
    up = (oldKeyboardState.IsKeyDown(Keys.Up) &&
        (keyboardState.IsKeyUp(Keys.Up)));
    // Handle the D-Pad
    down |= (oldGamePadState.DPad.Down == ButtonState.Pressed) &&
            (gamepadState.DPad.Down == ButtonState.Released);
    up |= (oldGamePadState.DPad.Up == ButtonState.Pressed) &&
        (gamepadState.DPad.Up == ButtonState.Released);

    if (down || up)
    {
        audioComponent.PlayCue("menu_scroll");
    }

    if (down)
    {
        selectedIndex++;
        if (selectedIndex == menuItems.Count)
        {
            selectedIndex = 0;
        }
    }
    if (up)
    {
        selectedIndex--;
        if (selectedIndex == -1)
        {
            selectedIndex = menuItems.Count - 1;
        }
    }

    oldKeyboardState = keyboardState;
    oldGamePadState = gamepadState;

    base.Update(gameTime);
}
```

Finally, in the class constructor you must initialize all these things:

```
/// <summary>
/// Default constructor
/// </summary>
/// <param name="game">the main game object</param>
```

```
/// <param name="normalFont">Font for regular items</param>
/// <param name="selectedFont">Font for selected item</param>
public TextMenuComponent(Game game, SpriteFont normalFont,
    SpriteFont selectedFont) : base(game)
{
    regularFont = normalFont;
    this.selectedFont = selectedFont;
    menuItems = new StringCollection();

    // Get the current spritebatch
    spriteBatch = (SpriteBatch)
        Game.Services.GetService(typeof (SpriteBatch));

    // Get the current audiocomponent and play the background music
    audioComponent = (AudioComponent)
        Game.Services.GetService(typeof (AudioComponent));

    // Used for input handling
    oldKeyboardState = Keyboard.GetState();
    oldGamePadState = GamePad.GetState(PlayerIndex.One);
}
```

More for the Opening Screen

Like you did with the HelpScene, add a new class called StartScene, derived from
GameScene. In this scene, you have an initial animation with two sprites (the "Rock" and
"Rain" words), a menu, background music, and another sprite with the word "enhanced"
flashing on the screen. Start adding the following attributes to the StartScene class:

```
// Misc
protected TextMenuComponent menu;
protected readonly Texture2D elements;
// Audio
protected AudioComponent audioComponent;
protected Cue backMusic;
// SpriteBatch
protected SpriteBatch spriteBatch = null;
// GUI Stuff
protected Rectangle rockRect = new Rectangle(0, 0, 536, 131);
protected Vector2 rockPosition;
protected Rectangle rainRect = new Rectangle(120, 165, 517, 130);
protected Vector2 rainPosition;
```

```
protected Rectangle enhancedRect = new Rectangle(8, 304, 375, 144);
protected Vector2 enhancedPosition;
protected bool showEnhanced;
protected TimeSpan elapsedTime = TimeSpan.Zero;
```

The attributes rockRect, rainRect, and enhancedRect refer to the rectangle that contains the images for the "Rock," "Rain," and "enhanced" in the texture. The attributes rockPosition, rainPosition, and enhancedPosition contain the position of these items on the screen. Draw these images in your chosen positions, but change the position of the "Rock" and "Rain" sprites to obtain a nice initial animation. When the "Rock" and "Rain" words are in the right place, you'll flash the "enhanced" word on the screen and show the initial menu.

All this is done in the Update() method, as follows. Note the calculations for the Xbox 360 version, to handle the 16:9 screen width:

```
/// <summary>
/// Allows the GameComponent to update itself.
/// </summary>
/// <param name="gameTime">Provides a snapshot of timing values.</param>
public override void Update(GameTime gameTime)
{
    if (!menu.Visible)
    {
        if (rainPosition.X >= (Game.Window.ClientBounds.Width - 595)/2)
        {
            rainPosition.X -= 15;
        }

        if (rockPosition.X <= (Game.Window.ClientBounds.Width - 715)/2)
        {
            rockPosition.X += 15;
        }
        else
        {
            menu.Visible = true;
            menu.Enabled = true;

            backMusic.Play();
#if XBOX360
            enhancedPosition = new Vector2((rainPosition.X +
            rainRect.Width - enhancedRect.Width / 2), rainPosition.Y);
#else
            enhancedPosition =
```

```
                    new Vector2((rainPosition.X + rainRect.Width -
                    enhancedRect.Width/2) - 80, rainPosition.Y);
#endif
            showEnhanced = true;
        }
    }
    else
    {
        elapsedTime += gameTime.ElapsedGameTime;

        if (elapsedTime > TimeSpan.FromSeconds(1))
        {
            elapsedTime -= TimeSpan.FromSeconds(1);
            showEnhanced = !showEnhanced;
        }
    }

    base.Update(gameTime);
}
```

The Draw() method draws the sprites in your actual position and draws the
"enhanced" sprite if the "Rock" and "Rain" sprites are in their final position (controlled
by the showEnhanced attribute):

```
/// <summary>
/// Allows the GameComponent to draw itself.
/// </summary>
/// <param name="gameTime">Provides a snapshot of timing values.</param>
public override void Draw(GameTime gameTime)
{
    base.Draw(gameTime);

    spriteBatch.Draw(elements, rockPosition, rockRect, Color.White);
    spriteBatch.Draw(elements, rainPosition, rainRect, Color.White);
    if (showEnhanced)
    {
        spriteBatch.Draw(elements, enhancedPosition, enhancedRect,
                        Color.White);
    }
}
```

You need to do some more work here. The Show() method must put these sprites
in their initial position and start the audio effects. The Hide() method must stop the

background music; otherwise, this music will play in another scene, won't it? The code for these methods follows:

```
/// <summary>
/// Show the start scene
/// </summary>
public override void Show()
{
    audioComponent.PlayCue("newmeteor");
    backMusic = audioComponent.GetCue("startmusic");

    rockPosition.X = -1*rockRect.Width;
    rockPosition.Y = 40;
    rainPosition.X = Game.Window.ClientBounds.Width;
    rainPosition.Y = 180;
    // Put the menu centered in screen
    menu.Position = new Vector2((Game.Window.ClientBounds.Width -
                                menu.Width)/2, 330);

    // These elements will be visible when the "Rock Rain" title
    // is done.
    menu.Visible = false;
    menu.Enabled = false;
    showEnhanced = false;

    base.Show();
}

/// <summary>
/// Hide the start scene
/// </summary>
public override void Hide()
{
    backMusic.Stop(AudioStopOptions.Immediate);
    base.Hide();
}
```

And, in the constructor you must initialize everything, including the Menu component with the game options:

```
/// <summary>
/// Default Constructor
/// </summary>
```

```
/// <param name="game">Main game object</param>
/// <param name="smallFont">Font for the menu items</param>
/// <param name="largeFont">Font for the menu selected item</param>
/// <param name="background">Texture for background image</param>
/// <param name="elements">Texture with the foreground elements</param>
public StartScene(Game game, SpriteFont smallFont, SpriteFont largeFont,
                  Texture2D background,Texture2D elements)
    : base(game)
{
    this.elements = elements;
    Components.Add(new ImageComponent(game, background,
                                     ImageComponent.DrawMode.Center));

    // Create the Menu
    string[] items = {"One Player", "Two Players", "Help", "Quit"};
    menu = new TextMenuComponent(game, smallFont, largeFont);
    menu.SetMenuItems(items);
    Components.Add(menu);

    // Get the current spritebatch
    spriteBatch = (SpriteBatch) Game.Services.GetService(
                                   typeof (SpriteBatch));
    // Get the current audiocomponent and play the background music
    audioComponent = (AudioComponent)
        Game.Services.GetService(typeof(AudioComponent));
}
```

Now modify the code of the LoadContent() method in the Game1 class to load the content needed in this scene:

```
/// <summary>
/// LoadContent will be called once per game and is the place to load
/// all your content.
/// </summary>
protected override void LoadContent()
{
    // Create a new SpriteBatch, which can be used to draw textures.
    spriteBatch = new SpriteBatch(graphics.GraphicsDevice);
    Services.AddService(typeof (SpriteBatch), spriteBatch);
    // Create the Credits / Instruction Scene
    helpBackgroundTexture = Content.Load<Texture2D>("helpbackground");
    helpForegroundTexture = Content.Load<Texture2D>("helpForeground");
    helpScene = new HelpScene(this, helpBackgroundTexture,
```

```
                helpForegroundTexture);
        Components.Add(helpScene);

        // Create the Start Scene
        smallFont = Content.Load<SpriteFont>("menuSmall");
        largeFont = Content.Load<SpriteFont>("menuLarge");
        startBackgroundTexture = Content.Load<Texture2D>("startbackground");
        startElementsTexture = Content.Load<Texture2D>("startSceneElements");
        startScene = new StartScene(this, smallFont$, largeFont,
            startBackgroundTexture, startElementsTexture);
        Components.Add(startScene);

        startScene.Show();
        activeScene = startScene;
    }
}
```

Declare these objects in the Game1 class to see the scene in action:

```
protected StartScene startScene;
protected Texture2D startBackgroundTexture, startElementsTexture;
// Fonts
private SpriteFont smallFont, largeFont
```

Execute the program and you should see something similar to Figure 4-1.

Creating the Action Scene

Up to now you've only created the opening and help scenes of the game. The most important scene is still missing: the game scene itself! This scene will look like the first version of Rock Rain, with the addition of some game rule changes and two-player support.

Still, there is an interesting change: the use of animated sprites, in which you have an animation composed of many frames that are shown on the screen in a specific order and during a specific time, giving an animation illusion. A component for animated sprites is a common component in any game, so you start this scene by creating this component.

Creating a GameComponent to Animate Sprites

As seen in Chapter 2, animated sprites are a basic resource in any 2-D game. They allow you to have actors in the scene that are more than a single moving image, allowing you to give the illusion of animation, the same way it's done in TV cartoons. In Rock Rain's case, you're using animated sprites to animate your meteors, which now spin while they move on the screen. So, create a class called Sprite and use the code in Listing 4-2 for this GameComponent. This code is just an improved version of the code shown in Chapter 2. Put it inside the project's Core folder.

Listing 4-2. *The Sprite GameComponent*

```
#region Using Statements

using System;
using System.Collections.Generic;
using Microsoft.Xna.Framework;
using Microsoft.Xna.Framework.Graphics;

#endregion

namespace RockRainEnhanced.Core
{
    /// <summary>
    /// This is a GameComponent that implements an Animated Sprite.
    /// </summary>
    public class Sprite : DrawableGameComponent
    {
        private int activeFrame;
        private readonly Texture2D texture;
        private List<Rectangle> frames;

        protected Vector2 position;
        protected TimeSpan elapsedTime = TimeSpan.Zero;
        protected Rectangle currentFrame;
        protected long frameDelay;
        protected SpriteBatch sbBatch;

        /// <summary>
        /// Default construtor
        /// </summary>
        /// <param name="game">The game object</param>
        /// <param name="theTexture">Texture that contains the sprite frames</param>
        public Sprite(Game game, ref Texture2D theTexture)
            : base(game)
        {
```

```csharp
        texture = theTexture;
        activeFrame = 0;
    }


    /// <summary>
    /// List with the frames of the animation
    /// </summary>
    public List<Rectangle> Frames
    {
        get { return frames; }
        set { frames = value; }
    }


    /// <summary>
    /// Allows the GameComponent to perform any initialization it needs to
    /// before starting to run.  This is where it can query for any required
    ///  services and load content.
    /// </summary>
    public override void Initialize()
    {
        // Get the current spritebatch
        sbBatch = (SpriteBatch) Game.Services.GetService(typeof (SpriteBatch));

        base.Initialize();
    }


    /// <summary>
    /// Allows the GameComponent to update itself.
    /// </summary>
    /// <param name="gameTime">Provides a snapshot of timing values.</param>
    public override void Update(GameTime gameTime)
    {
        elapsedTime += gameTime.ElapsedGameTime;

        // it's time for a next frame?
        if (elapsedTime > TimeSpan.FromMilliseconds(frameDelay))
        {
            elapsedTime -= TimeSpan.FromMilliseconds(frameDelay);
            activeFrame++;
            if (activeFrame == frames.Count)
            {
                activeFrame = 0;
```

```
            }
            // Get the current frame
            currentFrame = frames[activeFrame];
        }

        base.Update(gameTime);
    }

    /// <summary>
    /// Draw the sprite.
    /// </summary>
    /// <param name="gameTime">Provides a snapshot of timing values.</param>
    public override void Draw(GameTime gameTime)
    {
        sbBatch.Draw(texture, position, currentFrame, Color.White);

        base.Draw(gameTime);
    }
  }
}
```

The Update() method changes the current frame each *n* milliseconds to do the animation illusion, and the Draw() method draws the current frame in the current position in the screen. Now you'll use this class to create an animated sprite of the meteors. Create a class called Meteor and use the code in Listing 4-3.

Listing 4-3. *The Meteor GameComponent*

```
using System;
using System.Collections.Generic;
using Microsoft.Xna.Framework;
using Microsoft.Xna.Framework.Graphics;
using RockRainEnhanced.Core;

namespace RockRainEnhanced
{
    /// <summary>
    /// This class is the Animated Sprite for a Meteor
    /// </summary>
    public class Meteor : Sprite
    {
```

```csharp
// Vertical velocity
protected int Yspeed;
// Horizontal velocity
protected int Xspeed;
protected Random random;

// Unique ID for this meteor
private int index;

public Meteor(Game game, ref Texture2D theTexture) :
    base(game, ref theTexture)
{
    Frames = new List<Rectangle>();
    Rectangle frame = new Rectangle();
    frame.X = 468;
    frame.Y = 0;
    frame.Width = 49;
    frame.Height = 44;
    Frames.Add(frame);

    frame.Y = 50;
    Frames.Add(frame);

    frame.Y = 98;
    frame.Height = 45;
    Frames.Add(frame);

    frame.Y = 146;
    frame.Height = 49;
    Frames.Add(frame);

    frame.Y = 200;
    frame.Height = 44;
    Frames.Add(frame);

    frame.Y = 250;
    Frames.Add(frame);

    frame.Y = 299;
    Frames.Add(frame);
```

```
        frame.Y = 350;
        frame.Height = 49;
        Frames.Add(frame);

        // Initialize the random number generator and put the meteor in your
        // start position
        random = new Random(GetHashCode());
        PutinStartPosition();
    }


    /// <summary>
    /// Initialize Meteor Position and Velocity
    /// </summary>
    public void PutinStartPosition()
    {
        position.X = random.Next(Game.Window.ClientBounds.Width -
            currentFrame.Width);
        position.Y = 0;
        YSpeed = 1 + random.Next(9);
        XSpeed = random.Next(3) - 1;
    }


    /// <summary>
    /// Update the Meteor Position
    /// </summary>
    public override void Update(GameTime gameTime)
    {
        // Check if the meteor is still visible
        if ((position.Y >= Game.Window.ClientBounds.Height) ||
            (position.X >= Game.Window.ClientBounds.Width) ||
            (position.X <= 0))
        {
            PutinStartPosition();
        }

        // Move meteor
        position.Y += Yspeed;
        position.X += Xspeed;

        base.Update(gameTime);
    }
```

```csharp
        /// Vertical velocity
        /// </summary>
        public int YSpeed
        {
            get { return Yspeed; }
            set
            {
                Yspeed = value;
                frameDelay = 200 - (Yspeed * 5);
            }
        }

        /// <summary>
        /// Horizontal Velocity
        /// </summary>
        public int XSpeed
        {
            get { return Xspeed; }
            set { Xspeed = value; }
        }

        /// <summary>
        /// Meteor Identifier
        /// </summary>
        public int Index
        {
            get { return index; }
            set { index = value; }
        }

        /// <summary>
        /// Check if the meteor intersects with the specified rectangle
        /// </summary>
        /// <param name="rect">test rectangle</param>
        /// <returns>true, if has a collision</returns>
        public bool CheckCollision(Rectangle rect)
        {
            Rectangle spriterect =new Rectangle((int) position.X, (int) position.Y,
                currentFrame.Width, currentFrame.Height);
            return spriterect.Intersects(rect);
        }
    }
}
```

This class is similar to the first version in the previous chapter: only the code that adds the animation frames is in the constructor. All the rest follows the same previous logic. That is, the meteors will "fall," but now not like a static image, instead with an animation where they appear to spin. Cool, isn't it?

You also added a property Index to get a unique identifier for each meteor in the game, to be able to get a specified meteor when needed (you'll use this feature in the next version of Rock Rain).

Let's create one more GameComponent, this one only for design purposes, that will centralize all the meteor treatment. This class will be responsible for drawing and updating all the game's meteors, as well as doing the collision test and adding new meteors as time goes by. The advantage of having an object to manage other objects is that the game design becomes simpler and at the same time more efficient. For example, you don't need to pass through all the GameComponents to do a collision test as in the version in the previous chapter, but just through the GameComponents that are under control of this manager, which only controls the meteors. That way you gain a little performance benefit.

Add a class called MeteorsManager and add the code in Listing 4-4.

Listing 4-4. *The MeteorsManager GameComponent*

```
#region Using Statements

using System;
using System.Collections.Generic;
using Microsoft.Xna.Framework;
using Microsoft.Xna.Framework.Graphics;
using RockRainEnhanced.Core;

#endregion

namespace RockRainEnhanced
{
    /// <summary>
    /// This GameComponent implements a manager for all Meteors in the game.
    /// </summary>
    public class MeteorsManager : DrawableGameComponent
    {
        // List of active meteors
        protected List<Meteor> meteors;
        // Constant for initial meteor count
        private const int STARTMETEORCOUNT = 10;
        // Time for a new meteor
        private const int ADDMETEORTIME = 5000;
```

```csharp
protected Texture2D meteorTexture;
protected TimeSpan elapsedTime = TimeSpan.Zero;
protected AudioComponent audioComponent;


public MeteorsManager(Game game, ref Texture2D theTexture)
    : base(game)
{
    meteorTexture = theTexture;
    meteors = new List<Meteor>();
}


/// <summary>
/// Allows the GameComponent to perform any initialization it needs to
/// before starting to run.  This is where it can query for any required
/// services and load content.
/// </summary>
public override void Initialize()
{
    audioComponent = (AudioComponent)
        Game.Services.GetService(typeof (AudioComponent));

    meteors.Clear();

    Start();

    for (int i = 0; i < meteors.Count; i++)
    {
        meteors[i].Initialize();
    }

    base.Initialize();
}

/// <summary>
/// Start the Meteor Rain
/// </summary>
public void Start()
{
    // Initialize a counter
    elapsedTime = TimeSpan.Zero;
```

```csharp
    // Add the meteors
    for (int i = 0; i < STARTMETEORCOUNT; i++)
    {
        AddNewMeteor();
    }
}

/// <summary>
/// All Meteors in the game
/// </summary>
public List<Meteor> AllMeteors
{
    get { return meteors; }
}

/// <summary>
/// Check if it is time for a new meteor
/// </summary>
private void CheckforNewMeteor(GameTime gameTime)
{
    // Add a rock each ADDMETEORTIME
    elapsedTime += gameTime.ElapsedGameTime;

    if (elapsedTime > TimeSpan.FromMilliseconds(ADDMETEORTIME))
    {
        elapsedTime -= TimeSpan.FromMilliseconds(ADDMETEORTIME);

        AddNewMeteor();
        // Play a sound for a new meteor
        audioComponent.PlayCue("newmeteor");
    }
}

/// <summary>
/// Add a new meteor in the scene
/// </summary>
private void AddNewMeteor()
{
    Meteor newMeteor = new Meteor(Game, ref meteorTexture);
    newMeteor.Initialize();
    meteors.Add(newMeteor);
```

```csharp
        // Set the meteor identifier
        newMeteor.Index = meteors.Count - 1;


    }


    /// <summary>
    /// Allows the GameComponent to update itself.
    /// </summary>
    /// <param name="gameTime">Provides a snapshot of timing values.</param>
    public override void Update(GameTime gameTime)
    {
        CheckforNewMeteor(gameTime);

        // Update Meteors
        for (int i = 0; i < meteors.Count; i++)
        {
            meteors[i].Update(gameTime);
        }

        base.Update(gameTime);
    }


    /// <summary>
    /// Check if the ship collided with a meteor
    /// <returns>true, if has a collision</returns>
    /// </summary>
    public bool CheckForCollisions(Rectangle rect)
    {
        for (int i = 0; i < meteors.Count; i++)
        {
            if (meteors[i].CheckCollision(rect))
            {
                // BOOM !!
                audioComponent.PlayCue("explosion");

                // Put the meteor back to your initial position
                meteors[i].PutinStartPosition();

                return true;
            }
        }
```

```
                return false;
        }


        /// <summary>
        /// Allows the GameComponent to draw your content in the game screen
        /// </summary>
        public override void Draw(GameTime gameTime)
        {
            // Draw the meteors
            for (int i = 0; i < meteors.Count; i++)
            {
                meteors[i].Draw(gameTime);
            }

            base.Draw(gameTime);
        }
    }
}
```

Observe that this class contains a great deal of the code that was previously inside the Game1 class in the previous chapter, but essentially it does the same thing. You'll use this class later to compose the action scene.

■**Note** Overall, it's a good idea to create a management class for each group of GameComponents in a game. It's normal to see classes such as EnemyManager, WizardManager, and so on, because this puts all the complexity of this type of game element in only one class. This simplifies the code and maximizes the reuse of these components in other games.

Creating the Scoreboard

You still need to create one element of the action scene: the scoreboard. This scoreboard shows the quantity of points and energy of the player's ship. This class is simple: it only draws two lines of text on the screen. Add a class to the project called Score and add the code in Listing 4-5.

Listing 4-5. *The Score GameComponent*

```
#region Using Statements

using Microsoft.Xna.Framework;
using Microsoft.Xna.Framework.Graphics;

#endregion

namespace RockRainEnhanced
{
    /// <summary>
    /// This is a GameComponent that implements the Game Score.
    /// </summary>
    public class Score : DrawableGameComponent
    {
        // Spritebatch
        protected SpriteBatch spriteBatch = null;

        // Score Position
        protected Vector2 position = new Vector2();

        // Values
        protected int value;
        protected int power;

        protected readonly SpriteFont font;
        protected readonly Color fontColor;

        public Score(Game game, SpriteFont font, Color fontColor)
            : base(game)
        {
            this.font = font;
            this.fontColor = fontColor;
            // Get the current spritebatch
            spriteBatch = (SpriteBatch)
                        Game.Services.GetService(typeof (SpriteBatch));
        }

        /// <summary>
        /// Points value
        /// </summary>
```

```csharp
public int Value
{
    get { return value; }
    set { this.value = value; }
}

/// <summary>
/// Power Value
/// </summary>
public int Power
{
    get { return power; }
    set { power = value; }
}

/// <summary>
/// Position of component in screen
/// </summary>
public Vector2 Position
{
    get { return position; }
    set { position = value; }
}

/// <summary>
/// Allows the GameComponent to draw itself.
/// </summary>
/// <param name="gameTime">Provides a snapshot of timing values.</param>
public override void Draw(GameTime gameTime)
{
    string TextToDraw = string.Format("Score: {0}", value);

    // Draw the text shadow
    spriteBatch.DrawString(font, TextToDraw, new Vector2(position.X + 1,
                        position.Y + 1), Color.Black);
    // Draw the text item
    spriteBatch.DrawString(font, TextToDraw,
                        new Vector2(position.X, position.Y),
                        fontColor);

    float height = font.MeasureString(TextToDraw).Y;
    TextToDraw = string.Format("Power: {0}", power);
```

```
        // Draw the text shadow
        spriteBatch.DrawString(font, TextToDraw,
            new Vector2(position.X + 1, position.Y + 1 + height),
            Color.Black);
        // Draw the text item
        spriteBatch.DrawString(font, TextToDraw,
            new Vector2(position.X, position.Y + 1 + height),
            fontColor);

        base.Draw(gameTime);
    }
  }
}
```

Again, this looks like the code in the previous version, only this time it is encapsulated in a class and the text is now drawn with a little shadow under it, to enhance the legibility and give it a touch of style, like you did with the Menu component.

Creating the Energy Source

The change in Rock Rain's playability brings up the need for an interesting additional component. The player's ship now contains a finite energy source, which decreases over time and falls even more after a meteor collision. You have to provide a means for players to recharge their ships, so they can stay in the game longer, accumulating more points.

You'll create a new GameComponent, which looks like a small barrel of energy that shows up in regular intervals and "falls" together with the meteors. If the player touches it, it will refuel the ship with more energy. The idea is that the player keeps an eye out for this new element and tries to obtain it without hitting any incoming meteor.

Add a new class called PowerSource and add the code in Listing 4-6.

Listing 4-6. *The PowerSource GameComponent*

```
#region Using Statements

using System;
using System.Collections.Generic;
using Microsoft.Xna.Framework;
using Microsoft.Xna.Framework.Graphics;
using RockRainEnhanced.Core;

#endregion
```

```csharp
namespace RockRainEnhanced
{
    /// <summary>
    /// This is a GameComponent that implements Power Source Element.
    /// </summary>
    public class PowerSource : Sprite
    {
        protected Texture2D texture;
        protected Random random;

        public PowerSource(Game game, ref Texture2D theTexture)
            : base(game, ref theTexture)
        {
            texture = theTexture;

            Frames = new List<Rectangle>();
            Rectangle frame = new Rectangle();
            frame.X = 291;
            frame.Y = 17;
            frame.Width = 14;
            frame.Height = 12;
            Frames.Add(frame);

            frame.Y = 30;
            Frames.Add(frame);

            frame.Y = 43;
            Frames.Add(frame);

            frame.Y = 57;
            Frames.Add(frame);

            frame.Y = 70;
            Frames.Add(frame);

            frame.Y = 82;
            Frames.Add(frame);

            frameDelay = 200;

            // Initialize the random number generator and put the power
            // source in your start position
```

```
    random = new Random(GetHashCode());
    PutinStartPosition();
}


/// <summary>
/// Initialize Position and Velocity
/// </summary>
public void PutinStartPosition()
{
    position.X = random.Next(Game.Window.ClientBounds.Width -
        currentFrame.Width);
    position.Y = -10;
    Enabled = false;
}


public override void Update(GameTime gameTime)
{
    // Check if the power source is still visible
    if (position.Y >= Game.Window.ClientBounds.Height)
    {
        position.Y = 0;
        Enabled = false;
    }

    // Move
    position.Y += 1;

    base.Update(gameTime);
}


/// <summary>
/// Check if the object intersects with the specified rectangle
/// </summary>
/// <param name="rect">test rectangle</param>
/// <returns>true, if has a collision</returns>
public bool CheckCollision(Rectangle rect)
{
    Rectangle spriterect =
        new Rectangle((int) position.X, (int) position.Y,
        currentFrame.Width, currentFrame.Height);
    return spriterect.Intersects(rect);
}
```

```
        }
}
```

You did a similar thing with the Meteor class, creating an animation with the list of frames and updating its vertical position as time goes by, to give the "falling" effect.

Creating the Player's GameComponent

You're almost finished, but the main actor of the action scene is still missing: the player! In this new version, the code for the player's GameComponent is mostly the same as in the previous chapter, only with the addition of multiplayer support. This support differs from the previous version mainly in the treatment of energy, keyboard, points, and the way the player is drawn. The code of the Player class is in Listing 4-7.

Listing 4-7. *The Player GameComponent*

```
#region Using Statements

using System;
using Microsoft.Xna.Framework;
using Microsoft.Xna.Framework.Graphics;
using Microsoft.Xna.Framework.Input;

#endregion

namespace RockRainEnhanced
{
    /// <summary>
    /// This is a GameComponent that implements the player ship.
    /// </summary>
    public class Player : DrawableGameComponent
    {
        protected Texture2D texture;
        protected Rectangle spriteRectangle;
        protected Vector2 position;
        protected TimeSpan elapsedTime = TimeSpan.Zero;
        protected PlayerIndex playerIndex;

        // Screen Area
        protected Rectangle screenBounds;
```

```
        // Game Stuff
        protected int score;
        protected int power;
        private const int INITIALPOWER = 100;

        public Player(Game game, ref Texture2D theTexture, PlayerIndex playerID,
            Rectangle rectangle) : base(game)
        {
            texture = theTexture;
            position = new Vector2();
            playerIndex = playerID;

            // Create the source rectangle.
            // This represents where the sprite picture is in the surface
            spriteRectangle = rectangle;

#if XBOX360
    // On the 360, we need to take care about the TV "safe" area.
            screenBounds = new Rectangle((int)(Game.Window.ClientBounds.Width *
                0.03f),(int)(Game.Window.ClientBounds.Height * 0.03f),
                Game.Window.ClientBounds.Width -
                (int)(Game.Window.ClientBounds.Width * 0.03f),
                Game.Window.ClientBounds.Height -
                (int)(Game.Window.ClientBounds.Height * 0.03f));
#else
            screenBounds = new Rectangle(0, 0, Game.Window.ClientBounds.Width,
                Game.Window.ClientBounds.Height);
#endif
        }

        /// <summary>
        /// Put the ship in your start position in screen
        /// </summary>
        public void Reset()
        {
            if (playerIndex == PlayerIndex.One)
            {
                position.X = screenBounds.Width/3;
            }
            else
            {
```

```
            position.X = (int) (screenBounds.Width/1.5);
    }

    position.Y = screenBounds.Height - spriteRectangle.Height;
    score = 0;
    power = INITIALPOWER;
}

/// <summary>
/// Total Points of the Player
/// </summary>
public int Score
{
    get { return score; }
    set
    {
        if (value < 0)
        {
            score = 0;
        }
        else
        {
            score = value;
        }
    }
}

/// <summary>
/// Remaining Power
/// </summary>
public int Power
{
    get { return power; }
    set { power = value; }
}

/// <summary>
/// Update the ship position, points, and power
/// </summary>
public override void Update(GameTime gameTime)
{
    // Move the ship with the Xbox controller
```

```csharp
        GamePadState gamepadstatus = GamePad.GetState(playerIndex);
        position.Y += (int) ((gamepadstatus.ThumbSticks.Left.Y*3)*-2);
        position.X += (int) ((gamepadstatus.ThumbSticks.Left.X*3)*2);

        // Move the ship with the keyboard
        if (playerIndex == PlayerIndex.One)
        {
            HandlePlayer1KeyBoard();
        }
        else
        {
            HandlePlayer2KeyBoard();
        }

        // Keep the player inside the screen
        KeepInBound();

        // Update score
        elapsedTime += gameTime.ElapsedGameTime;

        if (elapsedTime > TimeSpan.FromSeconds(1))
        {
            elapsedTime -= TimeSpan.FromSeconds(1);
            score++;
            power--;
        }

        base.Update(gameTime);
    }

/// <summary>
/// Keep the ship inside the screen
/// </summary>
private void KeepInBound()
{
    if (position.X < screenBounds.Left)
    {
        position.X = screenBounds.Left;
    }
    if (position.X > screenBounds.Width - spriteRectangle.Width)
    {
        position.X = screenBounds.Width - spriteRectangle.Width;
```

```
        }
        if (position.Y < screenBounds.Top)
        {
            position.Y = screenBounds.Top;
        }
        if (position.Y > screenBounds.Height - spriteRectangle.Height)
        {
            position.Y = screenBounds.Height - spriteRectangle.Height;
        }
    }


    /// <summary>
    /// Handle the keys for the player 1 (arrow keys)
    /// </summary>
    private void HandlePlayer1KeyBoard()
    {
        KeyboardState keyboard = Keyboard.GetState();
        if (keyboard.IsKeyDown(Keys.Up))
        {
            position.Y -= 3;
        }
        if (keyboard.IsKeyDown(Keys.Down))
        {
            position.Y += 3;
        }
        if (keyboard.IsKeyDown(Keys.Left))
        {
            position.X -= 3;
        }
        if (keyboard.IsKeyDown(Keys.Right))
        {
            position.X += 3;
        }
    }


    /// <summary>
    /// Handle the keys for the player 2 (ASDW)
    /// </summary>
    private void HandlePlayer2KeyBoard()
    {
        KeyboardState keyboard = Keyboard.GetState();
        if (keyboard.IsKeyDown(Keys.W))
```

```
        {
            position.Y -= 3;
        }
        if (keyboard.IsKeyDown(Keys.S))
        {
            position.Y += 3;
        }
        if (keyboard.IsKeyDown(Keys.A))
        {
            position.X -= 3;
        }
        if (keyboard.IsKeyDown(Keys.D))
        {
            position.X += 3;
        }
    }


    /// <summary>
    /// Draw the ship sprite
    /// </summary>
    public override void Draw(GameTime gameTime)
    {
        // Get the current spritebatch
        SpriteBatch sBatch = (SpriteBatch)
            Game.Services.GetService(typeof (SpriteBatch));

        // Draw the ship
        sBatch.Draw(texture, position, spriteRectangle, Color.White);

        base.Draw(gameTime);
    }


    /// <summary>
    /// Get the bound rectangle of ship position in screen
    /// </summary>
    public Rectangle GetBounds()
    {
        return new Rectangle((int) position.X, (int) position.Y,
            spriteRectangle.Width, spriteRectangle.Height);
    }
    }
}
```

As you can see, this is practically the same class as in the previous chapter, but in the Update() method you handle the user input a little differently, testing the PlayerIndex to check for the correct gamepad or keyboard keys. In a multiplayer game, you'll instantiate two objects for this class with different PlayerIndexes and different rectangles in texture, for different ship sprites.

Bringing Everything Together

Now you have all the action scene components. The meteors, the score, and the player (or players) are ready to be put to work. Now add a class called ActionScene. This scene is the most complex scene of the game. It coordinates the action of all the components, as well as controls the game state, such as pause and gameOver.

Start declaring all elements of this scene, as follows:

```
// Basics
protected Texture2D actionTexture;
protected Cue backMusic;
protected SpriteBatch spriteBatch = null;

// Game Elements
protected Player player1;
protected Player player2;
protected MeteorsManager meteors;
protected PowerSource powerSource;
protected SimpleRumblePad rumblePad;
protected ImageComponent background;
protected Score scorePlayer1;
protected Score scorePlayer2;

// GUI Stuff
protected Vector2 pausePosition;
protected Vector2 gameoverPosition;
protected Rectangle pauseRect = new Rectangle(1, 120, 200, 44);
protected Rectangle gameoverRect = new Rectangle(1, 170, 350, 48);

// GameState elements
protected bool paused;
protected bool gameOver;
protected TimeSpan elapsedTime = TimeSpan.Zero;
protected bool twoPlayers;
```

It looks like the attributes from the game in the previous chapter, but you now have two Player instances (for a multiplayer game), two attributes for controlling the game state (paused and gameOver) and the components for Score, PowerSource, Meteors, and so on.

The constructor initializes all these objects, as follows:

```
/// <summary>
/// Default Constructor
/// </summary>
/// <param name="game">The main game object</param>
/// <param name="theTexture">Texture with the sprite elements</param>
/// <param name="backgroundTexture">Texture for the background</param>
/// <param name="font">Font used in the score</param>
public ActionScene(Game game, Texture2D theTexture,
    Texture2D backgroundTexture, SpriteFont font) : base(game)
{
    // Get the current audiocomponent and play the background music
    audioComponent = (AudioComponent)
        Game.Services.GetService(typeof (AudioComponent));

    background = new ImageComponent(game, backgroundTexture,
        ImageComponent.DrawMode.Stretch);
    Components.Add(background);

    actionTexture = theTexture;

    spriteBatch = (SpriteBatch)
        Game.Services.GetService(typeof (SpriteBatch));
    meteors = new MeteorsManager(Game, ref actionTexture);
    Components.Add(meteors);

    player1 = new Player(Game, ref actionTexture, PlayerIndex.One,
        new Rectangle(323, 15, 30, 30));
    player1.Initialize();
    Components.Add(player1);

    player2 = new Player(Game, ref actionTexture, PlayerIndex.Two,
        new Rectangle(360, 17, 30, 30));
    player2.Initialize();
    Components.Add(player2);

    scorePlayer1 = new Score(game, font, Color.Blue);
    scorePlayer1.Position = new Vector2(10, 10);
```

```
        Components.Add(scorePlayer1);
        scorePlayer2 = new Score(game, font, Color.Red);
        scorePlayer2.Position = new Vector2(
            Game.Window.ClientBounds.Width - 200, 10);
        Components.Add(scorePlayer2);

        rumblePad = new SimpleRumblePad(game);
        Components.Add(rumblePad);

        powerSource = new PowerSource(game, ref actionTexture);
        powerSource.Initialize();
        Components.Add(powerSource);
}
```

See how you create two instances for the Player class. For each player, just change
the PlayerIndex and the Rectangle of the image of the ship in the texture.

You also need to control the game state and define if the game is for one or two players,
or check if some of the players are already dead. Add these properties to the class:

```
/// <summary>
/// Indicate the 2-players game mode
/// </summary>
public bool TwoPlayers
{
    get { return twoPlayers; }
    set { twoPlayers = value; }
}

/// <summary>
/// True, if the game is in gameOver state
/// </summary>
public bool GameOver
{
    get { return gameOver; }
}

/// <summary>
/// Paused mode
/// </summary>
public bool Paused
{
    get { return paused; }
    set
```

```
    {
        paused = value;
        if (paused)
        {
            backMusic.Pause();
        }
        else
        {
            backMusic.Resume();
        }
    }
}
```

Like all the other scenes, you can use the Show() and Hide() methods to initialize and release scene components. In the Show() method you start playing the background music and setting the player2 status if you have a two-player game:

```
/// <summary>
/// Show the action scene
/// </summary>
public override void Show()
{
    backMusic = audioComponent.GetCue("backmusic");
    backMusic.Play();

    meteors.Initialize();
    powerSource.PutinStartPosition();

    player1.Reset();
    player2.Reset();

    paused = false;
    pausePosition.X = (Game.Window.ClientBounds.Width -
        pauseRect.Width)/2;
    pausePosition.Y = (Game.Window.ClientBounds.Height -
        pauseRect.Height)/2;

    gameOver = false;
    gameoverPosition.X = (Game.Window.ClientBounds.Width -
        gameoverRect.Width)/2;
    gameoverPosition.Y = (Game.Window.ClientBounds.Height -
        gameoverRect.Height)/2;
```

```
    // Is it a two-player game?
    player2.Visible = twoPlayers;
    player2.Enabled = twoPlayers;
    scorePlayer2.Visible = twoPlayers;
    scorePlayer2.Enabled = twoPlayers;

    base.Show();
}

/// <summary>
/// Hide the scene
/// </summary>
public override void Hide()
{
    // Stop the background music
    backMusic.Stop(AudioStopOptions.Immediate);
    // Stop the rumble
    rumblePad.Stop(PlayerIndex.One);
    rumblePad.Stop(PlayerIndex.Two);

    base.Hide();
}
```

And, as always, the Update() method synchronizes all these objects, checking the collisions and changing the game state for game over when some players die.

```
/// <summary>
/// Allows the GameComponent to update itself.
/// </summary>
/// <param name="gameTime">Provides a snapshot of timing values.</param>
public override void Update(GameTime gameTime)
{
    if ((!paused) && (!gameOver))
    {
        // Check collisions with meteors
        HandleDamages();

        // Check if a player gets a power boost
        HandlePowerSourceSprite(gameTime);

        // Update score
        scorePlayer1.Value = player1.Score;
        scorePlayer1.Power = player1.Power;
```

```
    if (twoPlayers)
    {
        scorePlayer2.Value = player2.Score;
        scorePlayer2.Power = player2.Power;
    }

    // Check if player is dead
    gameOver = ((player1.Power <= 0) || (player2.Power <= 0));
    if (gameOver)
    {
        player1.Visible = (player1.Power > 0);
        player2.Visible = (player2.Power > 0) && twoPlayers;
        // Stop the music
        backMusic.Stop(AudioStopOptions.Immediate);
        // Stop rumble
        rumblePad.Stop(PlayerIndex.One);
        rumblePad.Stop(PlayerIndex.Two);
    }

    // Update all other GameComponents
    base.Update(gameTime);
}

// In gameOver state, keep the meteors' animation
if (gameOver)
{
    meteors.Update(gameTime);
}
}
```

The HandleDamages() and HandlePowerSourceSprite() methods check the collisions with the meteors (and lose some player power), check the collision with the power source (and add some power to the player), and check if a player has zero or less power to end the game and put him or her in a game over state.

The HandleDamages() method is also similar to the collision test method from the previous chapter. Again, this method checks the collision with the players and meteors and one player with another player. For each collision the player loses ten points and ten power units:

```
/// <summary>
/// Handle collisions with a meteor
/// </summary>
private void HandleDamages()
```

```
{
    // Check Collision for player 1
    if (meteors.CheckForCollisions(player1.GetBounds()))
    {
        // Shake!
        rumblePad.RumblePad(PlayerIndex.One, 500, 1.0f, 1.0f);
        // Player penalty
        player1.Power -= 10;
        player1.Score -= 10;
    }

    // Check Collision for player 2
    if (twoPlayers)
    {
        if (meteors.CheckForCollisions(player2.GetBounds()))
        {
            // Shake!
            rumblePad.RumblePad(PlayerIndex.Two, 500, 1.0f, 1.0f);
            // Player penalty
            player2.Power -= 10;
            player2.Score -= 10;
        }

        // Check for collision between the players
        if (player1.GetBounds().Intersects(player2.GetBounds()))
        {
            rumblePad.RumblePad(PlayerIndex.One, 500, 1.0f, 1.0f);
            player1.Power -= 10;
            player1.Score -= 10;
            rumblePad.RumblePad(PlayerIndex.Two, 500, 1.0f, 1.0f);
            player2.Power -= 10;
            player2.Score -= 10;
        }
    }
}
```

The HandlePowerSourceSprite() method does the same job, but with the PowerSource sprite. If some player collides with this sprite, he or she gets 50 power units. The method also checks if it's time to send a new power source in the game, using an interval of 15 seconds.

```
/// <summary>
/// Handle power-up stuff
/// </summary>
private void HandlePowerSourceSprite(GameTime gameTime)
{
    if (powerSource.CheckCollision(player1.GetBounds()))
    {
        // Player 1 gets the power source
        audioComponent.PlayCue("powerget");
        elapsedTime = TimeSpan.Zero;
        powerSource.PutinStartPosition();
        player1.Power += 50;
    }

    if (twoPlayers)
    {
        // Player 2 gets the power source
        if (powerSource.CheckCollision(player2.GetBounds()))
        {
            audioComponent.PlayCue("powerget");
            elapsedTime = TimeSpan.Zero;
            powerSource.PutinStartPosition();
            player2.Power += 50;
        }
    }

    // Check for sending a new power source
    elapsedTime += gameTime.ElapsedGameTime;
    if (elapsedTime > TimeSpan.FromSeconds(15))
    {
        elapsedTime -= TimeSpan.FromSeconds(15);
        powerSource.Enabled = true;
    }
}
```

And finally, the Draw() method just draws some objects for a specified game state:

```
/// <summary>
/// Allows the GameComponent to draw itself.
/// </summary>
/// <param name="gameTime">Provides a snapshot of timing values.</param>
public override void Draw(GameTime gameTime)
{
```

```
            // Draw all GameComponents
            base.Draw(gameTime);

            if (paused)
            {
                // Draw the "pause" text
                spriteBatch.Draw(actionTexture, pausePosition, pauseRect,
                    Color.White);
            }
            if (gameOver)
            {
                // Draw the "gameover" text
                spriteBatch.Draw(actionTexture, gameoverPosition, gameoverRect,
                    Color.White);
            }
```

Observe that once again, a great deal of the game logic that you created in the previous chapter was kept. You only added the two-player support and two more game states: one when the user pauses the game (pressing the Enter key or pressing the A button on the Xbox 360 gamepad during the game), or when one of the players runs out of energy. When this happens, the game shows a message on the screen and waits for the player to press the Enter key or the A button on the Xbox 360 gamepad.

Navigating Between the Scenes

With all the scenes created, now you only need to show them according to users' wishes. Through the menu in the opening scene, users can show the help scene, the action scene (with one or two players), or just leave the game. Here, you'll use a technique in which you concentrate all the inputs that refer to the navigation or control of the scene states in one class. In this case you use the Game1 class, so that you have a central point where you shoot the scenes and control the Game1 class's state. Add the following code in the Game1 class:

```
private readonly GraphicsDeviceManager graphics;
private SpriteBatch spriteBatch;

// Textures
protected Texture2D helpBackgroundTexture, helpForegroundTexture;
protected Texture2D startBackgroundTexture, startElementsTexture;
protected Texture2D actionElementsTexture, actionBackgroundTexture;
// Game Scenes
protected HelpScene helpScene;
```

```
protected StartScene startScene;
protected ActionScene actionScene;
protected GameScene activeScene;

// Audio Stuff
private AudioComponent audioComponent;

// Fonts
private SpriteFont smallFont, largeFont, scoreFont;

// Used to handle input
protected KeyboardState oldKeyboardState;
protected GamePadState oldGamePadState;
```

In the LoadContent() method, add the code to create and load the content for the
ActionScene object:

```
// Create the action scene
actionElementsTexture = Content.Load<Texture2D>("rockrainenhanced");
actionBackgroundTexture = Content.Load<Texture2D>("SpaceBackground");
scoreFont = Content.Load<SpriteFont>("score");
actionScene = new ActionScene(this, actionElementsTexture,
    actionBackgroundTexture, scoreFont);
Components.Add(actionScene);

// Start the game in the start scene :)
startScene.Show();
activeScene = startScene;
```

Again, in this class you'll load all the game assets and initialize all the scenes, putting
the StartScene as the scene to be opened initially.

The Update() method handles all user input for each scene, and changes the active
scene if necessary:

```
/// <summary>
/// Allows the game to run logic such as updating the world,
/// checking for collisions, gathering input, and playing audio.
/// </summary>
/// <param name="gameTime">Provides a snapshot of timing values.</param>
protected override void Update(GameTime gameTime)
{
// Handle Game Inputs
    HandleScenesInput();
```

```
        base.Update(gameTime);
    }
```

HandleScenesInput() just calls the handler for the active scene in the game:

```
/// <summary>
/// Handle input of all game scenes
/// </summary>
private void HandleScenesInput()
{
    // Handle Start Scene Input
    if (activeScene == startScene)
    {
        HandleStartSceneInput();
    }
    // Handle Help Scene Input
    else if (activeScene == helpScene)
    {
        if (CheckEnterA())
        {
            ShowScene(startScene);
        }
    }
    // Handle Action Scene Input
    else if (activeScene == actionScene)
    {
        HandleActionInput();
    }
}
```

The CheckEnterA() method is a simple code to test the Enter key and the A button on an Xbox 360 gamepad:

```
/// <summary>
/// Check if the Enter Key or A button was pressed
/// </summary>
/// <returns>true, if Enter key or A button was pressed</returns>
private bool CheckEnterA()
{
    // Get the Keyboard and GamePad state
    GamePadState gamepadState = GamePad.GetState(PlayerIndex.One);
    KeyboardState keyboardState = Keyboard.GetState();
```

```
        bool result = (oldKeyboardState.IsKeyDown(Keys.Enter) &&
            (keyboardState.IsKeyUp(Keys.Enter)));
        result |= (oldGamePadState.Buttons.A == ButtonState.Pressed) &&
                (gamepadState.Buttons.A == ButtonState.Released);

        oldKeyboardState = keyboardState;
        oldGamePadState = gamepadState;

        return result;
}
```

The HandleStartSceneInput() shows the correct scene following the user selection in the menu. If a two-player game is selected, you just set the TwoPlayers attribute in the actionScene to true:

```
/// <summary>
/// Handle buttons and keyboard in StartScene
/// </summary>
private void HandleStartSceneInput()
{
    if (CheckEnterA())
    {
        audioComponent.PlayCue("menu_select3");
        switch (startScene.SelectedMenuIndex)
        {
            case 0:
                actionScene.TwoPlayers = false;
                ShowScene(actionScene);
                break;
            case 1:
                actionScene.TwoPlayers = true;
                ShowScene(actionScene);
                break;
            case 2:
                ShowScene(helpScene);
                break;
            case 3:
                Exit();
                break;
        }
    }
}
```

`HandleActionInput()` handles input in the action scene to pause and cancel a game, using a keyboard or an Xbox 360 gamepad:

```
/// <summary>
/// Check if the Enter Key or A button was pressed
/// </summary>
/// <returns>true, if Enter key or A button was pressed</returns>
private void HandleActionInput()
{
    // Get the Keyboard and GamePad state
    GamePadState gamepadState = GamePad.GetState(PlayerIndex.One);
    KeyboardState keyboardState = Keyboard.GetState();

    bool backKey = (oldKeyboardState.IsKeyDown(Keys.Escape) &&
        (keyboardState.IsKeyUp(Keys.Escape)));
    backKey |= (oldGamePadState.Buttons.Back == ButtonState.Pressed) &&
            (gamepadState.Buttons.Back == ButtonState.Released);

    bool enterKey = (oldKeyboardState.IsKeyDown(Keys.Enter) &&
        (keyboardState.IsKeyUp(Keys.Enter)));
    enterKey |= (oldGamePadState.Buttons.A == ButtonState.Pressed) &&
            (gamepadState.Buttons.A == ButtonState.Released);

    oldKeyboardState = keyboardState;
    oldGamePadState = gamepadState;

    if (enterKey)
    {
        if (actionScene.GameOver)
        {
            ShowScene(startScene);
        }
        else
        {
            audioComponent.PlayCue("menu_back");
            actionScene.Paused = !actionScene.Paused;
        }
    }

    if (backKey)
    {
        ShowScene(startScene);
```

```
    }
}
```

The ShowScene() method is just a helper to Show() a new scene and Hide() a previous scene, as follows:

```
/// <summary>
/// Open a new scene
/// </summary>
/// <param name="scene">Scene to be opened</param>
protected void ShowScene(GameScene scene)
{
    activeScene.Hide();
    activeScene = scene;
    scene.Show();
}
```

What about the Draw() method? Well, all elements of your game are GameComponents now, so just let XNA do its job:

```
/// <summary>
/// This is called when the game should draw itself.
/// </summary>
/// <param name="gameTime">Provides a snapshot of timing values.</param>
protected override void Draw(GameTime gameTime)
{
    // Begin..
    spriteBatch.Begin();

    // Draw all GameComponents..
    base.Draw(gameTime);

    // End.
    spriteBatch.End();
}
```

That's it. Compile and execute the game to see the final result. The architecture is flexible, and it's easy to add new features to your game, as you'll see in the next chapter. However, try putting new meteor types or new ways to acquire energy, for instance. You'll start to understand how games are "assembled" from GameComponents.

Summary

You started from a simple game and evolved that into a more elaborate game with simple techniques that are useful to any kind of game. You saw the value of the GameComponents and their reuse capability. Feel free to improve and change this game and build your own awesome version of Rock Rain!

CHAPTER 5

■■■

Basics of Game Networking

In this chapter you'll see basic concepts involved in creating games that support networking, so you'll be prepared to create a real multiplayer game in the next chapter.

Introducing Multiplayer Games

Online multiplayer games, also known as network-enabled games or simply networked games, are hard to code. Period.

That said, it's also important to state that, in XNA, this difficulty is not related to coding for connecting the machines (PCs or Xbox 360) or making them talk with each other. That's because XNA hides all complexities from you in this case, as it does with everything else in the framework.

Networked games are hard to code because there are many extra problems to deal with: your program will receive messages from the host or other players, send messages back to them, process the local player input, and perform the physics and artificial intelligence calculations, while not letting the screen freeze between each frame drawn (one of the worst things that might happen in a multiplayer game).

Fortunately, XNA can help us with most of the communication problems, such as providing ways to control the message flow between players and host to guarantee that no message is lost and that all messages arrive in the same order they were sent, if you want to. Nevertheless, there will still be some problems to solve.

Before discussing the details of XNA support for networking, let's look at some basic concepts about networked games and some of the most common problems faced when coding such games, in the next sections.

Choosing the Network Topology

The most common topologies for networked games are peer-to-peer and client/server connections, and because XNA network implementation is not tied to any type of connection, you can code any of these types depending on the way you organize your network code.

In peer-to-peer connections, every player is aware of every other player in the game, sending and receiving messages from, and to, all players, as illustrated in Figure 5-1.

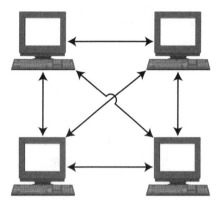

Figure 5-1. *Peer-to-peer connection*

The most obvious benefit of using this network organization is that you don't need a dedicated server to play the game, so every group of players can play it within their own local area network (LAN), or even through the Internet, as long as they know the addresses of the other members of the group.

In this type of connection, one of the players acts as a host, so all the new players connect to that player. However, once connected, the messages flow directly from one player to all the others. If the player who is also the host disconnects from the game, the game might stop or simply choose another player as the new host, depending on what the game developers defined.

The main problem you face when coding peer-to-peer games is that you can't have too many players in the same game session, because the number of messages will increase exponentially with every new player who joins. For instance, in Figure 5-1 we have 4 players, so every time a player needs to update his or her status (for example, move), you send 3 messages, one for each player. Because you have 4 players, during each game turn you exchange $4 \times 3 = 12$ messages. Making the same calculations with a 5-player game increases this to $5 \times 4 = 20$ messages per turn, and in a 6-player game you'll reach $6 \times 5 = 30$ messages.

Usually, having more than ten players in the same game session is not suggested, because every message can take dozens of bytes and you'll consume the bandwidth available in your network quickly. But it's still possible if the game development team can make the messages as small as possible; for example, passing only the players' inputs across the computers, and letting games on every player's machine calculate everything else from these inputs.

The second most common game network topology is client/server. In this kind of network, all players connect to a host, which usually processes the messages and does the game synchronization, sending messages back to each of the players, as presented in Figure 5-2.

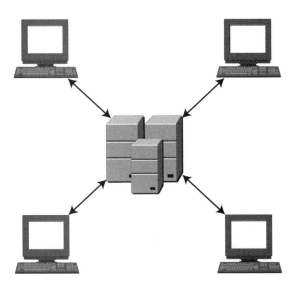

Figure 5-2. *Client/server connection*

Client/server games consume a lot less bandwidth per player, which allows you to send more data (and maybe create a more complex game). However, on the other hand, the player depends on having a host to connect to (so it usually can't be played on a home LAN).

When coding client/server games, you must decide which actions will take place on the host, and which actions will take place on the client machines. Is it better to put all the game physics and intelligence on the players' machines, using a host just as a forwarder of messages, or is it better to include all the game code on the host, leaving just the input gathering and rendering code on the players' machines?

There is no right answer for this question, because it depends largely on the game constraints and goals. When making your decision, you'll have to take into account how many players will be connected to the server, and how much it will cost the server processor to perform each activity (for all players). You also might need to verify the cost for each player's machine to do its own calculations against the bandwidth impact for doing all calculations on the server and passing the results to the players. Even when the server could do a specific operation better, you might decide to run it on the client if passing the results of the operation will use a large amount of the available bandwidth.

Besides these two types of topology, there are other types of network organization. Some are useful in game development, others are not. For example, in a ring topology each player sends messages to one specific player, creating a ring that will eventually return to the first player in the sequence, as shown in Figure 5-3.

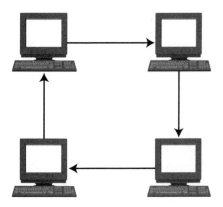

Figure 5-3. *Ring network topology*

This network organization is usually not practical for games, because the first player in the sequence would have to wait for the message to go around to every other player before it got back to him or her, which can easily lead to unacceptable waiting times.

Another example of a different approach is using network groups: each player exchanges messages only with the other players in his or her group, and the host (which could be a dedicated server or a player) exchanges information with other groups, when needed. The group organization is designed for the number of messages passed between the groups to be as small as possible. Figure 5-4 illustrates a game network topology based on groups.

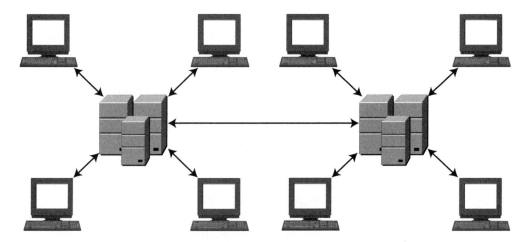

Figure 5-4. *A group-based network topology*

This approach is also used in network games, being a mix of the client/server and peer-to-peer topologies that tries to gather the benefits of each one.

In the next section we'll discuss some choices you must make when producing your network game project.

Turn-Based vs. Real-Time Games

This is probably one of the first decisions when thinking about multiplayer games, and probably the one that will have the greatest impact on your game project.

In turn-based games, each player will think about his or her move, do the proper action, and then pass the control to the next player. Although the first type of game that comes to mind is board games, such as chess or Monopoly, there are sophisticated action games based on turns, such as the old X-COM series, where you move each of your soldiers (using his energy to walk or fire), and then the enemies move, using the same rules.

Choosing this approach will save you a lot of headaches when trying to deal with the latency between your game messages, especially when running through the Internet, but might lead to a less than optimal game play because this type of game is unusual. Never choose this approach if you have many players (say, more than three or four, depending on the game pace), because if each player needs to wait more than a couple minutes to play again, the game will rapidly become uninteresting—except, of course, if the players actually expect a delay, like in a chess match. A practical idea is letting the players communicate with one another (by voice or by typing a message) even when it is not their turn, so you can improve the interaction between players and make the waiting less boring.

Creating continuous action multiplayer games that support remote players, like Halo, is challenging. That's mainly because you must transfer a certain amount of data within tight time frames, which unfortunately depends on the response time of something beyond your control—the network. At the same time, you need to make sure that all players have synchronized information, especially in fast-paced action games where players are fighting against one another.

One possible approach is to send all the data updates to each of the players, so that you can ensure that everyone has the most recent events on their machines. However, this approach consumes the entire bandwidth available even for few players.

In the other extreme, you can carefully calculate exactly which information should be sent to each player, and then send the minimum data needed. For instance, if another player is behind you or in another part of the game level, you can't see him or her, so you don't need to receive information from that player. Although it saves bandwidth, this approach consumes CPUs cycles on the players' machines by calculating the data to send, leaving fewer cycles to calculate the game physics and draw the graphics.

Then again, the best approach is to find a balance according to your game requirements. There is no right answer; just minimize the data while trying not to expend too much processing time on this minimization, and always keep in mind that your game will run on slower machines and might face unpredictably bad network response times.

In the next section we'll discuss another point you must think about when coding multiplayer games.

Some Technical Tips

In this section we include some technical tips you must keep in mind when coding a multiplayer game. Although this is not an exhaustive list, it presents some of the most common problems in such games, and it's a good starting point for anyone who wants to write a networked game.

Plan the Game Carefully Before Starting

If creating a good project is important to every game, when talking about multiplayer games a detailed project is a must. Because you'll have different programs, or at least different parts of the same program, interacting through the network, you must define every message that will be exchanged and every way the programs might process them.

It's crucial to the success of the game that you define where and *when* each process will occur, to guarantee that each player is synchronized. Programmers tend to forget these details, because in stand-alone programs everything occurs directly after the command is processed, although in multiplayer games this is not the case. For example, if you are coding a shooter game, one player can shoot another player's character and, almost at the same time, in the remote machine, the other player's character might be moving out of the firing range of the first player. If all processing occurs locally on each player's machine, the first player will see a successful shot. Although the message with the shot information did not reach the other player's machine, the remote player jumped out of the way, so the remote player will see the shot missing his or her character.

So, devising an algorithm that guarantees synchronization is as important as not using a lot of bandwidth. Considering that you might face bad response times when running across the Internet, this is challenging.

Code for Network Features from the Beginning

It's far better to code everything from the ground up than to try to adjust a stand-alone game to support networking, if it was not planned to do so. Even in a simple program you might face situations where adjusting the program will lead to a less than optimal result, compared to writing the game with networking in mind. So if you're planning to create a game that will support networking only in a second version, prepare all your code, from the first version, to be "network-friendly." For example, isolate the routines that deal with user input from the rest of the game, so you can change these routines to receive remote input later. Also, plan how to synchronize input from all players, even if in the first version all players are local.

> **Note** XNA network routines allow you to create games with more than one local player. The best approach, in this case, would be to use these routines right away, to create the first version of your game. That way, it would support networking from the start even if there is no support for remote players in the first version.

Define the Messages Types and Sizes Carefully

Bandwidth is a rare and expensive thing, so use it sparingly.

After defining all messages that your programs will exchange in the project phase, you have to draw the complete flow of a typical game cycle (the game's main loop, including the calls for the Update and Draw methods of your XNA Game class), so you can check if you are forgetting anything important. You must create this flow for at least two to three players, plus the server, if any exists, because some situations will occur with three players that don't occur with two.

After being sure that you aren't forgetting anything, you must go back and recheck every message to see if you are using the minimum space possible for each message, especially those that will be exchanged most frequently. For example, a single bit can be used as a flag, so a Byte can comprise up to eight flags. Also, a Byte takes 256 different values, so if your values are within this range, you can use the Byte data type instead of the Int16 one, which takes 2 bytes.

A final word on this: be sure that you know the real size of the data types you are using. For example, an Int32 takes 4 bytes, while an Int16 takes 2 bytes. Another interesting example refers to strings: they do *not* occupy the same amount of bytes as the number of characters. They have extra internal control bytes that help, for example, when defining the string's length.

> **Note** ANSI strings (one byte per character) are the default for most Western countries, but this does not suffice for writing every character in Eastern countries, such as the *kana* characters in Japan and China. That's because you have only 256 possible characters in ANSI. Unicode is the default for such countries, and in this case every character could be one of up to 65,536 different values—enough for any language.

Hide the Latency from the Player

Latency is the worst enemy of every multiplayer game programming team. And, even worse, there's no solution for this problem. It's not a bug, it's a fact of life, so you must learn—and code—to live with it.

Because you never know for sure how much time it'll take to receive the next message, you can use some tricks to distract the player while he or she waits. For example, say your game is a strategy game such as the Age of Empires series, where the player can give orders to game characters. However, the character will only move after the client machine receives confirmation from the host that the command has been received. So, you can make your characters say something ("Yes, master!" would suffice, although it's very innovative) just after the command is issued, so the player has the impression that the result is immediate, although it really will start (hopefully) a number of milliseconds later.

You can use this same idea with animations instead of sounds; the game character can start a little animation, such as making an "okay" sign with his hand or moving his head around as if looking for a way to start the command. This kind of trick is effective.

Another thing you can do, when facing extra-long waiting times for the next message, is let your program continue the action based on the last input, maybe at a lower rate. For example, if you know the speed and the direction of the other players' starships in a space battle game, you can suppose that they are still moving in the same direction, and move their spaceships a little following this supposition. However, as soon as the new message arrives, you must check and correct the other players' positions. This can be a challenge, even for experienced programmers, and can lead to problems in the game, such as a spaceship "jumping" from one place to another. You can solve this with a smoothing trick, by adjusting the position in more than one game cycle, but this trick will add extra complexity to your game.

The important thing about latency is that while it'll probably always be a problem, players didn't, don't, and won't ever accept latency in games. Few things are worse for a player than receiving a pop-up window with a message such as "waiting for the answer from the host." So, your team will have to spend some hours on this topic at the game project stage, if you are planning to do a serious multiplayer game.

Note XNA provides a way to simulate latency so you can easily test your program in "real conditions," with `NetworkSession.SimulatedLatency`. You can also simulate a percentage of message loss between computers, another common problem, with `NetworkSession.SimulatedPacketLoss`. You won't use these commands in this chapter, but it's important for you to know they exist when testing your network games.

Include Single-Player Features in Your Multiplayer Game

Many players don't like, or simply don't have the money or the time, to play games with other players. Many games that are solely multiplayer have failed, so be careful if you want to follow this approach.

We'll give a simple example: Halo is a great game, and multiplayer features give a whole new experience for the players, as everyone who has played it knows. Just imagine now if Halo had no history, no computer-controlled characters, and was restricted to death-match and other player-against-player options. It would surely still be a good game given its details, but would hardly be a great game.

Another simple example is the Net Rumble starter kit, released with XNA 2.0. It's a nice game, but if you play alone, all you have is a spaceship with some floating rocks to shoot, with no goal—no fun at all. Coding a computer-controlled ship might be a challenge for starters, but will surely make a real difference if you want to play alone, or even if you want to test the game while coding with no partners.

Remember: having computer-controlled characters is useful even in network games, so you'd better spend some time thinking about this in your games!

Use Different Threads to Handle Network Messages

It's a simple but important tip: having a specific thread dedicated to message sending and receiving, and another thread or threads to deal with the game physics and artificial intelligence gives you more flexibility to hide the latency and get the most from your hardware, be it PC or Xbox.

Although it's beyond the scope of this book to talk about multithreading, you must keep this tip in mind if you plan to create more advanced games.

Test, Test, Test!

Multiplayer games have extra sources of errors, and sometimes the errors are harder to find and fix, so testing from the beginning is a real must.

The first tests you must do are about message delivering and handling, to check if your code will behave accordingly if a network packet is lost or if it receives the packets in a different order than the order in which they were sent.

▨Note XNA allows you to choose if you want the framework to guarantee the reliability of the packets (so no message is ever lost), using the `SendDataOptions.Reliable` flag, and the packet order (so the messages always arrive in the same order they were sent), with `SendDataOptions.InOrder`. Although it might sound good to always have the messages arriving, and in order, setting both flags might lead to greater latency times, because the XNA Framework will do extra controls and eventually resend messages. The better approach is to create a game that doesn't rely on these features.

Multiplayer game reliability is always a problem. Just imagine you have created a game that has an uptime of 99.9 percent. This means that your game can run, on the average, for 23 hours and 59 minutes without crashing, having a minute out on each day. Sound good enough?

Well, if you have ten players in your game, in ten different machines, they will probably not crash at the same time. So, if you divide 24 hours by 10 you see that you might have a crash every 2 hours and 24 minutes. If your program is good enough, the other players can continue playing—even if it's kind of frustrating when playing in a team to see a companion freezing or disappearing from the team.

So, when coding your next network game, keep these figures in mind, and follow our tip: test, test, and test. And after that, test it all over again.

Introducing XNA Networking

XNA 2.0 offers a set of functions and components through the `Microsoft.Xna.Framework. GamerServices` and the `Microsoft.Xna.Framework.Net` namespaces, which enable the creation of multiplayer game hosts (that other players can connect to), handle the connections and message exchanging between players and the host, and include many extra features, such as native support for voice communications.

In the next sections you'll create a simple class to illustrate the basic features needed to implement simple multiplayer games, so you'll be ready to explore these concepts further in the next chapter, and later on your own.

Although coding a complete multiplayer game might be challenging, the basic steps are simple for creating a multiplayer host, where other players can connect. The game host can be a player, in a peer-to-peer game, or a server machine, if you are using the client/server approach. There are four steps to create a host:

1. Sign in a gamer (with a local or remote profile).

2. Create a session, establishing its properties, including available slots.

3. Wait for other players to join and be ready.

4. Change the session state to "Game Started."

Similarly, you can resume the creation of a game client in four simple steps, which are valid for both peer-to-peer and client/server games:

1. Sign in a gamer (with a local or remote profile).

2. Find any sessions with empty slots to join.

3. Join the session.

4. Change the player state to "Ready."

In the next section, we'll present the NetworkHelper class, which you'll create to help your program use XNA's basic network features.

Starting the Gamer Services Component

In 2002, Microsoft created Xbox LIVE (officially spelled with all caps), an online service for distributing game content (such as demos, trailers, and extra content for games) and connecting Xbox players. The ability to play your console games with remote players, display your high scores online, and much more led to a widespread adoption of LIVE. This made Microsoft extend the online service for Windows Games in 2007, with the launching of Games for Windows—LIVE. In XNA 2.0 you can connect to both services, depending on the platform your game is running on.

The XNA programming team packed all the complexity of manipulating LIVE profiles in the GamerServices namespace, making it simple for developers to use LIVE capabilities such as creating local accounts, connecting to a LIVE profile, and also use many available LIVE Guide user interface screens to manipulate gamer information.

The easiest way to get access to LIVE features is through the GamerServicesComponent that, when created in a game, runs the Gamer Services pump at regular intervals. This allows your game, for instance, to respond to user interaction such as presenting the LIVE Guide when the user presses the Home key.

Let's see this in action in a simple project. Start by creating a new Windows Game project, naming it XNADemo. Then, open the Game1 class and include the following code line in the class constructor, just after the line that sets the content root directory:

```
Components.Add(new GamerServicesComponent(this));
```

Run the game now. If you already have a LIVE profile configured for automatic login, your profile will sign in, and you'll see a button on the center bottom of the blank game screen, as shown in Figure 5-5.

Figure 5-5. *The automatic gamer login feature*

If you don't have a local profile, LIVE will automatically display a Welcome screen (see Figure 5-6), and let you create a new gamer profile. If for any reason the screen presented in Figure 5-6 doesn't show up, pressing the Home key makes it pop up.

Figure 5-6. *The LIVE Guide Create New Profile screen*

Choose Create New Profile in this screen. The LIVE Guide presents a new screen, where you can name your new profile (see Figure 5-7).

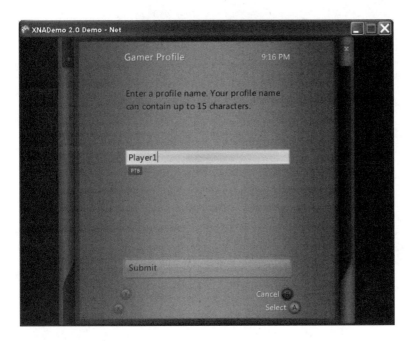

Figure 5-7. *The LIVE Guide Gamer Profile screen*

Choose a name for your profile and click Submit in this screen. This profile name (which you can modify later) will be used to identify you when playing network games.

After clicking Send, your local profile will be created and the LIVE Guide will navigate to the next screen, presented in Figure 5-8.

In this last screen, three buttons allow you to do several things. Clicking Join LIVE opens Internet Explorer and navigates to the Game for Windows—LIVE site. Customize Profile enables you to configure your profile (for example, the profile image) according to your preferences. You can close the window by clicking the Done button.

After configuring your profile, and joining LIVE if you want—and we recommend you do so—click the Done button and let's go on coding our sample!

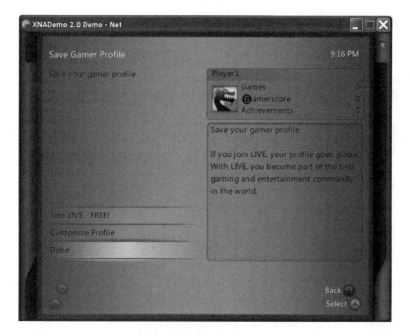

Figure 5-8. *The Live Guide Profile Created screen*

Defining the NetworkHelper Class

When creating a real project, you need to choose which approach to creating the network supporting classes is the best. For this chapter, where all you want is to understand the networking concepts, let's keep things as simple as possible. Because the client and the host programs usually have many common features, you'll create a single class, grouping all XNA network routines.

Open the project created in the previous section and click the project name in the Solution Explorer window with the right button. In the presented pop-up menu, choose Add ➤ Class to create a new, empty class, and name it NetworkHelper.

Include the references to the Microsoft.Xna.Framework.Net and Microsoft.Xna.Framework.GamerServices namespaces in the beginning of the class, and you're ready to go. The next code snippet presents the new class:

```
using System;
using Microsoft.Xna.Framework.Net;
using Microsoft.Xna.Framework.GamerServices;

namespace XNADemo
{
    class clsNetWorkHelper
```

```
    {
    }
}
```

In the next sections, you'll follow the previous steps to create a host, using them as a guide to create methods and properties in your network helper class. As a reminder, the steps are: sign in a gamer, create a session, wait for other players to join and be ready, and then change the session state to Game Started.

Signing in a Gamer

In the section "Starting the Gamer Services Component," you already created a local profile with automatic sign-in, so in fact you don't need to code anything else to sign in a gamer. However, because your goal here is to learn, you'll create a method named SignInGamer, on the NetworkHelper class, that allows you to display the LIVE Guide screens programmatically:

```
public void SignInGamer()
{
    if (!Guide.IsVisible)
    {
        Guide.ShowSignIn(1, false);
    }
}
```

In the previous code fragment you used the Guide class to show the LIVE Guide. This class is the entry point to any operation related to the LIVE Guide, and contains methods to present the Guide, show message boxes, and handle text entry and other interface elements. These methods work both in Xbox 360 and Windows.

In the code sample, at first you check if the Guide is visible and, if not, present it through the ShowSignIn method. This method takes two arguments: the number of panes displayed for gamers' sign-in (always 1 in Windows; 1, 2, or 4 in Xbox 360), and a flag indicating if only online profiles should be displayed or not. In this case, you are choosing to present one pane, and to display both online and offline profiles.

Now, if you want to display the LIVE Guide—for example, when the user presses the F1 key on the keyboard—you can create a network helper object and call this method. To do this, you must define the new object in the Game1 class:

```
NetworkHelper networkHelper;
```

Then, in the Initialize method of the Game1 class, you must create the object:

```
networkHelper = new NetworkHelper();
```

Finally, you must call the method in the Update method of the Game1 class, which will look like this after your adjustment:

```
protected override void Update(GameTime gameTime)
{
    // Allows the game to exit
    if (GamePad.GetState(PlayerIndex.One).Buttons.Back ==
        ButtonState.Pressed)
        this.Exit();

    //  Presents the LIVE Guide to sign in
    if (Keyboard.GetState().IsKeyDown(Keys.F1))
        networkHelper.SignInGamer();

    base.Update(gameTime);
}
```

Run the program now and press the F1 key on the keyboard. The LIVE Guide pops up.

Now that you have a signed-in player, the next step is to create a session. Let's do it in the next section.

Creating a Session

The XNA Framework NetworkSession class represents a multiplayer session, and is used to create, find, join, and end sessions. It also offers a series of properties that allow you to gather information about the current session.

Note XNA Framework 2.0 can only start one Games for Windows—LIVE network support program per machine, so you need to run your sample on two machines to test it—one for creating the session, and the second one to find and join the session.

To create a new session, you'll use the NetworkSession.Create method, which receives up to five parameters:

- The session type, which can be NetworkSessionType.Local (no networking, used for split-screen games, only works for Xbox 360), NetworkSessionType.SystemLink (connects two machines, Xbox 360 or PC, in the same subnet), NetworkSessionType.PlayerMatch (allows connection through the LIVE servers) and NetworkSessionType.Ranked (used for ranked commercial games that passed Xbox LIVE certification).

- The maximum number of local (in the same machine) players.

- The numbers of slots for players on this session (from 2 to a maximum of 31 players).

- The number of private slots (optional parameter), stating how many of the session slots are reserved for players who join through invitation. If this number is equal to the number of session slots, the session will only accept invited players.

- The session properties (optional parameter): a collection of custom properties that you can use to define any game-specific values, such as the game difficulty level or the time limit for the session. These properties, stored as a NetworkSessionProperties class, are also used to filter the results when searching for sessions to join.

To create the session, you'll define some private class-level variables and code a new method, CreateSession, in your NetworkHelper class:

```
private NetworkSession session = null;  //  The game session
private int maximumGamers = 2;  // Only 2 will play
private int maximumLocalPlayers = 1;  //  no split-screen, only remote players

public void CreateSession()
{
    if (session == null)
    {
        session = NetworkSession.Create(NetworkSessionType.SystemLink,
                                        maximumLocalPlayers,
                                        maximumGamers);
    }
}
```

Creating a multiplayer game session in XNA is simple as that: only one command and you're good to go!

However, for this session to work, processing the network packets properly, you'll need to call its Update method on every game update cycle. To do this, include an Update method on your NetworkHelper class:

```
public void Update()
{
    if (session != null)
        session.Update();
}
```

The best way to call this method in every game loop cycle is by including the following line at the beginning of the Game1 Update method:

```
networkHelper.Update();
```

Now your session is created and ready to process network messages. You might also want to configure some details about the session behavior. For instance, you can include the following lines just after the session creation:

```
// If the host goes out, another machine will assume as a new host
session.AllowHostMigration = true;
// Allow players to join a game in progress
session.AllowJoinInProgress = true;
```

You can also configure your NetworkHelper class to answer to session events. To see what is going on, create a new read-only string property for your class, Message, and code the session event handlers to set this property properly:

```
// Message regarding the session's current state
private String message = "Waiting for user command...";
public String Message
{
    get { return message; }
}
```

Now that the message property is set up, let's include the event hooks in the CreateSession method, after the session creation, by incorporating the following lines:

```
session.GamerJoined +=
            new EventHandler<GamerJoinedEventArgs>(session_GamerJoined);
session.GamerLeft +=
            new EventHandler<GamerLeftEventArgs>(session_GamerLeft);
session.GameStarted +=
            new EventHandler<GameStartedEventArgs>(session_GameStarted);
session.GameEnded +=
            new EventHandler<GameEndedEventArgs>(session_GameEnded);
session.SessionEnded +=
            new EventHandler<NetworkSessionEndedEventArgs>(session_SessionEnded);
session.HostChanged +=
            new EventHandler<HostChangedEventArgs>(session_HostChanged);
```

In the previous code excerpt, you inform the session object that you'll handle every single event that it offers. However, you must keep in mind this is not necessary: you should code only the relevant events according to your game logic. For example, if you set the session property `AllowHostMigration` to `False`, the `HostChanged` event will never happen.

Getting back to our example, all you need for now is to set the `message` property you just created properly, so you can code the game's main class to write it on the game window and then be able to see when each event happens.

The next listing presents the code snippets for setting the `message` property on each event you created the hook for:

```
void session_GamerJoined(object sender, GamerJoinedEventArgs e)
{
    if (e.Gamer.IsHost)
        message = "The Host started the session!";
    else
        message = "Gamer " + e.Gamer.Tag + " joined the session!";
}

void session_GamerLeft(object sender, GamerLeftEventArgs e)
{
    message = "Gamer " + e.Gamer.Tag + " left the session!";
}

void session_GameStarted(object sender, GameStartedEventArgs e)
{
    message = "Game Started";
 }

void session_HostChanged(object sender, HostChangedEventArgs e)
{
    message = "Host changed from " + e.OldHost.Tag + " to " + e.NewHost.Tag;
}

 void session_SessionEnded(object sender, NetworkSessionEndedEventArgs e)
{
    message = "The session has ended";
}

void session_GameEnded(object sender, GameEndedEventArgs e)
{
    message = "Game Over";
}
```

The session events have self-explanatory names: the GamerJoined event happens every time a new gamer joins the session, so you must include the proper code for new player initialization there. The GamerLeft event occurs when a gamer leaves the session, so in your games you must include the code for gracefully allowing the game to continue without that player, or maybe the code to end the game, in this event, and so on.

To finish coding for session creation, you only need to write the code in the Update method of the Game1 class to start a session (let's say, when the user presses the F2 key on the keyboard:

```
// Creates a Session
if (Keyboard.GetState().IsKeyDown(Keys.F2))
    networkHelper.CreateSession();
```

Your program is ready to go, but if you want to see the message with the session state, of course you need to code for it. Right-click your project in the Solution Explorer and choose Add ➤ New Item, including a new SpriteFont in your project (name it Arial). Include the following line at the beginning of the Game1 class to declare the SpriteFont:

```
SpriteFont Arial;
```

Then, load the file you just included in the project by including the following line in the LoadContent method of the Game1 class:

```
Arial = Content.Load<SpriteFont>("Arial");
```

Now, all you need is to use the SpriteBatch the XNA Framework kindly created for you to draw the message using your SpriteFont, in the Draw method of the Game1 class:

```
// Show the current session state
spriteBatch.Begin();
spriteBatch.DrawString(Arial, "Game State: " + networkHelper.Message,
                                new Vector2(20, lineHeight), Color.Yellow);
spriteBatch.End();
```

Run your program now, and press F1 (or the Start button on your gamepad) to bring up the player sign-in screen. Sign in from this screen and close it, then press F2 to start a new session. You can see the result—not quite impressive—in Figure 5-9.

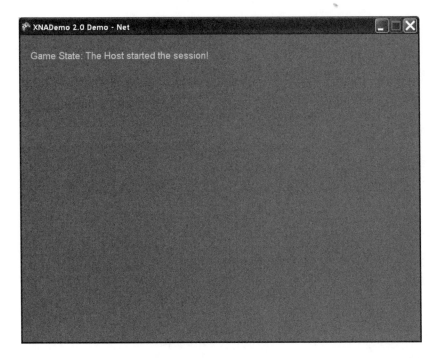

Figure 5-9. *Game screen with a "The Host started the session!" message*

In the next section, you'll code the client-side routines used to find and join sessions.

Finding and Joining a Session Synchronously

Connecting synchronously to an existing session is almost as easy as creating a session, with straightforward code: you need to search for available sessions using the Find method of the NetworkSession object, then check if a session has empty slots for you to connect, and finally you need to join the session found.

By including the next code piece in your NetworkHelper class, you'll be able to make your sample search and join game sessions:

```
public void FindSession()
{
    // all sessions found
    AvailableNetworkSessionCollection availableSessions;
    // the session we'll join
    AvailableNetworkSession availableSession = null;
```

```
    availableSessions = NetworkSession.Find(NetworkSessionType.SystemLink,
        maximumLocalPlayers, null);

    // Get a session with available gamer slots
    foreach (AvailableNetworkSession curSession in availableSessions)
    {
        int TotalSessionSlots = curSession.OpenPublicGamerSlots +
                                        curSession.OpenPrivateGamerSlots;
        if (TotalSessionSlots > curSession.CurrentGamerCount)
            availableSession = curSession;
    }

    // if a session was found, connect to it
    if (availableSession != null)
    {
        message = "Found an available session at host " +
                            availableSession.HostGamertag;
        session = NetworkSession.Join(availableSession);
    }
    else
        message = "No sessions found!";
}
```

Let's review the code, step by step, to understand its details.

First, you define two variables that will receive objects that help you find and manage sessions: AvailableNetworkSessionCollection, which is a collection of sessions, as returned from the NetworkSession.Find method; and AvailableNetworkSession, which is an item of such a collection.

■**Note** The AvailableNetworkSession object is different from the NetworkSession object. It is only a reference to an available session, with properties that describe a session. You can use it to create a NetworkSession object through the NetworkSession.Join method.

After retrieving these objects, you use the NetworkSession.Find method to retrieve the collection of available sessions. This method receives three parameters: the network session type you are searching for (these types were discussed in the previous session); the maximum number of players; and a collection of NetworkSessionProperties custom properties, which must match the properties used in the session creation. In this example, because you created a session with no custom properties, you can simply pass null as this last argument.

After retrieving the available sessions, the previous code loops through these sessions and checks if any of them have empty slots for you to sign in, comparing the sum of the available session properties OpenPublicGamerSlots and OpenPrivateGamerSlots with the total gamers already signed in to the session, given by the CurrentGamerCount property.

Finally, you set the message NetworkHelper property with the corresponding message (stating if you did or didn't find a session to join). If you find a session with empty slots, you join the session using the NetworkSession.Join method, passing the available session found as a parameter.

To finish coding for session finding, now you need to adjust the Update method of the Game1 class to call your Find method. You can fire the session to find when the user presses the F3 key on the keyboard through the following code:

```
// Looks for a Session
if (Keyboard.GetState().IsKeyDown(Keys.F3))
    networkHelper.FindSession();
```

To test your program, you'll need two machines. Run the program on both machines, and follow the steps presented in the section "Creating a Session" on the first computer.

On the second computer, run the program, press the F1 key to be sure that there's a signed-in player (otherwise the session finding will fail), and then press F3 to find a session. If both computers are in the same subnet, XNA will be able to find the session and the screen will present the message "Found an available session at host XXX," where XXX is the gamer tag signed in to the host machine, as presented in Figure 5-10.

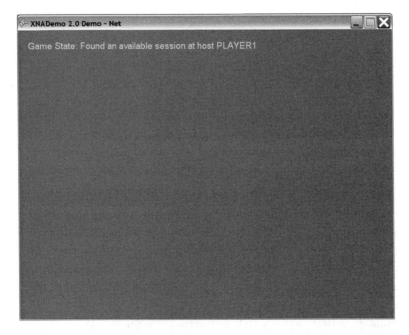

Figure 5-10. *Game screen with a "Found an available session . . ." message*

■**Tip** The AvailableNetworkSession object has a property, QualityOfService, which is filled with information about the quality of the connection after the XNA Framework gathers this data (check the isAvailable property of this class to check if data is already gathered). This class has four properties, which present the minimum and average round-trip time for the network packets, and the available bandwidth from the host to the local machine and from the local machine to the host.

In the next section, you'll see how to find sessions asynchronously.

Finding and Joining a Session Asynchronously

Coding for asynchronous session searching is an approach commonly used in games because you usually don't want to freeze the game and the player options when searching for available sessions. The basic idea for session finding and joining is the same as you saw in the previous section. However, here you'll use the BeginFind and EndFind NetworkSession methods, which respectively start a session search, indicating the function to be called when the searching is ended, and get the results from the search.

The next code sample, to be included in your NetworkHelper class, defines a new variable used to store and track the status of the asynchronous operation, and a method that will call BeginFind to start the session searching:

```
IAsyncResult AsyncSessionFind = null;
public void AsyncFindSession()
{
    message = "Asynchronous search started!";
    if (AsyncSessionFind == null)
    {
        AsyncSessionFind = NetworkSession.BeginFind(
            NetworkSessionType.SystemLink,  maximumLocalPlayers, null,
            new AsyncCallback(session_SessionFound), null);
    }
}
```

BeginFind receives the same parameters from the Find method discussed in the previous section (session type, maximum number of players, and custom session properties), plus the address of the callback function (which is called when the search results are ready). BeginFind also receives an object used to store the state of the asynchronous operation (let's not bother about this last one right now; it's fine just to pass a null value).

In the previous code sample, you passed session_SessionFound as the callback function for BeginFind. The next code excerpt presents the code for the callback function that, as you'll see, is very similar to your previously coded FindSession method:

```
public void session_SessionFound(IAsyncResult result)
{
  // all sessions found
  AvailableNetworkSessionCollection availableSessions;
  // the session we will join
  AvailableNetworkSession availableSession = null;

    if (AsyncSessionFind.IsCompleted)
    {
        availableSessions = NetworkSession.EndFind(result);

        // Look for a session with available gamer slots
        foreach (AvailableNetworkSession curSession in
                availableSessions)
        {
            int TotalSessionSlots = curSession.OpenPublicGamerSlots +
                                curSession.OpenPrivateGamerSlots;
            if (TotalSessionSlots > curSession.CurrentGamerCount)
                availableSession = curSession;
        }

        // if a session was found, connect to it
        if (availableSession != null)
        {
            message = "Found an available session at host" +
                        availableSession.HostGamertag;
            session = NetworkSession.Join(availableSession);
        }
        else
            message = "No sessions found!";

        // Reset the session finding result
        AsyncSessionFind = null;
    }
}
```

The previous code excerpt is almost identical to your FindSession synchronous method; in fact, only three lines are different: the test to check the AsyncSessionFind. IsCompleted property to see if the results are already available; using NetworkSession. EndFind (instead of NetworkSession.Find) to retrieve the available sessions collection; and finally the last line of the listing, where you simply reset the AsyncSessionFind result variable. So, if you understand the synchronous session searching concepts, you have few new things to learn when dealing with asynchronous ones.

All you need to do now is to revise the Update method of the Game1 class to call the new asynchronous session-finding method, by including the following lines:

```
// Find a session asynchronously
if (Keyboard.GetState().IsKeyDown(Keys.F4))
    networkHelper.AsyncFindSession();
```

You can test the new code by executing again the steps you used in the previous section to join a session synchronously, except that you press the F4 key instead of the F3 one. On the client machine you'll see the message "Asynchronous search started!" followed, a few seconds later, by the message that states the result of the session searching.

Now that you have two machines with signed-in gamers, the first one creating a session and acting as a host, and the second one joining the session created, it's time to inform XNA that you are ready to go, and start the game!

Starting the Game

A game session, in XNA, has three possible states, informed by its SessionState property:

- NetworkSessionState.Lobby: A session in this state means that the local machine has joined a session and is ready to start, but is waiting for other players to join and the host to start the game. The host knows when all players are ready by checking the IsEveryoneReady property of the session object; it can check the number of signed-in gamers by consulting Gamer.SignedInGamers.Count.

- NetworkSessionState.Playing: When the host starts the game, by calling the StartGame method of the session object, the GameStarted session event is fired for all players, and the session state changes from Lobby to Playing.

- NetworkSessionState.Ended: Similarly, the host calls the EndGame method of the session object to finish a game, firing the GameEnded session event for all players and changing the session state from Playing to Ended.

So, once you have all players connected in the same session, you need every player to report that he or she is ready and to include the code in the host to start and end the game.

Signaling that all local players (maximum one in Windows, up to four in Xbox 360) are ready is easy through the session object, which has a collection with references to all local gamers' profiles. The next code sample shows a new method for your NetworkHelper class that does this job:

```
public void SetPlayerReady ()
{
    foreach (LocalNetworkGamer gamer in session.LocalGamers)
        gamer.IsReady = true;
}
```

Although you can use this method in a real game, in this sample you only have two players, so you don't need to wait for other players to join. As soon as the second machine joins a session, the host can start the game. To do this, you can include an extra line on the gamerJoined event to start the game as soon as the host detects that another player joined the game, as presented in the following code snippet:

```
void session_GamerJoined(object sender, GamerJoinedEventArgs e)
{
    if (e.Gamer.IsHost)
    {
        message = "The Host started the session!";
    }
    else
    {
        message = "Gamer " + e.Gamer.Tag + " joined the session!";
        // Other played joined, start the game!
        session.StartGame();
    }
}
```

If you run your program now on your two test machines, pressing F2 on the host machine and pressing F3 or F4 to find the session on the second machine, the host machine will automatically start the game and present the Game Started message (which you coded in the GameStarted event of the session object in the earlier section "Creating a Session").

At this point, you have two machines connected in the same game. Following the general guidelines presented in this section, you can easily extend the sample by writing the code to end the game by calling the session.EndGame() method.

All you need to know now is how to send data from one machine to another, and you'll have all the basic knowledge needed to include network support in your games.

Handling Messages

Sending and receiving messages is simply a matter of calling the SendData and ReceiveData methods of the LocalNetworkGamer class, which represents a local player.

Both methods can handle arrays of bytes or a packet writer, which is a binary data streamer. It receives basic data types and transforms them into an array of bytes, in an efficient way. Because dealing with packet writers is easier, let's work with them. Start by creating a new class-level variable in your NetworkHelper class, named packetWriter:

```
PacketWriter packetWriter = new PacketWriter();
```

You can now use this packet writer to stream your messages to one or all the other remote players by looping through your session's LocalGamers collection and calling the SendData method, as follows:

```
public void SendMessage(string key)
{
    foreach (LocalNetworkGamer localPlayer in session.LocalGamers)
    {
        packetWriter.Write(key);
        localPlayer.SendData(packetWriter, SendDataOptions.None);
        message = "Sending message: " + key;
    }
}
```

The SendData method can define the reliability and the order reinforcement for the message in its SendDataOptions parameter, which can be set to None (packet sent with no guarantees), InOrder (packet sent in order, but a packet loss might happen), Reliable (packet always reaches its destination, but might arrive out of order), and ReliableInOrder (no packet loss, and all packets are delivered in the same order they were sent). Remember what we said in the beginning of this chapter: decide which option is best for your game.

Besides this, the SendData method has overloads that receive an extra NetworkGamer parameter, which allows your game to send messages to a specific player. If this parameter is not reported, the message is delivered to all signed-in players.

In the SendMessage method, you are packing only one string, but you could pack a number of variables, depending on your game logic. For example, if you want to send the left thumbstick and both triggers' state to all other players, you can write your packet according to the next code fragment:

```
GamePadState GamePad1 = GamePad.GetState(PlayerIndex.One);
packetWriter.Write(GamePad1.Triggers.Left);
packetWriter.Write(GamePad1.Triggers.Right);
packetWriter.Write(GamePad1.ThumbSticks.Left);
```

The method to receive messages is just as simple: you'll loop through the local gamers' collection and check if there is any available message. If so, you need to call the ReceiveData method of the LocalNetworkGamer object until you consume all available data.

ReceiveData returns arrays of bytes or a packetReader (the counterpart of packetWriter, used to write the packet), and also a NetworkGamer object with data from the remote player, which you can use to test if you want to process the message or not, depending on the game logic.

The next code excerpt presents a simple implementation of a routine that consumes messages from other players:

```
PacketReader packetReader = new PacketReader();
public void ReceiveMessage()
{
    NetworkGamer remotePlayer;  // The sender of the message

    foreach (LocalNetworkGamer localPlayer in session.LocalGamers)
    {
        // While there is data available for us, keep reading
        while (localPlayer.IsDataAvailable)
        {
            localPlayer.ReceiveData(packetReader, out remotePlayer);
            // Ignore input from local players
            if (!remotePlayer.IsLocal)
                message = "Received message: " +
                            packetReader.ReadString();
        }
    }
}
```

The send and receive routines of your game must write and read the same data structures, in the same order. Getting back to our later example, if you want to read the left thumbstick and both triggers' data, you need to write your packed reading code as follows:

```
remoteThumbstick = packetReader.ReadVector2();
remoteLeftTrigger = packetReader.ReadSingle();
remoteRightTrigger = packetReader.ReadSingle();
```

Now that your sending and writing routines are in place, you need to call them from the Update method of the Game1 class, to test them. Because you only want to send and receive messages when the game is running, create a new property for the NetworkHelper class that returns the current session state:

```
public NetworkSessionState SessionState
{
    get
```

```
    {
        if (session == null)
            return NetworkSessionState.Ended;
        else
            return session.SessionState;
    }
}
```

Now, let's include the calls for sending and receiving messages in the Update method, when the session is in "Playing" state:

```
if (networkHelper.SessionState == NetworkSessionState.Playing)
{
    // Send any key pressed to the remote player
    foreach (Keys key in Keyboard.GetState().GetPressedKeys())
        networkHelper.SendMessage(key.ToString());

    // Receive the keys from the remote player
    networkHelper.ReceiveMessage();
}
```

To test your program, run the test from the previous section, until you have two machines connected and the game started. At this point, press any key and you'll see the message "Sending message:" plus the key pressed on the first machine, and the message "Received message:" plus the key pressed on the remote machine in the second one.

A Final Touch

While we presented the various concepts through this chapter, you programmed a lot of keys to have a special meaning. To help you when testing your program, what about updating the Draw method of the Game1 class to present some helper messages stating the meaning of each key? Just update this method to reflect the next code example:

```
protected override void Draw(GameTime gameTime)
{
    graphics.GraphicsDevice.Clear(Color.CornflowerBlue);

    // Show the current session state
    spriteBatch.Begin();
    spriteBatch.DrawString(Arial, "Game State: " +
                networkHelper.Message,
                new Vector2(20, 20), Color.Yellow);
    spriteBatch.DrawString(Arial, "Press:", new Vector2(20, 100),
```

```
                Color.Snow);
        spriteBatch.DrawString(Arial, " - F1 to sign in",
                    new Vector2(20, 120), Color.Snow);
        spriteBatch.DrawString(Arial, " - F2 to create a session",
                    new Vector2(20, 140), Color.Snow);
        spriteBatch.DrawString(Arial, " - F3 to find a session",
                    new Vector2(20, 160), Color.Snow);
        spriteBatch.DrawString(Arial, " - F4 to asynchronously find a
session",
                    new Vector2(20, 180), Color.Snow);

        spriteBatch.DrawString(Arial, "After the game starts, press other
keys to send messages",
                    new Vector2(20, 220), Color.Snow);
        spriteBatch.End();

        base.Draw(gameTime);
}
```

Now, when you start the game, you have a quick reference for all keys that have some special meaning, as presented in Figure 5-11.

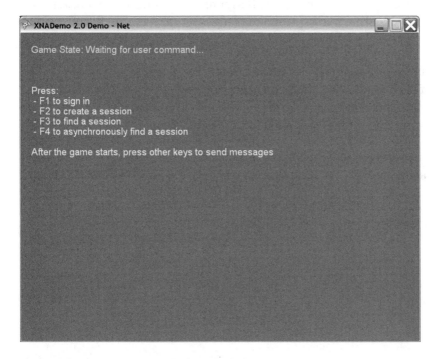

Figure 5-11. *Game screen with the next helper messages*

Remember, when testing this application, that you need to execute the commands in order: sign in a gamer, create a session, join a session (only on the other machine), set the players as "ready," and start sending and receiving messages. In the sample you coded in this chapter, you have to be careful about this, but in your games, you need to ensure, for example, that you never try to create or find a session if there is no signed-in player.

That's it for this chapter. In the next section we'll revisit the main points we've discussed.

Summary

In this chapter we started by presenting some generic concepts involved in creating networked games. Planning carefully and testing the networked games thoroughly are probably the most important points, because there are many more extra error sources than in local, single-player ones.

As for XNA network features, everything is pretty simple:

- When you include the Gamer Services component in your game, you automatically have access to all LIVE Guide features.

- To host a session, all you need to do is call the NetworkSession.Create method.

- Joining a session on a remote computer is as simple as calling the NetworkSession. Find method (to look for a session) and the NetworkSession.Join method (to join a session).

- Starting and ending a game is also simple: when the host calls the StartGame method of the session object, all players enter the game playing state, and receive a GameStarted event. The GameEnd method generates opposite results, firing a GameEnded event and setting the session to a game ended state.

- Sending messages is just as easy, by using the PacketWriter and PacketReader classes and the SendData and ReceiveData methods of the LocalNetworkGamer class.

In the next chapter, you'll explore the XNA networking concepts you learned here to create a network-enabled version of the Rock Rain game.

CHAPTER 6

■ ■ ■

Rock Rain Live!

The game in Chapter 4 mainly showed a playability change, allowing a match between two players on the same PC or on the same Xbox 360 console. This is nice, but how about being able to play with your friend on the other side of the world? And what about matches with one player running on a PC and another one on an Xbox 360? Wouldn't that be cool?

We'll use the concepts in the previous chapter and add a networked multiplayer feature to Rock Rain, called Multiplayer Online. We'll call this new version Rock Rain *Live*.

Planning Rock Rain Live

Rock Rain Enhanced already implements many of the features that you need for a new Multiplayer Online version of Rock Rain. What you'll do is add a new item in the game's starting screen menu that leads to another scene with the options of network games (create a game, join a game's session, and so on). With this new scene, the start scene will look like Figure 6-1.

Still, you have to think a little beforehand about how your game will work in a network. You saw in the previous chapter that XNA offers all the support for data transport between the players through a network, be it a local network or through LIVE. It's simple to send and receive data in a synchronized and safe way, but the main question is: *what* should you send or receive between the two players to create a network match?

Remember that Rock Rain is a game in which you must dodge the meteors (and the other player) and try to get the energy source to remain as long as possible in the game. So, the two players must be synchronized so that they see the same meteors, the other player's score, the energy source, and so on. That is, they must share the same *state* of the game.

Remember Chapter 2? There, we talked a little about game state; controlling this state is one of the most important tasks in any game. In Rock Rain Live's case, besides controlling this state, you also have to think about how to *synchronize* this state between the two players who will be playing a match through a local network or through the LIVE network from Microsoft.

Figure 6-1. *The new start scene*

In this game, you'll use a client/server architecture, described in the previous chapter, where one of the players is the game's server, offering the synchrony services of the game state itself. You'll call that player the *local player*. The other player is the game's client, consuming the data from the server to show the correct status of the game to the other player. You'll call that player the *remote player*.

It seems obvious, then, that the remote player will always consume information from the local player to obtain the game state. The remote player will always ask the state of the game, obtaining from the local player the score of the game, the meteors' positions, and so on. That is, the local player will always have "control" of the game state, and it's up to him or her to change this state (add a new meteor, for instance).

However, the remote player controls a new game state: its own position on the screen. So, you'll also have to inform the local player of the remote player's position, so that the game state stays synchronized between the two players.

This information exchange indeed involves a lot of code, but it's not complicated. Next, you'll create all the communication protocols to send the game state information between the players in a simple but powerful way, which can be changed or extended to other games.

Adding the Support for Network Games

Thanks to the excellent XNA network support, adding these new features to Rock Rain Enhanced is simple. Actually, you can copy all the game project code from Chapter 4 and change its name to Rock Rain Live. Also, change the classes' namespace name to RockRainLive (using Visual Studio's refactoring tool if you wish). Then add the following line in the Game1 class constructor:

```
// Add Live Support
Components.Add(new GamerServicesComponent(this));
```

Also add the namespace reference:

```
using Microsoft.Xna.Framework.GamerServices;
```

Execute the game. It's the same old version of Rock Rain. Now press the Home key on the keyboard or the Guide button on the Xbox 360 gamepad and you'll see a host of new features.

Now you can start to implement your new version of Rock Rain.

Changing the Opening Screen

Since the screen flow is now different, you have to change the opening screen to reflect the new Network Game option, which initially involves a menu change. So, change the StartScene class constructor and change the line where you created the menu, as follows:

```
// Create the Menu
string[] items = {"One Player", "Two Players", "Network Game",
                  "Help", "Quit"};
```

Because you added a new item, you have to change the HandleStartSceneInput() method of the Game1 class so that you update the indices of the menu options that open the help screen, and of the option that quits the game:

```
/// <summary>
/// Handle buttons and keyboard in StartScene
/// </summary>
private void HandleStartSceneInput()
{
    if (CheckEnterA())
    {
        audioComponent.PlayCue("menu_select3");
        switch (startScene.SelectedMenuIndex)
```

```
        {
            case 0:
                actionScene.TwoPlayers = false;
                ShowScene(actionScene);
                break;
            case 1:
                actionScene.TwoPlayers = true;
                ShowScene(actionScene);
                break;
            case 3:
                ShowScene(helpScene);
                break;
            case 4:
                Exit();
                break;
        }
    }
}
```

Also, in the HandleScenesInput() method of the Game1 class (which manipulates the input of all scenes), you should also add the manipulation support for this new scene:

```
/// <summary>
/// Handle input of all game scenes
/// </summary>
private void HandleScenesInput()
{
    // Handle Start Scene Input
    if (activeScene == startScene)
    {
        HandleStartSceneInput();
    }
    // Handle Help Scene input
    else if (activeScene == helpScene)
    {
        if (CheckEnterA())
        {
            ShowScene(startScene);
        }
    }
    // Handle Action Scene Input
    else if (activeScene == actionScene)
    {
```

```
        HandleActionInput();
    }
    else
    {
        // Handle Network Scene input
        HandleNetworkSceneInput();
    }
}
```

Let's create the method that will manipulate the network's scene input. You'll return to this method next:

```
/// <summary>
/// Handle Network Scene menu
/// </summary>
private void HandleNetworkSceneInput()
{
}
```

The guide that you saw in the previous chapter adds a series of services to your game, and when it's opened your game should not capture the user's inputs, because this could confuse the player. Therefore, also change the Update() method of the Game1 class, as follows, so you don't capture the user's inputs when the guide is opened:

```
/// <summary>
/// Allows the game to run logic such as updating the world,
/// checking for collisions, gathering input, and playing audio.
/// </summary>
/// <param name="gameTime">Provides a snapshot of timing values.</param>
protected override void Update(GameTime gameTime)
{
    // Handle Game Inputs
    if (!Guide.IsVisible)
    {
        HandleScenesInput();
    }

    base.Update(gameTime);
}
```

Execute the game and everything should work normally, except the Network Game option does nothing. You'll make this option open the multiplayer game scene later.

Creating the Network Game Scene

Now you'll create the scene that allows you to create a session or join a session of a network game. Similar to what you previously did in Chapter 4, add a new public class called NetworkScene and derive it from GameScene (in the RockRain.Core namespace) so that you have a new scene class. First, add the namespace reference for the network support:

```
using Microsoft.Xna.Framework.GamerServices;
```

In this scene you only have a background image, a menu, and a text line to show the messages related to the connection with the other player and background music. In it you can choose, through the menu, to start a new network game (creating a server), join a game that's already started, or log in to the network and return to the previous scene. Each option opens up a new menu, in such a way that you need to track this scene's state so that you can show the correct menu. The following enumeration creates the possible state of this scene:

```
// Scene State
public enum NetworkGameState
{
    idle = 1,
    joining = 2,
    creating = 3
}
```

As already mentioned, in this scene you have a menu, a background texture, and a blinking message. Declare the objects necessary to compose this scene:

```
// Misc
protected TextMenuComponent menu;
private readonly SpriteFont messageFont;
private Vector2 messagePosition,messageShadowPosition;
private string message;
protected TimeSpan elapsedTime = TimeSpan.Zero;

// SpriteBatch
protected SpriteBatch spriteBatch = null;

// Scene state
private NetworkGameState state;
// Used for message blink
private bool showMessage = true;
```

In the constructor, only initialize these objects, like you did with all the scenes throughout Chapter 4:

```
/// <summary>
/// Default Constructor
/// </summary>
/// <param name="game">Main game object</param>
/// <param name="smallFont">Font for the menu items</param>
/// <param name="largeFont">Font for the menu selected item</param>
/// <param name="background">Texture for background image</param>
public NetworkScene(Game game, SpriteFont smallFont, SpriteFont largeFont,
                    Texture2D background) : base(game)
{
    messageFont = largeFont;
    Components.Add(new ImageComponent(game, background,
                                ImageComponent.DrawMode.Stretch));

    // Create the menu component
    menu = new TextMenuComponent(game, smallFont, largeFont);
    Components.Add(menu);

    // Get the current spritebatch
    spriteBatch = (SpriteBatch)Game.Services.GetService(
                                typeof(SpriteBatch));
}
```

The scene state must also be the same when the user opens it:

```
/// <summary>
/// Show Scene
/// </summary>
public override void Show()
{
    state = NetworkGameState.idle;

    base.Show();
}
```

The menu components largely perform the drawing of the scene itself, for images that were already added to the scene. You only need to draw the message text that keeps blinking, the same way you did in the scene of the game's beginning, in Chapter 4. See that the message is also drawn twice to give a shadow effect:

```
/// <summary>
/// Allows the game component to draw your content in game screen
/// </summary>
public override void Draw(GameTime gameTime)
{
    base.Draw(gameTime);

    if (!string.IsNullOrEmpty(message) && showMessage)
    {
        DrawMessage();
    }
}


/// <summary>
/// Helper draws notification messages before calling blocking
/// network methods.
/// </summary>
void DrawMessage()
{
    // Draw the shadow
    spriteBatch.DrawString(messageFont, message, messageShadowPosition,
        Color.Black);

    // Draw the message
    spriteBatch.DrawString(messageFont, message, messagePosition,
        Color.DarkOrange);
}
```

You should expose the message attribute of the class so that the program is able to tell the scene in which the message will be showed. You use this message to show text such as "connecting…" or "connection terminated":

```
/// <summary>
/// Text of the message line
/// </summary>
public string Message
{
    get { return message; }
    set
    {
        message = value;
        // Calculate the message position
        messagePosition = new Vector2();
```

```
    messagePosition.X = (Game.Window.ClientBounds.Width -
        messageFont.MeasureString(message).X)/2;
    messagePosition.Y = 130;

    // Calculate the message shadow position
    messageShadowPosition = messagePosition;
    messageShadowPosition.Y++;
    messageShadowPosition.X--;


    }
}
```

On the other hand, the Update() method is only responsible for controlling the time to create the blink effect of the message on the screen and updating the menu to reflect the scene's current status:

```
/// <summary>
/// Allows the game component to update itself.
/// </summary>
/// <param name="gameTime">Provides a snapshot of timing values.</param>
public override void Update(GameTime gameTime)
{
    elapsedTime += gameTime.ElapsedGameTime;

    if (elapsedTime > TimeSpan.FromSeconds(1))
    {
        elapsedTime -= TimeSpan.FromSeconds(1);
        showMessage = !showMessage;
    }

    // Set the menu for the current state
    UpdateMenus();

    base.Update(gameTime);
}
```

The UpdateMenus() method only creates the menu for the current status. In particular, you create a menu when there is no user logged into the network, so that the user can log in before creating or joining a game:

```
/// <summary>
/// Build a menu for each scene state and network status
/// </summary>
```

```
private void UpdateMenus()
{
    if (Gamer.SignedInGamers.Count == 0)
    {
        string[] items = {"Sign in", "Back"};
        menu.SetMenuItems(items);
    }
    else
    {
        if (state == NetworkGameState.idle)
        {
            string[] items = {"Join a System Link Game",
                "Create a System Link Game", "Sign out", "Back"};
            menu.SetMenuItems(items);
        }
        if (state == NetworkGameState.creating)
        {
            string[] items = { "Cancel"};
            menu.SetMenuItems(items);
        }
    }

    // Put the menu centered in screen
    menu.Position = new Vector2((Game.Window.ClientBounds.Width -
                               menu.Width) / 2, 330);
}
```

And like you've always done, expose the menu option selected so that the Game1 class is able to execute the options the user selects. Also, expose the scene state so that the Game1 class is also able to change it when needed. Then, add the following code to the NetworkScene class:

```
/// <summary>
/// Gets the selected menu option
/// </summary>
public int SelectedMenuIndex
{
    get { return menu.SelectedIndex; }
}

/// <summary>
/// Scene state
/// </summary>
```

```
public NetworkGameState State
{
    get { return state; }
    set
    {
        state = value;
        menu.SelectedIndex = 0;
    }
}
```

Now you can use this scene in your game. Start by adding the declaration to a NetworkScene object in the Game1 class:

```
protected NetworkScene networkScene;
```

Then add the background texture of this new scene:

```
protected Texture2D networkBackgroundTexture;
```

You can find the background images for this project in the Source Code/Download area of the Apress web site at http://www.apress.com. Add these images to the Content folder and change the LoadContent() method, adding the following lines to load the background texture and create the network scene object:

```
// Create the Network Scene
networkBackgroundTexture = Content.Load<Texture2D>("NetworkBackground");
networkScene = new NetworkScene(this,smallFont,largeFont,
                        networkBackgroundTexture);
Components.Add(networkScene);
```

Now, you only need to show this scene when the user selects it from the initial scene menu. So, add the following code to the switch found in the HandleStartSceneInput() method in the Game1 class:

```
case 2:
    ShowScene(networkScene);
    break;
```

Execute the program. Select the Network Game option and you see something like Figure 6-2.

Figure 6-2. *The network game scene*

Now you'll go back to the HandleNetworkSceneInput() method and implement the methods that create and join a session of a network game.

Controlling the Input to the Scene

As you previously saw, the HandleNetworkSceneInput() method deals with all input originating from the menu for this scene; its code follows. You only separated the menu treatment for the two distinct situations when we discussed creating a network game: when the user is connected and when he's not connected to the network.

```
/// <summary>
/// Handle Network Scene menu
/// </summary>
private void HandleNetworkSceneInput()
{
    if (CheckEnterA())
    {
```

```
        audioComponent.PlayCue("menu_select3");
        if (Gamer.SignedInGamers.Count == 0)
        {
            HandleNotSigned();
        }
        else
        {
            HandleSigned();
        }
    }
}
```

The HandleNotSigned() method contains all the code for the menu when it's showing the options for a not-connected player, and the HandleSigned() method contains the options for a connected user.

All a not-connected user can do is connect to the network or go back to the initial scene. So, the HandleNotSigned() method is simple:

```
/// <summary>
/// Handle Network Scene menu for an unsigned user
/// </summary>
private void HandleNotSigned()
{
    switch (networkScene.SelectedMenuIndex)
    {
        case 0:
            if (!Guide.IsVisible)
            {
                Guide.ShowSignIn(1, false);
                break;
            }
            break;
        case 1:
            ShowScene(startScene);
            break;
    }
}
```

However, a user connected to the network can create a new game, join an already created session, change the authenticated user, or go back to the initial scene.

If this connected user is creating a game, he or she can also cancel the wait for the other player. You implement these situations in the HandleSigned() method, as follows:

```csharp
/// <summary>
/// Handle Network Scene menu for a signed user
/// </summary>
private void HandleSigned()
{
    switch (networkScene.State)
    {
        case NetworkScene.NetworkGameState.idle:
            switch (networkScene.SelectedMenuIndex)
            {
                case 0:
                    // Join a network game
                    JoinSession();
                    break;
                case 1:
                    // Create a network game
                    CreateSession();
                    break;
                case 2:
                    // Show the guide to change user
                    if (!Guide.IsVisible)
                    {
                        Guide.ShowSignIn(1, false);
                        break;
                    }
                    break;
                case 3:
                    // Back to start scene
                    ShowScene(startScene);
                    break;
            }
            break;
        case NetworkScene.NetworkGameState.creating:
            // Close the session created
            CloseSession();
            // Wait for a new command
            networkScene.State = NetworkScene.NetworkGameState.idle;
            networkScene.Message = "";
            break;
    }
}
```

Notice the CreateSession(), JoinSession(), and CloseSession() methods. These methods are common to all network games, and in fact start and end all the communication between the players. You'll implement them soon, but let's first create a class to help you with the network services necessary for Rock Rain Live.

The NetworkHelper Class

You saw in the previous chapter that all the network services in your XNA game are centralized in the NetworkSession class. With it, you used objects from the PacketWriter and PacketReader classes to write and read network data. For organization purposes, you'll create a class that encapsulates all the necessary data transport functionality, using these classes, so that you have only one object you can use to send and read data from the server and the client, and to the server and the client. This class is simple—just add a new class called NetworkHelper to the project, and add the following code:

```
using Microsoft.Xna.Framework.Net;

namespace RockRainLive
{
    /// <summary>
    /// Helper for network services
    /// </summary>
    class NetworkHelper
    {
        // NetworkStuff
        private NetworkSession networkSession;
        private readonly PacketWriter serverPacketWriter = new PacketWriter();
        private readonly PacketReader serverPacketReader = new PacketReader();
        private readonly PacketWriter clientPacketWriter = new PacketWriter();
        private readonly PacketReader clientPacketReader = new PacketReader();

        /// <summary>
        /// The active network session
        /// </summary>
        public NetworkSession NetworkGameSession
        {
            get { return networkSession; }
            set { networkSession = value; }
        }
```

```csharp
/// <summary>
/// Writer for the server data
/// </summary>
public PacketWriter ServerPacketWriter
{
    get { return serverPacketWriter; }
}

/// <summary>
/// Writer for the client data
/// </summary>
public PacketWriter ClientPacketWriter
{
    get { return clientPacketWriter; }
}

/// <summary>
/// Reader for the client data
/// </summary>
public PacketReader ClientPacketReader
{
    get { return clientPacketReader; }
}

/// <summary>
/// Reader for the server data
/// </summary>
public PacketReader ServerPacketReader
{
    get { return serverPacketReader; }
}

/// <summary>
/// Send all server data
/// </summary>
public void SendServerData()
{
    if (ServerPacketWriter.Length > 0)
    {
        // Send the combined data to everyone in the session.
        LocalNetworkGamer server = (LocalNetworkGamer) networkSession.Host;
```

```csharp
            server.SendData(ServerPacketWriter, SendDataOptions.InOrder);
        }
    }


    /// <summary>
    /// Read server data
    /// </summary>
    public NetworkGamer ReadServerData(LocalNetworkGamer gamer)
    {
        NetworkGamer sender;

        // Read a single packet from the network.
        gamer.ReceiveData(ServerPacketReader, out sender);
        return sender;
    }


    /// <summary>
    /// Send all client data
    /// </summary>
    public void SendClientData()
    {
        if (ClientPacketWriter.Length > 0)
        {
            // The first player is always running in the server...
            networkSession.LocalGamers[0].SendData(clientPacketWriter,
                                              SendDataOptions.InOrder,
                                              networkSession.Host);
        }
    }


    /// <summary>
    /// Read the Client Data
    /// </summary>
    public NetworkGamer ReadClientData(LocalNetworkGamer gamer)
    {
        NetworkGamer sender;

        // Read a single packet from the network.
        gamer.ReceiveData(ClientPacketReader, out sender);
        return sender;
    }
    }
}
```

This class contains your `NetworkSession` object, as well as methods to send and read the data packages through the `PacketWriter` and `PacketReader` objects, both for the client and for the server. You'll use this class to implement your communication protocol in the next section. For now, you'll initialize the `NetworkSession` object of this class, like you did in the previous chapter, to create a game session, join an existing session, or terminate a session. That is, you'll implement the `CreateSession()`, `JoinSession()`, and `CloseSession()` methods that we talked about earlier.

Creating the Game Sessions

Now you'll start adding the network support to your game. You'll initially create all the network session support for your new game so that later you can send and receive data between the client and the server. Then you'll declare an object for the `NetworkHelper` class that you created, as well as the constants for the maximum number of local players and for the game session. Add the attributes to the `Game1` class:

```
// Network stuff
private readonly NetworkHelper networkHelper;
private const int maxLocalPlayers = 1;
private const int maxSessionPlayers = 2;
```

Then, add a reference to the network's support classes:

```
using Microsoft.Xna.Framework.Net;
```

Then, initialize the `networkHelper` object in the class constructor. Add it also to the Game Services because the various classes of your game will use it later on:

```
networkHelper = new NetworkHelper();
Services.AddService(typeof(NetworkHelper), networkHelper);
```

You can use this class already. First, create the method that creates the network game session. This method is called when the user selects the corresponding option in the network scene:

```
/// <summary>
/// Create a session for a game server
/// </summary>
private void CreateSession()
{
    networkHelper.NetworkGameSession = NetworkSession.Create(
                                NetworkSessionType.SystemLink,
                                maxLocalPlayers, maxSessionPlayers);
```

```
    HookSessionEvents();
    networkScene.State = NetworkScene.NetworkGameState.creating;
    networkScene.Message = "Waiting another player...";
}
```

▪**Note** This Rock Rain version can create games for local network usage, called *SystemLink* in XNA. The procedures for the game creation using the Xbox LIVE network are exactly the same, but require that *both* players have the Creator's Club signature (even on the PC). This makes its professional use difficult, so we won't cover this kind of connection in this book.

You created a session using the Create() method of the NetworkSession class, according to what you learned in the previous chapter. You also initialized the network scene object to reflect the action that you just took, setting its state to creating and showing a message that you were waiting for the other player to join the session.

The HookSessionEvents() method signs some events that you need to handle for the session control, also according to what you saw in the previous chapter. In this Rock Rain version you handle the events that happen when the player joins a game and when the player terminates the session:

```
/// <summary>
/// After creating or joining a network session, we must subscribe to
/// some events so we will be notified when the session changes state.
/// </summary>
void HookSessionEvents()
{
    networkHelper.NetworkGameSession.GamerJoined +=
        GamerJoinedEventHandler;
    networkHelper.NetworkGameSession.SessionEnded +=
        SessionEndedEventHandler;
}
```

So, when the session is terminated, the preceding code calls the SessionEndedEventHandler() method to display the game's network scene again, showing an error message that was sent as the reason for the session to end (using the EndReason attribute of the NetworkSessionEndedEventArgs class that is passed as a method parameter), as follows:

```
// <summary>
/// Event handler notifies us when the network session has ended.
/// </summary>
```

```
void SessionEndedEventHandler(object sender, NetworkSessionEndedEventArgs e)
{
    networkScene.Message = e.EndReason.ToString();
    networkScene.State = NetworkScene.NetworkGameState.idle;

    CloseSession();

    if (activeScene != networkScene)
    {
        ShowScene(networkScene);
    }
}
```

In the `GamerJoinedEventHandler()` method, which is called when the player (local or remote) joins a game session, you only check if all (two) players have already joined the session to start the game itself. This activates the action scene for both players and associates the player to his or her corresponding `Player` object, which you'll subsequently use to differentiate the local player from the remote player:

```
/// <summary>
/// This event handler will be called whenever a new gamer joins the
/// session.
/// </summary>
void GamerJoinedEventHandler(object sender, GamerJoinedEventArgs e)
{
    // Associate the ship with the joined player
    if (actionScene.Player1.Gamer == null)
    {
        actionScene.Player1.Gamer = e.Gamer;
    }
    else
    {
        actionScene.Player2.Gamer = e.Gamer;
    }

    if (networkHelper.NetworkGameSession.AllGamers.Count ==
        maxSessionPlayers)
    {
        actionScene.TwoPlayers = true;
        ShowScene(actionScene);
    }
}
```

The method to terminate the session just releases the NetworkSession object, the same way it did in the previous chapter:

```
/// <summary>
/// Quit the game session
/// </summary>
private void CloseSession()
{
    networkHelper.NetworkGameSession.Dispose();
    networkHelper.NetworkGameSession = null;
}
```

There's only the method to join a game session left. The code is practically the same as in the previous chapter; you only add some messages to the network scene based on the success or not of joining the game:

```
/// <summary>
/// Joins an existing network session.
/// </summary>
void JoinSession()
{
    networkScene.Message = "Joining a game...";
    networkScene.State = NetworkScene.NetworkGameState.joining;

    try
    {
        // Search for sessions.
        using (AvailableNetworkSessionCollection availableSessions =
                    NetworkSession.Find(NetworkSessionType.SystemLink,
                                    maxLocalPlayers, null))
        {
            if (availableSessions.Count == 0)
            {
                networkScene.Message = "No network sessions found.";
                networkScene.State = NetworkScene.NetworkGameState.idle;
                return;
            }

            // Join the first session we found.
            networkHelper.NetworkGameSession = NetworkSession.Join(
                                    availableSessions[0]);
```

```
            HookSessionEvents();
        }
    }
    catch (Exception e)
    {
        networkScene.Message = e.Message;
        networkScene.State = NetworkScene.NetworkGameState.idle;
    }
}
```

Now that you can create, terminate, and join a session in progress for a network game, you already have all the necessary structure to be able to send and receive data. You should now start to think about what your communication protocol will be. We'll cover that in the following section.

Let's Talk

A communication protocol is a "language" spoken between the client and the server. It defines the way the messages are sent and received so that with this message exchange you can keep your game state in sync.

You saw in the previous chapter that these messages are sent and received through PacketWriter and PacketReader class objects, respectively. You can send or receive any kind of data with these classes, but you need to define a protocol so that this communication is done efficiently.

Imagine the following situation. You're playing in a network with a friend on the other side of the world and you suddenly pause the game. You have to tell the other player somehow that you paused, and therefore his game must also pause, so that he doesn't obtain any advantage while you're on the toilet. How do you "tell" the other player that you paused, and how do you let the player know when you return to the game?

In the case of Rock Rain, your protocol is simple. Each message that you send to the other player is composed of a header with a character that explains which message is being sent, followed by the message itself. In the case of pausing the game, you send a message as in Table 6-1.

Table 6-1. *The Pause Message*

Header	Message
'P'	true or false, according to the pause status

If the player pauses, you send the message in Table 6-2 to the other player.

Table 6-2. *The Message Sent When the Player Pauses the Game*

Header	Message
'P'	true

When the player releases the pause, you send the message in Table 6-3.

Table 6-3. *The Message Sent When the Player Releases the Game*

Header	Message
'P'	false

So, when you detect that the user wants to pause or stop the pause, you should send this data to the PacketWriter object corresponding to the client or to the server, depending on which one wants to change the pause state. To do this, change the HandleActionInput() method of the Game1 class and add the following lines:

```
if (enterKey)
{
    if (actionScene.GameOver)
    {
        ShowScene(startScene);
    }
    else
    {
        audioComponent.PlayCue("menu_back");
        actionScene.Paused = !actionScene.Paused;
        // Send the pause command to the other Player
        if (networkHelper.NetworkGameSession != null)
        {
            // If we are the server, send using the server packets
            if (networkHelper.NetworkGameSession.IsHost)
            {
                networkHelper.ServerPacketWriter.Write('P');
                networkHelper.ServerPacketWriter.Write(
                                            actionScene.Paused);
            }
            else
            {
                networkHelper.ClientPacketWriter.Write('P');
                networkHelper.ClientPacketWriter.Write(
```

```
                                                    actionScene.Paused);
                }
            }


        }
        if (backKey)
        {
            if (networkHelper.NetworkGameSession != null)
            {
                CloseSession();
                networkScene.State = NetworkScene.NetworkGameState.idle;
                networkScene.Message = "";
                ShowScene(networkScene);
            }
            else
            {
                ShowScene(startScene);
            }
        }
    }
}
```

■**Note** Be careful when defining the format of your messages. The network traffic has a lot of influence on the performance of an online game. Overall, keep the least possible amount of traffic, so that the server doesn't keep processing messages for too long. Besides the client/server model, XNA offers the peer-to-peer (P2P) model, which might be more adequate for games with excessive message exchange or with large states, such as the Massive Multiplayer Online type of games.

See that you put the message header first ('P') in the ClientPacketWriter or in the ServerPacketWriter, then include the message itself (actionScene.Paused) so that the message is now formatted and ready to be sent.

You also added new code in the treatment of the Back key. If it's activated during a network game, it makes the game terminate the connection and return to the network scene, instead of simply returning to the initial scene.

Now you need to read this message, interpret it, and change the game state (pause or not) according to the message content. It's good design to keep the method that deals with the messages close to the class that contains the game state itself. In Rock Rain's case it's the class that represents the action scene.

Before you do anything else, you need your NetworkHelper object. So, declare it in the ActionScene class:

```
// Network Stuff
private readonly NetworkHelper networkHelper;
```

Initialize it in the class constructor:

```
// Get the current server state for a networked multiplayer game
networkHelper = (NetworkHelper)
    Game.Services.GetService(typeof (NetworkHelper));
```

Now you'll create two methods in the ActionScene class: one to interpret the messages that come from the client, and another one for the server messages. So, add the following method in the ActionScene class:

```
/// <summary>
///  Handle all data incoming from the client
/// </summary>
public void HandleClientData()
{
    while (networkHelper.ClientPacketReader.PeekChar() != -1)
    {
        char header = networkHelper.ClientPacketReader.ReadChar();
        switch (header)
        {
            case 'P':
                Paused = networkHelper.ClientPacketReader.ReadBoolean();
                break;
        }
    }
}
```

This method will be called when you need to interpret any message originating from the remote player (client). Note that the while condition loops through all PacketReaders of the client to read all messages, the same way you did in the previous chapter, and interprets them accordingly. In the case of a 'P' message, for a pause, all you do is assign the value of the message to the Paused attribute for the scene, which pauses the game or not.

For the pause message that comes from the server, the code is practically the same:

```
/// <summary>
///  Handle all data incoming from the server
/// </summary>
public void HandleServerData()
{
    while (networkHelper.ServerPacketReader.PeekChar() != -1)
```

```
    {
        char header = networkHelper.ServerPacketReader.ReadChar();
        switch (header)
        {
            case 'P':
                Paused = networkHelper.ServerPacketReader.ReadBoolean();
                break;
        }
    }
}
```

Except, the difference is now that you used the server's `PacketReader`. Note that because the server maintains the game state, many new messages are created and interpreted here, while on the client only this pause message and another message with the position of the remote player are sent. We'll go back to these methods later.

Now you need to call these methods in some moments; that is, you need to put all the sending and receiving of the network data in the game's loop. The same way you did in the previous chapter, add this in the `Update()` method of the `Game1` class, and use the methods of the `NetworkHelper` class that send and receive data. So, add the following code to the `Update()` method of the `Game1` class:

```
// Handle the network session
if (networkHelper.NetworkGameSession != null)
{
    // Only send if we are not the server. There is no point sending
    // packets to ourselves, because we already know what they will
    // contain!
    if (!networkHelper.NetworkGameSession.IsHost)
    {
        networkHelper.SendClientData();
    }
    else
    {
        // If we are the server, transmit the game state
        networkHelper.SendServerData();
    }

    // Pump the data
    networkHelper.NetworkGameSession.Update();

    // Read any incoming network packets.
    foreach (LocalNetworkGamer gamer in
            networkHelper.NetworkGameSession.LocalGamers)
```

```
        {
            // Keep reading as long as incoming packets are available.
            while (gamer.IsDataAvailable)
            {
                NetworkGamer sender;
                if (gamer.IsHost)
                {
                    sender = networkHelper.ReadClientData(gamer);
                    if (!sender.IsLocal)
                    {
                        actionScene.HandleClientData();
                    }
                }
                else
                {
                    sender = networkHelper.ReadServerData(gamer);
                    if (!sender.IsLocal)
                    {
                        actionScene.HandleServerData();
                    }
                }
            }
        }
    }

}
```

So, for each game loop, you're always reading and sending the necessary data packages.

You also need to expose the Player objects to associate the network Gamer class for each player who joins the game session. So, add the following code:

```
public Player Player1
{
    get { return player1; }
}

public Player Player2
{
    get { return player2; }
}
```

Now let's add new messages to the other game states.

Synchronizing the Players

What defines a player's state? It's not only the player's position on the screen, but also his or her score and energy level. So, you need to inform the other player of his or her opponent's status so that the game stays synchronized. Create a new message for this, as in Table 6-4.

Table 6-4. *The Player's Status Message*

Header	Message
'S'	Position, Score, Energy

The 'S' message sends all the necessary information for a player, and both players (the local player, player1, and remote player, player2) must send their status through the network.

For the remote player, add the following code in the HandleClientData() method of the ActionScene class:

```
case 'S':
    player2.Position =
        networkHelper.ClientPacketReader.ReadVector2();
    player2.Power =
        networkHelper.ClientPacketReader.ReadInt32();
    player2.Score =
        networkHelper.ClientPacketReader.ReadInt32();
    break;
```

That is, if it's the 'S' message, it will be followed by the player's position (a Vector2 object) and by the player's score and energy level (Int32 objects). You only need to update the player2 object's attributes with these values.

Similarly, add the following code to deal with the player's movement on the server side—in this case, in the HandleServerData() method:

```
case 'S':
    player1.Position =
        networkHelper.ServerPacketReader.ReadVector2();
    player1.Power =
        networkHelper.ServerPacketReader.ReadInt32();
    player1.Score =
        networkHelper.ServerPacketReader.ReadInt32();
    break;
```

You must alter the Player class (which represents the player1 and player2 objects) to send the player's position through the network. In fact, the class must change to stop any alterations of its state by the remote player. If alterations are allowed (such as changing the position), a message must send this change to the server.

Adding Network Support to the Player Class

If you're adding network support, you also need your instance of the NetworkHelper class. So, declare it in the Player class:

```
// Network Stuff
private readonly NetworkHelper networkHelper;
```

Then, initialize it in the class constructor:

```
// Get the current server state for a networked multiplayer game
networkHelper = (NetworkHelper)
    Game.Services.GetService(typeof (NetworkHelper));
```

Now let's change the Update() method of this class so that it sends the 'S' message, with the ship's status. Change the code of the method as follows:

```
if (networkHelper.NetworkGameSession != null)
{
    if (gamer.IsLocal)
    {
        // Local gamers always use the main gamepad and keyboard keys
        HandleInput(PlayerIndex.One);
        UpdateShip(gameTime);
        UpdateNetworkData();
    }
}
else
{
    HandleInput(playerIndex);
    UpdateShip(gameTime);
}
```

Note that only the messages to the local player are sent, because you don't need to send the remote player's changes to him or her. Also, in the case of a multiplayer game via network, the two players don't need to divide the keyboard or use two gamepads, so they always use the same gamepad or keyboard keys.

The following `UpdateNetworkData()` method creates the messages that will be sent:

```
/// <summary>
/// Update server data with the ship info
/// </summary>
private void UpdateNetworkData()
{
    if (networkHelper.NetworkGameSession.IsHost)
    {
        networkHelper.ServerPacketWriter.Write('S');
        networkHelper.ServerPacketWriter.Write(position);
        networkHelper.ServerPacketWriter.Write(power);
        networkHelper.ServerPacketWriter.Write(score);
    }
    else
    {
        networkHelper.ClientPacketWriter.Write('S');
        networkHelper.ClientPacketWriter.Write(position);
        networkHelper.ClientPacketWriter.Write(power);
        networkHelper.ClientPacketWriter.Write(score);

    }
}
```

That adds the message data in the corresponding `PacketWriter`, the same way you did before. The code you added to the `Update()` method of the `Game1` class also sends this data, and the `HandleClientData()` and `HandleServerData()` methods of the `ActionScene` class handle it, the same way they handle the pause message. In this way, you'll add the network support to all the other objects that contain some game state.

Adding Network Support to the PowerSource Class

The `PowerSource` class, which represents the item that gives the energy to the player, also contains an important state in the game: its position. Through this position and the other players' positions, you know if any player managed to get any energy during a match.

So, create a message to tell the position about this item (see Table 6-5).

Table 6-5. *The Power Source Position Message*

Header	Message
'L'	Position

This state is only kept on the server. Then, add the following code to the HandleServerData() method of the ActionScene class:

```
case 'L':
    powerSource.Position =
        networkHelper.ServerPacketReader.ReadVector2();
    break;
```

Think it's repetitive? Great! Next, add an attribute of the NetworkHelper type and initialize it in the PowerSource class constructor, the same way you did with the Player class, and change the Update() method as follows:

```
/// <summary>
/// Allows the game component to update itself.
/// </summary>
/// <param name="gameTime">Provides a snapshot of timing values.</param>
public override void Update(GameTime gameTime)
{
    if ((networkHelper.NetworkGameSession == null) ||
        (networkHelper.NetworkGameSession.IsHost))
    {
        // Check if the meteor is still visible
        if (position.Y >= Game.Window.ClientBounds.Height)
        {
            PutinStartPosition();
        }

        // Move
        position.Y += 1;

        networkHelper.ServerPacketWriter.Write('L');
        networkHelper.ServerPacketWriter.Write(position);
    }

    base.Update(gameTime);
}
```

That is, the Update() method only updates the position of the object that is running on the server side. The HandleServerData() method sets the position of the object on the client side with the data sent by the instance that runs on the server, so that both stay synchronized.

You already synchronized the players, the energy source, and the game pause. Only the meteors are left.

Adding Network Support for the Meteors

The game's meteors are represented by two distinct classes: the Meteor class, which represents the sprite of the meteor itself, and the MeteorsManager class, which represents the entire meteor field in the game. Each of them changes the game state in its own way, and you'll alter its code to add the network game support separately.

In the Meteor class, only the PutinStartPosition() and Update() methods change the attributes of an instance. So, you'll change these methods. But which message will be sent to represent a meteor state?

In Rock Rain, each meteor only updates its position on the screen, so you can send a message as in Table 6-6.

Table 6-6. *The Meteor Position Message*

Header	Message
'R'	Index, Position

Each meteor on the screen sends that message, to inform the client of its position in the game. Because the value of the Index property can identify each meteor, let's send them together so that the client knows about which meteor position it's being informed.

First, add and initialize an instance of the NetworkHelper class, the same way you already did. Change the PutinStartPosition() method:

```
/// <summary>
/// Initialize Meteor Position and Velocity
/// </summary>
public void PutinStartPosition()
{
    // Only the server can set the meteor attributes
    if ((networkHelper.NetworkGameSession == null) ||
        (networkHelper.NetworkGameSession.IsHost))
    {
        position.X = random.Next(Game.Window.ClientBounds.Width -
                                 currentFrame.Width);
        position.Y = 0;
        YSpeed = 1 + random.Next(9);
        XSpeed = random.Next(3) - 1;
    }
}
```

Following is the code for the Update() method:

```
/// <summary>
/// Update the Meteor Position
/// </summary>
public override void Update(GameTime gameTime)
{
    // Check if the meteor is still visible
    if ((position.Y >= Game.Window.ClientBounds.Height) ||
        (position.X >= Game.Window.ClientBounds.Width) ||
        (position.X <= 0))
    {
        PutinStartPosition();
    }

    // Move meteor
    position.Y += Yspeed;
    position.X += Xspeed;

    // Send the meteor info to the client
    if ((networkHelper.NetworkGameSession != null) &&
        (networkHelper.NetworkGameSession.IsHost))
    {
        networkHelper.ServerPacketWriter.Write('R');
        networkHelper.ServerPacketWriter.Write(index);
        networkHelper.ServerPacketWriter.Write(position);
    }

    base.Update(gameTime);
}
```

This is also a message that is only sent by the server, so you handle it in the HandleServerData() method of the ActionScene class, like you did with the other messages:

```
case 'R':
    int meteorId = networkHelper.ServerPacketReader.ReadInt32();
    meteors.AllMeteors[meteorId].Position =
        networkHelper.ServerPacketReader.ReadVector2();
    break;
```

In the preceding code, you just set the position of the specified meteor with the position sent in the message. Because you're doing this for each meteor, you'll then synchronize the position of all of them during the game.

Another state change situation occurs when a new meteor is added to the scene. The MeteorsManager class performs this operation. The client must be notified about a new object added by the server, so that the client can see a new meteor with the same characteristics.

So, add and initialize an instance of the `NetworkHelper` object and change the `Start()` method of the `MeteorsManager` class:

```
/// <summary>
/// Start the Meteors' Rain
/// </summary>
public void Start()
{
    if ((networkHelper.NetworkGameSession == null) ||
        (networkHelper.NetworkGameSession.IsHost))
    {
        // Initialize a counter
        elapsedTime = TimeSpan.Zero;

        // Add the meteors
        for (int i = 0; i < STARTMETEORCOUNT; i++)
        {
            AddNewMeteor();
        }
    }
}
```

This way, only the server is able to add new meteors, and when a new meteor is added you must send a message to inform the client. This message contains the attributes of a meteor (see Table 6-7).

Table 6-7. *The Meteor Status Message*

Header	Message
'M'	Index, Position, Horizontal Speed, Vertical Speed

Then, change the `AddNewMeteor()` method to send a message with the other attributes of the new meteor:

```
/// <summary>
/// Add a new meteor in the scene
/// </summary>
/// <returns>the new meteor</returns>
private Meteor AddNewMeteor()
{
```

```
    Meteor newMeteor = new Meteor(Game, ref meteorTexture);
    newMeteor.Initialize();
    meteors.Add(newMeteor);
    newMeteor.Index = meteors.Count-1;

    // Send the new meteor info to the client
    if ((networkHelper.NetworkGameSession != null) &&
        (networkHelper.NetworkGameSession.IsHost))
    {
        networkHelper.ServerPacketWriter.Write('M');
        networkHelper.ServerPacketWriter.Write(newMeteor.Index);
        networkHelper.ServerPacketWriter.Write(newMeteor.Position);
        networkHelper.ServerPacketWriter.Write(newMeteor.XSpeed);
        networkHelper.ServerPacketWriter.Write(newMeteor.YSpeed);
    }

    return newMeteor;
}
```

And again handle this message in the `HandleServerData()` event of the `ActionScene` class so that a new meteor is added to the client's meteor list:

```
case 'M':
    int index = networkHelper.ServerPacketReader.ReadInt32();
    Vector2 position =
        networkHelper.ServerPacketReader.ReadVector2();
    int xspeed = networkHelper.ServerPacketReader.ReadInt32();
    int yspeed = networkHelper.ServerPacketReader.ReadInt32();
    meteors.AddNewMeteor(index,position,xspeed,yspeed);
    break;
```

Now, the motion as well as the addition of new meteors are synchronized with the client.

There's still a third point where the game state is changed: when the `Update()` method checks if it's necessary to add a new meteor. Only the server can execute this operation, so change the method as follows:

```
// Only the server can add new meteors
if ((networkHelper.NetworkGameSession == null) ||
    (networkHelper.NetworkGameSession.IsHost))
{
    CheckforNewMeteor(gameTime);
}
```

That's it! All the objects are now synchronized, and the server will control all the game state and send it to the client so it keeps the game synchronized. The client will receive all the messages and change the status of its objects according to the content of these messages, to maintain an online match the same way as if you were beside your opponent. Figure 6-3 demonstrates the message traffic between the players. Now call that friend of yours who lives in Japan for a Rock Rain match!

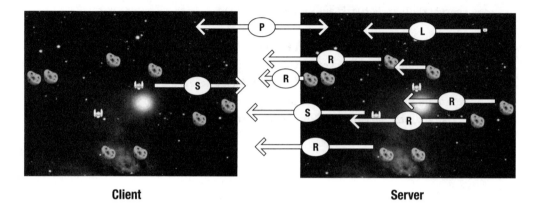

Client   Server

Figure 6-3. *The chat between server and client*

Summary

In this chapter you saw the basic principles of how to plan and create an online multi-player game. Correct definitions for the protocol and sending messages are essential for keeping the game state synchronized between the various players. XNA offers powerful classes so that this work becomes simple and you don't have to worry about the details of sending and receiving data through the network.

How about now adding a new feature to send messages between the players? Or, how about adding support for three or four players? Try and you'll see that it's not hard to make Rock Rain a Massive Multiplayer Online game.

CHAPTER 7

■ ■ ■

3-D Game Programming Basics

In this chapter you'll see basic concepts involved in creating 3-D games and create a simple program that explores these concepts, to prepare you to create a complete 3-D game in the next chapter.

3-D Coordinate Systems and Projections

In Chapter 2 we talked about 2-D coordinate systems, including a special case of such systems: the screen coordinate systems. When talking about 3-D coordinate systems, though, you need to comprehend a lot of extra concepts to understand what is involved in defining a 3-D virtual object and transforming such an object into the 2-D representation that is presented on the screen. First, you'll learn the basics of these concepts, then see how to apply them in a game using XNA.

When dealing with three Cartesian dimensions, there are two types of coordinate systems: left-handed and right-handed. These names refer to the Z axis's position relative to the X and Y axes. To determine this position, point the fingers of one hand to the X axis's positive direction and move them in a counterclockwise direction to the Y axis's positive position. The Z axis's direction is the direction your thumb points to. Figure 7-1 illustrates this concept.

To put it a different way, in the left-handed coordinate system, the Z value gets bigger (the positive direction) when you go from the screen to a point away from you (considering that the X axis and the Y axis are on the computer screen). The right-handed 3-D system is the opposite: the Z values increase toward you from the screen.

The XNA Framework works, by default, in a right-handed coordinate system—which, it's worth noting, is different from DirectX's default. This means that negative values for Z are visible, and the more negative they are for a given object, the farther the object is from the screen. Positive values are not shown, unless you change your "camera position," as you'll see later in this chapter.

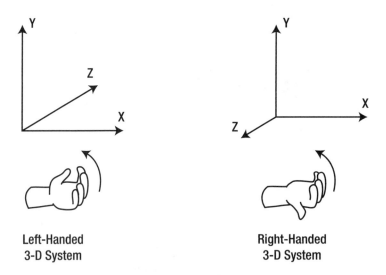

Left-Handed
3-D System

Right-Handed
3-D System

Figure 7-1. *The Cartesian 3-D coordinate systems*

Now that you understand 3-D coordinate systems, the next step to explore is how you can map 3-D objects to your computer's 2-D screen.

Fortunately, XNA does all the hard mathematical work for this mapping, but you still have to understand the concept of *projections* and how they apply to XNA to issue the basic instructions for how to present the objects onscreen.

Similarly to other gaming libraries, XNA supports two different types of projections:

- *Perspective projection*: The most common type of projection, it takes the Z distance into account and adjusts the objects accordingly. This projection makes objects appear smaller when far from the screen. Depending on the position, the objects also appear deformed, like in the real world. For example, the sides of a cube that are closer to the screen seem bigger than the farther ones. Figure 7-2 shows a graphical representation of the perspective projection.

- *Orthogonal projection*: In this type of projection, the Z component is just ignored, and the objects don't get bigger when closer to the screen or smaller when they are farther away. This projection is mostly used for 2-D games (which use a "fake" 3-D, just to put some sprites over others) or simpler 3-D games. Figure 7-3 presents orthogonal projection.

You'll see later in this chapter how to use each projection type in XNA. However, before you start coding, you need to understand how 3-D objects are represented in a game. That's exactly what you'll do in the next section.

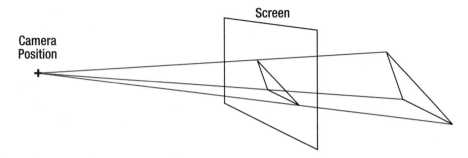

Figure 7-2. *Perspective projection*

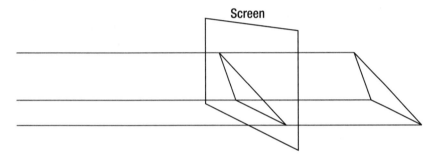

Figure 7-3. *Orthogonal projection*

Vertices and Primitives

The most basic part of a 3-D object is a vertex. Mathematically, vertices are represented solely by their 3-D coordinates (which are mapped to the Vector3 data type in XNA), but in XNA they include extra information, such as color, texture, or normal vector information, depending on the vertex format used. Table 7-1 presents the vertex definitions provided by the XNA Framework.

Table 7-1. *Vertex Format Structure Definition in XNA*

Vertex Format	Description
VertexPositionColor	Defines a vertex with position and rendering color
VertexPositionTexture	Defines a vertex with position and texture coordinates, which specify how to map a given texture over this vertex, with (0,0) being the upper-left coordinate of the texture, and (1,1) the bottom-right limit of the texture
VertexPositionColorTexture	Defines a vertex with position, color, and texture coordinates
VertexPositionNormalTexture	Defines a vertex with position and the normal vector

Besides the vertices' position and additional data, when creating 3-D objects you also need to specify how XNA will connect these vertices, according to different drawing primitives.

Drawing primitives, or 3-D primitives, define to XNA how a vertices collection (known in XNA as a *vertex buffer*) will be rendered when the drawing functions are called. The vertices can be drawn as a set of disconnected points, as a set of lines, or as triangles.

The triangle is used as a base to create any other 2-D or 3-D objects. This is because a primitive defined with only three points is guaranteed to be in a single plane, and to be convex (a line connecting any two points inside a triangle is always fully inside the triangle, which doesn't happen in some figures with four vertices). These characteristics are the key to performing the fastest rendering possible by the graphics cards, which always use triangles as the base rendering primitives.

So, for example, if you want to draw a square onscreen, you'll have to use two triangles. If you want to create a cube, you'll use 12 triangles (2 for each facet), as shown in Figure 7-4.

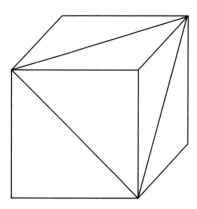

Figure 7-4. *A cube made with triangles*

In XNA, the graphics device object has a method named DrawPrimitives that is used to draw a vertex buffer according to a specific primitive type, defined by the PrimitiveType enumeration:

- PointList: Each vertex is rendered isolated from the others, so you can see a list of floating points. Figure 7-5 presents a set of vertices rendered as a point list.

- LineList: The vertices are rendered in pairs, with lines connecting each pair. This call fails if you fail to pass a vertex buffer with an even number of vertices. Figure 7-6 illustrates the use of a line list primitive type.

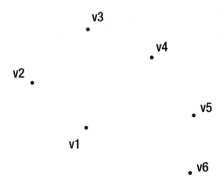

Figure 7-5. *Vertices rendered as a point list*

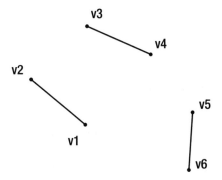

Figure 7-6. *The same vertices rendered as a line list*

- LineStrip: All the vertices in the buffer are rendered as a single, connected line. This can be useful when debugging, because this primitive type allows you to see a wireframe image of your objects, regardless of the number of vertices. Figure 7-7 presents a line strip primitive type sample.

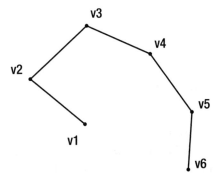

Figure 7-7. *The same vertices rendered as a line strip*

- TriangleList: The vertices are rendered in groups of three, as isolated triangles. This provides you with the greatest flexibility when rendering complex scenes, but there's the drawback of having duplicated vertices if you want to draw connected triangles. Figure 7-8 shows the use of the triangle list primitive type to render vertices.

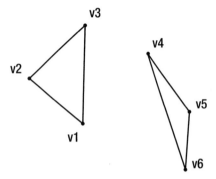

Figure 7-8. *The same vertices rendered as a triangle list*

- TriangleStrip: You use this primitive type when drawing connected triangles. It's more efficient for rendering scenes, because you don't have to repeat the duplicated vertices. Every new vertex (after the first two) added to the buffer creates a new triangle, using the last two vertices. Figure 7-9 presents a triangle strip primitive type example.

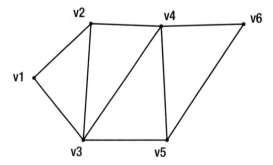

Figure 7-9. *The same vertices rendered as a triangle strip*

- TriangleFan: In this primitive, all the triangles share a common vertex—the first one in the buffer—and each new vertex added creates a new triangle, using the first vertex and the last defined one. Figure 7-10 illustrates the last of the primitive types, the triangle fan.

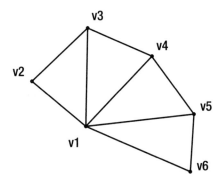

Figure 7-10. *The same vertices rendered as a triangle fan*

■**Note** When drawing triangles, you need to take special care about the triangle vertex ordering if you want XNA to know correctly which triangles are facing the camera and which ones are not. This is important when drawing complex objects such as a donut, for example. To determine the "front" side of a triangle, follow its vertices, from the first to the last one according to their definition order, with the fingers of your right hand. Your thumb will point to the front side of the triangle, just like you did with the right-handed coordinate system in Figure 7-1. The back side of the triangle can be drawn or not, according to the CullMode setting of the RenderState class, so you need to create all the triangles of an object following the same order.

Vectors, Matrices, and 3-D Transformations

Before you're ready to create your first 3-D program, there are still some important concepts to learn. Understanding the importance of 3-D vectors and matrices is possibly the most important one of all.

It's important to understand that *vectors*, besides storing the positional values, provide many helper methods that will come in handy when creating your games. Vector3 is the most commonly used vector in 3-D games, and some of its most important methods are as follows:

- Vector3.Distance: Given two points, return a float representing the distance between them.

- Vector3.Add *and* Vector3.Subtract: Add and subtract two vectors.

- Vector3.Multiply *and* Vector3.Divide: Multiply and divide two vectors, or a vector by a float value.

- Vector3.Clamp: Constrain the vector components into a given range—useful when defining lights or matrices' values that only support values among a given range.

- Vector3.Lerp: Calculate the linear interpolation between two vectors.

- Vector3.SmoothStep: Interpolate two vectors according to a float given as a weight value.

Besides these methods, Vector3 offers a series of shortcuts for special vectors, such as Vector.Zero for an empty vector, Vector3.Up for the (0,1,0) vector, Vector3.Right for the (1,0,0) vector, and others. Vector2 and Vector4 provide similar methods and shortcuts.

Many of these methods and shortcuts, as you'll see in this chapter and the next ones, are used when defining matrices and executing 3-D operations.

Matrices are the base for defining rotation, scaling, or translation of an object in the 3-D world. Because matrices are used to define any 3-D transformations, they are also used to define the operations needed to simulate the projections (we talked about projections in the previous sections) and to transform the 3-D scene according to the camera position and facing direction.

You'll see examples of each of these uses when creating your sample program. For now, let's see the use of transformation matrices to do a simple translation, and then extrapolate the idea for more complex operations. This will help you understand the importance of the use of matrices in 3-D programs.

Suppose you want to move a triangle up the Y axis, as shown in Figure 7-11.

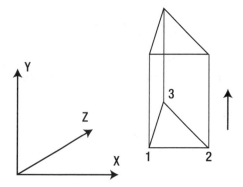

Figure 7-11. *Moving a triangle on the Y axis*

Let's assume that the coordinates of the triangle vertices are as follows:

Vertex	X	Y	Z
1	50	10	0
2	70	10	0
3	55	25	0

To translate 40 units over the Y axis's positive direction, all you need to do is to sum 40 to each Y position, and you have the new coordinates for the vertices, shown here:

Vertex	X	Y	Z
1	50	50	0
2	70	50	0
3	55	65	0

You can achieve the same results by representing each vertex as a matrix with one row and four columns, with the vertex coordinates as the first three columns and one as the value in the last one. You then multiply this matrix to a special matrix, constructed to produce the translation transformation to the vertex matrix.

Figure 7-12 presents the same operation applied to the first vertex.

$$
\begin{matrix} x & y & z \\ [50 & 10 & 0 & 1] \end{matrix} \times
\begin{bmatrix} 1 & 0 & 0 & 0 \\ 0 & 1 & 0 & 0 \\ 0 & 0 & 1 & 0 \\ 0 & 40 & 0 & 1 \end{bmatrix}
= \begin{matrix} x' & y' & z' \\ [50 & 50 & 0 & 1] \end{matrix}
$$

Figure 7-12. *Applying a matrix multiplication to a 3-D vertex*

A little explanation about multiplication for matrices: to calculate the resulting matrix, you must take each value in the row of the first matrix, multiply them by each of the values in the corresponding column in the second matrix, and then perform the sum of all results. So, in the previous sample, the calculations are as follows:

$x' = (50 \times 1) + (10 \times 0) + (0 \times 0) + (1 \times 0) = 50$

$y' = (50 \times 0) + (10 \times 1) + (0 \times 0) + (1 \times 40) = 50$

$z' = (50 \times 0) + (10 \times 0) + (0 \times 1) + (1 \times 0) = 0$

We don't want to get into much more detail here. It's enough to say that you can perform translations by putting the desired values for translation over the X, Y, and Z in the last row of the transformation matrix. You can perform scaling by replacing the 1s on the diagonal with fractional values (to shrink) or values bigger than 1 (to expand), and perform rotation around any axis using a combination of sine and cosine values in specific positions in the matrix.

So, what's the big deal about using matrices? One of the biggest benefits is that you can perform complex operations by multiplying their corresponding transformation matrices. You can then apply the resulting matrix over each vertex on the 3-D model, so you can perform all operations over the model by multiplying its vertices for only one matrix, instead of calculating each transformation for each vertex.

Better than that: all graphics cards have built-in algorithms to multiply matrices, so this multiplication consumes little processing power.

Considering that complex 3-D objects may have thousands of vertices, doing the transformations with as low a processing cost as possible is a must, and matrices are the way to do this.

Luckily enough, you don't need to understand all these mathematical details to use matrices and execute 3-D transformations in your program. All game programming libraries (from OpenGL to DirectX) offer ready-to-use matrix manipulation functions, and XNA is no exception. Through the `Matrix` class, many matrix operations are available, such as the following:

- `Matrix.CreateRotationX`, `Matrix.CreateRotationY`, *and* `Matrix.CreateRotationZ`: Creates a rotation matrix for each of the axes.

- `Matrix.Translation`: Creates a translation matrix (one or more axes).

- `Matrix.Scale`: Creates a scale matrix (one or more axes).

- `Matrix.CreateLookAt`: Creates a view matrix used to position the camera, by setting the 3-D position of the camera, the 3-D position it is facing, and which direction is "up" for the camera.

- `Matrix.CreatePerspectiveFieldOfView`: Creates a projection matrix that uses a perspective view, by setting the angle of viewing ("field of view"), the aspect ratio (see the following note), and the near and far plane, which limit which part of the 3-D scene is drawn. See Figure 7-13 to better understand these concepts. Similarly, you have two extra methods, `CreatePerspectiveOffCenter` and `CreatePerspective`, which also create matrices for perspective projection, using different parameters.

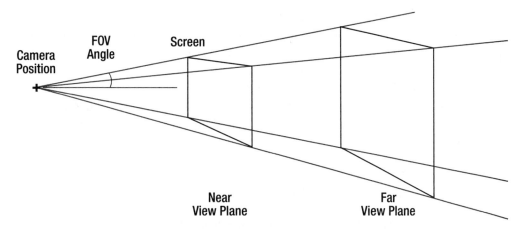

Figure 7-13. *A perspective projection definition*

■**Note** When creating projection matrices, XNA methods also expect you to pass the aspect ratio as a parameter. Aspect ratio is the ratio used to map the 3-D projection to screen coordinates, usually the width of the screen divided by the height of the screen. This ratio is needed because the pixels are not squared (normally they are more tall than wide), so a sphere can appear like an egg if the aspect ratio is not correctly defined. A concept closely related to the aspect ratio is the viewport, which is the portion of the 3-D scene that will be drawn when rendering the scene. Because the viewport is a property of the device, in XNA the aspect ratio is usually defined as `device.Viewport.Width` / `device.Viewport.Height`.

- `Matrix.CreateOrthographic`: Creates a matrix used in orthogonal, or *orthographic*, projection. This method receives the width, height, and near and far plane that define the orthographic projection, and has a similar method— `CreateOrthographicOffCenter`—which creates the orthogonal projection matrix where the center of the 3-D scene does not map to the center of the screen.

You'll see the use of some of these functions in this chapter's sample code, and others in the next chapter, when creating a complete 3-D game.

Lights, Camera . . . Effects!

If you thought that defining and playing around with a camera and lights is something reserved for complex games, think again. XNA makes it simple to deal with a camera, lights, and "special effects," but you also need to know the basics about these to create even a simple 3-D game. After all, without a camera and lights, how can you see what was constructed in your 3-D scene?

In this section you'll only get a high-level view of those features, just enough to give you the ability to go on to the next chapter and create a simple game. Just remember that you can do a lot of exciting things with lights, effects, and camera movement, so you can dig into those topics when you master the basics.

XNA's BasicEffect class fulfills all your needs for not only basic games, but also for some complex games. This class offers properties and methods that let you define the final details to render your 3-D scene. Following are some of the most important properties of this class:

- View: The view matrix, which defines the camera position and direction. Usually created using Matrix.CreateLookAt.

- Projection: The projection matrix that's used to map the 3-D scene coordinates to screen coordinates. Usually created through Matrix.CreatePerspective, Matrix.CreateOrthographic, or similar methods.

- World: The *world matrix*, which is used to apply transformations to all objects in the 3-D scene.

- LightingEnabled: If False, the scene is rendered using a base light that illuminates all sides of all objects equally. If True, the light properties of BasicEffect will be used to light the scene.

- EnableDefaultLighting: This method turns on a single, white directional light without requiring any extra light configuration.

- AmbientLightColor: Defines the color of the *ambient light*, which illuminates all sides of all objects equally. It's only used when rendering if LightingEnabled is set to True.

- DirectionalLight0, DirectionalLight1, *and* DirectionalLight2: Defines up to three directional lights used by the effect when rendering. Each directional light is defined by its specular color (color of the light that will have a perfect, mirror-like reflection), its diffuse color (color of the light that will be reflected diffusely), and the light direction. These properties are only used if LightingEnabled is set to True.

- FogColor, FogStart, *and* FogEnd: Lets you define a "fog" for the scene, so objects in the fog range appear to be seen through a dense smoke. You can specify the fog color, along with the distance in which the fog begins and ends.

Along with these properties, BasicEffect provides functionality that lets you render the 3-D scene properly. The following code fragment presents a blueprint for what your program needs to do to render the scene properly, assuming that effect is a BasicEffect object that was properly initialized:

```
effect.Begin();
foreach(EffectPass CurrentPass in effect.CurrentTechnique.Passes)
{
   CurrentPass.Begin();
   // Include here the code for drawing the scene using this effect
   CurrentPass.End();
}
effect.End();
```

In this code, you tell the effect to Begin its processing, then loop through a collection of all EffectPass of the current technique used (there's also a collection of effect techniques). You also need to start and end each of the passes of the technique. Finally, you need to tell the effect to End the processing.

At first sight, the previous code might seem a bit too much for a simple rendering effect. However, you need to remember that BasicEffect is a special case of the Effect class, which is powerful and flexible, and gives programmers all the control they need to manipulate advanced effect techniques, such as the use of custom-made shaders.

Because BasicEffect is simpler, but is still an Effect, you must use the previous code in every program you create. However, you don't need to worry about which types of techniques a program can use, or what passes can comprise each of these techniques—you'll just use this code as a blueprint, because for now the important point is to understand what conveniences BasicEffect can provide you through its properties. If you need to dig into more details about effects, refer to "How to: Create and Apply Custom Effects" in XNA Game Studio 1.0 Refresh help.

Drawing the 3-D Axis in XNA

To exemplify the concepts seen in the previous sections, in this section you'll create code to draw a line over each of the 3-D axes, and the X, Y, and Z near these lines, so you can see for yourself the results of creating and manipulating a 3-D scene.

The steps for creating and rendering 3-D objects in XNA can be summarized as follows:

1. Define the vertex type you'll use (position plus color, texture, and so on).

2. Create a vertices array and fill it with the vertices' data.

3. Create a vertex buffer and fill it with the vertices previously created.

4. Define the effect to be used, with projection and view matrices and the light sources, if any.

5. Inform the device which vertices you'll use.

6. Using the effect, draw the vertex buffer using a specific primitive type.

All the concepts involved in these steps were previously explained in this chapter, so if something is not quite clear, browse back through the previous pages before entering the code.

To better organize your code, create a new class named cls3Daxis. This class has some methods with the same names of the by now well-known Game1.cs class, provided for you when you create a new XNA Windows Program solution: LoadContent, UnloadContent, and Draw, so you can call these methods from the main game class ones.

Create the new class and include code for three private properties: device, vertexBuffer, and effect, also creating the class constructor with code to receive and store the graphics device. You'll need the graphics device for the rendering operations, and you must also create the vertex buffer and the effect at the class level so you can create them in the LoadContent method and release them in UnloadContent. The initial code for the class is as follows:

```
class cls3DAxis
{
    private GraphicsDevice device;
    private VertexBuffer vertexBuffer;
    private BasicEffect effect;

    public cls3DAxis(GraphicsDevice graphicsDevice)
    {
        device = graphicsDevice;
    }
}
```

Coding the Vertices and the Vertex Buffer

You'll now code a private helper method for this class, named Create3Daxis, which creates the 3-D axis and fills the vertex buffer. This enables you to fulfill the first three steps of the summary list we just defined.

The next code sample presents a first version of the method, which simply creates three lines representing each of the 3-D axes, going from axisLength negative position to axisLength positive position in each axis. For example, if axisLength is 1, for the X axis you'll draw a line from (-1, 0, 0) to (1, 0, 0).

```
private void Create3DAxis()
{
    //  size of 3-D Axis
```

```
    float axisLength = 1f;
    // Number of vertices we'll use
    int vertexCount = 6;

    VertexPositionColor[] vertices = new VertexPositionColor[vertexCount];
    // X axis
    vertices[0] = new VertexPositionColor(new Vector3(-axisLength, 0.0f, 0.0f),
        Color.White);
    vertices[1] = new VertexPositionColor(new Vector3(axisLength, 0.0f, 0.0f),
        Color.White);
    // Y axis
    vertices[2] = new VertexPositionColor(new Vector3(0.0f, -axisLength, 0.0f),
        Color.White);
    vertices[3] = new VertexPositionColor(new Vector3(0.0f, axisLength, 0.0f),
        Color.White);
    // Z axis
    vertices[4] = new VertexPositionColor(new Vector3(0.0f, 0.0f, -axisLength),
        Color.White);
    vertices[5] = new VertexPositionColor(new Vector3(0.0f, 0.0f, axisLength),
        Color.White);

    // fill the vertex buffer with the vertices
    vertexBuffer = new VertexBuffer(device,
                            vertexCount * VertexPositionColor.SizeInBytes,
                            BufferUsage.WriteOnly);
    vertexBuffer.SetData<VertexPositionColor>(vertices);
}
```

As you can see, for this sample you used a vertex defined by its position and color, and defined all vertex colors as white. When drawing these vertices you'll use the line list primitive type, so every pair of vertices, in the order they were defined, will become a line.

In the last part of the previous code, you created the vertex buffer, passing the graphics device, the size of the vertex buffer (calculated by the vertices' count multiplied by the size of each vertex, given by VertexPositionColor.SizeInBytes), and the behavior of your buffer (you'll just write the vertices and use them later).

After creating the buffer, in the last code line, you set the vertices' data by calling the SetData method of the vertex buffer, which receives the vertices' array you created and the vertices' format (also called *custom vertex format* or *flexible vertex format*).

To create the letters over the positive edge of each of the axes, you need to create new line segments that will form each letter. In such cases, the best you can do is to draw a little sketch so you can calculate the vertices' position for every line, in every letter. Look at the distances presented in Figure 7-14 and compare them with the next code sample, which presents the complete Create3Daxis function. Make sure you understand how the X, Y, and Z letters are drawn.

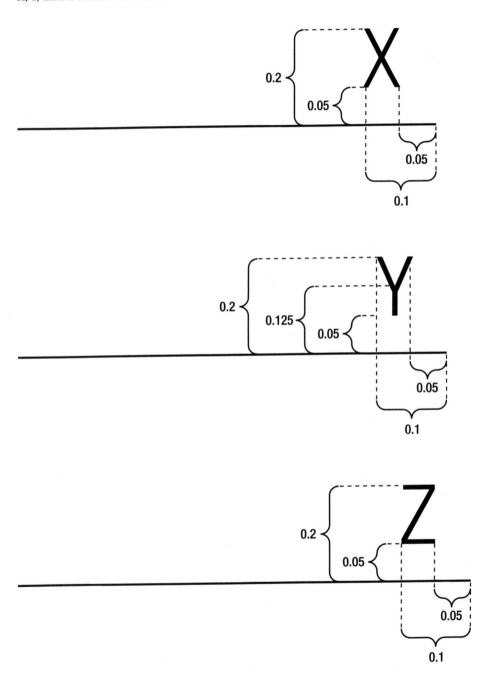

Figure 7-14. *A sketch showing the dimensions to create each axis letter*

In case you're wondering how we came up with the values presented in Figure 7-14, the answer is easy: trial and error! If you don't like the way the characters look, just adjust the values until you find the desired effect.

```
private void Create3DAxis()
{
    //  size of 3-D Axis
    float axisLength = 1f;
    //  Number of vertices we'll use
    int vertexCount = 22;

    VertexPositionColor[] vertices = new VertexPositionColor[vertexCount];
    // X axis
    vertices[0] = new VertexPositionColor(
                new Vector3(-axisLength, 0.0f, 0.0f), Color.White);
    vertices[1] = new VertexPositionColor(
                new Vector3(axisLength, 0.0f, 0.0f), Color.White);
    // Y axis
    vertices[2] = new VertexPositionColor(
                new Vector3(0.0f, -axisLength, 0.0f), Color.White);
    vertices[3] = new VertexPositionColor(
                new Vector3(0.0f, axisLength, 0.0f), Color.White);
    // Z axis
    vertices[4] = new VertexPositionColor(
                new Vector3(0.0f, 0.0f, -axisLength), Color.White);
    vertices[5] = new VertexPositionColor(
                new Vector3(0.0f, 0.0f, axisLength), Color.White);

    //  "X" letter near X axis
    vertices[6] = new VertexPositionColor(
                new Vector3(axisLength - 0.1f, 0.05f, 0.0f), Color.White);
    vertices[7] = new VertexPositionColor(
                new Vector3(axisLength - 0.05f, 0.2f, 0.0f), Color.White);
    vertices[8] = new VertexPositionColor(
                new Vector3(axisLength - 0.05f, 0.05f, 0.0f), Color.White);
    vertices[9] = new VertexPositionColor(
                new Vector3(axisLength - 0.1f, 0.2f, 0.0f), Color.White);

    //  "Y" letter near Y axis
    vertices[10] = new VertexPositionColor(
                new Vector3(0.075f, axisLength - 0.125f, 0.0f), Color.White);
    vertices[11] = new VertexPositionColor(
```

```
                            new Vector3(0.075f, axisLength - 0.2f, 0.0f), Color.White);
        vertices[12] = new VertexPositionColor(
                            new Vector3(0.075f, axisLength - 0.125f, 0.0f), Color.White);
        vertices[13] = new VertexPositionColor(
                            new Vector3(0.1f, axisLength - 0.05f, 0.0f), Color.White);
        vertices[14] = new VertexPositionColor(
                            new Vector3(0.075f, axisLength - 0.125f, 0.0f), Color.White);
        vertices[15] = new VertexPositionColor(
                            new Vector3(0.05f, axisLength - 0.05f, 0.0f), Color.White);

        //  "Z" letter near Z axis
        vertices[16] = new VertexPositionColor(
                            new Vector3(0.0f, 0.05f, axisLength - 0.1f), Color.White);
        vertices[17] = new VertexPositionColor(
                            new Vector3(0.0f, 0.05f, axisLength - 0.05f), Color.White);
        vertices[18] = new VertexPositionColor(
                            new Vector3(0.0f, 0.05f, axisLength - 0.1f), Color.White);
        vertices[19] = new VertexPositionColor(
                            new Vector3(0.0f, 0.2f, axisLength - 0.05f), Color.White);
        vertices[20] = new VertexPositionColor(
                            new Vector3(0.0f, 0.2f, axisLength - 0.1f), Color.White);
        vertices[21] = new VertexPositionColor(
                            new Vector3(0.0f, 0.2f, axisLength - 0.05f), Color.White);

        //  fill the vertex buffer with the vertices
        vertexBuffer = new VertexBuffer(device,
                        vertexCount * VertexPositionColor.SizeInBytes,
                        ResourceUsage.WriteOnly,
                        ResourceManagementMode.Automatic);
        vertexBuffer.SetData<VertexPositionColor>(vertices);
}
```

You also need to create code in the LoadContent method to call the Create3Daxis, and in UnloadContent to free the vertex buffer property in the cls3Daxis class, as shown in the next code sample.

```
public void LoadContent()
{
    //  Create the 3-D axis
    Create3DAxis();
}
public void UnloadContent()
{
```

```
    if (vertexBuffer != null)
    {
        vertexBuffer.Dispose();
        vertexBuffer = null;
    }
}
```

This concludes the code for creating and freeing up the used resources from memory (disposing) the 3-D axis's vertices. However, you can't run the program yet: you still need to code the basic effect that defines how the rendering is done, and include calls for the cls3Daxis class in the program's main class, Game1.

In the next section you'll finish the cls3Daxis class, setting the effect properties you need to display the axis.

Coding a Basic Effect and Rendering the 3-D Scene

You saw earlier in this chapter that BasicEffect is a class XNA provides to help you create effects for rendering 3-D scenes, and includes many properties that let you define the camera position, the projection to be used, and the light sources used, for example.

The next code sample shows the complete code for the LoadContent method, including creation and configuration for a simple basic effect, which will meet the needs for your programs. All functions and properties presented were previously explained; you might want to refer back to the section "Lights, Camera . . . Effects!" to refresh some details if you find yourself getting a little lost:

```
public void LoadContent()
{
    // Create the effect that will be used to draw the axis
    effect = new BasicEffect(device, null);

    // Calculate the effect aspect ratio, projection, and view matrix
    float aspectRatio = (float)device.Viewport.Width / device.Viewport.Height;
    effect.View = Matrix.CreateLookAt(new Vector3(0.0f, 2.0f, 2.0f), Vector3.Zero,
                        Vector3.Up);
    effect.Projection = Matrix.CreatePerspectiveFieldOfView(
                    MathHelper.ToRadians(45.0f),
                    aspectRatio, 1.0f, 10.0f);
    effect.LightingEnabled = false;

    // Create the 3-D axis
    Create3DAxis();
}
```

It's worth it to highlight the meaning of some parameters on the presented functions. In the CreateLookAt method, you're creating the camera two units up (Y axis) from the (0,0,0) position, and two units outside the screen (Z axis; Z negative values are onscreen, visible values, so positive values are placed out of the screen); "looking at" the Zero vector (0,0,0), and setting Y as "up" with Vector3.Up.

You then create a perspective projection matrix, "looking" in a 45-degree angle as "field of view." The rendering happens for objects from 1 to 10 units from the screen (Z values from –1 to –10).

At last, you disable lighting, so the whole scene is rendered with a simple and omni-directional default light, which generates no gradients or shades.

The UnloadContent method also needs be completed to include the disposal of the effect object, as presented in the next code sample:

```
public void UnloadContent()
{
    if (vertexBuffer != null)
    {
        vertexBuffer.Dispose();
        vertexBuffer = null;
    }

    if (effect != null)
    {
        effect.Dispose();
        effect = null;
    }
}
```

Now that you've set up the vertex buffer and the effect, you need to code the Draw method of the cls3Daxis class, which will use the effect to draw the scene, following the blueprint code presented in the earlier section "Lights, Camera . . . Effects!"

In the next code fragment you configure the device to use the vertices format you are using (vertices defined by their position and color). Then, you set the device vertices stream to your vertex buffer, defining the starting point in this stream (start reading from the first vertex) and the size of each vertex element. Once the device is configured, you enter the drawing loop, and call device.DrawPrimitives for every pass of the current effect technique (as explained earlier in this chapter), stating that you are drawing 11 lines (made of 22 vertices).

```
public void Draw()
{
    // Create a vertex declaration to be used when drawing the vertices
    device.VertexDeclaration = new VertexDeclaration(device,
```

```
                              VertexPositionColor.VertexElements);
    // Set the vertex source
    device.Vertices[0].SetSource(vertexBuffer, 0, VertexPositionColor.SizeInBytes);

    // Draw the 3-D axis
    effect.Begin();
    foreach(EffectPass CurrentPass in effect.CurrentTechnique.Passes)
    {
        CurrentPass.Begin();
        // We are drawing 22 vertices, grouped in 11 lines
        device.DrawPrimitives(PrimitiveType.LineList, 0, 11);
        CurrentPass.End();
    }
    effect.End();
}
```

This code concludes the cls3Daxis class. All you need to do now is call this class's methods from within the Game1 main class, and you'll be able to see the 3-D axis. You'll do this in the next section.

Coding the Main Program Calls

In the previous section, you created the cls3Daxis class, which provides methods with the same names of the main class of XNA programs: LoadContent, UnloadContent, and Draw.

To use this class, let's now create a new, empty XNA Windows Game project. The Game1 class is generated automatically for you. You need to define an object of the cls3Daxis class, initialize it, and call the corresponding methods on the Game1 class. The code for the updated methods is as follows:

```
GraphicsDeviceManager graphics;

// 3-D objects
cls3DAxis my3DAxis;

protected override void Initialize()
{
    my3DAxis = new cls3DAxis(graphics.GraphicsDevice);
    base.Initialize();
}


protected override void LoadContent()
{
```

```
    // Create the 3-D axis
    my3DAxis.LoadGraphicsContent();
}

protected override void UnloadContent()
{
    //  Free the resources allocated for 3-D drawing
    my3DAxis.UnloadContent();

}

protected override void Draw(GameTime gameTime)
{
    graphics.GraphicsDevice.Clear(Color.CornflowerBlue);
    // Draw the 3-D axis
    my3DAxis.Draw();
    base.Draw(gameTime);
}
```

Figure 7-15 presents the result of running the code now.

The result presented in Figure 7-15 might not look as you expected: you are only able to see the X and Y axes, and this certainly doesn't seem too much like 3-D . . . This is because the camera position is aligned with the Z axis, so this axis is hidden behind the Y axis, and the letter Z is not drawn because it's behind the camera.

You could simply adjust the camera position in the cls3Daxis class, but let's do a little better, while exploring a new concept: the world matrix.

The world matrix, as explained when we talked about effects, is a property of the Effect class that contains transformations that are applied to all scene objects when rendering.

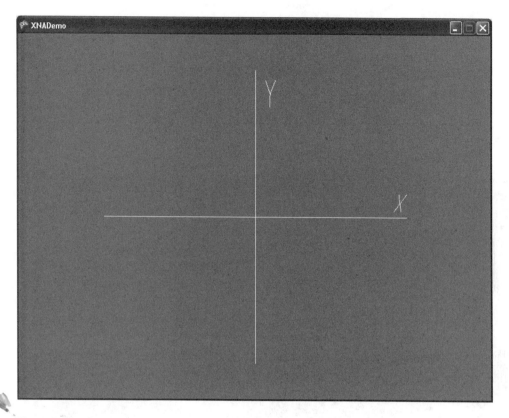

Figure 7-15. *The 3-D axis*

Let's then use the world matrix to make your 3-D axis drawing spin, so you can see the result of rotating a 3-D scene. You can do this in three easy steps:

1. Create a new property in the cls3Daxis class to store the current world matrix, defaulting to an identity matrix (a matrix that doesn't perform any transformation):

```
public Matrix worldMatrix = Matrix.Identity;
```

2. Include a new line in the Draw method of this class to update the effect's World property to this matrix, so the effect receives the updated matrix and is able to use it to transform the axis drawing:

```
effect.World = worldMatrix;
```

3. Include a new line in the Update method of the Game1 class to update the cls3Daxis worldMatrix property, incrementing the world rotation angle in every update:

```
my3DAxis.worldMatrix *= Matrix.CreateRotationY(0.01f) *
                                    Matrix.CreateRotationX(0.01f);
```

Running your program now, you can see the nice result of spinning the 3-D axis, as shown in Figure 7-16.

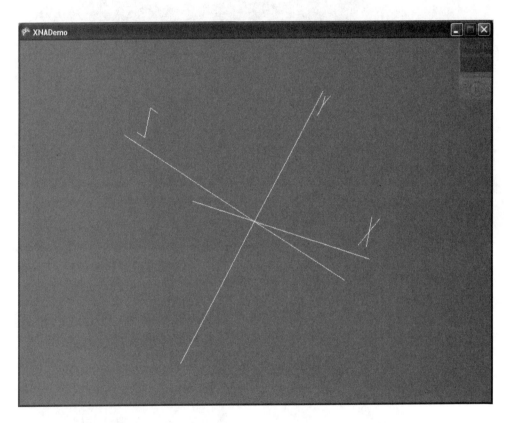

Figure 7-16. *The spinning 3-D axis*

Models and Meshes

Playing around with vertices and drawing primitives is cool, but if you want to create a game with complex 3-D objects, this would be hardly the best choice.

In Chapter 1 you saw that XNA's Content Pipeline supports many file formats, including 3-D object definition X and FBX files. These files store the definition of 3-D objects, known as a *3-D model* or simply *model*.

As a simple definition, you can say a model is a hierarchy of meshes, which can be rendered independently, and a *mesh* is a collection of interconnected vertices, along with some rendering information. XNA provides special classes to manipulate models and meshes: Model and ModelMesh.

To create a program that manipulates models, you must first load a model as new content into your sample program.

To do this, right-click the project in Solution Explorer and choose Add ➤ Existing Content, change the file type to Content Pipeline Files, and select an X or FBX file. In this section you'll use the Cube.X file, a simple file with a cube definition that comes with the DirectX Software Development Kit (SDK), which can be downloaded from the Microsoft site (http://www.microsoft.com/directx).

Once the content is in your project, you must declare a model variable to hold the reference to this content, at the Game1 class level:

```
Model myModel;
```

In the LoadContent method, you need to include a single line that loads the model:

```
myModel = Content.Load<Model>("Cube");
```

Finally, you must include a loop in the Draw method to run through all meshes in the model and draw each one. Although there is only one mesh in this simple model, using this approach makes the code ready to draw complex models:

```
// Loop through each mesh of the model
foreach (ModelMesh mesh in myModel.Meshes)
{
    // Draw the current mesh
    mesh.Draw();
}
```

If you run your program now, you can see the mesh already loaded, along with the spinning 3-D axis created in the previous section, as shown in Figure 7-17.

The image in Figure 7-17 is not very exciting, because two details don't let the image appear like a cube: first, the camera is upright on one of the cube faces, so all you see is a square. Besides, there's no lighting enabled, so every face is illuminated exactly the same way. There's no shading to help you see the difference between one face and another.

To work around these problems, you need to rotate the model to a better position (and maybe do some scaling, so it doesn't hide the axis), and apply lights to the model rendering.

Figure 7-17. *The first view of a 3-D model (cube)*

If you remember the BasicEffect class you used in the previous section, you're right: with BasicEffect you can apply transformations to the object (through the World property), set the Projection and the View matrices (which are a must for every effect), and turn on a default light source with little effort, as you saw when we talked about effects earlier in this chapter. You can use the same projection and camera view matrices you used for cls3Daxis; a rotation of 45 degrees in both the X and Y axes will turn the cube so you can see three of its faces.

To use the effect to render the 3-D object, you must remember that a model is composed of many meshes, so you need to loop through all the meshes to apply the effect to all. Besides that, a mesh has a collection of effects, so it can render different parts of the mesh with different effects—a useful thing for complex meshes. Because you might have many effects for a single mesh, you need to have a second loop, running through all effects of each mesh, to be certain you'll apply the same effect in all mesh parts.

In a simple model such as your cube, you have only one mesh, and only one effect on this mesh. However, creating generic code allows you to use the same program for more complex models.

The final code with the effect creation and use follows. You must place it in the LoadContent method:

```
// Calculate the aspect ratio for the model
float aspectRatio = (float)graphics.GraphicsDevice.Viewport.Width /
                        graphics.GraphicsDevice.Viewport.Height;


//  Configure basic lighting and do a simple rotation for the model
//     (so it can be seen onscreen)
foreach (ModelMesh mesh in myModel.Meshes)
    foreach (BasicEffect effect in mesh.Effects)
    {
        //  Rotate and make the model a little smaller (50%)
        effect.World = Matrix.CreateScale(0.5f) *
            Matrix.CreateRotationX(MathHelper.ToRadians(45.0f)) *
            Matrix.CreateRotationY(MathHelper.ToRadians(45.0f));
        //  Set the projection matrix for the model
        effect.Projection = Matrix.CreatePerspectiveFieldOfView(
                MathHelper.ToRadians(45.0f),
                aspectRatio, 1.0f, 10.0f);
        effect.View = Matrix.CreateLookAt(new Vector3(0.0f, 0.0f, 3.0f),
                Vector3.Zero, Vector3.Up);
        effect.EnableDefaultLighting();
    }
```

Figure 7-18 presents the result of running the program with the newly created effect.

Note You don't have to bother to load textures if your model uses them: model files already include information about the textures they use. Because this information includes the path where the texture files should be, you only need to know this path and then copy the texture files to the corresponding path. You can find out the texture paths by examining the model files (in a text editor, for example), or by including the model in the project and compiling it. XNA Game Studio presents the Content Pipeline path errors stating where the model looked for the textures.

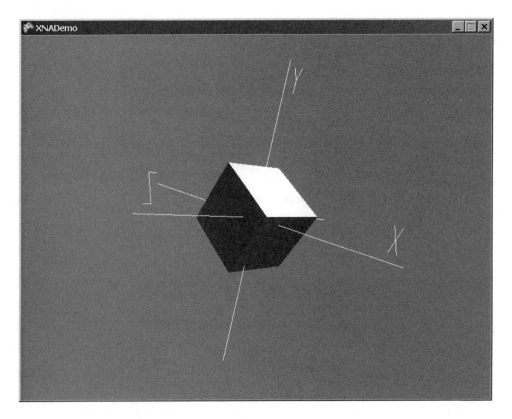

Figure 7-18. *The rotated, scaled, and lightened cube*

Summary

In this chapter you learned the basics of 3-D graphics programming. Although XNA provides you with many premade classes and methods that lower the program's complexity, there are still a lot of concepts to understand.

Be sure you understand the following concepts before you go on to the next chapter:

- What vertices are and what type of information can be used when defining them

- What a vertex buffer is and how to use it

- Why matrices are important, and how to use them to perform transformations in 3-D objects

- What the projection matrix is, which types of projections XNA supports, and how to use them

- What the view matrix is and how you create it in XNA

- What the world matrix is, and how to use it to perform operations in all 3-D scenes

- What models and meshes are, and how to load and render them in XNA

In the next chapter you'll create a complete 3-D game, so you'll be able to exercise and explore these concepts.

■ ■ ■

CHAPTER 8

Rendering Pipeline, Shaders, and Effects

In this chapter you'll learn some of the concepts related to the rendering pipeline, shaders, and effects. The rendering pipeline is responsible for processing a 3-D representation of a scene, which generates a 2-D image as output. You can use shaders to program some stages of the rendering pipeline, and effects to encapsulate shaders and configurations for the fixed stages of the rendering pipeline.

Rendering Pipeline

Before you can visualize a 3-D scene, this scene must be transformed into an image: a matrix of pixels. In this way, a 3-D scene can be shown on an ordinary monitor. The process used to transform a scene description into an image is called *rendering*. Figure 8-1 shows a high-level diagram of the rendering pipeline used by XNA.

The objects in a 3-D scene are described through their meshes, while the object's mesh is described by its vertices. The vertices in a mesh can have many different attributes, such as position, color, normal, and texture coordinate.

In the beginning of the rendering process, the vertices of the object's mesh are sent to the rendering pipeline, where they go through the stages of vertex processing, rasterization, and pixel processing. At the end of this process, many pixels are generated that are ready to be stored in the scene's final image. A last stage in the rendering pipeline, the output merger, defines which pixels are effectively stored in the final image and which are discarded. This decision is based on the pixel depth, transparency, and some other attributes.

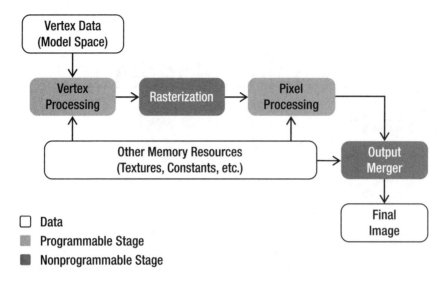

Figure 8-1. *XNA rendering pipeline*

Rendering Pipeline: Fixed or Programmable

In the old versions of the DirectX and OpenGL application programming interfaces (APIs), all the stages of the rendering pipeline were fixed (preprogrammed). This means that preprogrammed processing was made over all the data sent to be rendered. This forced all games to use the same rendering process, allowing them to change only a few fixed parameters. The result was the release of many game titles with similar graphics.

With the introduction of the Graphics Processing Units (GPUs), it became possible to program some of the stages of the rendering pipeline. Programming these stages became possible through the creation of small programs called *shaders*. The shaders allow you to define which data is input and output from each programmable stage of the GPU, as well as the processing that is made inside each stage. Using shaders, you can create many new effects for games that weren't possible using the fixed pipeline.

XNA Rendering Pipeline

In XNA, you must use shaders to render any object! The use of shaders is needed in XNA because it doesn't support the full-fixed (preprogrammable) rendering pipeline. This occurs because XNA was made to target Windows and the Xbox 360 platform, but the Xbox 360 hardware doesn't support the full-fixed rendering pipeline. Notice that the rendering pipeline of the Xbox 360 still has some fixed stages, such as Rasterization and Output Merger, shown in Figure 8-1.

To ease game development without needing to program shaders, XNA provides some helper classes that encapsulate the use of shaders. For example, you can use the SpriteBatch class to draw 2-D sprites, and you can use the BasicEffect class to draw 3-D models. These two classes use shaders in a way that's transparent to you. One drawback of using these helper classes is that they only allow you to change a small number of parameters in the rendering, like the old fixed pipeline.

Shaders

Shaders are small programs that execute inside the GPU and define how the data is processed in the programmable stages of the rendering pipeline. You can use many languages for shader programming, including low-level languages (assembly) and high-level languages (C-like). In a general way, the shader code is similar to a mathematical equation, written using functions of the language.

Vertex Shader

The shader used in the vertex processing stage, shown in Figure 8-1, is called the *vertex shader*. You use the vertex shader to process the vertex's attributes of the rendered objects, generating a new set of attributes that are output from the vertex shader and sent to the next stage of the pipeline. The output attributes of the vertex shader aren't fixed and might vary in each shader, where the only necessary output attribute in a vertex shader is the final (transformed) vertex position.

Vertex shaders allow you to execute many tasks, such as solids deforming, skeletal animation, and particle motion.

Rasterization

The rasterization stage is executed between the vertex processing stage, where the vertex shader is applied, and the pixel processing stage, where the pixel shader is applied. In the rasterization stage, primitives are constructed from the vertices output from the vertex processing stage. The constructed primitives are then rasterized, transforming their vectorial representation (vertex positions) into a pixel representation.

Figure 8-2 illustrates a rasterized triangle, which generates many pixels. Note especially that the vertex attributes are linearly interpolated between all the generated pixels.

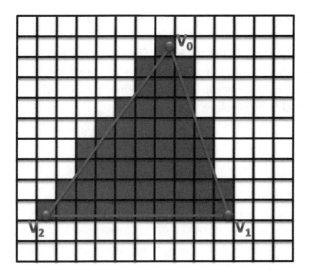

Figure 8-2. *Triangle rasterization. The gray quads represent the pixels generated.*

Pixel Shader

The pixels generated in the rasterization stage are sent to the pixel processing stage, which is programmable through the use of pixel shaders. Differing from the vertex shader, there are only two possible output attributes from the pixel shader: the pixel color, which is required, and the pixel depth, which is optional.

Pixel shaders allow you to execute many tasks, such as per-pixel lightening, texturing, and procedural texture generation. You can also use a pixel shader to apply postprocessing effects over an entire rendered scene, such as brightness, contrast, color saturation, and blur.

High Level Shading Language

XNA natively supports shader programming through Microsoft's High Level Shading Language (HLSL). HLSL has a small number of functions, which include math operations, texture access, and flow control. The types of data that HLSL supports are similar to those used in the C language, with the exception of vectors, matrices, and samplers.

Data Types

HLSL supports many different data types, including scalars, vectors, matrices, and samplers. Table 8-1 shows the scalar data types present in the language. Note that it is possible to create vectors and matrices for all the scalar types present in the language, such as float2, float4, bool3x3, double2x2, and so on.

Table 8-1. *HLSL Scalar Types*

Type	Value
bool	true or false
int	32-bit signed integer
half	16-bit floating point
float	32-bit floating point
double	64-bit floating point

Another data type present in HLSL is the `sampler` type, which is used to read (sample) data from textures. There are some different sampler types, such as `sampler`, `sampler1D`, `sampler2D`, and `sampler3D`, which are used to sample 1-D, 2-D, and 3-D textures. The sampler type has a few states associated with it that specify the texture to be sampled, the type of filtering used, and how the texture is addressed (wrapped). Following is an example of a sampler for a 2-D texture:

```
// Declares the input texture
texture skyTexture;

// Declares the sampler used to sample the skyTexture
sampler2D skySampler = sampler_state
{
    Texture = skyTexture;

    MinFilter = Linear;
    MagFilter = Linear;
    MipFilter = Linear;

    AddressU = Wrap;
    AddressV = Wrap;
    AddressW = Wrap;
}
```

The texture state represents the texture to be sampled, which can only be read through the use of a sampler. The `MinFilter`, `MagFilter`, and `MipFilter` are the filtering states, and the `AddressU`, `AddressV`, and `AddressW` are the addressing states. For further information, the documentation for the DirectX SDK (`http://msdn2.microsoft.com/en-us/library/bb509638.aspx`) has a complete reference of the data types present in HLSL.

Uniform and Varying Inputs

In HLSL, there are two types of input data types: uniform and varying. The uniform input data is the data that is constant in a shader during the processing of its entire input data. For example, during the rendering of a car, its texture and the world matrix are constant.

The uniform input data in a shader is usually declared as global variables, out of the scope of the functions in the beginning of the shader. The uniform variables are queried and set by the application, usually using their names.

The varying input data is the data that is changed in each execution of a shader. For example, during the car rendering all the vertices of the car model are sent to the vertex processing stage. Thus, each time the vertex shader executes it receives a vertex with different attributes (position, color, normal, and so on) as input. So, the vertex attributes are not constant during the rendering of the entire car. Differing from the uniform input data, you declare the varying input data using semantics.

Semantics

HLSL uses semantics to map input and output data to variables. For example, you use the POSITION0 semantic in the vertices' processing stage to map the position attribute of each vertex to a varying variable, as follows:

```
float4 vertexPosition : POSITION0;
```

The semantics are required in all varying input data (received from the application or passed between the rendering stages). For example, all the data output from the vertex shader that will be used in the pixel shader must be associated to a semantic. Semantics are not case sensitive and are specified after the variables' names using a colon (:). Table 8-2 shows some vertex shader semantics.

Table 8-2. *Vertex Shader Semantics*

Input	Description	Type
POSITION[n]	Vertex position in object space	float4
COLOR[n]	Diffuse and specular color	float4
NORMAL[n]	Normal vector	float4
TEXCOORD[n]	Texture coordinate	float4
TANGENT[n]	Tangent vector	float4
BINORMAL[n]	Binormal vector	float4
BLENDINDICES[n]	Bones blend indices	int4
BLENDWEIGHT[n]	Bones blend weight	float4

Input	Description	Type
Output	**Description**	**Type**
POSITION[n]	Position of a vertex in homogenous space (X, Y, Z, W)	float4
COLOR[n]	Diffuse or specular color	float4
TEXCOORD[n]	Texture coordinates	float4
FOG	Vertex fog	float

You use the input vertex shader semantics for varying data received by the vertex shader. Some commonly used semantics are POSITION, COLOR, NORMAL, and TEXTURE. You use the TANGENT and BINORMAL semantics if the vertex has tangent or *binormal* vectors, which are perpendicular vectors to the normal vertex. You use these three vectors to create a coordinate system that is planar to the object surface in a point (called tangent space). You use the BLENDINDICES and BLENDWEIGHT semantics when the vertices are linked to *bones*. Bones are used to deform the vertices of a mesh and will be explained in Chapter 11.

Notice that the [n] is an optional integer that defines the number of the resource to be used. For example, if a model has three textures, the [n] of its TEXTURE semantic varies between 0 and 2. So, TEXTURE0, TEXTURE1, and TEXTURE2 are valid input semantics for the vertex shader. Table 8-3 shows some pixel shader semantics.

Table 8-3. *Pixel Shader Semantics*

Input	Description	Type
COLOR[n]	Diffuse or specular color	float4
TEXCOORD[n]	Texture coordinates	float4
Output	**Description**	**Type**
COLOR[n]	Output color	float4
DEPTH[n]	Output depth	float

Because the pixel shader is executed after the rasterization stage, the available input semantics are the pixel color and some texture coordinates. The texture coordinates address the texture positions that are mapped into the current pixel. Note that you could also output custom data from the vertex shader using the texture coordinates.

The final data output from the pixel shader is the pixel color and depth, where the output of the pixel color is obligatory and the output of the pixel depth is optional.

Functions

HLSL allows the creation of functions with syntax like the C language, where each function has a declaration and a body. The function declaration contains the function name and return type, and might have a list of parameters. Also, the return type of a function may have a semantic associated to it. Following is shown the code of a function used as the entry point for the pixel shader. We'll show how to define which functions will be used as the entry point for the vertex and pixel shader in the section "Effects."

```
float4 simplePS(float4 inputColor : COLOR0) : COLOR0
{
    return inputColor * 0.5f;
}
```

Because the simplePS function is used as the entry point to the pixel shader, its parameters must have a semantic associated. In this case, the simplePS function scales the received color parameter by a factor of 0.5 and returns it as the final pixel color. Note that the parameters of the function can have other modifiers, such as in, out, and inout, which are used to define input, output, and input/output parameters.

Intrinsic Functions

HLSL has a small set of functions, which include math operations, texture access, and flow control. These functions are intrinsic functions because they're built into HLSL and don't necessarily map directly to the GPU assembly instructions. In fact, many of these functions are mapped to a few GPU assembly instructions, and they're likely to provide the best implementation for their task. Table 8-4 shows some of the functions present in HLSL.

Table 8-4. *Some HLSL Functions*

Function	Description
dot	Returns the dot product of two vectors
cross	Returns the cross product of two floating-point, 3-D vectors
lerp	Performs a linear interpolation between two values
mul	Performs matrix multiplication between X and Y
normalize	Normalizes the specified floating-point vector
pow	Returns X to the power of Y
reflect	Returns the reflection vector, given the entering ray direction and the surface normal

Function	Description
refract	Returns a refraction vector using an entering ray direction, a surface normal, and a refraction index
saturate	Clamps the specified value within the range of 0 to 1
tex2d	Performs a 2-D texture lookup
tex3d	Performs a 3-D volume texture lookup

Creating a Simple Shader

In this section you'll create your first shader using HLSL. First, you should declare the uniform and varying variables of the shader:

```
// Matrix received from the application - Uniform
// (World * View * Projection)
float4x4 matWVP : WorldViewProjection;

// Struct used for the input vertex - Varying
struct vertexInput
{
    float4 position : POSITION0;
};

// Struct used to pass the VS output to the PS input - Varying
struct vertexOutput
{
    float4 hposition : POSITION;
    float3 color : COLOR0;
};
```

In the previous code, you used the vertexInput struct to pass data from the application to the vertex shader, and you used the vertexOutput struct to pass data from the vertex shader to the pixel shader.

The vertexInput struct has a unique attribute: the vertex position. The vertexOutput struct has two attributes, which are the vertex's final position and color. So, the vertex shader function receives the vertex position and must output its final position and color.

Notice that the vertex position output by the vertex shader is not accessible by the pixel shader. Next, declare the function used as the vertex shader's entry point:

```
// Vertex shader code
pixelInput SimpleVS(vertexInput IN)
{
```

```
    pixelInput OUT;

    // Transform the vertex position
    OUT.hposition = mul(IN.position, matWVP);
    OUT.color = float3(1.0f, 1.0f, 0.0f);
    return OUT;
}
```

In the SimpleVS function, you calculate the output vertex position by transforming (multiplying) it by the matWVP matrix (which is the combination of the world, view, and projection matrix). The output vertex color is set as yellow, RGB (1, 1, 0). Finally, you should declare the function used as the pixel shader's entry point:

```
// Pixel shader code
float4 SimplePS(pixelInput IN) : COLOR0
{
    return float4(IN.color.rgb, 1.0f);
}
```

The pixel shader created just returns the color received from the vertex processing stage. This color will be used as the final pixel color.

Effects

Effects are entities that can store different shaders, techniques, and configurations for the fixed stages of the rendering pipeline. Besides the shaders, an effect must have one or more *techniques*. A technique is used to specify how the shaders, inside the effect, should be compiled and linked for the rendering. For example, because an effect could have many vertex and pixel shaders, each technique could define a different combination (linkage) of vertex and pixel shaders. Techniques can also have more than one pass, where the entire rendering process is repeated for each pass. Furthermore, inside a technique it is possible to configure some parameters of the rasterization and output merger stages.

The use of effects facilitates the shaders' programming, making it possible to reuse shader code in different techniques, and also create different techniques targeting low-end and high-end GPUs. Following is the code for a technique:

```
technique basicShader
{
    pass p0
    {
        VertexShader = compile vs_2_0 SimpleVS();
```

```
        PixelShader = compile ps_2_0 SimplePS();
    }
}
```

The basicShader technique has just one pass, called p0. Inside each pass you define which function will be used as the vertex shader and pixel shader entry point. In this case you're using the SimpleVS function as the vertex shader entry point and the SimplePS function as the pixel shader entry point. You also need to define which shader model should be used to compile the shaders. In this case you're using the shader model 2.0.

The shader models have evolved since DirectX 8.1, and XNA supports shader models up to 3.0. Each shader model has different features and allows the creation of shaders with a different number of instructions. For example, the dynamic flow control operations (if, while, and so on) on the vertex shader and pixel shader are only available in the shader model version 3.0 or higher. Table 8-5 presents the number of instruction slots available on each shader model. Notice that each HLSL function can use one or more instruction slots, because they are not direct-mapped to the GPU assembly instructions.

Table 8-5. *Number of Instruction Slots on the Shader Models*

Shader Version	Instruction Slots
VS_1_1	128
VS_2_0	256
VS_2_A	256
VS_3_0	>= 512
PS_1_1	12 (4 texture and 8 arithmetic)
PS_2_0	96 (32 texture and 64 arithmetic)
PS_2_A	512
PS_3_0	>= 512

Using Effects with XNA

Effects in XNA are treated as game assets, just like models and textures. All the effects are processed through the XNA Content Pipeline, generating manageable objects that the content manager can load at runtime.

You use XNA's Effect class to represent an effect. This class allows you to configure the effect's parameters, select the current effect technique, and use the effect for rendering. The following code illustrates how to load and configure an effect with XNA:

```
// XNA Effect object
Effect effect;

// Load the effect
effect = content.Load<Effect>("/effects/lightEffect");

// Set the technique
effect.CurrentTechnique = lightEffect.Techniques["basicLight"];

// Configure effect parameters
effect.Parameters["lightPosition"].SetValue(new Vector3(0.0f, 40.0f, 0.0f));
effect.Parameters["lightColor"].SetValue(Vector3.One);
```

In the previous code, you initially load the lightEffect effect using the content
manager. Then you define which technique of the effect will be used—in this case,
the basicLight technique. Finally, you set the effect parameters: lightPosition and
lightColor. The following code shows how to draw an object using the loaded effect:

```
// First begin the effect
effect.Begin();

// Remember that the effect can have many passes
foreach (EffectPass pass in effect.CurrentTechnique.Passes)
{
    pass.Begin();
    // PUT YOUR DRAWING CODE HERE
    pass.End();
}

// Finally, end the effect
effect.End();
```

To draw a model using an effect, you first need to begin its effect and then go through
all the passes of its technique. For each pass, you need to begin the pass, draw the model,
and end the pass. Finally, you need to end the effect. The effect pass is represented by
XNA's EffectPass class, and is accessed through the CurrentTechnique property of the
Effect class. If you want to change an effect parameter after the beginning of a pass, you
need to call the CommitChanges method of the Effect class to update the changes.

The steps previously shown are only necessary if you're going to draw a model by
yourself. If you use one of the XNA classes, such as the ModelMesh class, it will automatically draw the model using its associated effect.

Helper Effects

When an effect is loaded through the content manager, you don't know what parameters or techniques it has. Also, to modify an effect parameter you must first query this parameter inside the effect, and then modify it.

To ease the management of custom-created effects, you're going to create a unique helper class for each of them. Each effect helper class will store a reference for all the effect parameters, avoiding the overhead of constant querying for the parameters. Also, all effect parameters will be visible through the effect class's properties, avoiding trying to query invalid parameters. You use the following code to configure the effect parameter lightPosition:

```
effect.Parameters["lightPosition"].SetValue(new Vector3(0.0f, 40.0f, 0.0f));
```

In the previous code, when you alter the lightPosition parameter, a query is made inside the effect for the lightPosition paramenter. Here you have two problems: an overhead to query for this parameter, and a possible query for an invalid parameter. Using helper classes, you can avoid these problems. The following code shows how to store a reference for the effect parameter and change its value:

```
EffectParameter param1 = effect.Parameters["lightPosition"];

// Render loop
{
    param1.SetValue(new Vector3(0.0f, 40.0f, 0.0f));
    // Draw model
    ... ...
}
```

Futhermore, you can create a Visual Studio plug-in to generate the effect helper classes automatically.

Materials

Materials store the parameters used to configure an effect. For example, you can render two surfaces using an effect that applies a texture to each of them. In this case, the material of each surface is its texture, which you use to configure the effect used to render the surfaces. So, if the two surfaces share the same material, you could set the desired effect and the desired material, and render both surfaces in sequence by avoiding changing the effect that is currently set or its parameters.

To ease the configuration of the helper effect classes, you're also going to create some material classes. The two basic material classes that you'll create are the LightMaterial class, which stores the surface properties used for lighting (diffuse color, specular color, and specular power), and the TextureMaterial class, which stores a texture map and tile used to apply a texture to a surface. You could use these two basic material classes to create more complex types of materials, such as a multitexturing material. Following is the complete code for the LightMaterial class:

```
public class LightMaterial
{
    // Material properties - Diffuse and Specular color
    Vector3 diffuseColor;
    Vector3 specularColor;
    // Specular power (Shininess)
    float specularPower;

    // Properties
    public Vector3 DiffuseColor
    {
        get { return diffuseColor; }
        set { diffuseColor = value; }
    }
    public Vector3 SpecularColor
    {
        get { return specularColor; }
        set { specularColor = value; }
    }

    public float SpecularPower
    {
        get { return specularPower; }
        set { specularPower = value; }
    }

    public LightMaterial (Vector3 diffuseColor, Vector3 specularColor,
        float specularPower)
    {
        this.diffuseColor = diffuseColor;
        this.specularColor = specularColor;
        this.specularPower = specularPower;
    }
}
```

You store the light's diffuse and specular colors as an XNA Vector3 in the diffuseColor and specularColor attributes of the LightMaterial class, respectively. You store the light's specular power (or shininess) as a float value, in the specularPower attribute of the class. Note that the (X, Y, Z) components of the color vector represent a color in the RGB format. You also need to create properties to set and retrieve the light's diffuse color, specular color, and specular power. Following is the complete code for the TextureMaterial class:

```
public class TextureMaterial
{
    // Texture
    Texture2D texture;
    // Texture UV tile
    Vector2 uvTile;

    // Properties
    public Texture2D Texture
    {
        get { return texture; }
        set { texture = value; }
    }
    public Vector2 UVTile
    {
        get { return uvTile; }
        set { uvTile = value; }
    }

    public TextureMaterial(Texture2D texture, Vector2 uvTile)
    {
        this.texture = texture;
        this.uvTile = uvTile;
    }
}
```

You store the texture as an XNA Texture2D in the texture attribute of the TextureMaterial class, and the texture UV tile as an XNA Vector2 in the uvTile attribute of the class. As in the LightMaterial class, you need to create properties to set and retrieve the texture and its UV tile.

Shader Authoring Tools

During shader development, you constantly need to modify your shader, adjust its parameters, and test it using different assets (models, textures, and so on). This process can also be slow and tiring if you need to recompile and execute your game every time you change something in one of its shaders. To help you during shader development, you can use a shader authoring tool.

One of the best tools available for shader authoring is NVIDIA's FX Composer 2.0. FX Composer 2.0 is a cross-platform integrated development environment (IDE) for shader authoring that programmers and technical artists can use. It supports a few shader languages, including HLSL, and many types of assets, such as COLLADA, FBX, X, 3DS, and OBJ. Using FX Composer, you can also watch the results of your shader in real time while you're developing and modifying it. Figure 8-3 shows the FX Composer 2.0 IDE.

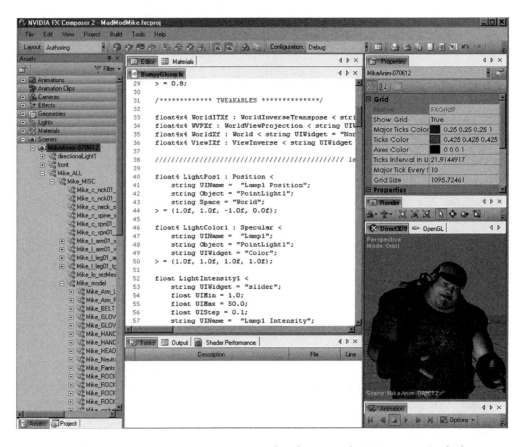

Figure 8-3. *The NVIDIA FX Composer 2.0 IDE. Other features of FX Composer include scene management, shader performance analysis, and many available samples. You can download FX Composer at the NVIDIA developer web site: http://developer.nvidia.com.*

Summary

In this chapter, you learned about the fixed and the programmable rendering pipeline, its stages, and how to use them to process the description of a 3-D scene and output a 2-D image.

You also learned how to create shaders to program the programmable stages of the GPU, and how you can encapsulate these shaders in effects. Using effects, you can also configure the fixed stages of the rendering pipeline and specify how the shaders are compiled and combined (linked) for use.

Finally, you learned how to load, configure, and use effects with XNA. After the Content Pipeline processes the effects, you can easily load and use them.

Now that you've reviewed some basic concepts of shaders and effects, you can start drawing some 3-D models. In the following chapters, you'll create more complex effects to render 3-D models, where for each effect you'll also create a new helper effect class that will use the created material classes.

CHAPTER 9

■■■

Lights, Camera, Transformations!

In this chapter you're going to create a basic framework to manage cameras, lights, and object transformations. A 3-D scene might have many cameras, lights, and objects scattered around it. Because you might have a few different types of cameras and lights in your scene, creating base classes and managers for them is very helpful. For the objects in the scene, it's useful to create a class to store its transformation: translation, rotation, and scale. The basic concepts related to transformations, cameras, and lights were presented in Chapter 7; here you're going to create some classes to represent and manage these objects. You'll use the classes created in this chapter in Chapters 10, 11, and 12.

Cameras

Depending on the genre of the game that you're going to create, you might want to use a different type of camera, such as a fixed-position camera, a first-person camera, a third-person camera, a Real Time Strategy (RTS) camera, and so on. With so many different types of cameras, it is helpful to create a basic camera that can be extended to create more specific types of cameras.

BaseCamera Class

In this section you're going to create a generic base class for the cameras, named BaseCamera. This class will handle the camera view and projection matrices and its visualization volume, a *frustum* (truncated pyramid). You can use the camera's frustum to identify which objects are not inside the camera's visualization volume, keeping these objects out of the rendering process. The camera's frustum is generated based on the camera's view and projection matrices.

Camera Perspective Projection

The BaseCamera class only supports perspective projection. You'll create the
SetPerspectiveFov method to set the camera's perspective projection, and the Projection
property to retrieve it. You can use the following code to create and update the camera
perspective projection matrix:

```
// Perspective projection parameters
float fovy;
float aspectRatio;
float nearPlane;
float farPlane;

// Matrices and flags
protected bool needUpdateProjection;
protected bool needUpdateFrustum;
protected Matrix projectionMatrix;

// Get the camera projection matrix
public Matrix Projection
{
    get
    {
        if (needUpdateProjection)  UpdateProjection();
        return projectionMatrix;
    }
}

// Set the camera perspective projection
public void SetPerspectiveFov(float fovy, float aspectRatio, float nearPlane,
    float farPlane)
{
    this.fovy = fovy;
    this.aspectRatio = aspectRatio;
    this.nearPlane = nearPlane;
    this.farPlane = farPlane;
    needUpdateProjection = true;
}

// Update the camera perspective projection matrix
protected virtual void UpdateProjection()
{
    // Create a perspective field of view matrix
```

```
    projectionMatrix = Matrix.CreatePerspectiveFieldOfView(
        MathHelper.ToRadians(fovy), aspectRatio, nearPlane, farPlane);
    needUpdateProjection = false;
    needUpdateFrustum = true;
}
```

The method `SetPerspectiveFov` stores the new perspective projection parameters but does not generate the new projection matrix. Instead, it sets the `needUpdateProjection` variable as `true`, indicating that the projection matrix needs to be updated before it can be used. When the perspective projection is retrieved through the `Projection` property, it will update the projection matrix if needed. Finally, inside the `UpdateProjection` method you generate the new perspective projection matrix using the `CreatePerspectiveFieldOfView` method of XNA's `Matrix` class.

Notice that the camera's frustum needs to be updated whenever the projection matrix is updated.

Camera View (Position and Orientation)

The view matrix stores the camera's position and orientation in the world. You'll create the `SetLookAt` method to set the camera view matrix, and the `View` property to retrieve it. You can use the following code to modify and update the camera's view matrix:

```
// Position and target
Vector3 position;
Vector3 target;

// Orientation vectors
Vector3 headingVec;
Vector3 strafeVec;
Vector3 upVec;

// Matrices and flags
protected bool needUpdateView;
protected bool needUpdateFrustum;
protected Matrix viewMatrix;

// Get the camera view matrix
public Matrix View
{
    get
    {
        if (needUpdateView)  UpdateView();
```

```
        return viewMatrix;
    }
}


// Set the camera view
public void SetLookAt(Vector3 cameraPos, Vector3 cameraTarget, Vector3 cameraUp)
{
    this.position = cameraPos;
    this.target = cameraTarget;
    this.upVec = cameraUp;

    // Calculate the camera axes (heading, upVector, and strafeVector)
    headingVec = cameraTarget - cameraPos;
    headingVec.Normalize();
    upVec = cameraUp;
    strafeVec = Vector3.Cross(headingVec, upVec);
    needUpdateView = true;
}


// Update the camera view
protected virtual void UpdateView()
{
    viewMatrix = Matrix.CreateLookAt(position, target, upVec);
    needUpdateView = false;
    needUpdateFrustum = true;
}
```

The SetLookAt method stores the new view parameters of the camera, but like the SetPerspectiveFov method, it lets the view matrix be further generated when the view matrix is retrieved through the View property. This method also calculates the three vectors that compose the camera's coordinate system and that are used to orient the camera. We'll explain how to calculate these vectors in more detail in the next section.

Last, inside the UpdateView method you generate the new view matrix using the CreateLookAt method of XNA's Matrix class. Notice that the camera's frustum needs to be updated whenever the view matrix is updated.

Camera Coordinate System

Every time you change the camera's configuration through the SetLookAt method, you need to calculate the three camera coordinate system vectors: heading (Z axis), strafe (X axis), and up (Y axis). Figure 9-1 illustrates the camera's coordinate systems placed in the world coordinates system. Notice that because these vectors compose the camera's coordinate system, they must be *unitary* and perpendicular vectors. You can use unitary vectors to represent directions, because the size of the vector doesn't matter in this case. For more information about coordinate systems, refer to Chapter 7.

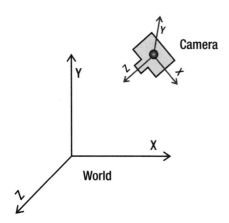

Figure 9-1. *Camera's coordinate system placed in the world coordinates system. The camera's X, Y, and Z axes are represented respectively by the strafe, up, and heading vectors of the BaseCamera class.*

The heading vector is the direction from the camera's position to its target position, and you can calculate it by subtracting the camera's position from its target position. The up vector defines the camera's up direction and is used to orient the camera. For example, you can use the vector (0, 1, 0) to orient the camera up as the world's Y axis. You can calculate the last vector (the strafe vector) by finding a vector that is perpendicular to the heading and up vectors. The vector cross product is an operation that calculates a vector that's perpendicular to two other vectors at the same time. You'll use the cross product between the heading and up vectors to calculate the camera's strafe vector. To calculate a cross product you can use the Cross method of XNA's Vector3 class. Notice that the vectors used in the cross product operation must be unitary vectors, and the order in which they are passed to the Cross method changes the direction of the resulting vector.

Another important thing to notice is that in this case, the up vector is user-defined and not necessarily perpendicular to the heading vector, although it is perpendicular to the strafe vector. If you do want to make sure the up vector is perpendicular to the heading vector, after calculating the strafe vector you must calculate a new up vector by a cross product between the heading and strafe vectors.

These three vectors form the camera's coordinate system, and are used whenever you need to transform the camera based on its axes; for example, whenever you need to move the camera towards the direction it is heading.

Camera Frustum

You'll represent the camera's frustum using XNA's BoundingFrustum class. XNA has some classes to represent bounding volumes, such as BoundingBox (an axis-aligned box), BoundingSphere, and BoundingFrustum. Each of these classes has collision test methods, which you can use to check the intersection between them. So, using the XNA BoundingFrustum class you already have methods to check the intersection with some different objects.

You'll create the UpdateFrustum method to generate the camera's frustum, and the Frustum property to retrieve it. You can generate the camera's frustum by combining the camera's view and projection matrices and using it to construct a new XNA BoundingFrustum. You can use the following code to build the camera's frustum:

```
public BoundingFrustum Frustum
{
    get
    {
        if (needUpdateProjection)
            UpdateProjection();
        if (needUpdateView)
            UpdateView();
        if (needUpdateFrustum)
            UpdateFrustum();

        return frustum;
    }
}

protected virtual void UpdateFrustum()
{
    frustum = new BoundingFrustum(viewMatrix * projectionMatrix);

    needUpdateFrustum = false;
}
```

Finally, the BaseCamera class has the abstract method Update that defines how the camera should be updated. Each camera that extends the BaseCamera class must implement this method. The Update method's signature follows:

```
public abstract void Update(GameTime time);
```

Third-Person Camera

In this section you'll extend the BaseCamera class, created in the previous section, to create a more specific type of camera: a third-person camera. For this type of camera, you'll create a class named ThirdPersonCamera, which extends the BaseCamera class. The third-person camera's goal is to follow an object while it moves, and the distance in which the camera follows an object must be variable. Otherwise, it would appear that the object is bound to the camera.

To make the camera follow an object, for example the player-controlled character, you need to define some parameters, such as chase position (the position the camera must follow); chase direction (the direction used to follow the chase position); chase speed; and minimum, desired, and maximum distances between the camera and the object. Figure 9-2 illustrates some of the parameters that need to be configured.

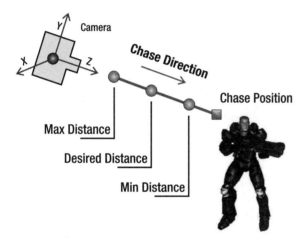

Figure 9-2. *For the third-person camera, the square is the camera's chase position, and the dots are the camera's maximum, desired, and minimum allowed positions.*

Setting Chase Parameters

In the ThirdPersonCamera class, you create the SetChaseParameters method to set the camera's chase parameters that are not frequently updated: the chase distances and speed. You can configure the chase position and direction parameters, which are more frequently updated, through properties:

```
// Chase parameters
float desiredChaseDistance;
float minChaseDistance;
float maxChaseDistance;
float chaseSpeed;
```

```
Vector3 chasePosition;
public Vector3 ChasePosition
{
    get { return chasePosition; }
    set { chasePosition = value; }
}

Vector3 chaseDirection;
public Vector3 ChaseDirection
{
    get { return chaseDirection; }
    set { chaseDirection = value; }
}

public void SetChaseParameters(float chaseSpeed,
    float desiredChaseDistance, float minChaseDistance, float maxChaseDistance){
    this.chaseSpeed = chaseSpeed;
    this.desiredChaseDistance = desiredChaseDistance;
    this.minChaseDistance = minChaseDistance;
    this.maxChaseDistance = maxChaseDistance;
}
```

Updating the Camera's Position

Every time the camera is updated, its position needs to be recalculated. The desired camera position is equal to the camera's chase position, minus the chase direction, multiplied by the chase distance (which is the distance between the camera and the chase position), as shown in Figure 9-2. The desired camera position would be the camera's final position if it were placed at a fixed distance from the chase position. However, to allow the camera to move smoothly, the distance between the camera and the chase position may vary between a minimum and maximum range (defined in the attributes minChaseDistance and maxChaseDistance). This way, the new camera position is calculated through a linear interpolation between its current position and its desired position. You can see the "Linear Interpolation" note for more details.

```
Vector3 targetPosition = chasePosition;
Vector3 desiredCameraPosition = chasePosition -
    chaseDirection * desiredChaseDistance;

float interpolatedSpeed = MathHelper.Clamp(chaseSpeed *
    elapsedTimeSeconds, 0.0f, 1.0f);
```

```
desiredCameraPosition = Vector3.Lerp(position, desiredCameraPosition,
    interpolatedSpeed);
```

The weight used to interpolate the camera's position is calculated based on the time elapsed since the last update and the camera speed. However, because the interpolation weight must be between 0 and 1, you need to clamp its value. XNA's Vector3 class has a Lerp method that helps you interpolate vectors.

LINEAR INTERPOLATION

A linear interpolation is an interpolation between two values that varies linearly according to a defined weight, where the weight is usually a float number defined between 0 and 1. For example, a linear interpolation between the numbers 10 and 20 using the weight value 0.5 results in the value 15, while a linear interpolation using the weights 0 and 1 results in the values 10 and 20. Also, a linear interpolation between two 3-D vectors interpolates the value of each component of the vectors (X, Y, Z) linearly.

Create the UpdateFollowPosition method to update the camera's position. Following is the code for the UpdateFollowPosition method:

```
private void UpdateFollowPosition(float elapsedTimeSeconds,
    bool interpolate)
{
    Vector3 targetPosition = chasePosition;
    Vector3 desiredCameraPosition = chasePosition- chaseDirection *
        desiredChaseDistance;

    if (interpolate)
    {
        float interpolatedSpeed = MathHelper.Clamp(
            chaseSpeed * elapsedTimeSeconds, 0.0f, 1.0f);
        desiredCameraPosition = Vector3.Lerp(position,
            desiredCameraPosition, interpolatedSpeed);

        // Clamp the min and max follow distances
        Vector3 targetVector = desiredCameraPosition - targetPosition;
        float targetLength = targetVector.Length();
        targetVector /= targetLength;
        if (targetLength < minChaseDistance)
        {
            desiredCameraPosition = targetPosition +
                targetVector * minChaseDistance;
```

```
        }
        else if (targetLength > maxChaseDistance)
        {
            desiredCameraPosition = targetPosition +
                targetVector * maxChaseDistance;
        }
    }

    // Needed to recalculate heading, strafe, and up vectors
    SetLookAt(desiredCameraPosition, targetPosition, upVec);
}
```

The `UpdateFollowPosition` method has the `interpolate` parameter, which defines whether the camera will be placed at its desired position (if the `interpolate` value is `false`), or will be smoothly interpolated to the desired position. When the camera chases an object for the first time, you must set the `interpolate` value as `false`, forcing the camera to start at its desired position.

When the final camera position is calculated by interpolating its current position with its desired position, you need to check if the distance from the camera to the chase position is between the minimum and maximum chase distances defined, as shown in Figure 9-2. If the distance is smaller than the minimum, you set it to the minimum allowed distance. Otherwise, if the camera distance is greater than the maximum distance, you set it to the maximum allowed distance. These tests are important and they ensure that the camera can chase objects that have a greater speed than the camera.

Rotating the Camera Around the Target

The last feature you'll add to the camera is the ability to rotate it around its target. For that feature, you'll add two new attributes and a property to the `ThirdPersonCamera` class:

```
// Maximum allowed rotation
public static float MAX_ROTATE = 30.0f;

// Current rotation angle over the camera axes (heading, up, and strafe)
Vector3 eyeRotate;

// Rotation velocity over the camera axes
Vector3 eyeRotateVelocity;
public Vector3 EyeRotateVelocity
{
    get { return eyeRotateVelocity; }
    set { eyeRotateVelocity = value; }
}
```

The allowed camera rotation range is defined between the -MAX_ROTATE and MAX_ROTATE values, and if the camera rotation is outside this range it is clamped. The eyeRotate vector stores the current camera rotation, where the X, Y, and Z components of this vector represent the angle of the rotation around the camera's strafe, up, and heading axes. Finally, the eyeRotateVelocity vector stores the velocity in which the camera rotation angle is updated.

To calculate the camera view matrix taking into account the camera rotation, you'll need to overwrite the UpdateView method of the BaseCamera class. Remember that the UpdateView method is called when the camera view matrix is retrieved through the View property, and needs to be updated. Following is the code for the UpdateView method of the ThirdPersonCamera class:

```
protected override void UpdateView()
{
    Vector3 newPosition = Position - Target;

    // Calculate the new camera position, rotating it around its axes
    newPosition = Vector3.Transform(newPosition,
        Matrix.CreateFromAxisAngle(UpVector,
            MathHelper.ToRadians(eyeRotate.Y)) *
        Matrix.CreateFromAxisAngle(StrafeVector,
            MathHelper.ToRadians(eyeRotate.X)) *
        Matrix.CreateFromAxisAngle(HeadingVector,
            MathHelper.ToRadians(eyeRotate.Z))
        );

    viewMatrix = Matrix.CreateLookAt(newPosition + Target,
        Target, UpVector);

    needUpdateView = false;
    needUpdateFrustum = true;
}
```

In the overwritten UpdateView method, you need to calculate the camera's position considering its rotation. The camera rotation is stored in the eyeRotation attribute and is relative to its axes. To rotate the camera around its own axes you'll need to create a rotation matrix that rotates around an arbitrary axis. You can create this matrix using the CreateFromAxisAngle method of XNA's Matrix class. Then, you can calculate the final matrix used to rotate the camera by combining the matrices that rotate the camera around its Y, X, and Z axes in order.

Updating the Camera

You must implement a final method in the ThirdPersonCamera class: the Update method. The Update method is an abstract method of the BaseCamera class, which is called every time the camera needs to be updated. Inside the Update method you need to update the camera's attributes, as well as call the methods used to update the camera. Note that the UpdateView and UpdateProjection methods use the camera's attributes to update the camera's view and projection matrix. These methods are only called when the view and projection matrices are retrieved through properties and need to be updated. Following is the code for the Update method of the ThirdPersonCamera class:

```
public override void Update(GameTime time)
{
    float elapsedTimeSeconds =
        (float)time.ElapsedGameTime.TotalSeconds;

    // Update the follow position
    UpdateFollowPosition(elapsedTimeSeconds, !isFirstTimeChase);
    if (isFirstTimeChase)
    {
        eyeRotate = Vector3.Zero;
        isFirstTimeChase = false;
    }

    // Calculate the new rotation based on the rotation speed
    if (eyeRotateVelocity != Vector3.Zero)
    {
        eyeRotate += eyeRotateVelocity * elapsedTimeSeconds;
        eyeRotate.X = MathHelper.Clamp(eyeRotate.X,
            -MAX_ROTATE, MAX_ROTATE);
        eyeRotate.Y = MathHelper.Clamp(eyeRotate.Y,
            -MAX_ROTATE, MAX_ROTATE);
        eyeRotate.Z = MathHelper.Clamp(eyeRotate.Z,
            -MAX_ROTATE, MAX_ROTATE);
        needUpdateView = true;
    }
}
```

In the Update method, you first update the camera's position using the UpdateFollowPosition method. Then you calculate the camera's current rotation based on its rotation velocity and the elapsed time since the last update.

Lights

Lights make a big contribution to the realism of a game. A game scene can have various light sources scattered around it, which can be, for example, activated or deactivated dynamically depending on the player's position. The main drawback of placing many lights in a scene is that the higher the number of light sources, the higher the processing needed to render the scene. Some types of light sources used in games are directional light (for example, sunlight), spotlight (as the name says), and point light (a point that emits light in all directions).

Base Light

In this section you'll create a base class for all the lights, named BaseLight. The BaseLight class doesn't have any methods, besides its constructor, and because the light sources don't share many resources, you only store the light source color inside this class:

```
// Light diffuse and specular color
Vector3 color;
public Vector3 Color
{
    get { return color; }
    set { color = value; }
}
```

The color attribute of the BaseLight class is used as the color of the diffuse and specular components of the light. Another alternative would be to store the colors of the diffuse and specular components separately. Note that the (X, Y, Z) components of the color vector are used to represent a color in the RGB format. Also, note that the lights don't have an ambient component. You'll later define the color of the light's ambient component globally for the entire scene, not for every light source.

Point Light/Ominidirectional Light

In this section you'll extend the BaseLight class to create a more specific type of light: a point light (or ominidirectional light). Point lights are easy to handle, and you can use them to light up your scenes. For this type of light, you'll create a class named PointLight, which extends the BaseLight class.

Point lights are so simple that you only need to store the light position inside the PointLight class:

```
// Omnidirectional light position
Vector3 position;
public Vector3 Position
{
    get { return position;  }
    set { position = value;  }
}
```

Besides their position, you could also store the range of the point lights, which you could use to calculate the light's attenuation. However, to simplify the illumination calculus, only the light position is stored.

Camera and Light Manager

To ease the camera and light management for the game, you'll create two different managers: one for cameras and another for lights.

Camera Manager

In this section you'll create a class to manage the cameras, named `CameraManager`. The camera manager allows many cameras to be placed in the scene, managing which camera is active at a determined time. The active camera is the camera from where the scene is observed. Following is the complete code for the `CameraManager` class:

```
public class CameraManager
{
    // Active camera index and reference
    int activeCameraIndex;
    BaseCamera activeCamera;
    // Sorted list containing all cameras
    SortedList<string, BaseCamera> cameras;

    #region Properties
    public int ActiveCameraIndex
    {
        get { return activeCameraIndex; }
    }
    public BaseCamera ActiveCamera
    {
        get { return activeCamera;  }
    }
```

```
public BaseCamera this[int index]
{
    get { return cameras.Values[index];  }
}
public BaseCamera this[string id]
{
    get { return cameras[id]; }
}
public int Count
{
    get { return cameras.Count;  }
}
#endregion

public CameraManager()
{
    cameras = new SortedList<string, BaseCamera>(4);
    activeCameraIndex = -1;
}

public void SetActiveCamera(int cameraIndex)
{
    activeCameraIndex = cameraIndex;
    activeCamera = cameras[cameras.Keys[cameraIndex]];
}

public void SetActiveCamera(string id)
{
    activeCameraIndex = cameras.IndexOfKey(id);
    activeCamera = cameras[id];
}

public void Clear()
{
    cameras.Clear();
    activeCamera = null;
    activeCameraIndex = -1;
}

public void Add(string id, BaseCamera camera)
{
    cameras.Add(id, camera);
```

```
        if (activeCamera == null)
        {
            activeCamera = camera;
            activeCameraIndex = -1;
        }
    }

    public void Remove(string id)
    {
        cameras.Remove(id);
    }
}
```

In the `CameraManager` class, the cameras are stored in a `SortedList`, which has a string containing the camera name as its key. With that, the cameras can be accessed through an integer's index or by its name. Note that the index used to access the cameras doesn't represent the order in which they were added to the camera manager. The `CameraManager` class provides methods for the addition and removal of cameras, as well as methods to define the active camera.

Light Manager

In this section you'll create a class to manage the lights, named `LightManager`. Similar to the camera manager, the light manager allows you to add various lights to a scene. But, differently from the camera manager, all the lights added to the light manager are considered to be active. You'll store a global ambient light color inside the `LightManager` class, instead of storing an ambient color for each light in the scene. Following is the complete code for the `LightManager` class:

```
public class LightManager
{
    // Global ambient component of the scene
    Vector3 ambientLightColor;
    // Sorted list containing all lights
    SortedList<string, BaseLight> lights;

    #region Properties
    public Vector3 AmbientLightColor
    {
        get { return ambientLightColor; }
        set { ambientLightColor = value; }
    }
```

```
    public BaseLight this[int index]
    {
        get { return lights.Values[index]; }
    }
    public BaseLight this[string id]
    {
        get { return lights[id]; }
    }
    public int Count
    {
        get { return lights.Count; }
    }
    #endregion

    public LightManager()
    {
        lights = new SortedList<string, BaseLight>();
    }

    public void Clear()
    {
        lights.Clear();
    }

    public void Add(string id, BaseLight light)
    {
        lights.Add(id, light);
    }

    public void Remove(string id)
    {
        lights.Remove(id);
    }
}
```

In the LightManager class, the lights are stored in a SortedList, similar to the CameraManager class. In this way, the lights can be accessed through an integer's index or by its name. The LightManager class provides methods for adding and removing lights.

Object Transformation

Transformations are an important tool in object manipulation. They allow you to position, orient, deform, and apply other types of transformations to the objects. Among the various types of transformations, the most commonly used are translation, rotation, and scale.

To help handle the transformation of the objects, you'll create a class named Transformation. This class stores the objects' translation, rotation, and scale, and creates a matrix that holds the combination of all these transformations, as shown in the following code:

```
// Translate
Vector3 translate;
// Rotate around the (X, Y, Z) world axes
Vector3 rotate;
// Scale the X, Y, Z axes
Vector3 scale;
bool needUpdate;
// Store the combination of the transformations
Matrix matrix;

public Vector3 Translate
{
    get { return translate; }
    set { translate = value; needUpdate = true; }
}
public Vector3 Rotate
{
    get { return rotate; }
    set { rotate = value; needUpdate = true; }
}
public Vector3 Scale
{
    get { return scale; }
    set { scale = value; needUpdate = true; }
}

public Matrix Matrix
{
    get
    {
        if (needUpdate)
```

```
    {
        // Compute the final matrix (Scale * Rotate * Translate)
        matrix = Matrix.CreateScale(scale) *
            Matrix.CreateRotationY(MathHelper.ToRadians(rotate.Y)) *
            Matrix.CreateRotationX(MathHelper.ToRadians(rotate.X)) *
            Matrix.CreateRotationZ(MathHelper.ToRadians(rotate.Z)) *
            Matrix.CreateTranslation(translate);
        needUpdate = false;
    }

    return matrix;
    }
}
```

In the `Transformation` class, the translation, rotation, and scale transformations are stored as XNA's `Vector3` respectively in the `translate`, `rotate`, and `scale` attributes, and you can set and retrieve them through properties. The `matrix` attribute stores the combination of the translation, rotation, and scale transformation as XNA's `Matrix`, and you can use it to apply these transformations over an object. You can set and retrieve the `matrix` attribute through the `Matrix` property, and it is recalculated whenever the translate, rotate, or scale transformation is updated.

You can use the `CreateTranslate`, `CreateRotation`, and `CreateScale` methods of XNA's `Matrix` class to generate the matrices used to translate, rotate, and scale an object. Notice that the object's transformation matrix is calculated by combining the scale, rotation, and translation transformations, in this order. Because the matrix product is not commutative, the order in which you combine the transformations is very important. The correct order to transform an object is first scale, then rotate, and finally translate.

Summary

In this chapter you created a basic framework to handle cameras, lights, and transformations, which are common objects used in a game. You learned how to structure the camera and light classes hierarchically by having a base class that stores the common attributes and methods of the classes and that could be extended to create specific types of the base class. Using this concept, you extended the base camera class to create a third-person camera, and extended the base light class to create a point light. Finally, you created some managers to handle the cameras and lights in a scene.

CHAPTER 10

■■■

Generating a Terrain

In this chapter you'll learn how to create a 3-D terrain from a height map. Terrains are a good way to represent outdoor environments, and an efficient way to represent a terrain is through the use of height maps. To give a photorealistic look to the terrain, you're also going to learn how to create an effect that uses multitexturing and normal mapping, which you'll use to render the terrain.

At the end of the chapter you'll create some auxiliary methods for the terrain, used to query the height of a position over the terrain, and check the collision between a ray and the terrain.

Height Maps

Height maps are 2-D maps used to store the height of a terrain. They're usually stored in 8-bit grayscale images, where each point of the image stores the terrain's height at that position. Figure 10-1 shows an image of a height map.

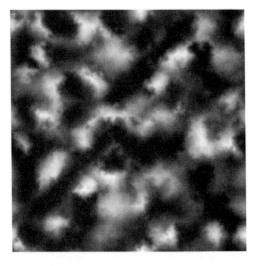

Figure 10-1. *An example of a height map*

To build a terrain from a height map, you first need to build a vertex grid with the same dimensions as the height map, and then use the height value of each point (pixel) on the height map as the height of a vertex on the vertex grid. For example, you can use a height map with a 6 × 6 pixel resolution to displace the height of each vertex in a 6 × 6 vertex grid.

Besides its position, each vertex on the grid contains other attributes needed for rendering, such as normal and texture coordinate. Figure 10-2 illustrates a vertex grid with 6 × 6 vertices created over the world plane XZ, where the height of each vertex is relative to the world's Y axis.

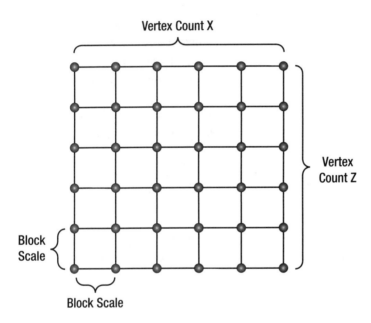

Figure 10-2. *A 6 × 6 vertex grid created over the XZ plane*

In a vertex grid you should define a distance between each pair of vertices (vertically and horizontally). This distance is represented by the "Block Scale" in Figure 10-2. A small distance between the vertices allows smooth transitions between the vertices' heights over the vertex grid but reduces the grid size, while a big distance between the vertices increases the grid size but can yield sharp transitions between the vertices' heights. This way, if the distance between each pair of vertices (vertically and horizontally) is 1 meter, the total size of the generated terrain will be 255 × 255 meters.

As the terrain's height map is usually stored in 8-bit images, its height values vary between 0 and 255, where 0 (black color) represents the lowest possible height for a vertex and 255 (white color) represents the highest possible height. You can raise this interval using a scale factor, which is multiplied by the default height value, increasing its range. This provides a bigger height interval, but with less precision between the values.

Figure 10-3 shows a 3-D terrain built from the height map of Figure 10-1, rendered in wireframe (up) and solid (low).

Note that for the rendered terrain shown in Figure 10-3, the normal and the texture coordinate were calculated for each vertex, allowing correct illumination and texturing of the terrain.

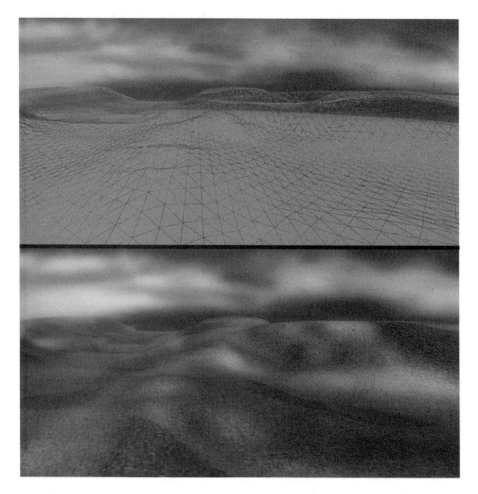

Figure 10-3. *Terrain generated from the height map in Figure 10-1 in wireframe and solid rendering*

Generating a Height Map

You can build or obtain height maps in different ways. You can find different kinds of height maps all over the Internet, including height maps of real places (cities, and so on). Because height maps are grayscale images, you can use any image editor tool to build or edit your own height maps. Also, some tools allow procedural generation of the terrain's height map from user-defined parameters.

One of the simplest and fastest ways to build height maps is through the use of procedural generation tools such as Terragen (http://www.planetside.co.uk/terragen/). Terragen allows the generation of a height map from various user-defined parameters, such as terrain size, realism, smoothing, glaciation, and canyonism. One advantage of Terragen is that you can use it freely for noncommercial applications. An artist can also refine the height map generated from Terragen at a later time.

Another tool you can use to create height maps is EarthSculptor (http://www.earthsculptor.com/). EarthSculptor has some internal tools for 3-D modeling of terrains, and it allows saving the terrain model as a height map.

Height Map File Format

The height map file format you'll use is the RAW format. This format is easy to read because it doesn't have a header with image information such as image type and size. The RAW files are simple binary files that only contain data about the height of the terrain. In an 8-bit height map, each byte inside the RAW file represents the height of a vertex.

Terrain Class

In this section you'll create the class to handle the terrain, named Terrain class, where you'll initially create methods to load a height map, generate its 3-D mesh, and draw it. Further, you'll add new methods to this class, used to query the terrain's height at a point and check for collisions.

Loading the Terrain Height Map

The first step to generate the terrain is to read its data from a height map. As the height map is stored as a RAW file, you can use a FileStream to read its data and store it in a byte array. Notice that because the height map doesn't have a header, you need to know its size, and it must match with the vertex's grid size. You can use the following code to read and store the height map data:

```
// Open a height map file
FileStream fileStream = File.OpenRead(heightmapFileName);

int heightmapSize = vertexCountX * vertexCountZ;
```

```
// Read the height map data
heightmap = new byte[heightmapSize];
fileStream.Read(heightmap, 0, heightmapSize);
fileStream.Close();
```

In the preceding code, you're reading and storing a height map with the same size of the vertex grid you're going to create. You define the size of the vertex grid through the vertexCountX and vertexCountZ variables, which are parameters used to load the height map. The vertexCountX defines the number of vertices per row (over the X axis) of the vertex grid and the vertexCountZ defines the number of vertices per column (over the Z axis).

You store the height map data in the heightmap variable, which is an attribute of the Terrain class. Note that you'll need the height map data later to be able to query the height of a position over the terrain. After reading the height map data, you can generate the terrain's mesh using its data. You create the GenerateTerrainMesh method to generate the terrain's mesh, which is composed of indices and vertices. The GenerateTerrainMesh method must be called after the height map has been loaded.

```
// Generate terrain mesh
GenerateTerrainMesh();
```

You can also store the terrain transformations (translate, rotate, and scale) inside the Terrain class, using the Transformation class created in Chapter 9. To do that, add a new attribute of type Transformation to the Terrain class, and name it transformation. Then, when the terrain's height map is loaded you must instantiate a new Transformation:

```
transformation = new Transformation();
```

Finally, you should load a custom effect for the terrain and encapsulate it in a TerrainEffect object. As described in Chapter 9, you should create a helper class for each effect that you create, to help you manage and modify the effect parameters. The TerrainMaterial class is another class you create to configure the terrain effect:

```
// Load effect
effect = new TerrainEffect(
    Game.Content.Load<Effect>(TerrainEffect.EFFECT_FILENAME));
terrainMaterial = new TerrainMaterial();
```

The custom effect that you created for the terrain provides a more realistic rendering using multitexturing and normal mapping. Multitexturing allows different textures to be applied over the same surface, while normal mapping allows you to increase the terrain's details without increasing its mesh complexity. You'll create the effect used to render the terrain at the end of this chapter. Following is the code for the Load method of the Terrain class:

```
public void Load(string heightmapFileName, int vertexCountX, int vertexCountZ,
    float blockScale, float heightScale)
{
    if (!isInitialized) Initialize();

    this.vertexCountX = vertexCountX;
    this.vertexCountZ = vertexCountZ;
    this.blockScale = blockScale;
    this.heightScale = heightScale;

    // Open height map file
    FileStream fileStream = File.OpenRead(Game.Content.RootDirectory +
        "/" + GameAssetsPath.TERRAINS_PATH + heightmapFileName);

    // Read height map data
    int heightmapSize = vertexCountX * vertexCountZ;
    heightmap = new byte[heightmapSize];
    fileStream.Read(heightmap, 0, heightmapSize);
    fileStream.Close();

    // Generate terrain mesh
    GenerateTerrainMesh();
    // Instantiate a new transformation for the terrain
    transformation = new Transformation();

    // Load effect
    effect = new TerrainEffect(
        Game.Content.Load<Effect>(TerrainEffect.EFFECT_FILENAME));
    material = new TerrainMaterial();
}
```

The Load method receives as a parameter the height map's file name; the terrain size in number of vertices (along the X and Z axes); the block scale, which represents the distance between the vertices; and a height scale value, used to scale the height of the terrain. All these parameters, with the exception of the height map file name, are stored in the Terrain class, respectively, in the attributes vertexCountX, vertexCountZ, blockScale, and heightScale.

Generating the Terrain's Mesh

To generate the terrain's mesh, you need to generate its vertices and indices. The mesh's indices store the order in which the mesh's vertices should be combined to generate triangles. Meanwhile, each mesh's vertex contains a spatial coordinate and stores some attributes needed for rendering, such as normal and texture coordinate. You should generate the mesh's indices prior to its vertices because you can only calculate some of the vertex attributes, such as the vertex normal, if you know which vertices are used in each triangle.

You'll create two separate methods to generate the mesh's indices and vertices, respectively named GenerateTerrainIndices and GenerateTerrainVertices. You'll call these methods from the GenerateTerrain method to generate the mesh's vertices and indices. Then, you'll create an XNA VertexBuffer to store the mesh's vertices and an XNA IndexBuffer to store the mesh's indices. Vertex and index buffers are memory buffers that store its data in system memory and copy it to the video memory as needed. Use the following code for the GenerateTerrain method, which calls the GenerateTerrainIndices and GenerateTerrainVertices methods to generate the indices and vertices of the terrain's mesh. Following is the code for the GenerateTerrainMesh method:

```
private void GenerateTerrainMesh()
{
    numVertices = vertexCountX * vertexCountZ;
    numTriangles = (vertexCountX - 1) * (vertexCountZ - 1) * 2;

    // You must generate the terrain indices first
    int[] indices = GenerateTerrainIndices();

    // Then, generate terrain vertices
    VertexPositionNormalTangentBinormal[] vertices =
        GenerateTerrainVertices(indices);

    // Create a vertex buffers to hold all the vertices
    vb = new VertexBuffer(GraphicsDevice, numVertices *
        VertexPositionNormalTangentBinormal.SizeInBytes, BufferUsage.WriteOnly);
    vb.SetData<VertexPositionNormalTangentBinormal>(vertices);

    // Create an index buffers to hold all the indices
    ib = new IndexBuffer(GraphicsDevice, numTriangles * 3 * sizeof(int),
        BufferUsage.WriteOnly, IndexElementSize.ThirtyTwoBits);
    ib.SetData<int>(indices);
}
```

Notice that the terrain vertices are stored as an array of the VertexPositionNormalTangentBinormal struct. You must create this helper struct to store the vertex data because you'll need to store the position, texture coordinate, normal, tangent, and binormal of each vertex, and XNA doesn't have a class that stores all these vertex attributes. Following is the code for the VertexPositionNormalTangentBinormal struct:

```
public struct VertexPositionNormalTangentBinormal
{
    public Vector3 Position;
    public Vector3 Normal;
    public Vector2 TextureCoordinate;
    public Vector3 Tanget;
    public Vector3 Binormal;

    public static int SizeInBytes
    {
        get { return (3 + 3 + 2 + 3 + 3) * sizeof(float); }
    }

    public static VertexElement[] VertexElements = new VertexElement[] {
        new VertexElement(0, 0, VertexElementFormat.Vector3,
                            VertexElementMethod.Default,
                            VertexElementUsage.Position, 0),
        new VertexElement(0, 12, VertexElementFormat.Vector3,
                            VertexElementMethod.Default,
                            VertexElementUsage.Normal, 0),
        new VertexElement(0, 24, VertexElementFormat.Vector2,
                            VertexElementMethod.Default,
                            VertexElementUsage.TextureCoordinate, 0),
        new VertexElement(0, 32, VertexElementFormat.Vector3,
                            VertexElementMethod.Default,
                            VertexElementUsage.Tangent, 0),
        new VertexElement(0, 44, VertexElementFormat.Vector3,
                            VertexElementMethod.Default,
                            VertexElementUsage.Binormal, 0)
    };
}
```

The VertexPositionNormalTangentBinormal struct has all the attributes that you need for a vertex: position, texture coordinate, normal, tangent, and binormal. This structure also declares a VertexElement array containing the format of the vertex data, which has the type and size of each element in the vertex.

Generating the Mesh's Indices

In this section you'll create the GenerateTerrainIndices method to generate the indices of the terrain's mesh. The mesh's indices define in which order the vertices should be combined to generate triangles. Figure 10-4 shows the indices of the vertices in a grid and how they are combined to form triangles.

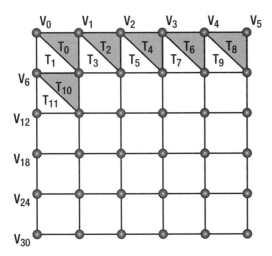

Figure 10-4. *Indexing grid vertices to create triangles*

Each quad in the terrain has two triangles: a gray triangle and a white triangle. In the first quad of the grid the gray triangle has the vertices 0, 1, and 7, while the white triangle has the vertices 0, 7, and 6. Notice that the order of the triangle's indices is important: it should be clockwise, because the XNA pipeline culls counterclockwise triangles by default.

Notice that there is a pattern between the indices used to create the triangles, where the indices of the first and second triangles of every quadrant follow the same order, as shown in the next equation.

$$T_{bottom} = V_{[Index]}, V_{[Index+1]}, V_{[Index+VertexCountX+1]}$$
$$T_{top} = V_{[Index]}, V_{[Index+VertexCountX+1]}, V_{[Index+VertexCountX]}$$

In the preceding equation, the VertexCountX variable is equal to the number of vertices per row in the vertex grid. Using the preceding equation, you can loop through all the quadrants of the vertex grid, generating the indices of its triangles. You'll generate the mesh's indices as an array of integers that have three values for each triangle. Following is the code for the GenerateTerrainIndices method:

```
private int[] GenerateTerrainIndices()
{
    int numIndices = numTriangles * 3;
    int[] indices = new int[numIndices];

    int indicesCount = 0;
    for (int i = 0; i < (vertexCountZ - 1); i++)
    {
        for (int j = 0; j < (vertexCountX - 1); j++)
        {
            int index = j + i * vertexCountZ;

            // First triangle
            indices[indicesCount++] = index;
            indices[indicesCount++] = index + 1;
            indices[indicesCount++] = index + vertexCountX + 1;
            // Second triangle
            indices[indicesCount++] = index + vertexCountX + 1;
            indices[indicesCount++] = index + vertexCountX;
            indices[indicesCount++] = index;
        }
    }
    return indices;
}
```

Generating Vertices' Position and Texture Coordinate

In this section you'll create the GenerateTerrainVertices method to generate the mesh's
vertices. You'll place the terrain vertices over the world's XZ plane, centering the terrain at
the world position (0, 0). To do that, you first need to calculate half the terrain size along
the X and Z axes, and then set the terrain's start position at minus its half size along the
X and Z axes (-halfTerrainWidth, -halfTerrainDepth).

You can calculate the terrain size through the terrain attributes: vertexCountX, which
stores the number of vertices of the terrain along the X axis; vertexCountZ, which stores
the number of vertices of the terrain along the Z axis; and blockScale, which stores the
distance between the vertices in the X and Z axes. After calculating the terrain size, you
just need to divide it by two, as shown next:

```
float terrainWidth = (vertexCountX - 1) * blockScale;
float terrainDepth = (vertexCountZ - 1) * blockScale;
float halfTerrainWidth = terrainWidth * 0.5f;
float halfTerrainDepth = terrainDepth * 0.5f;
```

You can generate the terrain's vertex grid beginning at the terrain's start position and going over each row of the vertex grid, placing the vertices (going from –X to +X), where each row is placed in a different grid column (going from –Z to +Z). In this way, the grid's vertices have its position incremented along the X and Z axes according to the block scale that you defined, as shown in Figure 10-2. While placing the vertices, you'll use the previously stored height map data to set the vertex height along the Y axis. You'll also scale the height of the terrain by multiplying the height of each vertex by a scale factor: the heightScale attribute of the Terrain class. You can use the following code to correctly position the vertices over the terrain's vertex grid:

```
for (float i = -halfTerrainDepth; i <= halfTerrainDepth; i += blockScale)
    for (float j = -halfTerrainWidth; j <= halfTerrainWidth; j += blockScale)
        Position = (j, heightmap[vertexCount] * heightScale, i)
```

Each vertex also has a U and V texture coordinate that should vary between (0, 0) and (1, 1), where (0, 0) is the initial texture coordinate and (1, 1) the final texture coordinate. Figure 10-5 shows the texture coordinates of some vertices in a grid.

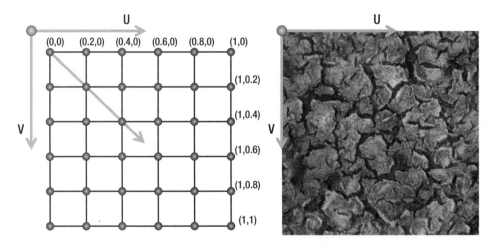

Figure 10-5. *(Left) The texture coordinates for a grid of vertices. (Right) The UV axes over a texture map.*

To calculate the correct texture coordinate for each vertex in the terrain, you first need to calculate the increment of the texture coordinate in the UV axis. You do so by dividing the maximum texture coordinate value (1.0) by the number of vertices minus 1, in each axis:

```
float tu = 0; float tv = 0;
float tuDerivative = 1.0f / (vertexCountX - 1);
float tvDerivative = 1.0f / (vertexCountZ - 1);
```

Then, you go through each vertex, setting its texture coordinate and incrementing it. Besides the position and texture coordinate, you still need to calculate the normal, tangent, and binormal for each vertex. To do that, create the GenerateTerrainNormals and GenerateTerrainTangentBinormal methods, which you call at the end of the GenerateTerrainVertices method. Next is the complete code for the GenerateTerrainVertices method:

```
private VertexPositionNormalTangentBinormal[] GenerateTerrainVertices(
    int[] terrainIndices)
{
    float halfTerrainWidth = (vertexCountX - 1) * blockScale * 0.5f;
    float halfTerrainDepth = (vertexCountZ - 1) * blockScale * 0.5f;

    // Texture coordinates
    float tu = 0;
    float tv = 0;
    float tuDerivative = 1.0f / (vertexCountX - 1);
    float tvDerivative = 1.0f / (vertexCountZ - 1);

    int vertexCount = 0;
    // Create the vertex array
    VertexPositionNormalTangentBinormal[] vertices =
        new VertexPositionNormalTangentBinormal[vertexCountX * vertexCountZ];

    // Set position and texture coordinate of each vertex
    for (float i = -halfTerrainDepth; i <= halfTerrainDepth; i += blockScale)
    {
        tu = 0.0f;
        for (float j = -halfTerrainWidth; j <= halfTerrainWidth; j += blockScale)
        {
            // Set vertex position and UV
            vertices[vertexCount].Position =
                new Vector3(j, heightmap[vertexCount] * heightScale, i);
            vertices[vertexCount].TextureCoordinate = new Vector2(tu, tv);

            tu += tuDerivative;
            vertexCount++;
        }
        tv += tvDerivative;
    }
```

```
// Generate vertices' normal, tangent, and binormal
GenerateTerrainNormals(vertices, terrainIndices);
GenerateTerrainTangentBinormal(vertices, terrainIndices);

return vertices;
}
```

Generating Vertices' Normal

The normal vector of each vertex in a triangle is equal to the normal vector of the triangle. So, to calculate the normal of the vertices in a triangle you need to calculate the normal of the triangle. You could calculate the triangle normal by a cross product between two vectors formed by its vertices, such as (v1 – v0) and (v2 – v0), because the cross product returns a vector perpendicular to these two vectors.

Because one to six different triangles can share each vertex in a vertex grid, the normal of each vertex is the sum of the normals of the triangles that share this vertex. Thus, you need to calculate the normal vector for each triangle and sum it to the normal of the vertices of this triangle. Last, you must normalize the normal of each vertex, making them unitary length. Normal vectors are used in lighting calculations, and they must be unitary length to yield correct lighting. You use the following code for the GenerateTerrainNormals method to generate the normal of the terrain's vertices:

```
private void GenerateTerrainNormals(VertexPositionNormalTangentBinormal[] vertices,
    int[] indices)
{
    for (int i = 0; i < indices.Length; i += 3)
    {
        // Get the vertex position (v1, v2, and v3)
        Vector3 v1 = vertices[indices[i]].Position;
        Vector3 v2 = vertices[indices[i + 1]].Position;
        Vector3 v3 = vertices[indices[i + 2]].Position;

        // Calculate vectors v1->v3 and v1->v2 and the normal as a cross product
        Vector3 vu = v3 - v1;
        Vector3 vt = v2 - v1;
        Vector3 normal = Vector3.Cross(vu, vt);
        normal.Normalize();

        // Sum this normal with the current vertex normal of the tree vertices
        vertices[indices[i]].Normal += normal;
        vertices[indices[i + 1]].Normal += normal;
```

```
            vertices[indices[i + 2]].Normal += normal;
    }

    // After calculating all the normals, normalize them
    for (int i = 0; i < vertices.Length; i++)
        vertices[i].Normal.Normalize();
}
```

Generating Vertices' Tangent and Binormal

The custom effect you'll create for the terrain uses a technique named *normal mapping*, which allows increasing the terrain details without increasing its mesh complexity. To use the normal mapping technique, every mesh's vertex must have tangent, binormal, and normal vectors. The tangent, binormal, and normal vectors are perpendiculars and they form the tangent base. Figure 10-6 illustrates the tangent, binormal, and normal vectors for different points of two different surfaces.

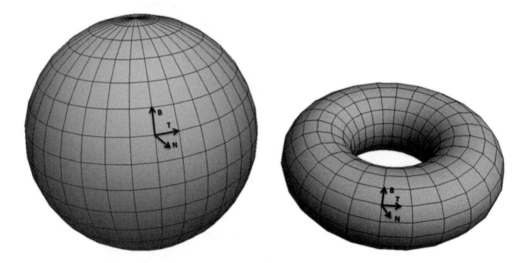

Figure 10-6. *Tangent, binormal, and normal vectors*

You can calculate the tangent vector of each vertex in the vertex grid, as the vector that starts at this vertex and ends in the next vertex of the grid. This way the tangent vector is oriented with the grid's X axis. Notice that the tangent vector of the last vertex in a line on the grid is calculated as a vector that starts in the penultimate vertex of the line and ends in the last vertex.

After calculating the tangent vector, you can obtain the binormal vector by a cross product between the vertices' tangent and normal. Figure 10-7 shows the tangent, binormal, and normal vectors of a flat grid of vertices.

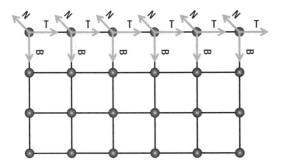

Figure 10-7. *Tangent, binormal, and normal vectors of some vertices in a flat grid*

Use the following code for the GenerateTerrainTangentBinormal method to calculate the vertices' tangent and binormal vectors:

```
public void GenerateTerrainTangentBinormal(
    VertexPositionNormalTangentBinormal[] vertices, int[] indices)
{
    for (int i = 0; i < vertexCountZ; i++)
    {
        for (int j = 0; j < vertexCountX; j++)
        {
            int vertexIndex = j + i * vertexCountX;
            Vector3 v1 = vertices[vertexIndex].Position;

            // Calculate the tangent vector
            if (j < vertexCountX - 1)
            {
                Vector3 v2 = vertices[vertexIndex + 1].Position;
                vertices[vertexIndex].Tanget = (v2 - v1);
            }
            // Special case: Last vertex of the plane in the X axis
            else
            {
                Vector3 v2 = vertices[vertexIndex - 1].Position;
                vertices[vertexIndex].Tanget = (v1 - v2);
            }
```

```
                // Calculate binormal as a cross product (Tangent x Normal)
                vertices[vertexIndex].Tanget.Normalize();
                vertices[vertexIndex].Binormal = Vector3.Cross(
                    vertices[vertexIndex].Tanget, vertices[vertexIndex].Normal);
            }
        }
    }
```

Terrain Effect

For the terrain rendering, you'll create a custom effect that uses multitexturing and nor-mal mapping. The multitexturing allows you to combine and use some different textures over the terrain, while the normal mapping allows you to add small-scale details to the terrain. Next, we're going to discuss the use of the multitexturing and normal mapping techniques, and then you're going to create the terrain effect.

Multitexturing

Using multitexturing, you can apply different layers of textures over the terrain, such as sand, grass, rocks, snow, and so on. Then, you can generate the terrain's texture by com-bining all these textures. For example, some parts of the terrain could have grass, others rocks, and some parts sand and grass, or snow and rocks, and so on. Figure 10-8 shows how some textures are combined to form a new texture.

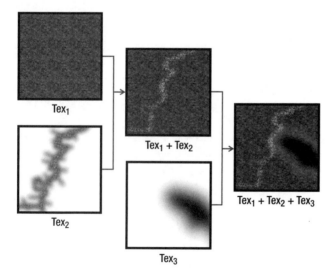

Figure 10-8. *Multitexturing—combining three different textures to form a new one*

In the terrain effect you're going to create, you'll combine the terrain textures based on a separate texture, named alpha map, which defines the intensity of each texture over the terrain. In this case, the alpha map is an RGBA texture, with 8 bits per channel, and you're using each texture channel to store the intensity of a different texture layer.

Normal Mapping

Using the the normal mapping technique, you can add small-scale details to the terrain's mesh without needing to modify or increase the complexity of its mesh. You can also use other more precise and complex techniques to highly increase the mesh details, such as relief mapping, parallax occlusion mapping, and cone step mapping.

In normal mapping, you modify the surface normals based on a map of normals, named normal map. Then you do the surface lighting using the modified normals, allowing small details to be simulated on the surface, as shown in Figure 10-9.

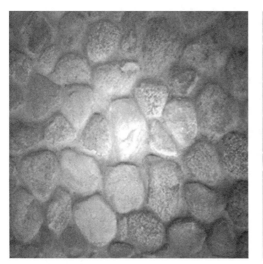 

Figure 10-9. *(Left) Only texturing. (Right) Texturing plus normal mapping.*

The normal map used by the normal mapping technique is an RGB texture, where each component of the texture represents the X, Y, and Z components of the new surface normal. Notice that the normal X, Y, and Z axes aren't on the world coordinates. Instead, they're placed in the tangent base coordinates. In that way, the normal map is independent of the surface and could be applied to any type of object. Also, that is why you need to calculate the tangent, binormal, and normal vectors for each vertex.

One of the weaknesses of the normal mapping technique is that when the surface is visualized from grazing angles (the angle between the surface normal and a viewer close to 90 degrees), the surface will seem flat.

Terrain Effect—Vertex Processing

The effect you're going to create for terrain rendering will support two omnidirectional light sources, multitexturing with four diffuse textures, and normal mapping. In total, the terrain effect will use six textures: four textures for the diffuse color, one alpha map, and a normal map. The alpha map defines how the diffuse textures will be combined to form the final terrain color.

Let's begin constructing the effect through its vertex shader. The vertex shader receives a structure containing the vertex position, texture coordinate, and tangent base (tangent, binormal, and normal vectors):

```
struct a2v
{
    float4 position   : POSITION;
    float2 uv0             : TEXCOORD0;
    float3 tangen  t  : TANGENT;
    float3 binormal : BINORMAL;
    float3 normal     : NORMAL;
};
```

The output of the vertex shader contains the vertex's final position, the coordinate of the six textures used, the view vector, and the two lighting vectors (all the vectors are in the tangent space):

```
struct v2f
{
    float4 hposition           : POSITION;
    float4 uv1_2                   : TEXCOORD0;
    float4 uv3_4                   : TEXCOORD1;
    float4 uv5_6                   : TEXCOORD2;
    float3 eyeVec              : TEXCOORD4;
    float3 lightVec1        : TEXCOORD5;
    float3 lightVec2        : TEXCOORD6;
};
```

Inside the vertex processing, the first thing you should do is calculate the final position of every vertex, transforming it by combining the world, view, and projection matrices:

```
OUT.hposition = mul(IN.position, matWVP);  // Vertex position in homogeneous space
```

Then you calculate the tangent base, combine it with the world matrix, and calculate its inverse matrix (in this case, the inverse matrix is equal to the transpose matrix). You use the tangentSpace matrix to transform a vector from the world space to the tangent space:

```
float3x3 tangentSpace = float3x3(IN.tangent, IN.binormal, IN.normal);
tangentSpace = mul(tangentSpace, matW);
tangentSpace = transpose(tangentSpace);
```

Now you should calculate the view vector and the two lighting vectors and transform their coordinate to the tangent space (transforming them using the tangentSpace matrix):

```
float3 worldPosition = mul(IN.position, matW).xyz;
OUT.eyeVec = mul(matVI[3].xyz - worldPosition, tangentSpace);
OUT.lightVec1 = mul(light1Position - worldPosition, tangentSpace);
OUT.lightVec2 = mul(light2Position - worldPosition, tangentSpace);
```

Last, calculate all the texture coordinates using the default texture coordinate of the surface and some tile factors:

```
OUT.uv1_2 = float4(IN.uv0 * uv1Tile, IN.uv0 * uv2Tile);
OUT.uv3_4 = float4(IN.uv0 * uv3Tile, IN.uv0 * uv4Tile);
OUT.uv5_6 = float4(IN.uv0 * uvBumpTile, IN.uv0);
```

Next, the complete vertex processing code is shown:

```
v2f TerrainVS(a2v IN)
{
    v2f OUT;
    OUT.hposition = mul(IN.position, matWVP);
// Vertex position in homogeneous space

    // Calculate the tangent basis
    float3x3 tangentSpace = float3x3(IN.tangent, IN.binormal, IN.normal);
    tangentSpace = mul(tangentSpace, matW);
    tangentSpace = transpose(tangentSpace);
    // Calculate eye and light vector in tangent space
    float3 worldPosition = mul(IN.position, matW).xyz;
    OUT.eyeVec = mul(matVI[3].xyz - worldPosition, tangentSpace);
    OUT.lightVec1 = mul(light1Position - worldPosition, tangentSpace);
    OUT.lightVec2 = mul(light2Position - worldPosition, tangentSpace);
    // Multitexturing
    OUT.uv1_2 = float4(IN.uv0 * uv1Tile, IN.uv0 * uv2Tile);
    OUT.uv3_4 = float4(IN.uv0 * uv3Tile, IN.uv0 * uv4Tile);
    OUT.uv5_6 = float4(IN.uv0 * uvBumpTile, IN.uv0);
    return OUT;
}
```

Terrain Effect—Pixel Processing

All the data received in the pixel shader is interpolated values output from the vertex shader. The first thing you're going to do in the pixel shader is normalize all the vectors, making sure that they remain unitary. Remember that all these vectors must be unitary to yield correct lighting.

```
float3 eyeVec = normalize(IN.eyeVec);
float3 lightVec1 = normalize(IN.lightVec1);
float3 lightVec2 = normalize(IN.lightVec2);
float3 halfwayVec1 = normalize(lightVec1 + eyeVec);
float3 halfwayVec2 = normalize(lightVec2 + eyeVec);
```

Next, read the normal map and normalize its value to the -1 to 1 interval. This is needed because the values stored in the texture are in the 0.0 to 1.0 range, but they are used to represent negative and positive values:

```
float3 normal = tex2D(normalSampler, IN.uv5_6.xy);
normal.xy = normal.xy * 2.0 - 1.0;
normal.z = sqrt(1.0 - dot(normal.xy, normal.xy));
```

At this point you have all the necessary vectors for the lighting calculation. You'll do the lighting calculation using the Phong equation, which is usually implemented in the graphics APIs. The created phongShading function implements the Phong equation and returns a diffuse and specular component for each specified light source.

```
float3 diffuseColor1, diffuseColor2, specularColor1, specularColor2;
phongShading(normal, lightVec1, halfwayVec1, light1Color,
    diffuseColor1, specularColor1);
phongShading(normal, lightVec2, halfwayVec2, light2Color,
    diffuseColor2, specularColor2);
```

Besides the lighting, you should calculate the texture color for each pixel. You calculate this color by sampling and combining the four diffuse textures that are applied to the terrain according to the alpha map texture. Each component of the alpha map stores a value used to linearly interpolate between the colors of the diffuse textures:

```
float3 color1 = tex2D(diffuseSampler1, IN.uv1_2.xy);
float3 color2 = tex2D(diffuseSampler2, IN.uv1_2.zw);
float3 color3 = tex2D(diffuseSampler3, IN.uv3_4.xy);
float3 color4 = tex2D(diffuseSampler4, IN.uv3_4.zw);
float4 alpha = tex2D(alphaSampler, IN.uv5_6.zw);
// Combine using the alpha map
float3 combinedColor = lerp(color1, color2, alpha.x);
```

```
combinedColor = lerp(combinedColor , color3, alpha.y);
combinedColor = lerp(combinedColor , color4, alpha.z);
```

Finally, you calculate the final color of each pixel, combining its texture color with the diffuse and specular light that is reflected from the pixel according to its material:

```
float4 finalColor;
finalColor.a = 1.0f;
finalColor.rgb = combinedColor * ( (diffuseColor1 + diffuseColor2) *
    materialDiffuseColor + ambientLightColor) + (specularColor1 +
    specularColor2) * materialSpecularColor;
```

The final pixel shader code and the Phong method are shown next. The book *Real-Time Rendering*, 2nd ed., by Tomas Akenine-Möller and Eric Haines (AK Peters, Ltd., 2002) is a good reference for a deep understading of the Phong algorithm and the normal mapping technique.

```
void phongShading(in float3 normal, in float3 lightVec, in float3 halfwayVec,
    in float3 lightColor, out float3 diffuseColor, out float3 specularColor)
{
    float diffuseInt = saturate(dot(normal, lightVec));
    diffuseColor = diffuseInt * lightColor;
    float specularInt = saturate(dot(normal, halfwayVec));
    specularInt = pow(specularInt, specularPower);
    specularColor = specularInt * lightColor;
}


float4 TerrainPS(v2f IN) : COLOR0
{
    float3 eyeVec = normalize(IN.eyeVec);
    float3 lightVec1 = normalize(IN.lightVec1);
    float3 lightVec2 = normalize(IN.lightVec2);
    float3 halfwayVec1 = normalize(lightVec1 + eyeVec);
    float3 halfwayVec2 = normalize(lightVec2 + eyeVec);

    // Normal mapping
    float3 normal = tex2D(normalSampler, IN.uv5_6.xy);
    normal.xy = normal.xy * 2.0 - 1.0;
    normal.z = sqrt(1.0 - dot(normal.xy, normal.xy));

    // Calculate diffuse and specular color for each light
    float3 diffuseColor1, diffuseColor2, specularColor1, specularColor2;
    phongShading(normal, lightVec1, halfwayVec1, light1Color,
```

```
        diffuseColor1, specularColor1);
    phongShading(normal, lightVec2, halfwayVec2, light2Color,
        diffuseColor2, specularColor2);

    // Combine the diffuse textures using the alpha map
    float3 color1 = tex2D(diffuseSampler1, IN.uv1_2.xy);
    float3 color2 = tex2D(diffuseSampler2, IN.uv1_2.zw);
    float3 color3 = tex2D(diffuseSampler3, IN.uv3_4.xy);
    float3 color4 = tex2D(diffuseSampler4, IN.uv3_4.zw);
    float4 alpha = tex2D(alphaSampler, IN.uv5_6.zw);
    float3 combinedColor = lerp(color1, color2, alpha.x);
    combinedColor = lerp(combinedColor , color3, alpha.y);
    combinedColor = lerp(combinedColor , color4, alpha.z);

    // Calculate the final color
    float4 finalColor;
    finalColor.a = 1.0f;
    finalColor.rgb = combinedColor * ( (diffuseColor1 + diffuseColor2) *
        materialDiffuseColor + ambientLightColor) + (specularColor1 +
        specularColor2) * materialSpecularColor;

    return finalColor;
}
```

Setting the Effect Material

To manage the terrain effect, you'll create the TerrainEffect class. The helper classes help you modify and manage the effect parameters, as explained in Chapter 8. You'll also create the TerrainMaterial class, to help you configure the terrain effect. The code of the TerrainEffect class is omitted for simplicity because inside this class you just need to query and store all the parameters of the effect.

The TerrainMaterial class stores the surface material as an attribute of type LightMaterial and the surface textures as some attributes of type TextureMaterial. Following is the code for the TerrainMaterial class:

```
public class TerrainMaterial
{
    // Surface material
    LightMaterial lightMaterial;
```

```csharp
// Diffuse Textures
TextureMaterial diffuseTexture1;
TextureMaterial diffuseTexture2;
TextureMaterial diffuseTexture3;
TextureMaterial diffuseTexture4;

// Alpha map
TextureMaterial alphaMapTexture;

// Normal map
TextureMaterial normalMapTexture;

// Properties
public LightMaterial LightMaterial
{
    get { return lightMaterial; }
    set { lightMaterial = value; }
}

public TextureMaterial DiffuseTexture1
{
    get { return diffuseTexture1; }
    set { diffuseTexture1 = value; }
}

public TextureMaterial DiffuseTexture2
{
    get { return diffuseTexture2; }
    set { diffuseTexture2 = value; }
}

public TextureMaterial DiffuseTexture3
{
    get { return diffuseTexture3; }
    set { diffuseTexture3 = value; }
}

public TextureMaterial DiffuseTexture4
{
    get { return diffuseTexture4; }
    set { diffuseTexture4 = value; }
}
```

```
    public TextureMaterial AlphaMapTexture
    {
        get { return alphaMapTexture; }
        set { alphaMapTexture = value; }
    }

    public TextureMaterial NormalMapTexture
    {
        get { return normalMapTexture; }
        set { normalMapTexture = value; }
    }

    public TerrainMaterial()
    {
    }
}
```

To configure the terrain effect, inside the `Terrain` class you'll create the `SetEffectMaterial` method. You'll use this method to configure all the effect parameters, through the `TerrainEffect` helper class, before the terrain rendering.

In your scene you'll manage the cameras and lights using the `CameraManager` and `LightManager` classes, created in Chapter 9. You can add these classes to the service container of the `Game` class. In this way, any class that has a reference to the `Game` class could query for these resources any time at runtime. The service container helps maintain loose coupling between the objects. Using the service container, you can get the light manager and obtain the scene lights, which are used by the effect, by getting the two first lights from the light manager (`LightManager`):

```
// Get the light manager
LightManager lightManager = Game.Services.GetService(
    typeof(LightManager)) as LightManager;

// Get the first two lights from the light manager
PointLight light0 = lightManager[0] as PointLight;
PointLight light1 = lightManager[1] as PointLight;

// Lights
effect.AmbientLightColor = lightManager.AmbientLightColor;
effect.Light1Position = light0.Position;
effect.Light1Color = light0.Color;
effect.Light2Position = light1.Position;
effect.Light2Color = light1.Color;
```

Using the service container you can get the camera manager (CameraManager) and obtain the active camera from it, and you can read the terrain transformation from its transformation attribute of type Transformation:

```
// Get the camera manager
cameraManager = Game.Services.GetService(
    typeof(CameraManager)) as CameraManager;

// Set the camera view and projection
effect.View = cameraManager.ActiveCamera.View;
effect.Projection = cameraManager.ActiveCamera.Projection;

// Set the terrain transformation
effect.World = transformation.Matrix;
```

Finally, you configure the terrain material and the textures through the LightMaterial and TextureMaterial attributes of the TerrainMaterial classes. Following is the code for the SetEffectMaterial method:

```
private void SetEffectMaterial()
{
    // Get the light manager
    LightManager lightManager = Game.Services.GetService(
        typeof(LightManager)) as LightManager;

    // Get the first two lights from the light manager
    PointLight light0 = lightManager[0] as PointLight;
    PointLight light1 = lightManager[1] as PointLight;
    // Lights
    effect.AmbientLightColor = lightManager.AmbientLightColor;
    effect.Light1Position = light0.Position;
    effect.Light1Color = light0.Color;
    effect.Light2Position = light1.Position;
    effect.Light2Color = light1.Color;

    // Get the camera manager
    cameraManager = Game.Services.GetService(
        typeof(CameraManager)) as CameraManager;

    // Set the camera view and projection
    effect.View = cameraManager.ActiveCamera.View;
    effect.Projection = cameraManager.ActiveCamera.Projection;
```

```
    // Set the terrain transformation
    effect.World = transformation.Matrix;

    // Material
    effect.DiffuseColor = terrainMaterial.LightMaterial.DiffuseColor;
    effect.SpecularColor = terrainMaterial.LightMaterial.SpecularColor;
    effect.SpecularPower = terrainMaterial.LightMaterial.SpecularPower;
    // Textures
    effect.DiffuseTexture1 = terrainMaterial.DiffuseTexture1.Texture;
    effect.DiffuseTexture2 = terrainMaterial.DiffuseTexture2.Texture;
    effect.DiffuseTexture3 = terrainMaterial.DiffuseTexture3.Texture;
    effect.DiffuseTexture4 = terrainMaterial.DiffuseTexture4.Texture;
    effect.NormalMapTexture = terrainMaterial.NormalMapTexture.Texture;
    effect.AlphaMapTexture = terrainMaterial.AlphaMapTexture.Texture;
    // Textures UVs
    effect.TextureUV1Tile = terrainMaterial.DiffuseTexture1.UVTile;
    effect.TextureUV2Tile = terrainMaterial.DiffuseTexture2.UVTile;
    effect.TextureUV3Tile = terrainMaterial.DiffuseTexture3.UVTile;
    effect.TextureUV4Tile = terrainMaterial.DiffuseTexture4.UVTile;
    effect.TextureUVNormalTile = material.NormalMapTexture.UVTile;
}
```

Drawing the Terrain

To draw the terrain, you initially need to call the SetEffectMaterial method, which configures the terrain effect. Then you set the terrain's vertex buffer, the index buffers, and
the vertex declaration on the graphics device. You use the vertex declaration to inform
the graphics device about the vertex format you're using, so that it can correctly process
the vertices:

```
// Set mesh vertex and index buffer
GraphicsDevice.Vertices[0].SetSource(vb, 0,
    VertexPositionNormalTangentBinormal.SizeInBytes);
GraphicsDevice.Indices = ib;

// Set the vertex declaration
GraphicsDevice.VertexDeclaration = new VertexDeclaration(GraphicsDevice,
    VertexPositionNormalTangentBinormal.VertexElements);
```

The next step is to begin the effects and go over all the effects' passes, drawing the terrain for each pass. To draw the terrain's mesh, you use the `DrawIndexedPrimitives` method of XNA's `GraphicsDevice`. You use this method because you're drawing a primitive that has indices. Following is the complete code for the `Draw` method from the `Terrain` class:

```
public override void Draw(GameTime time)
{
    // Configure TerrainEffect
    SetEffectMaterial();

    // Set mesh vertex and index buffer
    GraphicsDevice.Vertices[0].SetSource(vb, 0,
        VertexPositionNormalTangentBinormal.SizeInBytes);
    GraphicsDevice.Indices = ib;

    // Set the vertex declaration
    GraphicsDevice.VertexDeclaration = new VertexDeclaration(GraphicsDevice,
        VertexPositionNormalTangentBinormal.VertexElements);

    effect.Begin();
    // Loop through all effect passes
    foreach (EffectPass pass in effect.CurrentTechniquePasses)
    {
        pass.Begin();
        // Draw the mesh
        GraphicsDevice.DrawIndexedPrimitives(PrimitiveType.TriangleList,
            0, 0, numVertices, 0, numTriangles);
        pass.End();
    }
    effect.End();
}
```

Figure 10-10 shows the final result of the terrain rendering. Notice that the terrain surface is flat. However, the normal map used adds the detail of a stone pattern over the surface.

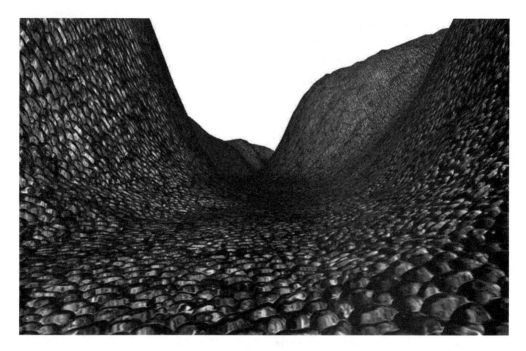

Figure 10-10. *Final result of the terrain rendering*

Querying the Terrain's Height

To guarantee that all scene objects remain over the terrain, you should be able to query the terrain's height at any position, and then position the objects over the terrain. You can get the height of a vertex in the terrain from the terrain's height map, and you can calculate the height of any position over the terrain from the terrain's vertices.

To query the height of the terrain at an arbitrary world position, you first need to calculate this position relative to the terrain's vertex grid. You can do this by subtracting the queried world's position from the initial terrain position, making sure to consider the terrain transformations such as translations. Then you need to know in which quadrant of the terrain grid the position you are querying is located, which you can do by dividing the calculated position (relative to the terrain) by the terrain's block scale.

Figure 10-11 shows an object in the world position (52, 48), where its position in the terrain grid is (1, 1). Notice that you aren't considering the object position over the Y axis (which represents its height over the terrain), because the terrain is constructed over the XZ plane, and the value you're looking for is relative to this axis.

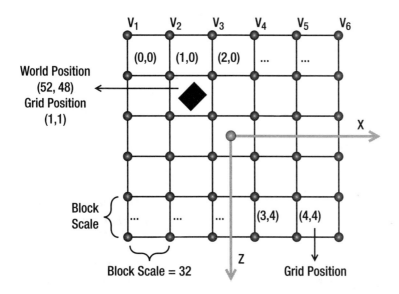

Figure 10-11. *Object position relative to the terrain grid*

The code to calculate the position of an object over the terrain grid follows:

```
// Get the position relative to the terrain grid
Vector2 positionInGrid = new Vector2(
    positionX - (StartPosition.X + Transformation.Translate.X),
    positionZ - (StartPosition.Y + Transformation.Translate.Z));

// Calculate the grid position
Vector2 blockPosition = new Vector2(
    (int)(positionInGrid.X / blockScale),
    (int)(positionInGrid.Y / blockScale));
```

After you calculate in which quadrant of the grid the position you are querying is, you should calculate in which triangle of this block it is. You can do this by calculating the position of the object inside the block and verifying if its position in the X axis is higher than its position in the Z axis. When the object's X position is higher than the Z position, the object will be found on the top triangle; otherwise, if the value is smaller the object will be found on the bottom triangle, as shown in Figure 10-12.

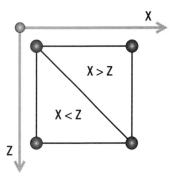

Figure 10-12. *A block in the terrain grid. If the X position inside the block is bigger than the Z position, the object is in the top triangle. Otherwise, the object is in the bottom triangle.*

After finding in which triangle the object is positioned, you can obtain the height of a position inside this triangle through a linear interpolation of the height of the triangle's vertices. Use the following code for the GetHeight method to calculate the height of a terrain's position:

```
private float GetHeight(float positionX, float positionZ)
{
    float height = -999999.0f;
    if (heightmap == null) return height;

    // Get the position relative to the terrain grid
    Vector2 positionInGrid = new Vector2(
        positionX - (StartPosition.X + Transformation.Translate.X),
        positionZ - (StartPosition.Y + Transformation.Translate.Z));

    // Calculate the grid position
    Vector2 blockPosition = new Vector2(
        (int)(positionInGrid.X / blockScale),
        (int)(positionInGrid.Y / blockScale));

    // Check if the object is inside the grid
    if (blockPosition.X >= 0 && blockPosition.X < (vertexCountX - 1) &&
        blockPosition.Y >= 0 && blockPosition.Y < (vertexCountZ - 1))
    {
        Vector2 blockOffset = new Vector2(
            blockPosition.X - (int)blockPosition.X,
            blockPosition.Y - (int)blockPosition.Y);
```

```
        // Get the height of the four vertices of the grid block
        int vertexIndex = (int)blockPosition.X +
            (int)blockPosition.Y * vertexCountX;
        float height1 = heightmap[vertexIndex + 1];
        float height2 = heightmap[vertexIndex];
        float height3 = heightmap[vertexIndex + vertexCountX + 1];
        float height4 = heightmap[vertexIndex + vertexCountX];

        // Top triangle
        float heightIncX, heightIncY;
        if (blockOffset.X > blockOffset.Y)
        {
            heightIncX = height1 - height2;
            heightIncY = height3 - height1;
        }
        // Bottom triangle
        else
        {
            heightIncX = height3 - height4;
            heightIncY = height4 - height2;
        }

        // Linear interpolation to find the height inside the triangle
        float lerpHeight = height2 + heightIncX * blockOffset.X +
            heightIncY * blockOffset.Y;
        height = lerpHeight * heightScale;
    }
    return height;
}
```

Notice that you use this method only to ensure that all scene objects are positioned over the terrain. To produce a realistic interaction between the objects and the terrain you would need to implement a physics system.

Ray and Terrain Collision

To detect when an object in the scene intercepts a part of the terrain, you need to create some collision test methods. One useful collision test is between a ray and the terrain. For example, if an object is moving in the scene, you can trace a ray in the direction in which this object is moving and get the distance between it and the terrain.

To check the ray and terrain collision, you'll do a collision test between the ray and the terrain's height map, instead of testing the ray against the terrain's mesh (many triangles). The collision test will be divided in two parts. In the first part, you'll do a linear search on the ray until you find a point outside (above) and another inside (below) the terrain. Then, you'll perform a binary search between these two points to find the exact collision point with the terrain. Figure 10-13 illustrates the linear search processes, where the nearest points outside and inside the terrain are found.

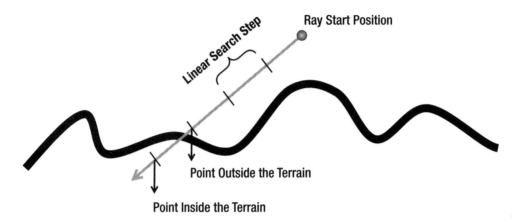

Figure 10-13. *Linear search used to find one point inside and another outside the terrain*

You can use the following code to perform the linear search on the terrain:

```
// A good ray step is half of the blockScale
Vector3 rayStep = ray.Direction * blockScale * 0.5f;
Vector3 rayStartPosition = ray.Position;

// Linear search - Loop until find a point inside and outside the terrain
Vector3 lastRayPosition = ray.Position;
ray.Position += rayStep;
float height = GetHeight(ray.Position);
while (ray.Position.Y > height && height >= 0)
{
    lastRayPosition = ray.Position;
    ray.Position += rayStep;
    height = GetHeight(ray.Position);
}
```

After the linear search, the lastRayPosition variable stores the position outside the terrain and the ray variable stores the position inside the terrain. You then need to make a binary search between these two points to find the closest point to the terrain. You make this search with a fixed number of steps, where 32 steps are enough for a good level of precision. The code for the binary search follows:

```
Vector3 startPosition = lastRayPosition;
Vector3 endPosition = ray.Position;

// Binary search with 32 steps. Try to find the exact collision point
for (int i = 0; i < 32; i++)
{
    // Binary search pass
    Vector3 middlePoint = (startPosition + endPosition) * 0.5f;
    if (middlePoint.Y < height) endPosition = middlePoint;
    else startPosition = middlePoint;
}

Vector3 collisionPoint = (startPosition + endPosition) * 0.5f;
```

You then create the Intersects method to check the intersection of a ray and the terrain. The Intersects method returns the distance between the ray's start point and the terrain's collision point, and if there is no collision with the terrain, the method will return null. Following is the code for the Intersects method of the Terrain class:

```
public float? Intersects(Ray ray)
{
    float? collisionDistance = null;
    Vector3 rayStep = ray.Direction * blockScale * 0.5f;
    Vector3 rayStartPosition = ray.Position;

    // Linear search - Loop until find a point inside and outside the terrain
    Vector3 lastRayPosition = ray.Position;
    ray.Position += rayStep;
    float height = GetHeight(ray.Position);
    while (ray.Position.Y > height && height >= 0)
    {
        lastRayPosition = ray.Position;
        ray.Position += rayStep;
        height = GetHeight(ray.Position);
    }

    // If the ray collides with the terrain
    if (height >= 0)
    {
```

```
        Vector3 startPosition = lastRayPosition;
        Vector3 endPosition = ray.Position;

        // Binary search. Find the exact collision point
        for (int i = 0; i < 32; i++)
        {
            // Binary search pass
            Vector3 middlePoint = (startPosition + endPosition) * 0.5f;
            if (middlePoint.Y < height) endPosition = middlePoint;
            else startPosition = middlePoint;
        }
        Vector3 collisionPoint = (startPosition + endPosition) * 0.5f;
        collisionDistance = Vector3.Distance(rayStartPosition, collisionPoint);
    }
    return collisionDistance;
}
```

Summary

In this chapter you learned all the steps needed to create a terrain from a height map and draw it. You first learned what height maps are and how to use them to represent the terrain. Then, you learned how to create a vertex grid to represent the terrain's mesh and how to use the height map values to change the height of the vertices of the grid. For each vertex in the vertex grid, you also learned how to calculate its attributes needed for multitexturing, lighting, and normal mapping. Finally, you learned how to create an effect for the terrain rendering, which uses multitexturing and normal mapping. Besides all this, you also learned how to create some auxiliary methods to query the height of a position over the terrain and check the collision between a ray and the terrain.

CHAPTER 11

■■■

Skeletal Animation

Although the game scenery is mainly composed of static objects, you might want to use some animated models for animated characters—the player and the nonplayable characters (NPCs)—in your game. You can create animated models in different ways. For example, in a racing game the car might be an animated model because its wheels rotate as the vehicle moves. You can easily reproduce this type of animation just by rotating the car's wheels over its axis. However, when you need to animate a character (running, jumping, falling, and so on), the animation process becomes more complex because you need to modify the character's mesh. Figure 11-1 shows the animation sequence of a character walking.

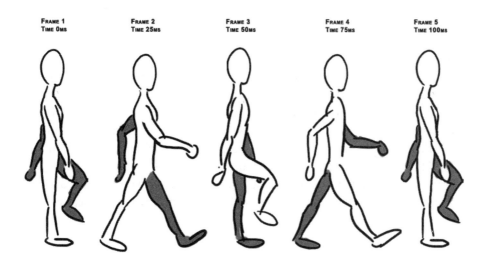

Figure 11-1. *In this animation of a character walking, the model's mesh has to be modified over each frame. Courtesy of Hugo Beyer (http://www.hugobeyer.com).*

The animation in Figure 11-1 is composed of five different frames (or keyframes), where each frame represents a different configuration of the character. Each animation frame also has a time, which defines when the model configuration needs to be changed.

Finally, to be able to loop through the animation, the first animation frame and the last animation frame must be the same frame or be in sequence.

Types of Animations

There are two main types of animation: keyframed animations and skeletal animations. Each type of animation is used in different situations and has its advantages and disadvantages.

Keyframed Animation

In keyframed animation, you store a static model mesh for each frame of the animation. If you were to animate the model in Figure 11-1, you would have to export four different static meshes and change the mesh that is drawn in each time frame. This animation is called *keyframed* because only the key frames of the animation are exported. For example, in the animation in Figure 11-1, you can have many intermediate frames between the first and second animation frame, which are used to make the animation smooth. However, you don't necessarily need to export them because you can obtain them by interpolating the first and second frame. For example, in a linear interpolation, the position of each vertex in the mesh is interpolated linearly between the first and second frame.

One of the advantages of the keyframed animation is that it's fast, because nothing needs to be calculated during the animation. All the animation frames are stored in memory, and during the animation you only need to change the model that is drawn each time. One of the disadvantages of this method is that it's necessary to store all the model meshes in memory so they're quickly drawn. If a model has hundreds of animation frames, it's necessary to store its mesh hundreds of times. In a scene with hundreds of animated models, where all of them share the same animation, the keyframed method can be useful. The use of keyframed animated models with XNA is simple, because XNA already has the classes needed to handle static models. Therefore, you can treat a keyframed animation model in XNA as an array of static models, using the Model class, for example.

Skeletal Animation

Another way to animate the model is through skeletal animation. In this process, you need to build a skeleton for the model, composed of some bones, and then connect every vertex of the mesh to a bone on that skeleton. Therefore, as the skeleton animates the mesh it's linked to, it animates too, following the skeleton's animation.

To build the model's mesh, skeleton, and animations, you can use different modeling tools that support skeletal (or bone) animation, such as 3ds Max, Maya, Blender, and others. After you create the model, you also need to export it to a format that supports skeletal animation. Among the model formats that XNA supports natively, the formats X (DirectX File) and FBX (Autodesk) support skeletal animation. Notice that the skeletal animation is also *keyframed*, meaning that only the key frames of the skeleton animations are exported. As in the keyframed animation, you can also interpolate the animation frames of the skeleton. Figure 11-2 illustrates a model with its mesh and skeleton.

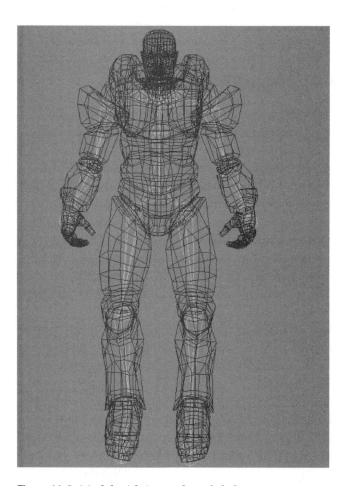

Figure 11-2. *Model with its mesh and skeleton*

Skeletal animation has more advantages over keyframed animation. It allows animations to be easily blended, allowing you to apply different animations over the model at the same time. For example, you could apply two different animations to the model in Figure 11-2, where one animation would make the model walk and another animation would make the model look around (rotating its neck). Skeletal animation also allows a bone from one object to be linked to a bone in another object. For example, if you have a character that wields a sword, you would connect the bone in the sword to the character's hand bone, which makes the sword move as the character's hand moves. Nowadays, skeletal animation is more widely used than keyframed animation. Keeping that in mind, we'll focus on skeletal animations.

XNA doesn't natively support skeletal animation. Although XNA's Content Pipeline is capable of importing models with skeletal animation, the default model processor is only capable of processing the model's mesh and skeleton, discarding the model's animation. In addition, the export format of the model's skeleton might not be adequate and optimized to be used during the animation process.

Skeleton and Bone Representation

Before we detail how to work with skeletal animation in XNA, it's important that you understand how the skeleton model is constructed and how its bones are represented and stored.

There are two different ways to store the model's skeleton. The first one uses bones and the second uses joints. For example, 3ds Max represents a skeleton using its bones, while Maya represents a skeleton using its joints. However, when the model is exported to an XNA-compatible format (X or FBX format) there is no difference between them and the skeleton is represented by its bones. In this chapter, you'll use bones to represent and store the skeleton, where each bone has an initial position and orientation, and the size of each bone is defined as the distance between its position and the position of a child bone. This bone representation creates the necessity of having an end bone (of zero size) to define the end of the skeleton.

The bone's orientation and position define its configuration. Figure 11-3 illustrates a skeleton's arm representation using bones. Notice that it is necessary to have an End Bone after the Hand Bone to define the hand bone's size and the end of the skeleton's arm.

The position and orientation of each bone is related to its ancestor. For example, the hand's orientation and position are defined according to the orientation and position defined by the forearm, which has its orientation and position defined by the upper arm, repeating the same process until the root bone is reached. With this concept, you can see that modifying any bone affects all the descendants of this bone. If the left shoulder bone was moved, all its descendants would be moved too.

To store the skeleton, you need to store the configuration (orientation and position) of every bone and the hierarchy of these bones inside the skeleton. The hierarchy is needed to calculate the absolute configuration of a bone at any given time. You can store the configuration of a bone as a matrix, and the skeleton hierarchy as a list with references to the ancestor of each bone.

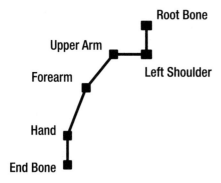

Figure 11-3. *Arm bones of a skeleton. The hierarchy begins in the Root Bone and the end is defined by the End Bone, where each bone is a descendent of the previous bone. All the bones begin at the position shown by a square, and they end at the next bone's starting point (the following square).*

Skeletal Animation in XNA

XNA has a well-defined Content Pipeline, which is separated in different layers and provides importers, processors, compilers (content writers), and readers (content readers) for the game assets. Because XNA's Content Pipeline does not have full support for models with skeletal animation, you need to extend the Content Pipeline, adding support for skeletal animation. Notice that the Content Pipeline partially supports skeletal animation, because it can import the skeletal animation data from the X and FBX files, but it doesn't process all the skeletal animation data that is imported. Figure 11-4 shows a simplified diagram of the Content Pipeline classes that are used to import, process, compile, and read model files.

First, the models are imported by their respective content importer, where each content importer converts the input model's data to an XNA document object model (DOM) format. In this way, after the models have been imported, they are all in the same format and can be processed by their respective content processor, the ModelProcessor. The output of the model importers is a root NodeContent object, which describe a graphics type that has its own coordinate system and can have children. Two classes extend the NodeContent class: MeshContent and BoneContent. So, the root NodeContent object output from a model importer might have some NodeContent, MeshContent, and BoneContent children.

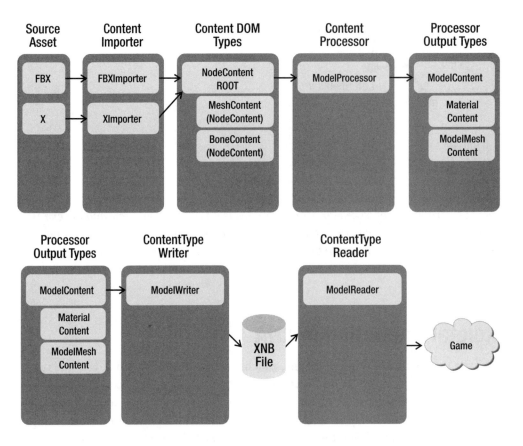

Figure 11-4. *The XNA Content Pipeline—classes used to import, process, compile, and read the game models*

The ModelProcessor receives as a parameter the root NodeContent object, output by the model importer, and returns a ModelContent object. The ModelContent object returned by the ModelProcessor has the processed model data, which needs to be stored into an XNB binary file. To be able to store the ModelContent object into an XNB file, the ModelContent and each object inside of it must have its own ContentTypeWriter. The ContentTypeWriter defines how the data of each object is written into the XNB file. Finally, at runtime the ContentManager uses a ContentTypeReader for each object to read its data from the XNB binary file and return a Model object.

To add support for skeletal animation in XNA, you need to extend the default model processor, creating a new one capable of processing and storing the model's skeleton and animations. Besides that, you need to create some classes to store the skeletal animation data (model's skeleton and animations) and some ContentTypeWriter and ContentTypeReader classes to write and read this data.

Figure 11-5 shows the classes that you need to create to extend the Content Pipeline, adding support to models with skeletal animation. The classes that you need to create are marked in red in Figure 11-5.

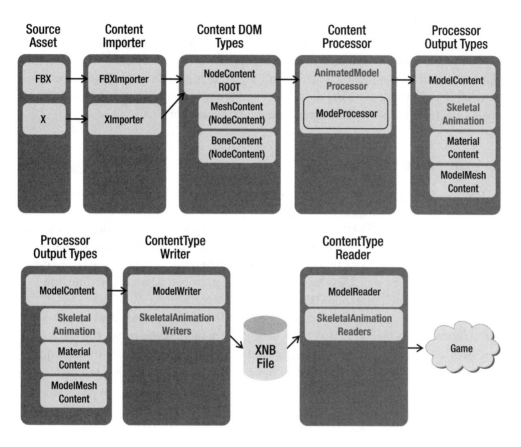

Figure 11-5. *An extension of the Content Pipeline shown in Figure 11-4, which supports models with skeletal animation*

You'll create the classes used to store the skeletal animation data in a separate library, because they'll be used by the animated model processor to store the skeletal animation data and by the game application to load this data at runtime. To store the skeletal animation classes, create a new Windows Game Library project named AnimationModelContentWin. The model processor will use the classes of this library on the Windows platform to store the skeletal animation data. If your game was targeted to the Windows platform, this library would also be used to load the skeletal animation data in runtime.

If you're targeting the Xbox 360, you need to create one more project: an Xbox 360 Game Library named AnimationModelContentXbox. This library contains the same files as the AnimationModelContentWin library, but Xbox 360 applications use it to load the skeletal animation at runtime. You need the `AnimationModelContentWin` project even if you're targeting the Xbox 360 platform, because the original model files are imported and processed on the Windows platform, needing a Windows library to store the model data.

You'll create three different classes to store the skeletal animation data: `Keyframe`, `AnimationData`, and `AnimatedModelData`. The `Keyframe` class stores an animation frame of a skeletal animation, where each animation frame stores a new configuration for a bone in the skeleton. The `AnimationData` class stores an array of keyframes, which compose a complete animation (such as running, jumping, and so on). Finally, the `AnimatedModelData` class stores the model skeleton (bones and hierarchy) and an array of type `AnimatedModelData`, containing all the model animations.

Keyframe Class

The `Keyframe` class is responsible for storing an animation frame of a bone in the skeleton. An animation frame must have a reference for the animated bone, the new configuration (position and orientation) of the referenced bone, and the time in which this new configuration should be applied. Notice that you use the keyframes to modify the original bone configuration, changing its current configuration to a new one. You store the bone configuration as a matrix using XNA's `Matrix` class, and you store the animation time (the time in which this keyframe should be applied) as a `TimeSpan`.

In the `AnimatedModelData` class you store the model's skeleton as an array of bones, which is constructed through a depth traverse of the model's skeleton. So, you can store the reference for the bone that will be animated as an integer that represents the index of the bone in the `bones` array of the `AnimatedModelData` class. The `Keyframe` class code follows:

```
public class Keyframe : IComparable
{
    int boneIndex;
    TimeSpan time;
    Matrix transform;

    // Properties...
    public TimeSpan Time
    {
        get { return time; }
        set { time = value; }
    }

    public int Bone
    {
        get { return boneIndex; }
```

```
        set { boneIndex = value; }
    }
    public Matrix Transform
    {
        get { return transform; }
        set { transform = value; }
    }

    public Keyframe(TimeSpan time, int boneIndex, Matrix transform)
    {
        this.time = time;
        this.boneIndex = boneIndex;
        this.transform = transform;
    }

    public int CompareTo(object obj)
    {
        Keyframe keyframe = obj as Keyframe;
        if (obj == null)
            throw new ArgumentException("Object is not a Keyframe.");

        return time.CompareTo(keyframe.Time);
    }
}
```

In the Keyframe class, you're implementing the interface IComparable to be able to compare Keyframe objects. The Keyframe objects are compared based on their time: their time attribute. You'll use this comparison further to sort the keyframes according to their time frame.

AnimationData Class

The AnimationData class is responsible for storing a complete model animation (such as running, jumping, and so on). You store each animation as an array of type Keyframe, and besides its keyframes you also store other useful data such as the animation name and duration. The code for the AnimationData class follows:

```
public class AnimationData
{
    string name;
    TimeSpan duration;
    Keyframe[] keyframes;
```

```
    public string Name
    {
        get { return name; }
        set { name = value; }
    }

    public TimeSpan Duration
    {
        get { return duration; }
        set { duration = value; }
    }

    public Keyframe[] Keyframes
    {
        get { return keyframes; }
        set { keyframes = value; }
    }

    public AnimationData(string name, TimeSpan duration,
        Keyframe[] keyframes)
    {
        this.name = name;
        this.duration = duration;
        this.keyframes = keyframes;
    }
}
```

AnimatedModelData Class

The AnimatedModelData class is responsible for storing the model's skeleton and animations. You store the model skeleton as an array of bones, where each bone is represented as a matrix. You construct the bone array through a depth traverse of the model's skeleton. The depth traversal starts in the root bone of the skeleton and goes to the deepest bone. When it finds the deepest bone in a path, the traversal comes back and tries to find another possible path, then travels to the deepest bone again. For example, a depth traverse of the hierarchy of Figure 11-6 returns the array Root Bone, Neck, Left Shoulder, Left Forearm, Left Hand, Left End Bone, Right Shoulder, Right Forearm, Right Hand, and Right End Bone.

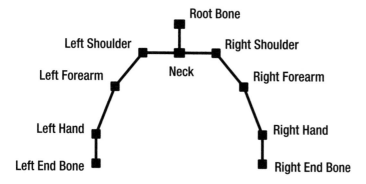

Figure 11-6. *An example of a skeleton hierarchy*

You store the skeleton's bones in its *bind pose* configuration. The bind pose is the pose in which the bones were linked to the model's mesh and is the starting pose of any animation. When the model is not being animated or when the animation starts, all the model's bones are found in the bind pose.

In the AnimatedModelData class, you should create two attributes of type XNA Matrix array for storing the skeleton's bones, one attribute of type int array for storing the skeleton's bones hierarchy, and one attribute of type AnimationData array for storing the model's animation. The AnimatedModelData class code follows:

```
public class AnimatedModelData
{
    Matrix[] bonesBindPose;
    Matrix[] bonesInverseBindPose;
    int[] bonesParent;

    AnimationData[] animations;

    // Properties ...
    public int[] BonesParent
    {
        get { return bonesParent; }
        set { bonesParent = value; }
    }

    public Matrix[] BonesBindPose
    {
        get { return bonesBindPose; }
        set { bonesBindPose = value; }
    }
```

```
public Matrix[] BonesInverseBindPose
{
    get { return bonesInverseBindPose; }
    set { bonesInverseBindPose = value; }
}

public AnimationData[] Animations
{
    get { return animations; }
    set { animations = value; }
}

public AnimatedModelData(Matrix[] bonesBindPose,
    Matrix[] bonesInverseBindPose, int[] bonesParent,
    AnimationData[] animations)
{
    this.bonesParent = bonesParent;
    this.bonesBindPose = bonesBindPose;
    this.bonesInverseBindPose = bonesInverseBindPose;
    this.animations = animations;
}
}
```

In the AnimatedModelData class, the bonesBindPose attribute stores an array containing the local configuration (related to its ancestor) of each skeleton's bone in its bind pose, the bonesInverseBindPose attribute stores an array containing the inverse absolute configuration (not related to its ancestor) of each skeleton's bone in its bind pose, and the bonesParent attribute stores the index of the parent of each bone. Finally, the animations attribute stores the model's animations.

You use the inverse absolute configuration of a bone to transform the vertices that are linked to this bone from its default coordinate system (the model coordinate system) to the coordinate system of this bone, needed to animate (transform) the vertices. We'll explain this process in more detail in the section "Skeletal Animation Equations."

Animated Model Processor

Now you need to create a new model processor that extends the default XNA model processor. You'll use this new processor to process the animated models, extract their skeleton and animations, and store them as an AnimatedModelData object.

To create the new model processor you should create a new Content Pipeline Extension Library project named AnimatedModelProcessorWin. The Content Pipeline Extension

Library project comes with a new content processor class, and automatically adds the Content Pipeline assembly (Microsoft.Xna.Framework.Content.Pipeline) to the project. Because you're going to use the AnimatedModelContentWin library (that you created in the last section) to store the animation data, you need to add its assembly to the project too. Following is the code for the new content processor class that is created with the Content Pipeline Extension project:

```
[ContentProcessor]
public class ContentProcessor1 : ContentProcessor<TInput, TOutput>
{
    public override TOutput Process(TInput input,
        ContentProcessorContext context)
    {
        // TODO
        throw new NotImplementedException();
    }
}
```

The default content processor class extends the ContentProcessor class, which is the base class for any Content Pipeline processor, and it's used to process an object of the type TInput outputting a new object of the type TOutput. Because you aren't interested in creating a new content processor but in extending the features of an existing one, you must extend an existing content processor instead of the ContentProcessor class. In this case, you'll extend XNA's ModelProcessor class, which is the default model processor class. Also, you're going to rename your new content processor class to AnimatedModelProcessor. Following is the base structure of your new model processor—the AnimatedModelProcessor class:

```
[ContentProcessor]
public class AnimatedModelProcessor : ModelProcessor
{
    public static string TEXTURES_PATH = "Textures/";
    public static string EFFECTS_PATH = "Effects/";
    public static string EFFECT_FILENAME = "AnimatedModel.fx";

    public override ModelContent Process(NodeContent input,
            ContentProcessorContext context)
    {
        ...
    }
```

```
        protected override MaterialContent ConvertMaterial(
            MaterialContent material, ContentProcessorContext context)
        {
            ...
        }
}
```

The ModelProcessor class has many methods that you can overwrite, where you only need to overwrite the Process and ConvertMaterial methods to process the animated models. The main method called to process a model is the Process method. This method needs to convert a NodeContent object—which has the meshes, skeleton, and animations of the model—into a ModelContent object—which stores the data for an XNA Model object. Besides the Process method, the ConvertMaterial method is called to process the model's materials.

Overwriting the Default Process Method

In this section you'll overwrite the Process method of the ModelProcessor class, which is called to process the model. Also, you'll create two new methods to extract the model's skeleton and animations: the ExtractSkeletonAndAnimations method and the ExtractAnimations method, where the ExtractAnimations method is called inside the ExtractSkeletonAndAnimations method. Following is the code for the overwritten Process method:

```
public override ModelContent Process(NodeContent input,
    ContentProcessorContext context)
{
    // Process the model with the default processor
    ModelContent model = base.Process(input, context);

    // Now extract the model skeleton and all its animations
    AnimatedModelData animatedModelData =
        ExtractSkeletonAndAnimations(input, context);

    // Stores the skeletal animation data in the model
    Dictionary<string, object> dictionary = new Dictionary<string, object>();
    dictionary.Add("AnimatedModelData", animatedModelData);
    model.Tag = dictionary;

    return model;
}
```

At the beginning of the Process method, you call the Process method of the base class, the ModelProcessor. Then you call the ExtractSkeletonAndAnimations method, which processes the input NodeContent and returns an AnimatedModelData object containing the model's skeleton and animations. Finally, you create a dictionary that maps a string into an object, add the AnimatedModelData to this dictionary, and set it in the Tag property of the resulting ModelContent object. XNA's Model class has a Tag property that enables custom user data to be added to the model. Using a dictionary as the Tag property, you can add many different custom objects to XNA's Model class, and query for any of them at runtime using a string.

Notice that the data you set in the Tag property of the ModelContent object is stored together with the model data in a binary XNB file. This data is retrieved when the model is loaded using the content manager.

Extracting the Model's Skeleton

The ExtractSkeletonAndAnimations method receives the root NodeContent object as input, which might have MeshContent and BoneContent objects as its children, as described before. To extract the model's skeleton, you first need to find the root bone of the skeleton inside the root NodeContent, then you need to depth traverse the skeleton, creating a list of bones. XNA's MeshHelper class provides some methods to help you in this process:

```
// Find the root bone node
BoneContent skeleton = MeshHelper.FindSkeleton(input);
// Transform the hierarchy in a list (depth traversal)
IList<BoneContent> boneList = MeshHelper.FlattenSkeleton(skeleton);
```

You can find the root bone of the skeleton using the FindSkeleton method of the MeshHelper class. Then you need to transform the skeleton tree into a list, using a deep search. You do this using the FlattenSkeleton method of the MeshHelper class. The result is a list of bones, where each bone is an object of the BoneContent class. Notice that the bones in this list are in the same order as they are indexed by the mesh's vertices.

For each bone in the created list, you want to store its local configuration in the bind pose, its inverse absolute configuration in the bind pose, and the index of its parent. You can read the local and absolute configuration of a bone from the Transform and AbsoluteTransform properties of the BoneContent objects, and you can calculate the inverse absolute configuration of the bone using the Invert method of XNA's Matrix class:

```
bonesBindPose[i] = boneList[i].Transform;
bonesInverseBindPose[i] = Matrix.Invert(boneList[i].AbsoluteTransform);
```

Following is the complete code for the ExtractSkeletonAndAnimations method:

```
private AnimatedModelData ExtractSkeletonAndAnimations(NodeContent input,
    ContentProcessorContext context)
{
    // Find the root bone node
    BoneContent skeleton = MeshHelper.FindSkeleton(input);

    // Transform the hierarchy in a list (depth traversal)
    IList<BoneContent> boneList =
        MeshHelper.FlattenSkeleton(skeleton);
    context.Logger.LogImportantMessage("{0} bones found.",
        boneList.Count);

    // Create skeleton bind pose, inverse bind pose, and parent array
    Matrix[] bonesBindPose = new Matrix[boneList.Count];
    Matrix[] bonesInverseBindPose = new Matrix[boneList.Count];
    int[] bonesParentIndex = new int[boneList.Count];
    List<string> boneNameList = new List<string>(boneList.Count);

    // Extract and store the data needed from the bone list
    for (int i = 0; i < boneList.Count; i++)
    {
        bonesBindPose[i] = boneList[i].Transform;
        bonesInverseBindPose[i] =
            Matrix.Invert(boneList[i].AbsoluteTransform);
        int parentIndex =
            boneNameList.IndexOf(boneList[i].Parent.Name);
        bonesParentIndex[i] = parentIndex;
        boneNameList.Add(boneList[i].Name);
    }

    // Extract all animations
    AnimationData[] animations = ExtractAnimations(
        skeleton.Animations, boneNameList, context);

    return new AnimatedModelData(bonesBindPose, bonesInverseBindPose,
        bonesParentIndex, animations);
}
```

After extracting the model's skeleton, you should call the ExtractAnimations method to extract the model's animations.

Extracting the Model's Animation

All the model's animations are stored as an animation dictionary that maps a string containing the animation name to an AnimationContent object, containing the animation data. You can access the animation dictionary from the Animations property of the root node of type BoneContent of the model's skeleton. Note that the Content Pipeline has its own classes to store the model's animation data: the AnimationContent, AnimationChannel, and AnimationKeyframe classes. The AnimationContent class stores a complete model animation as an array of AnimationChannel objects, where each AnimationChannel object stores the animation of a single bone as an array of AnimationKeyframe objects. Also, XNA's AnimationContent class stores the animation of each bone separately, while you are storing them together in a single array.

You can extract the model's animations going over all the AnimationContent objects of the animation dictionary, where for each animation found you need to go over all their bone channels (which can be accessed from the Channels property), extracting all the animation keyframes (which can be accessed from the Keyframes property). The code for the ExtractAnimations method follows:

```
private AnimationData[] ExtractAnimations(
    AnimationContentDictionary animationDictionary, List<string> boneNameList,
    ContentProcessorContext context)
{
    context.Logger.LogImportantMessage("{0} animations found.",
        animationDictionary.Count);

    AnimationData[] animations = new
        AnimationData[animationDictionary.Count];

    int count = 0;
    foreach (AnimationContent animationContent in animationDictionary.Values)
    {
        // Store all keyframes of the animation
        List<Keyframe> keyframes = new List<Keyframe>();

        // Go through all animation channels
        // Each bone has its own channel
        foreach (string animationKey in animationContent.Channels.Keys)
        {
            AnimationChannel animationChannel =
                animationContent.Channels[animationKey];
            int boneIndex = boneNameList.IndexOf(animationKey);
```

```
                foreach (AnimationKeyframe keyframe in animationChannel)
                    keyframes.Add(new Keyframe(
                        keyframe.Time, boneIndex, keyframe.Transform));
            }

            // Sort all animation frames by time
            keyframes.Sort();
            animations[count++] = new AnimationData(animationContent.Name,
                animationContent.Duration, keyframes.ToArray());
        }

        return animations;
}
```

After all the keyframes of an animation have been stored, you need to sort them. As the keyframes are stored in a List, you can use the Sort method to sort them. Remember that you had previously implemented the IComparable interface in the Keyframe class, making the keyframes sorted by their time attribute.

Now you have the model's skeleton and animations extracted and stored in a friendly format, ready to be written to a binary XNB file.

■**Note** You can find more information about the List generic class and IComparable interface in C# help files, since they are provided by .NET Framework, not by XNA.

Reading and Writing Custom User Data

The AnimatedModelProcessor that you created stores the model's skeletal animation data using some custom user objects (AnimatedModelData, AnimationData, and Keyframe classes). The Content Pipeline needs to read and write these objects from a binary file, but the Content Pipeline doesn't know how to read or write your custom objects.

To define how the skeletal animation data should be read and written to a binary file, you must create a content type reader and a content type writer for each class you created to store the skeletal animation data. In this case, you need to create a new content type reader and a new content type writer for the AnimatedModelData, AnimationData, and Keyframe classes. You can create content type readers and writers by extending XNA's ContentTypeReader and ContentTypeWriter classes.

Content Type Writer

To create the content type writer you should add a new Content Type Writer item named
AnimatedModelDataWriter to the AnimatedModelProcessorWin project. The content type
writer classes only needed to be added to the model processor project. You'll add three
new classes to the content type writer file: the KeyframeWriter, AnimationDataWriter, and
AnimatedModelDataWriter classes, which are used to write the data for the Keyframe,
AnimationData, and AnimatedModelData classes. Each of these classes needs to extend the
ContentTypeWriter class and overwrite its Write method.

The Write method of the ContentTypeWriter class receives two parameters. The first
one is a ContentWriter, used to write the object's data into the binary file, and the second
is the object to be written. Inside the Write method, you must write all the attributes of
the class using the ContentWriter object. Note that the order in which the objects are
written in the binary file is important, and they must be the same order in which they
are read. Following is the code for the KeyframeWriter, AnimationDataWriter, and
AnimatedModelDataWriter classes:

```
[ContentTypeWriter]
public class KeyframeWriter : ContentTypeWriter<Keyframe>
{
    protected override void Write(ContentWriter output, Keyframe value)
    {
        output.WriteObject(value.Time);
        output.Write(value.Bone);
        output.Write(value.Transform);
    }

    public override string GetRuntimeReader(TargetPlatform targetPlatform)
    {
        return typeof(KeyframeReader).AssemblyQualifiedName;
    }
}


[ContentTypeWriter]
public class AnimationDataWriter : ContentTypeWriter<AnimationData>
{
    protected override void Write(ContentWriter output, AnimationData value)
    {
        output.Write(value.Name);
        output.WriteObject(value.Duration);
        output.WriteObject(value.Keyframes);
    }
```

```
        public override string GetRuntimeReader(TargetPlatform targetPlatform)
        {
            return typeof(AnimationDataReader).AssemblyQualifiedName;
        }
    }


    [ContentTypeWriter]
    public class AnimatedModelDataWriter : ContentTypeWriter<AnimatedModelData>
    {
        protected override void Write(ContentWriter output, AnimatedModelData value)
        {
            output.WriteObject(value.BonesBindPose);
            output.WriteObject(value.BonesInverseBindPose);
            output.WriteObject(value.BonesParent);
            output.WriteObject(value.Animations);
        }

        public override string GetRuntimeReader(TargetPlatform targetPlatform)
        {
            return typeof(AnimatedModelDataReader).AssemblyQualifiedName;
        }
    }
```

Content Type Reader

To create the content type reader you should add a new Content Type Reader item named AnimatedModelDataReader to the AnimatedModelContentWin project. Different from the content type writer classes, the game application needs the content type reader classes to load the animation data at runtime.

You need to create three new classes—the KeyframeReader, AnimationDataReader, and AnimatedModelDataReader classes—which are used to read the data of the Keyframe, AnimationData, and AnimatedModelData classes. Each of these classes needs to extend the ContentTypeReader class and overwrite the Read method.

The Read method of the ContentTypeReader class receives two parameters. The first one is a ContentReader, used to read the object's data from the binary file, and the second parameter is a reference for an existing instance of the object. The second parameter will be always null because you're creating the object. Again, notice that inside the Read method the objects must be read in the same order they were written. Following is the code for the KeyframeReader, AnimationDataReader, and AnimatedModelDataReader classes:

```
public class KeyframeReader : ContentTypeReader<Keyframe>
{
    protected override Keyframe Read(ContentReader input,
        Keyframe existingInstance)
    {
        TimeSpan time = input.ReadObject<TimeSpan>();
        int boneIndex = input.ReadInt32();
        Matrix transform = input.ReadMatrix();

        return new Keyframe(time, boneIndex, transform);
    }
}


public class AnimationDataReader : ContentTypeReader<AnimationData>
{
    protected override AnimationData Read(ContentReader input,
        AnimationData existingInstance)
    {
        string name = input.ReadString();
        TimeSpan duration = input.ReadObject<TimeSpan>();
        Keyframe[] keyframes = input.ReadObject<Keyframe[]>();

        return new AnimationData(name, duration, keyframes);
    }
}


public class AnimatedModelDataReader :
    ContentTypeReader<AnimatedModelData>
{
    protected override AnimatedModelData Read(ContentReader input,
        AnimatedModelData existingInstance)
    {
        Matrix[] bonesBindPose = input.ReadObject<Matrix[]>();
        Matrix[] bonesInverseBindPose = input.ReadObject<Matrix[]>();
        int[] bonesParent = input.ReadObject<int[]>();
        AnimationData[] animations =
            input.ReadObject<AnimationData[]>();

        return new AnimatedModelData(bonesBindPose,
            bonesInverseBindPose, bonesParent, animations);
    }
}
```

AnimatedModel Class

In this section you'll create the class used to handle the skeletal animation model at runtime, named `AnimatedModel`. This class will have methods to load an animated model, play and update an animation, and draw the model. You'll begin constructing the `AnimatedModel` class by declaring its attributes.

The animated model is loaded as an XNA `Model` object, which has a dictionary containing an `AnimatedModelData` object that you can access from its `Tag` property. In this way, the `Model` class contains the model's mesh and effects, while the `AnimatedModelData` class contains the model's skeleton and animations. You declare the `model` attribute of type `Model` and the `animatedModel` attribute of type `AnimatedModelData` to store the model data, and you store the model transformation (translate/rotate/scale) separately in an attribute of type `Transformation`.

```
Model model;
AnimatedModelData animatedModelData;
Transformation transformation;
```

You still need to declare some attributes to handle how the animations are reproduced. You need to store the current animation that is being played, as well as the current frame and time of this animation. You declare the `activeAnimation` attribute to store the current animation that is being played, and the `activeAnimationKeyframeIndex` and `activeAnimationTime` attributes to store the current animation frame and time respectively:

```
AnimationData activeAnimation;
int activeAnimationKeyframe;
TimeSpan activeAnimationTime;
```

You need to declare two other attributes to be able to configure the animation speed and enable animation looping—the `enableAnimationLoop` attribute and the `animationSpeed` attribute:

```
bool enableAnimationLoop;
float animationSpeed;
```

While the model is being animated, you use some temporary matrix arrays to calculate the final configuration of the skeleton's bones. You declare the `bones` attribute to store the local configuration of each bone, because the bones' configurations are modified as an animation is being played. You also declare the `bonesAbsolute` attribute to store the absolute configuration of each bone, calculated using the `bones` array and needed to animate the model at runtime. Finally, you declare the `bonesAnimation` attribute to store the final transformation of each bone, which combines the transformation needed to put the vertices in the coordinate system of the bone and animate them using the absolute configuration of each bone. We'll explain the skeletal animation in more detail in the section "Skeletal Animation Equations."

```
Matrix[] bones;
Matrix[] bonesAbsolute;
Matrix[] bonesAnimation;
```

To be able to apply custom transformation over the bones, you also declare another matrix array. You use these custom transformations to modify the skeleton's bones independently of the animation that is being played. For example, you could apply a custom rotation over the neck bone of a character's skeleton:

```
Matrix[] bonesTransform;
```

Last, you need to declare two attributes to store the animated model effect and material:

```
AnimatedModelEffect animatedModelEffect;
LightMaterial lightMaterial;
```

You create the `AnimatedModelEffect` class to encapsulate the animated model effect, and use the `LightMaterial` class, which you created in Chapter 8, to configure it.

Loading an Animated Model

The animated model is stored as an XNA `Model`, so the first step to load it is to load an XNA `Model` using the content manager. Then, you need to check if the loaded model is a valid animated model—whether it contains a dictionary with an `AnimatedModelData` object as the model's `Tag` property:

```
model = Game.Content.Load<Model>(
    GameAssetsPath.MODELS_PATH + modelFileName);

// Get the dictionary
Dictionary<string, object> modelTag =
    (Dictionary<string, object>)model.Tag;
if (modelTag == null)
    throw new InvalidOperationException(
        "This is not a valid animated model.");

// Get the AnimatedModelData from the dictionary
if (modelTag.ContainsKey("AnimatedModelData"))
    animatedModelData = (AnimatedModelData)
        modelTag["AnimatedModelData"];
```

```
else
    throw new InvalidOperationException(
        "This is not a valid animated model.");
```

After loading the model, you should initialize some variables used to configure and reproduce the model's animations. The default model animation is set as the first animation in the animations array of the AnimatedModelData object, and is stored in the activeAnimation attribute:

```
if (animatedModelData.Animations.Length > 0)
    activeAnimation = animatedModelData.Animations[0];
```

The current animation keyframe and time are stored respectively in the activeAnimationKeyframe and activeAnimationTime attributes. Last, you configure the animation speed through the animationSpeed attribute:

```
// Default animation configuration
animationSpeed = 1.0f;
activeAnimationKeyframe = 0;
activeAnimationTime = TimeSpan.Zero;
```

While the model is being animated, it uses some temporary matrix arrays to calculate the final configuration of each bone. You need to create these matrix arrays here, and their size needs to be equal to the number of bones in the model's skeleton. You should initialize the bones array with the bones' configuration stored in the AnimatedModelData, and the bonesTranformation with the identity matrix:

```
// Temporary matrices used to animate the bones
bones = new Matrix[animatedModelData.BonesBindPose.Length];
bonesAbsolute = new Matrix[animatedModelData.BonesBindPose.Length];
bonesAnimation = new Matrix[animatedModelData.BonesBindPose.Length];

// Used to apply custom transformation over the bones
bonesTransform = new Matrix[animatedModelData.BonesBindPose.Length];

for (int i = 0; i < bones.Length; i++)
{
    bones[i] = animatedModelData.BonesBindPose[i];
    bonesTransform[i] = Matrix.Identity;
}
```

Finally, you get the animated model effect of the model, and encapsulate it in an AnimatedModelEffect:

```
// Get the animated model effect - Shared by all meshes
animatedModelEffect = new AnimatedModelEffect(model.Meshes[0].Effects[0]);
// Create a default material
lightMaterial = new LightMaterial();
```

Note that the effect used to render the model is shared by all the model's meshes. Following is the complete code for the Load method of the AnimatedModel class:

```
public void Load(string modelFileName)
{
    if (!isInitialized)
        Initialize();

    model = Game.Content.Load<Model>(
        GameAssetsPath.MODELS_PATH + modelFileName);

    // Get the dictionary
    Dictionary<string, object> modelTag =
        (Dictionary<string, object>)model.Tag;
    if (modelTag == null) throw new InvalidOperationException(
        "This is not a valid animated model.");

    // Get the AnimatedModelData from the dictionary
    if (modelTag.ContainsKey("AnimatedModelData"))
        animatedModelData = (AnimatedModelData)
            modelTag["AnimatedModelData"];
    else
        throw new InvalidOperationException(
            "This is not a valid animated model.");

    // Default animation
    animationSpeed = 1.0f;
    activeAnimationKeyframe = 0;
    activeAnimationTime = TimeSpan.Zero;
    if (animatedModelData.Animations.Length > 0)
        activeAnimation = animatedModelData.Animations[0];

    // Temporary matrices used to animate the bones
    bones = new Matrix[animatedModelData.BonesBindPose.Length];
    bonesAbsolute = new
        Matrix[animatedModelData.BonesBindPose.Length];
    bonesAnimation = new
        Matrix[animatedModelData.BonesBindPose.Length];
```

```
    // Used to apply custom transformation over the bones
    bonesTransform = new
        Matrix[animatedModelData.BonesBindPose.Length];

    for (int i = 0; i < bones.Length; i++)
    {
        bones[i] = animatedModelData.BonesBindPose[i];
        bonesTransform[i] = Matrix.Identity;
    }

    // Get the animated model effect - Shared by all meshes
    animatedModelEffect = new AnimatedModelEffect(model.Meshes[0].Effects[0]);
    // Create a default material
    lightMaterial = new LightMaterial();
}
```

Skeletal Animation Equations

In this section you'll review some concepts and mathematical equations used in the skeletal animation. A skeletal animation is made of many keyframes, where each keyframe stores the configuration of a bone (its orientation and position) and the time frame in which this bone needs to be animated. At every time interval, you use one or more keyframes to alter the configuration of the skeleton's bones. Figure 11-7 illustrates an animation in the skeleton shown in Figure 11-3, where the Left Shoulder bone has its orientation changed, affecting all the other bones.

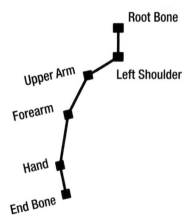

Figure 11-7. *Left Shoulder bone animation of the original skeleton shown in Figure 11-3. Notice that all the descendant bones have their configuration altered.*

To achieve the result in Figure 11-7, all you have to do is store a keyframe animation for the Left Shoulder bone. Although the configurations of all the Left Shoulder children have been changed, they are still the same relation to the Left Shoulder. In other words, you don't need to store the new configuration of the Left Shoulder children, because you can calculate them based on the new Left Shoulder configuration. So, when you need to update the model, you should calculate the absolute configuration of every bone and then transform the mesh's vertices using these bones. In the following sections we present some mathematical equations used to transform the model's mesh as the model is being animated. You'll further implement and use these mathematical equations to update and draw the model. To take advantage of the GPU, you'll implement some of these equations in the animated model's effects.

Transforming a Mesh's Vertex

Every vertex of the model contains the information about which bones affect its position, and the influence of these bones over the vertex. You can calculate the final position of a mesh's vertex, which is influenced by just one bone, with the following equation:

$$P_F = P'_0 \; [Bone \cdot W]$$

In the preceding equation, P_F is the vertex's final position, P'_0 is the vertex's initial position, Bone is the matrix that contains the absolute configuration of the bone that influences the vertex, and W is the weight of the influence of this bone over the vertex. Because the vertex is influenced by just one bone, the weight should be 1.0 (equivalent to 100 percent). This equation shows how you should calculate the vertex's final position: transform the vertex's initial position by the matrix that contains the bone's absolute configuration.

The vertex's initial position used in the preceding equation must be in the same coordinate system of the bone that is used to transform it, in its bind pose. Remember that when the vertices are linked to the skeleton's bones, all the bones are found in the bind pose position and all bone animations are applied over the initial bind pose of the skeleton. You can transform the vertex's initial position to the bone's bind pose coordinate system by multiplying the vertex's position by the inverse bone matrix, as shown in the following equation:

$$P'_0 = P_0 \; [Bone^{-1}_{BindPose}]$$

In the preceding equation, P'_0 is the initial position of the vertex in the bone's bind pose coordinate system, P_0 is the vertex position in the object coordinates system, and $Bone^{-1}_{BindPose}$ is the inverse matrix of the bone's absolute configuration in its bind pose. To place the vertex in the bone's coordinate system, you just have to multiply it by the inversed matrix of the bone in the bind pose. Using the two preceding equations, you can animate all the vertices of the mesh's model using its skeleton.

Combining Bone Transformations

The first equation in the preceding section doesn't allow more than one bone to affect a vertex, but in many situations you need a few different bones to affect a vertex. To calculate the final position of a vertex that is influenced by more than one bone, you need to calculate the final position of this vertex for each bone that influences it. Then you can calculate the vertex's final position by a sum of the vertex's final positions that you previously calculated. The following equation shows the calculation of the final position of a vertex that is affected by many bones:

$$P_F = \sum_{i=0}^{n-1} P'_0 \; [Bone_i \cdot W_i]$$

$$\sum_{i=0}^{n-1} W_i = 1$$

Notice that the sum of the weights used to transform the vertices in the preceding figure must equal 1. Finally, the following equation shows the complete equation used to transform the mesh's vertices:

$$P_F = P_0 \sum_{i=0}^{n-1} [Bone_{BindPose}^{-1} \cdot Bone_i \cdot W_i]$$

$$\sum_{i=0}^{n-1} W_i = 1$$

Notice that in the preceding equation you first calculate the average sum of the matrices used to transform the vertex, then the vertex is transformed once.

Animating the Model

During the model's animation, the code needs to constantly update the bones of the model's skeleton according to the animation keyframes, where the keyframe contains the new configuration of the bones in its local coordinates system, relative to its ancestor. You'll process the model animation using both the CPU and the GPU, where the CPU is responsible for calculating the bone matrix (matrix [Bone$^{-1}_{\text{BindPose}}$ * Bone$_i$], shown in the last equation in the preceding section), and the GPU is responsible for calculating the final matrix (shown in that last equation), and transforming the vertices.

To handle the animation process done on the CPU, you'll create an Update method for the AnimatedModel, and to handle the animation process done on the GPU, you'll create a new effect for the animated models.

AnimatedModel Update

In the CPU, you can divide the tasks to perform the model's animation into three main parts. First, you need to update the skeleton's bones according to the current animation that is being played and the elapsed time. Second, you calculate the absolute coordinate of each bone. Third, you calculate the final bone matrix used to transform the vertices.

You start the first part of the animation process by calculating the current animation time. This is done by incrementing the animation time by the elapsed time since the last update, where the elapsed time is scaled by the animation speed:

```
activeAnimationTime += new TimeSpan(
    (long)(time.ElapsedGameTime.Ticks * animationSpeed));
```

Then you check if the current animation has finished by comparing the activeAnimationTime with the duration of the current animation. If it has finished you can restart if you're resetting the animation time:

```
// Loop the animation
if (activeAnimationTime > activeAnimation.Duration && enableAnimationLoop)
{
    long elapsedTicks = activeAnimationTime.Ticks % activeAnimation.Duration.Ticks;
    activeAnimationTime = new TimeSpan(elapsedTicks);
    activeAnimationKeyframe = 0;
}
```

Next, you check if this is the first update of the animation. In this case, you need to restore the skeleton's bones to their bind pose:

```
// Put the bind pose in the bones in the beginning of the animation
if (activeAnimationKeyframe == 0)
{
    for (int i = 0; i < bones.Length; i++)
        bones[i] = animatedModelData.BonesBindPose[i];
}
```

To reproduce the animation, you loop through the keyframes of the current model animation, updating the model skeleton's bones when the `activeAnimationTime` is bigger than the keyframe time:

```
// Read all animation keyframes until the current time is reached
// That's possible because you have previously sorted the keyframes
int index = 0;
Keyframe[] keyframes = activeAnimation.Keyframes;
while (index < keyframes.Length && keyframes[index].Time <= activeAnimationTime)
{
    int boneIndex = keyframes[index].Bone;
    bones[boneIndex] = keyframes[index].Transform * bonesTransform[boneIndex];
    index++;
}
activeAnimationKeyframe = index - 1;
```

In the second part of the animation process you need to loop through all the bones' matrices and calculate the absolute configuration for each of them. Because the skeleton's bone array was constructed by a depth traverse, the parent of a bone in this array can't have an index bigger than its index. So, you can go through each element of the list in order, calculating its final position because the final position of its ancestor will already have been calculated. Notice that the first bone of the array is already in its absolute coordinate system (because it doesn't have a parent), but you transform it with a custom user matrix:

```
// Fill the bones with their absolute coordinate
bonesAbsolute[0] = bones[0] * parent;
for (int i = 1; i < bonesAnimation.Length; i++)
{
    int boneParent = animatedModelData.BonesParent[i];

    // Here we are transforming a child bone by its parent
    bonesAbsolute[i] = bones[i] * bonesAbsolute[boneParent];
}
```

Finally, you calculate the final position of each bone by multiplying the inverse transformation of the bone in its bind pose and its current absolute position:

```
// Before we can transform the mesh's vertices using the calculated
// bone matrix, we need to put the vertices in the coordinate system
// of the bone that is linked to it
for (int i = 0; i < bonesAnimation.Length; i++)
{
```

```
        bonesAnimation[i] = animatedModelData.BonesInverseBindPose[i] *
            bonesAbsolute[i];
}
```

Following is the complete code for the Update method of the AnimatedModel class:

```
private void UpdateAnimation(GameTime time, Matrix parent)
{
    activeAnimationTime += new TimeSpan(
        (long)(time.ElapsedGameTime.Ticks * animationSpeed));

    if (activeAnimation != null)
    {
        // Loop the animation
        if (activeAnimationTime >
            activeAnimation.Duration && enableAnimationLoop)
        {
            long elapsedTicks = activeAnimationTime.Ticks %
                activeAnimation.Duration.Ticks;
            activeAnimationTime = new TimeSpan(elapsedTicks);
            activeAnimationKeyframe = 0;
        }

        // Every time the animation starts put the local bind pose in
        // the bones array
        if (activeAnimationKeyframe == 0)
        {
            for (int i = 0; i < bones.Length; i++)
                bones[i] = animatedModelData.BonesBindPose[i];
        }

        // Play all animation keyframes until the current time
        // is reached. This is possible because we have sorted the
        // keyframes by time during the model processing
        int index = 0;
        Keyframe[] keyframes = activeAnimation.Keyframes;
        while (index < keyframes.Length &&
            keyframes[index].Time <= activeAnimationTime)
        {
            int boneIndex = keyframes[index].Bone;
            bones[boneIndex] = keyframes[index].Transform *
                bonesTransform[boneIndex];
            index++;
```

```
        }
        activeAnimationKeyframe = index - 1;
    }


    // Calculate the bones absolute coordinate
    bonesAbsolute[0] = bones[0] * parent;
    for (int i = 1; i < bonesAnimation.Length; i++)
    {
        int boneParent = animatedModelData.BonesParent[i];
        // Transform the bone configuration by its
        // parent configuration
        bonesAbsolute[i] = bones[i] * bonesAbsolute[boneParent];
    }


    // Before we can transform the vertices we
    // need to put the vertices in the coordinate system of the
    // bone that is linked to it
    for (int i = 0; i < bonesAnimation.Length; i++)
    {
        bonesAnimation[i] = animatedModelData.BonesInverseBindPose[i]
            * bonesAbsolute[i];
    }
}
```

AnimatedModel Effect

At every time interval, you need to animate (transform) the model's mesh according to
the skeleton model, whether via hardware (on the GPU) or software (on the CPU) processing. The advantage of transforming the model's mesh on the GPU is that it is usually
much faster than via software processing. In this section, you'll create an effect for the
animated model rendering that will transform the mesh's vertices in its vertex shader.
This effect will also support two omnidirectional light sources and texturing.

AnimatedModel Vertex Processing

Let's begin the construction of the effect through its vertex shader. The vertex shader
receives a structure containing the vertex position, normal, texture coordinate, and bone
index and weight. Each vertex has the indices of the bones that influence it and the
weight of these influences.

Notice that the vertex's indices and weight attributes were processed by the default XNA model processor, the ModelProcessor class:

```
struct a2v
{
    float4 position : POSITION;
    float3 normal : NORMAL;
    float2 uv0 : TEXCOORD0;
    float4 boneIndex : BLENDINDICES0;
    float4 boneWeight : BLENDWEIGHT0;
};
```

The output of the vertex shader contains the vertex's final position, normal, texture coordinate, view vector, and two lighting vectors:

```
struct v2f
{
    float4 hposition : POSITION;
    float2 uv0 : TEXCOORD0;
    float3 normal : TEXCOORD1;
    float3 lightVec1 : TEXCOORD2;
    float3 lightVec2 : TEXCOORD3;
    float3 eyeVec : TEXCOORD4;
};
```

Inside the vertex processing, you should first calculate the final bone matrix used to transform the vertex position and normal:

```
// Calculate the final bone transformation matrix
float4x4 matTransform = matBones[IN.boneIndex.x] * IN.boneWeight.x;
matTransform += matBones[IN.boneIndex.y] * IN.boneWeight.y;
matTransform += matBones[IN.boneIndex.z] * IN.boneWeight.z;
float finalWeight = 1.0f - (IN.boneWeight.x + IN.boneWeight.y + IN.boneWeight.z);
matTransform += matBones[IN.boneIndex.w] * finalWeight;
```

The matBones array is a uniform variable that contains a matrix with the configuration of each bone, and its maximum size is set according to the number of free constant registers on the GPU. In the shader that you're creating, and which is compiled with shader model 2.0, the maximum size of the matBones array is 58.

Next, you transform the vertex position and normal by the final bone matrix. After that, you transform it again by a matrix that combines the world, view, and projection transformations:

```
// Transform vertex and normal
float4 position = mul(IN.position, matTransform);
float3 normal = mul(IN.normal, matTransform);
OUT.hposition = mul(position, matWVP);
OUT.normal = mul(normal, matWV);
```

Last, you calculate the view vector and the two lighting vectors used to light the vertex:

```
// Calculate light and eye vectors
float4 worldPosition = mul(position, matW);
OUT.eyeVec = mul(matVI[3].xyz - worldPosition, matV);
OUT.lightVec1 = mul(light1Position - worldPosition, matV);
OUT.lightVec2 = mul(light2Position - worldPosition, matV);
OUT.uv0 = IN.uv0;
```

Next is the complete vertex processing code:

```
v2f animatedModelVS(a2v IN)
{
    v2f OUT;

    // Calculate the final bone transformation matrix
    float4x4 matTransform = matBones[IN.boneIndex.x] *
        IN.boneWeight.x;
    matTransform += matBones[IN.boneIndex.y] * IN.boneWeight.y;
    matTransform += matBones[IN.boneIndex.z] * IN.boneWeight.z;
    float finalWeight = 1.0f - (IN.boneWeight.x + IN.boneWeight.y +
        IN.boneWeight.z);
    matTransform += matBones[IN.boneIndex.w] * finalWeight;

    // Transform vertex and normal
    float4 position = mul(IN.position, matTransform);
    float3 normal = mul(IN.normal, matTransform);
    OUT.hposition = mul(position, matWVP);
    OUT.normal = mul(normal, matWV);

    // Calculate light and eye vectors
    float4 worldPosition = mul(position, matW);
    OUT.eyeVec = mul(matVI[3].xyz - worldPosition, matV);
    OUT.lightVec1 = mul(light1Position - worldPosition, matV);
```

```
OUT.lightVec2 = mul(light2Position - worldPosition, matV);
OUT.uv0 = IN.uv0;

return OUT;
}
```

AnimatedModel Pixel Processing

All the data received in the pixel shader is interpolated values output from the vertex shader. The first thing you do in the pixel shader is normalize all the vectors, making sure that they remain unitary:

```
// Normalize all input vectors
float3 normal = normalize(IN.normal);
float3 eyeVec = normalize(IN.eyeVec);
float3 lightVec1 = normalize(IN.lightVec1);
float3 lightVec2 = normalize(IN.lightVec2);
float3 halfVec1 = normalize(lightVec1 + eyeVec);
float3 halfVec2 = normalize(lightVec2 + eyeVec);
```

At this point, you have all the necessary vectors for the lighting calculation. You do the lighting calculation using the Phong equation, which is usually implemented in the graphics APIs. The created phongShading function implements the Phong equation and returns a diffuse and specular component for a specified light source. Note that these steps were performed in Chapter 10:

```
// Calculate diffuse and specular color for each light
float3 diffuseColor1, diffuseColor2;
float3 specularColor1, specularColor2;
phongShading(normal, lightVec1, halfwayVec1, light1Color,
    diffuseColor1, specularColor1);
phongShading(normal, lightVec2, halfwayVec2, light2Color,
    diffuseColor2, specularColor2);
```

Besides the lighting, the pixel color is read from its texture:

```
float4 materialColor = tex2D(diffuse1Sampler, IN.uv0);
```

Finally, you calculate the final color of each pixel, combining its color with the diffuse and specular components from the light sources:

```
float4 finalColor;
finalColor.a = 1.0f;
finalColor.rgb = materialColor *
    ( (diffuseColor1+diffuseColor2) * diffuseColor +
    ambientLightColor) + (specularColor1 + specularColor2) *
    specularColor ;
```

The code for the phongShading function is shown in Chapter 10, and the final pixel shader code follows:

```
float4 animatedModelPS(v2f IN): COLOR0
{
    // Normalize all input vectors
    float3 normal = normalize(IN.normal);
    float3 eyeVec = normalize(IN.eyeVec);
    float3 lightVec1 = normalize(IN.lightVec1);
    float3 lightVec2 = normalize(IN.lightVec2);
    float3 halfwayVec1 = normalize(lightVec1 + eyeVec);
    float3 halfwayVec2 = normalize(lightVec2 + eyeVec);

    // Calculate diffuse and specular color for each light
    float3 diffuseColor1, diffuseColor2;
    float3 specularColor1, specularColor2;
    phongShading(normal, lightVec1, halfwayVec1,
        light1Color, diffuseColor1, specularColor1);
    phongShading(normal, lightVec2, halfwayVec2,
        light2Color, diffuseColor2, specularColor2);

    // Read texture diffuse color
    float4 materialColor = tex2D(diffuse1Sampler, IN.uv0);

    // Phong lighting result
    float4 finalColor;
    finalColor.a = 1.0f;
    finalColor.rgb = materialColor *
        ( (diffuseColor1+diffuseColor2) * diffuseColor +
        ambientLightColor) + (specularColor1+specularColor2) *
        specularColor ;
    return finalColor;
}
```

Following is the code for the technique using the vertex and pixel shader created in the previous sections:

```
technique AnimatedModel
{
    pass p0
    {
        VertexShader = compile vs_2_0 animatedModelVS();
        PixelShader = compile ps_2_a animatedModelPS();
    }
}
```

Converting the Mesh Effect

You need to use the effect that you created in the preceding section to render the model. XNA's model processor has the ConvertMaterial method, which is called whenever a material of a model's mesh is found.

The ConvertMaterial method receives as a parameter a MaterialContent object that stores the material content used by the mesh. When a model is exported without an effect it only has some basic material configuration, such as the color and texture. In this case, the received MaterialContent is actually an instance of the BasicMaterialContent class. If the model has already been exported along with an effect, the received material is an instance of the EffectMaterialContent class.

To change the materials used in the model, you need to overwrite the ConvertMaterial method, and covert the BasicMaterialContent received to an EffectMaterialContent, containing the effect that you've created for the animated model. The following code shows the ConvertMaterial method, which you should add to the model processor class.

```
protected override MaterialContent ConvertMaterial(
    MaterialContent material, ContentProcessorContext context)
{
    BasicMaterialContent basicMaterial = material
        as BasicMaterialContent;
    if (basicMaterial == null)
        context.Logger.LogImportantMessage(
            "This mesh doesn't have a valid basic material.");

    // Only process meshes with basic material
    // Otherwise the mesh must use the correct effect (AnimatedModel.fx)
    if (basicMaterial != null)
    {
        EffectMaterialContent effectMaterial =
            new EffectMaterialContent();
```

```
            effectMaterial.Effect =
                new ExternalReference<EffectContent>(
                SHADERS_PATH + SHADER_FILENAME);

            // Correct the texture path
            if (basicMaterial.Texture != null)
            {
                string textureFileName = Path.GetFileName(
                    basicMaterial.Texture.Filename);
                effectMaterial.Textures.Add("diffuseTexture1",
                    new ExternalReference<TextureContent>(
                    TEXTURES_PATH + textureFileName));
            }

            return base.ConvertMaterial(effectMaterial, context);
        }
        else
            return base.ConvertMaterial(material, context);
}
```

When the BasicMaterialContent is converted to an EffectMaterialContent, the model texture used in the default material is passed again to the newly created effect.

Drawing the Model

Because the animated model is an XNA Model, it is simple to draw it. First, you need to configure the animated model's effects, then you just need to go through all its meshes, calling their Draw method. Following is the code for the Draw method of the AnimatedModel class:

```
public override void Draw(GameTime gameTime)
{
    SetEffectMaterial();
    for (int i = 0; i < model.Meshes.Count; i++)
    {
        model.Meshes[i].Draw();
    }
}
```

Summary

In this chapter you learned how to extend XNA's Content Pipeline by adding support to skeletal animation models, and how to create a class capable of handling the animated models at runtime. You also reviewed some concepts and mathematical equations behind the skeletal animation models.

In the next chapter you will see how to put together all concepts seen since Chapter 7 to create a real 3-D game, a simple third person shooter.

■ ■ ■

CHAPTER 12

Creating a Third-Person Shooter Game

In this chapter you're going to build a complete 3-D game using some of the concepts learned in Chapters 9, 10, and 11. You'll create a third-person shooter (TPS) game. First, you'll create a basic engine for the game containing all the required objects such as cameras, lights, terrains, and animated models. Then, you'll create all the gameplay and logic for the game.

Some FPS and TPS Examples

Today's gaming market is full of first-person shooter (FPS) and TPS games, such as Crysis, Gears of War, and Resident Evil 4. These games all share certain common characteristics. They tend to either partially or totally lack a user interface (UI) on the main screen (unlike older games in this genre, such as Doom), they contain a good selection of indoor and outdoor scenery for realism, and they have higher quality graphics than you'd find in a strategy or an RPG game to promote immersive game play.

Bearing these features in mind, you're now going to create a basic design to guide you through the creation of your own game.

Designing the Game

Before you start building the game you have to define a basic design for it that will help you with the development. The game design will be divided into three sections: "Defining the Game," "Gameplay," and "Technical Design." Note that this division was used by the authors and it is not intended to be used as a complete design document for a game. Aside from that, a small design document can be much more efficient than a document having dozens of pages.

Defining the Game

The game will be a TPS game, where the player will control a survivor of a human expedition that went to an unknown planet. The objective of the player is to avenge the death of his companions, fighting and destroying every living creature on this planet, where the game environment will be a completely outdoor scene. Now that you know what the game is, let's think a little bit about the gameplay.

Gameplay

The player will start the game equipped with a machine gun, ammunition, and the doable actions of running (forward and backward), jumping, and attacking (aiming and shooting). The player cannot move while aiming, and a sprite with a circle is used to show the target of the player's weapon. The player can be controlled using the Xbox 360 controller or the keyboard, where the game controls were created based on the principles of the game Resident Evil 4. Figure 12-1 shows the game controller.

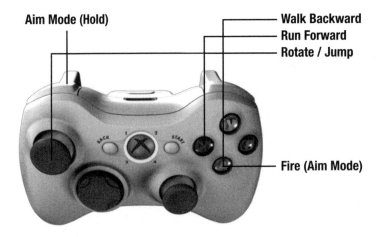

Figure 12-1. *The game controller*

In the Xbox 360, the left directional is used to rotate the player and jump (when clicked), while the X and A buttons move the player forward and backward. Button LB is used to enter into the aim mode, and while in the aim mode, the player cannot move and the A button is used to shoot.

The game map will have a few monsters (NPCs) scattered in different positions. Each monster will be randomly walking around the map until it sees the player or is attacked by the player. When this happens, the monster will chase the player, and after approaching him the monster will attack. Whenever the monster loses all its hit points, it will die. And if the player loses all his hit points, the game will be over.

Finally, the game UI will be as simple as possible. It will contain the player's health points, ammunition, and the number of remaining creatures alive on the planet.

Technical Design

Now you'll define some technical design items. To ease the building of the game, you'll divide the game code into three different namespaces: GameBase, GameLogic (or Gameplay), and Helpers.

The GameBase namespace contains the entire game engine, having objects such as cameras, lights, terrain, models, and effects. Notice that you created almost the entire game engine in Chapters 9, 10, and 11. The GameLogic namespace contains the logic of the game, including player logic, NPCs' artificial intelligence (AI), unit types, and others. The last one—the Helpers namespace—contains various helper objects, such as controller helper and random generator helper. Using these namespaces makes it easier to keep the game logic separate from the game engine, which helps you to develop, reuse, and maintain the game code.

Starting the Game Engine (GameBase)

You'll start constructing the XNA TPS game by creating its game engine, and then you'll work on its gameplay. Start the game development by creating a new Windows Game project named XNA TPS. In this new game project, create the folders GameBase, GameLogic, and Helpers. These folders will help you maintain the different parts of the game code separately, as described in the section "Technical Design." Besides the code, the game assets will be added to the Content project, which is inside the XNA TPS project.

You made most of the XNA TPS game engine in Chapters 9, 10, and 11. Here you'll add the classes that you created in the previous chapters to the GameBase namespace in the XNA TPS project.

Cameras, Lights, and Transformations

You made the Cameras, Lights, and Transformation classes in Chapter 9. To add these classes to the project, you first need to create the folders Cameras and Lights inside the GameBase folder. Then, add all the camera and light classes to the Cameras and Lights folders respectively, and the Transformation class to the GameBase folder.

Terrain

You created the Terrain class and its effect and material classes in Chapter 10. To add these classes to the project, you first need to create the Shapes, Materials, and Effects folders. Then add the Terrain class to the Shapes folder, the TerrainEffect class to the Effects folder, and all the material classes to the Materials folder. You also need to add the VertexPositionTangentBinormal class used by the Terrain class to the Helpers folder in the XNA TPS project.

Finally, add the terrain assets (height map, textures, and effects) to the XNA TPS Content project. To add these assets to the Content project, you create a few different folders: the Terrains folder, used to store the terrain's height map; the Textures folder, used to store the game textures; and the Effects folder, used to store the effects. After adding all the assets to their folders, remember to modify the properties of the terrain's height map, changing its Build Action property to None and its Copy to Output Directory property to Copy if Newer.

Animated Model

You created the animated model processor, content library, runtime class, and effects in Chapter 11. Instead of adding the animated model content processor and content library projects to the XNA TPS solution (which has the XNA TPS project), you could just add references to the compiled assemblies of these projects. To do that, in the XNA TPS project add a reference to the animated model content library, browsing the AnimatedModelContentWin binary (at AnimatedModelContentWin/bin/x86/Release/AnimatedModelContentWin.dll). In the Content project (inside the XNA TPS project) add a reference to the animated model content processor, browsing the AnimatedModelProcessorWin binary (at AnimatedModelProcessorWin/bin/x86/Release/AnimatedModelProcessorWin.dll). After referencing the content library and processor, add the AnimatedModel and AnimatedModelEffect classes to the XNA TPS project. Add the AnimatedModel class to the Shapes folder and the AnimatedModelEffect class to the Effects folder.

Finally, you need to add the animated model assets (model, textures, and effects) to the XNA TPS Content project. In the Content project, you just need to create a new folder named Models in which to put all the animated model files. You should add the animated model effect to the Effects folder and its textures to the Textures folder. After adding all the assets to the project, remember to change the content processor of the animated model files to the animated model processor.

Sky

In a game, the sky is used to create a background that covers all the scene objects, giving the sensation of infinite scenery around the player. Besides that, the sky also helps to place the player in the scene, allowing the player to have a notion of the environment around him. Notice that when we refer to the game's sky, we are talking about all the landscape surrounding the player. One way to create a landscape around the player would be to draw various objects around the scene, positioned far away from the player.

However, the cost of drawing these objects in real time would be high. Furthermore, these models would be positioned at such a great distance that they would not present a high level of detail.

A common way game designers use to create the landscape is to construct a solid that covers the entire scene. This solid can be a box, called SkyBox; a hemisphere, called SkyDome; or any other type of solid. The landscape around the player is then stored into textures that are mapped to the SkyBox or SkyDome. To give the feeling of an infinite horizon, the camera is always positioned in the center of the sky, moving with it.

SkyBox

In the SkyBox, the sky is created as a box, containing six faces, where each face has a different texture. The created box covers the entire scene, and all its faces are oriented to the inside of the cube—because you view the cube from its interior, not its exterior. Figure 12-2 illustrates the construction of a SkyBox.

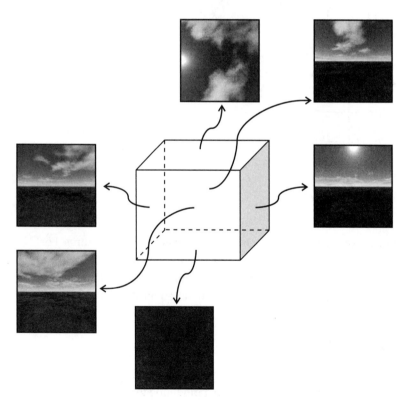

Figure 12-2. *A SkyBox*

Notice that the textures used in the Skybox must be continuous over its faces or the player will easily notice the box edges. One of the SkyBox's advantages is that it is simple to construct, and has only 12 triangles.

SkyDome

In the SkyDome, the sky is created as a hemisphere using only one texture, and is positioned above the scene. Figure 12-3 shows a wireframe model of a SkyDome.

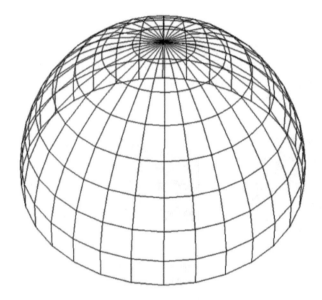

Figure 12-3. *A SkyDome model in wireframe*

One of the advantages of the SkyDome is that it's easy to animate its textures. For example, you could use two textures for the sky, using the first one for its background, and the second one to draw a second layer effect, such as moving clouds. One of the disadvantages of the SkyDome is that it has a much more detailed mesh than a SkyBox.

Creating a SkyDome Class

In your game you'll use a SkyDome to draw the scene's landscape. The SkyDome you'll use is a conventional 3-D model, previously made on a modeling tool and processed by the Content Pipeline. The sky model will be loaded and handled through XNA's Model class. Note that it is also possible to generate the sky model dynamically, instead of loading it.

In this section you'll create the class to load, update, and draw the sky model: the SkyDome class. You should create the SkyDome class inside the Shapes folder.

Loading the Sky

Because the SkyDome is an XNA Model, you simply need to use the content manager to load it. Following is the code for the Load method of the SkyDome class:

```
public void Load(string modelFileName)
{
    model = Content.Load<Model>(GameAssetsPath.MODELS_PATH
        + modelFileName);
}
```

Updating the Sky

Every time the sky is updated, you need to move its center position to the camera's position, ensuring that the camera remains positioned in the center of the sky. You can also rotate the sky model smoothly over the world's Y axis, giving the impression of a moving horizon around the player. Following is the code for the Update method of the SkyDome class:

```
public override void Update(GameTime time)
{
    BaseCamera camera = cameraManager.ActiveCamera;

    // Center the camera in the SkyDome
    transformation.Translate = new Vector3(camera.Position.X,
        0.0f, camera.Position.Z);

    // Rotate the SkyDome slightly
    transformation.Rotate += new Vector3(0,
        (float)time.ElapsedGameTime.TotalSeconds * 0.5f, 0);

    base.Update(time);
}
```

Drawing the Sky

The SkyDome model has a BasicEffect linked to it, which you can use to draw it. But before drawing the model, you need to configure its effect. First, set the sky texture that you want to use in the model (this is necessary because no texture was exported with the sky model). Then, set the model's world and the camera's view and projection matrices to the effect. Finally, draw the sky model.

Notice that it is important to disable the depth buffer before drawing the sky model; because the sky is the farthest drawing object you don't need to store its depth. Also, if you draw the sky model with the depth buffer enabled you might have precision problems when drawing distance objects. Following is the code for the SetEffectMaterial and Draw methods used to draw the sky:

```
private void SetEffectMaterial(BasicEffect basicEffect)
{
    BaseCamera activeCamera = cameraManager.ActiveCamera;

    // Texture Material
    basicEffect.Texture = textureMaterial.Texture;
    basicEffect.TextureEnabled = true;

    // Transformation
    basicEffect.World = transformation.Matrix;
    basicEffect.View = activeCamera.View;
    basicEffect.Projection = activeCamera.Projection;
}


public override void Draw(GameTime time)
{
    GraphicsDevice.RenderState.DepthBufferEnable = false;
    foreach (ModelMesh modelMesh in model.Meshes)
    {
        // We are only rendering models with BasicEffect
        foreach (BasicEffect basicEffect in modelMesh.Effects)
            SetEffectMaterial(basicEffect);

        modelMesh.Draw();
    }
    GraphicsDevice.RenderState.DepthBufferEnable = true;

    base.Draw(time);
}
```

Helper Classes

In this section you'll create some helper classes to manage the game input and settings, and to generate random values. You'll create all these classes inside the Helpers namespace.

Creating an Input Helper

In the section "Gameplay," we noted that your game can be played using the keyboard or the Xbox 360 gamepad. The XNA Framework has all the classes that you need to manage the input through the keyboard, gamepad, or mouse (only supported in Windows). However, because you want to handle the keyboard and gamepad simultaneously, a helper class could be useful. Also, the XNA input classes lack some features, such as checking when a key is first pressed (pressed when it is released), which you can add to the input helper class. In this section you'll create a helper class for the keyboard and gamepad input, named InputHelper.

Because you can play your game using the gamepad, you first map all the game actions to the gamepad, and then map the gamepad buttons to some keyboard keys. For example, you can define that the gamepad's A button is used to make the player jump. Then you can map the keyboard's Space key to the gamepad's A button. If you try to map the game actions to the keyboard first, it can be difficult to map these keys back to the gamepad.

InputHelper Attributes and Constructor

The InputHelper class stores the state of the gamepad, the state of the keyboard, and the map of the gamepad buttons to the keyboard. The InputHelper class also stores the index of the current player, because each instance of the InputHelper class handles the input of only one player. So, if you have a two-player game, you need to have two InputHelper objects.

Notice that the current state and last state of the gamepad and keyboard are stored because you need them to check when a button or key is pressed for the first time. Following is the code for the attributes and constructor of the InputHelper class:

```
PlayerIndex playerIndex;

// Keyboard
KeyboardState keyboardState;
KeyboardState lastKeyboardState;
Dictionary<Buttons, Keys> keyboardMap;
```

```
// Gamepad
GamePadState gamePadState;
GamePadState lastGamePadState;

public InputHelper(PlayerIndex playerIndex)
    : this(playerIndex, null)
{
}

public InputHelper(PlayerIndex playerIndex,
    Dictionary<Buttons, Keys> keyboardMap)
{
    this.playerIndex = playerIndex;
    this.keyboardMap = keyboardMap;
}
```

The InputHelper constructor's parameters are the player index and the keyboard map. However, the keyboard map's parameter could be null, if you are not interested in using a keyboard.

Updating the Input

To update the input, you need to save the last read state of the keyboard and gamepad and then read their new state. Note that in XNA 2.0, the GetState method of the Keyboard class receives the index of the current player. Following is the code for the Update method of the InputHelper class:

```
public void Update()
{
    lastKeyboardState = keyboardState;
    keyboardState = Keyboard.GetState(playerIndex);

    lastGamePadState = gamePadState;
    gamePadState = GamePad.GetState(playerIndex);
}
```

Checking Pressed Keys

In XNA 2.0, both the KeyboardState and the GamePadState have a method to check whether a button or a key was pressed. Because you're handling the input through the gamepad and keyboard you need to check if the button or key was pressed in any of them, but you could avoid checking them both at the same time.

The InputHelper class only allows checking if a gamepad button is pressed, but it internally checks whether the button was pressed on the gamepad or on the keyboard. In this case, it first checks if the current player's gamepad is connected and if it is, it checks if a button was pressed on the gamepad. Otherwise, if the InputHelper class has a valid keyboard map, it will check if the keyboard key that is mapped to the gamepad button is pressed. Following is the code for the IsKeyPressed method of the InputHelper class:

```
public bool IsKeyPressed(Buttons button)
{
    bool pressed = false;

    if (gamePadState.IsConnected)
        pressed = gamePadState.IsButtonDown(button);
    else if (keyboardMap != null)
    {
        Keys key = keyboardMap[button];
        pressed = keyboardState.IsKeyDown(key);
    }
    return pressed;
}
```

Besides checking when a button is pressed, you also want to check if a button was pressed for the first time. To do that, you can check if the desired button is pressed but was released in the previous update. Following is the code for the IsKeyJustPressed method of the InputHelper class:

```
public bool IsKeyJustPressed(Buttons button)
{
    bool pressed = false;

    if (gamePadState.IsConnected)
        pressed = (gamePadState.IsButtonDown(button) &&
            lastGamePadState.IsButtonUp(button));
    else if (keyboardMap != null)
    {
        Keys key = keyboardMap[button];
        pressed = (keyboardState.IsKeyDown(key) &&
            lastKeyboardState.IsKeyUp(key));
    }

    return pressed;
}
```

Checking Analog Button State

You can use the IsKeyPressed and IsKeyJustPressed methods that you created for the InputHelper class to check whether a digital key is pressed or not. So, if you try to use these methods to retrieve the state of the analog sticks and triggers of the Xbox 360 gamepad you'll just get a Boolean result, whether the buttons are pressed or not.

In the XNA's GamePadState class, the position of each analog stick is retrieved as a Vector2 object, and the triggers' state as a float value. In your InputHelper class, you'll create some methods to retrieve the state of the gamepad's analog sticks in the same way it's done in the GamePadState class. Notice that you also need to properly handle the keyboard keys that are mapped to the analog sticks. Following is the code for the GetLeftThumbStick method of the InputHelper class, used to retrieve the position of the gamepad's left stick:

```
public Vector2 GetLeftThumbStick()
{
    Vector2 thumbPosition = Vector2.Zero;

    if (gamePadState.IsConnected)
        thumbPosition = gamePadState.ThumbSticks.Left;
    else if (keyboardMap != null)
    {
        if (keyboardState.IsKeyDown(
            keyboardMap[Buttons.LeftThumbstickUp]))
            thumbPosition.Y = 1;
        else if (keyboardState.IsKeyDown(
            keyboardMap[Buttons.LeftThumbstickDown]))
            thumbPosition.Y = -1;
        if (keyboardState.IsKeyDown(
            keyboardMap[Buttons.LeftThumbstickRight]))
            thumbPosition.X = 1;
        else if (keyboardState.IsKeyDown(
            keyboardMap[Buttons.LeftThumbstickLeft]))
            thumbPosition.X = -1;
    }
    return thumbPosition;
}
```

In the GetLeftThumbStick method you take the same approach you did in the IsKeyPressed method: you first check if the gamepad is connected, and if it is, you just return the desired value. Otherwise, you check the state of the keyboard keys that are mapped to the left analog stick (up, down, left, and right) and return a Vector2 containing the resulting analog stick position.

Besides the `GetLeftThumbStick` method, you also need to create the `GetRightThumbStick` method to retrieve the position of the gamepad's right stick. Following is the code for the `GetRightThumbStick` method:

```
public Vector2 GetRightThumbStick()
{
    Vector2 thumbPosition = Vector2.Zero;

    if (gamePadState.IsConnected)
        thumbPosition = gamePadState.ThumbSticks.Right;
    else if (keyboardMap != null)
    {
        if (keyboardState.IsKeyDown(
            keyboardMap[Buttons.RightThumbstickUp]))
            thumbPosition.Y = 1;
        else if (keyboardState.IsKeyDown(
            keyboardMap[Buttons.RightThumbstickDown]))
            thumbPosition.Y = -1;
        if (keyboardState.IsKeyDown(
            keyboardMap[Buttons.RightThumbstickRight]))
            thumbPosition.X = 1;
        else if (keyboardState.IsKeyDown(
            keyboardMap[Buttons.RightThumbstickLeft]))
            thumbPosition.X = -1;
    }

    return thumbPosition;
}
```

Settings Manager

You might want to configure different settings for your game on each computer you are running, such as screen resolution, full screen mode, and keyboard map. These settings can be stored and read from files, so you don't need to reconfigure your game every time you run it. To do that, you'll create some structures to store the game settings, and a helper class to help you store and read these settings from a file. The game settings will be read and saved from an XML file. The XML format has the benefit of being human readable and can be modified in any text editor.

Start the construction of the settings manager by creating a new class named `SettingsManager` in the `Helpers` namespace. Inside the file created for the `SettingsManager` class, create a struct named `KeyboardSettings` to store the keyboard map. Following is the code for the `KeyboardSettings` struct:

```
[Serializable]
public struct KeyboardSettings
{
    public Keys A;
    public Keys B;
    public Keys X;
    public Keys Y;
    public Keys LeftShoulder;
    public Keys RightShoulder;
    public Keys LeftTrigger;
    public Keys RightTrigger;
    public Keys LeftStick;
    public Keys RightStick;
    public Keys Back;
    public Keys Start;

    public Keys DPadDown;
    public Keys DPadLeft;
    public Keys DPadRight;
    public Keys DPadUp;

    public Keys LeftThumbstickDown;
    public Keys LeftThumbstickLeft;
    public Keys LeftThumbstickRight;
    public Keys LeftThumbstickUp;
    public Keys RightThumbstickDown;
    public Keys RightThumbstickLeft;
    public Keys RightThumbstickRight;
    public Keys RightThumbstickUp;
}
```

In KeyboardSettings, you created an attribute of type Keys for each gamepad button that can be mapped to a keyboard key. Next, create the main game settings structure, named GameSettings. Following is the code for the GameSettings struct:

```
[Serializable]
public struct GameSettings
{
    public bool PreferredFullScreen;
    public int PreferredWindowWidth;
    public int PreferredWindowHeight;
```

```
    public KeyboardSettings[] KeyboardSettings;
}
```

The game settings structure stores the screen resolution, full screen mode, and an array of keyboard settings, used to map the gamepad buttons to the keyboard. Finally, you should create two methods inside the SettingsManager class to read and save the game settings. Because you don't need a specific instance of the SettingsManager class, you should make it and its methods static. Following is the code for the Read method of the SettingsManager class:

```
public static GameSettings Read(string settingsFilename)
{
    GameSettings gameSettings;
    Stream stream = File.OpenRead(settingsFilename);
    XmlSerializer serializer =
        new XmlSerializer(typeof(GameSettings));

    gameSettings = (GameSettings)serializer.Deserialize(stream);
    return gameSettings;
}
```

The Read method receives the name of the settings file to be read, and then it uses the File class to open the file, and the XmlSerializer to transform the XML document into an object of the type GameSettings. You can save the GameSettings data into an XML file in a similar way that you used to read it. Following is the code for the Save method of the SettingsManager class:

```
public static void Save(string settingsFilename, GameSettings gameSettings)
{
    Stream stream = File.OpenWrite(settingsFilename);
    XmlSerializer serializer = new
        XmlSerializer(typeof(GameSettings));

    serializer.Serialize(stream, gameSettings);
}
```

Last, you'll create a method to transform the KeyboardSettings structure into a dictionary that maps a gamepad button to a key. The InputHelper class that you created needs this dictionary, instead of a KeyboardSettings, to map the gamepad buttons to the keyboard. Creating this dictionary is simple: add an entry to the dictionary for each gamepad button, mapping it to the key that is stored in the KeyboardSettings structure. Following is the code for the GetKeyboardDictionary, used to transform KeyboardSettings into a dictionary:

```
public static Dictionary<Buttons, Keys>
    GetKeyboardDictionary(KeyboardSettings keyboard)
{
    Dictionary<Buttons, Keys> dictionary =
        new Dictionary<Buttons, Keys>();

    dictionary.Add(Buttons.A, keyboard.A);
    dictionary.Add(Buttons.B, keyboard.B);
    dictionary.Add(Buttons.X, keyboard.X);
    dictionary.Add(Buttons.Y, keyboard.Y);
    dictionary.Add(Buttons.LeftShoulder, keyboard.LeftShoulder);
    dictionary.Add(Buttons.RightShoulder, keyboard.RightShoulder);
    dictionary.Add(Buttons.LeftTrigger, keyboard.LeftTrigger);
    dictionary.Add(Buttons.RightTrigger, keyboard.RightTrigger);
    dictionary.Add(Buttons.LeftStick, keyboard.LeftStick);
    dictionary.Add(Buttons.RightStick, keyboard.RightStick);
    dictionary.Add(Buttons.Back, keyboard.Back);
    dictionary.Add(Buttons.Start, keyboard.Start);
    dictionary.Add(Buttons.DPadDown, keyboard.DPadDown);
    dictionary.Add(Buttons.DPadLeft, keyboard.DPadLeft);
    dictionary.Add(Buttons.DPadRight, keyboard.DPadRight);
    dictionary.Add(Buttons.DPadUp, keyboard.DPadUp);
    dictionary.Add(Buttons.LeftThumbstickDown,
        keyboard.LeftThumbstickDown);
    dictionary.Add(Buttons.LeftThumbstickLeft,
        keyboard.LeftThumbstickLeft);
    dictionary.Add(Buttons.LeftThumbstickRight,
        keyboard.LeftThumbstickRight);
    dictionary.Add(Buttons.LeftThumbstickUp,
        keyboard.LeftThumbstickUp);
    dictionary.Add(Buttons.RightThumbstickDown,
        keyboard.RightThumbstickDown);
    dictionary.Add(Buttons.RightThumbstickLeft,
        keyboard.RightThumbstickLeft);
    dictionary.Add(Buttons.RightThumbstickRight,
        keyboard.RightThumbstickRight);
    dictionary.Add(Buttons.RightThumbstickUp,
        keyboard.RightThumbstickUp);

    return dictionary;
}
```

Random Helper

To help you generate random values and random positions over the game terrain—used to randomly position the enemies—you'll create a RandomHelper class inside the Helpers namespace. The RandomHelper class and all its attributes and methods will be static.

Inside the RandomHelper class, declare a public attribute of type Random, named RandomGenerator. The RandomGenerator will be used as the main random generator by all the game classes. Next, to generate a random position over the game terrain—constructed over the XZ plane—create a method named GeneratePositionXZ. Inside the GeneratePositionXZ method, you need to generate a random value for the X and Z axes according to a distance parameter. To generate a random number, use the Random class's Next method. The Next method of the Random class generates a positive random value that is lower than the value passed as its parameter. Because the center of the game terrain is positioned at the scene origin (0,0,0), your GeneratePositionXZ method must generate positive and negative values to reach all the terrain. You can do that by subtracting the random values generated by half their maximum value. Following is the complete code for the RandomHelper class:

```
public static class RandomHelper
{
    public static Random RandomGenerator = new Random();

    public static Vector3 GeneratePositionXZ(int distance)
    {
        float posX = (RandomGenerator.Next(distance * 201)
            - distance * 100) * 0.01f;
        float posZ = (RandomGenerator.Next(distance * 201)
            - distance * 100) * 0.01f;

        return new Vector3(posX, 0, posZ);
    }
}
```

Creating the Game Logic

For each unit type in the game—player, player weapon, enemy (NPC)—you'll create a class in the GameLogic namespace. A game unit needs to store its attributes (for example: speed, hit points, damage, and so on) and its logic (states and actions). Besides the logic of the game units, you'll construct the main game logic, which defines the game controls and how the units are updated and drawn, outside the GameLogic namespace in the GameScreen class. You'll create the GameScreen class at the end of this chapter.

Before you start constructing the game logic classes, let's review some of the game-play features described before:

The player will start the game equipped with a machine gun, ammunition, and the doable actions of running (forward and backward), jumping, and attacking (aiming and shooting).

Each monster will be randomly walking around the map until it sees the player or is attacked by the player. When this happens, the monster will chase the player, and after approaching him the monster will attack. Whenever the monster loses all its hit points, it will die. And if the player loses all hit points, the game will be over.

From the gameplay description, you can see that both the player and the enemies share some common attributes and actions, such as having hit points, moving over a terrain, being able to cause and receive damage, being drawn as animated models, and so on. Because of these common characteristics between the player and the enemies, you can create a generic base class from them with their common attributes and methods. Then you create the player and enemy classes by extending this base class.

TerrainUnit

In this section you'll create the base class for the game units that are animated models, move over the terrain, and are able to cause and receive damage. Create a new class in the GameLogic namespace and name it TerrainUnit. Begin constructing the TerrainUnit class by declaring some of the common attributes shared by the units, which are their hit points and speed:

```
// Basic attributes (Life and Speed)
int life;
int maxLife;
float speed;
```

You'll draw the TerrainUnit as an animated model using the AnimatedModel class. So, declare an attribute of type AnimatedModel to store the TerrainUnit animated model. Next, declare an attribute of type int to store the current unit's animation, which you further need to properly control and change the unit's animation.

Each unit also needs a bounding box and bounding sphere volumes used for collision, represented through the XNA's BoundingBox and BoundingSphere classes. The collision volumes of the unit are the collision volumes of its animated model, which are created by the animated model's content processor. Because the collision volumes of the animated model are transformed as the unit moves around the map, you need a copy of them inside the TerrainUnit class. To identify when the collision volumes need to be updated, create the needUpdateCollision flag:

```
// Animated model
AnimatedModel animatedModel;
int currentAnimationId;

// Collision volumes
BoundingBox boundingBox;
BoundingSphere boundingSphere;
bool needUpdateCollision;
```

Note that the animated model processor created in Chapter 11 doesn't create the collision volumes for the animated models, but in the "Unit Collision Volume" section you'll extend the animated model processor, creating a new one capable of generating the collision volumes for the models.

Each unit has two velocities—a linear velocity and an angular velocity—where the linear velocity is used to update the unit's position (or translation) and the angular velocity is used to update the unit's orientation (or rotation). The angular and linear velocities are represented as a 3-D vector, and in the angular velocity each component of this vector represents the angular velocity around the X, Y, and Z world axes. The last velocity that acts over the unit is gravity. The axis of gravity is globally defined as the world's Y axis (0, 1, 0). The gravity velocity may have a negative value (when the unit is falling) and a positive value (when the unit is jumping):

```
// Velocities and gravity
Vector3 linearVelocity;
Vector3 angularVelocity;
float gravityVelocity;
```

You store the unit's orientation similarly to the camera's orientation, using three orientation vectors: headingVec, strafeVec, and upVec. These vectors are oriented respectively to the front, right side, and top of the unit. You use these vectors whenever you want to move a unit according to its axes. For example, if you wanted a unit to move backward you would set its linear velocity as the negative headingVec:

```
// Unit coordinate system
Vector3 headingVec;
Vector3 strafeVec;
Vector3 upVec;
```

To identify when the unit is over the terrain or is alive, or if you need to adjust some jump modifications, create some flags:

```
// Some flags
bool isOnTerrain;
bool isDead;
bool adjustJumpChanges;
```

Creating and Loading the Unit

The TerrainUnit class extends the DrawableGameComponent class, which needs a Game instance to be constructed. So, the TerrainUnit constructor must receive a Game as a parameter and use it in the constructor of its base class (the DrawableGameComponent). Its attributes are initialized inside the constructor of the TerrainUnit class. Following is the constructor code for the TerrainUnit class:

```
public TerrainUnit(Game game)
    : base(game)
{
    gravityVelocity = 0.0f;
    isOnTerrain = false;
    isDead = false;
    adjustJumpChanges = false;

    needUpdateCollision = true;
}
```

To load the unit's animated model, create a Load method. The Load method receives the animated model's file name, loads the model, places the model above the terrain, and updates its orientation vectors. Following is the code for the Load method:

```
protected void Load(string unitModelFileName)
{
    animatedModel = new AnimatedModel(Game);
    animatedModel.Initialize();
    animatedModel.Load(unitModelFileName);

    // Put the player above the terrain
    UpdateHeight(0);
    isOnTerrain = true;

    NormalizeBaseVectors();
}
```

Making the Unit Jump

One of the unit's actions is jumping, which makes the unit move upwards and then downwards. The velocity that acts over the unit and makes it moves down is the gravity velocity. In the game the gravity velocity is a negative scalar value that acts over the gravity axis, which points to the world's Y axis (0, 1, 0). So, to make the unit jump you could change the value of the gravity velocity that acts over it to a positive value, which makes the unit move upward. Then, while the unit is in the air, you slowly reduce the gravity velocity until it has a negative value again, which makes the unit move downwards. Notice that to make a smooth jump, you need to define a minimum and maximum value for the gravity velocity. So, when the unit is falling its velocity decreases until it reaches its minimum value.

While the unit is jumping, it moves faster than while it is walking. In this case, the camera's chase velocity is not enough to chase a unit while it jumps. To solve this problem, whenever a unit jumps, the camera's chase velocity is increased and when the unit reaches the ground it is restored. You can also increase the unit's speed while it jumps, allowing it to jump bigger distances. Following is the code for the Jump method:

```
public void Jump(float jumpHeight)
{
    if (isOnTerrain)
    {
        // Update camera chase speed and unit speed
        ThirdPersonCamera camera = cameraManager.ActiveCamera
            as ThirdPersonCamera;
        camera.ChaseSpeed *= 4.0f;
        speed *= 1.5f;
        adjustJumpChanges = true;

        // Set the gravity velocity
        gravityVelocity = (float)GRAVITY_ACCELERATION *
            jumpHeight * 0.1f;
        isOnTerrain = false;
    }
}
```

Before the unit can jump you need to check if it is positioned over the terrain, avoiding having the unit jump while it is in the air. The Jump method receives a parameter that is the height value that you want the unit to jump. Notice that after changing the camera's chase speed and unit speed you set the adjustJumpChanges flag as true, reporting that these modifications need to be restored.

Updating the Unit's Height

The units created based on the `TerrainUnit` class are units that move over the game terrain. These units need to have their height updated every time you update their position to ensure that they remain over the terrain. When a unit moves to a new position, the terrain's height in this new position could be equal to, higher, or lower than the unit's previous height, as shown in Figure 12-4.

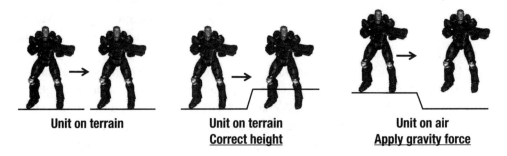

Unit on terrain   **Unit on terrain**   **Unit on air**

Correct height   **Apply gravity force**

Figure 12-4. *Moving the unit over the terrain*

If the terrain's height at the new unit position is equal to or higher than the unit's current height, the unit is over the terrain. In this case, you need to set the unit's height as the terrain's height in that position. Otherwise, the unit is in the air and you need to decrement the gravity velocity that acts over the unit. To update the unit's height, according to its position over the terrain, you'll create the `UpdateHeight` method.

Notice that to make sure that the unit is over the terrain you need to verify if the gravity velocity is not positive. If the gravity velocity is positive, the unit is moving upward and you cannot assume that it is over the terrain. Following is the code for the `UpdateHeight` method:

```
// Transformation property
public virtual Transformation Transformation
{
    get { return animatedModel.Transformation; }
    set { animatedModel.Transformation = value; }
}

private void UpdateHeight(float elapsedTimeSeconds)
{
    // Get terrain height
    float terrainHeight = terrain.GetHeight(Transformation.Translate);
    Vector3 newPosition = Transformation.Translate;
```

```
    // Unit is on terrain
    if (Transformation.Translate.Y <= terrainHeight &&
        gravityVelocity <= 0)
    {
        // Put the unit over the terrain
        isOnTerrain = true;
        gravityVelocity = 0.0f;
        newPosition.Y = terrainHeight;

        // Restore the changes made when the unit jumped
        if (adjustJumpChanges)
        {
            ThirdPersonCamera camera = cameraManager.ActiveCamera
                as ThirdPersonCamera;
            camera.ChaseSpeed /= 4.0f;
            speed /= 1.5f;
            adjustJumpChanges = false;
        }
    }
    // Unit is in the air
    else
    {
        // Decrement the gravity velocity
        if (gravityVelocity > MIN_GRAVITY)
            gravityVelocity -= GRAVITY_ACCELERATION *
                elapsedTimeSeconds;
        // Apply the gravity velocity
        newPosition.Y = Math.Max(terrainHeight,
            Transformation.Translate.Y+gravityVelocity);
    }

    // Update the unit position
    Transformation.Translate = heightTranslate;
}
```

Whenever the unit is over the terrain you verify if it is necessary to correct the changes that were made by the Jump method, through the adjustJumpChanges flag. Otherwise, if the gravityVelocity is bigger than the minimum gravity velocity you decrement it and move the player. Notice that all transformations applied on the unit are made through the Transformation property, which actually modifies its animated model transformation. This way, whenever you draw the animated model all the unit's transformations are already stored in it.

Updating the Unit

When updating the unit, you need to update its position and orientation (transformation), and its animated model. To update the unit's animated model you just have to call the Update method of the AnimatedModel class. To update the unit's position you calculate its displacement, based on its velocity and on the elapsed time since the last update, and add this displacement to its current position. The same is done to update its orientation, where the angular velocity is used to calculate the displacement on the unit's rotation. Following is the code for the Update and NormalizeBaseVectors methods:

```
public override void Update(GameTime time)
{
    // Update the animated model
    float elapsedTimeSeconds =
        (float)time.ElapsedGameTime.TotalSeconds;
    animatedModel.Update(time, Matrix.Identity);

    // Update the height and collision volumes if the unit moves
    if (linearVelocity != Vector3.Zero || gravityVelocity != 0.0f)
    {
        Transformation.Translate += linearVelocity *
            elapsedTimeSeconds * speed;
        UpdateHeight(elapsedTimeSeconds);
        needUpdateCollision = true;
    }

    // Update coordinate system when the unit rotates
    if (angularVelocity != Vector3.Zero)
    {
        Transformation.Rotate += angularVelocity *
            elapsedTimeSeconds * speed;
        NormalizeBaseVectors();
    }

    base.Update(time);
}

private void NormalizeBaseVectors()
{
    // Get the vectors from the animated model matrix
```

```
    headingVec = Transformation.Matrix.Forward;
    strafeVec = Transformation.Matrix.Right;
    upVec = Transformation.Matrix.Up;
}
```

In the Update method, you first update the unit's animated model, passing the elapsed time since the last update and a parent matrix used to transform the animated model. Because there is no need to transform the animated model, you can pass the identity matrix to update it. After that, you update the unit's linear and angular velocity. If the unit's linearVelocity or gravityVelocity is not zero, the unit is moving and you need to call the UpdateHeight method to assure that the unit is correctly positioned over the terrain. You also need to set the needUpdateCollision flag to true, to update the position of the unit's collision volumes.

Last, if the unit's angularVelocity is not zero, you call the NormalizeBaseVectors method to update its orientation vectors (heading, strafe, and up vectors). You can extract these vectors from the transformation matrix of the unit's animated model.

Unit Collision Volume

You can check the collision between the scene objects using some different approaches. An accurate approach would check the intersection between two objects using its mesh, which is composed of many triangles. This method is the most accurate one, but it is also the least efficient one. For example, to test the collision between two meshes having 2,000 triangles each, you would need to make 2000 * 2000 collision tests. Instead of testing the collision using the mesh of the objects, you can use collision volumes. Collision volumes provide a faster, although more inaccurate, way of checking the intersection between objects. In your game, you'll use two different collision volumes for each unit—a box and a sphere—to check its collision against other objects. When the collision volume is a box, it's called a *bounding box*, whereas when the volume is a sphere, it's called a *bounding sphere*.

You can build the box you'll use for the collision aligned to the world axes. In this case, the box is called an *axis-aligned bounding box* (AABB). One of the advantages of the AABB is that the collision test with it is simple. However, the AABB can't be rotated because it needs to keep its axes aligned with the world's axes. If the box used for collision is oriented with the unit's axes, it's then called an *object oriented bounding box* (OOBB). A collision test using an OOBB is slower than one using an AABB, but the OOBB provides a box that is always oriented with the unit. Figure 12-5 illustrates the creation of an AABB and an OOBB for a unit with two different orientations.

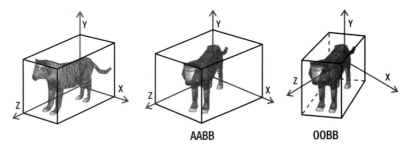

Figure 12-5. *Creating an AABB and an OOBB for a model. (Left) The AABB and the OOBB are the same when the model has the same orientation as the world. (Middle) The AABB created for the new model orientation. (Right) The OOBB created for the new model orientation.*

Because XNA already has a class to handle an AABB, you'll use it as the box volume for the unit. So, each unit will have an AABB and a bounding sphere volume, represented using XNA's `BoundingBox` and `BoundingSphere` classes.

The default model processor of the Content Pipeline generates a bounding sphere volume for each mesh present in a model that is processed. In this way, you have a bounding sphere for each model's mesh. You can avoid testing the collision with each mesh of the model, creating a bounding sphere for the entire model. Also, because the default model processor doesn't generate a bounding box (AABB) volume, you need to generate one for the model.

You can create the bounding box and bounding sphere for the unit by modifying its model processor, which is the `AnimatedModelProcessor` class created in Chapter 11. First, open the `AnimatedModelProcessor` class, which is inside the `AnimatedModelProcessorWin` project. Then, create a method named `GetModelVertices` to extract all the vertices of the model's meshes. You'll use these vertices to create the collision volumes of the model, through the `CreateFromPoints` method of XNA's `BoundingBox` and `BoundingSphere` classes. The `CreateFromPoints` method creates a volume for the model from its vertices. Following is the code for the `GetModelVertices` method:

```
private void GetModelVertices(NodeContent node,
    List<Vector3> vertexList)
{
    MeshContent meshContent = node as MeshContent;
    if (meshContent != null)
    {
        for (int i = 0; i < meshContent.Geometry.Count; i++)
        {
            GeometryContent geometryContent = meshContent.Geometry[i];
            for (int j = 0; j <
                geometryContent.Vertices.Positions.Count; j++)
```

```
            vertexList.Add(geometryContent.Vertices.Positions[j]);
        }
    }

    foreach (NodeContent child in node.Children)
        GetModelVertices(child, vertexList);
}
```

In the GetModelVertices method you travel through all the model nodes, starting at the root node, searching for the MeshContent nodes. The MeshContent nodes have the model's mesh data, from where you can extract the vertices of the mesh from its Geometry property. After processing a node you need to call the GetModelVertices method recursively and for its children, assuring that all nodes are processed. Note that all the vertices are stored in the vertexList variable of the type List<Vector3>.

At the end of the Process method of the AnimatedModelProcessor class, where you processed the model and extracted its skeletal animation data, you should call the GetModelVertices method and generate the collision volumes for its model. After generating the collision volumes for the model, you can store them in the model's Tag property. You can do that by adding the collision volumes to the dictionary that has the model's animation data, which is stored in the model's Tag property. Following is the code that you can use to generate the collision volumes:

```
// Extract all model's vertices
List<Vector3> vertexList = new List<Vector3>();
GetModelVertices(input, vertexList);

// Generate the collision volumes
BoundingBox modelBoundBox = BoundingBox.CreateFromPoints(vertexList);
BoundingSphere modelBoundSphere =
    BoundingSphere.CreateFromPoints(vertexList);

// Store everything in a dictionary
Dictionary<string, object> tagDictionary =
    new Dictionary<string, object>();
tagDictionary.Add("AnimatedModelData", animatedModelData);
tagDictionary.Add("ModelBoudingBox", modelBoundBox);
tagDictionary.Add("ModelBoudingSphere", modelBoundSphere);

// Set the dictionary as the model tag property
model.Tag = tagDictionary;
return model;
```

Unit Collision Tests

Each unit has a bounding box and a bounding sphere volume, which were previously created by the unit's animated model content processor, and that you'll use to perform a few collision tests. To make things simple, you're only going to perform two different collision tests with the units in your game. The first verifies when a ray collides with a unit and is used to check if a gunshot has hit the unit. The second verifies when the unit is inside the camera's visualization volume (a frustum) and is used to avoid updating and drawing the units that are not visible.

To check if a ray collides with a unit, you use the unit's bounding box, which is an AABB. In this case, the AABB should provide a more accurate collision volume for the unit's model than its bounding sphere. Notice that you need to apply the same transformations made over the unit (translations and rotations) to the unit's AABB before you can use it for collision tests. Moreover, you need to make sure that the model is aligned with the world's axes to use its AABB, which prohibits you from rotating the unit.

To tackle this, instead of transforming the model's AABB, you can inversely transform the ray that you are testing, guaranteeing that the AABB remains aligned with the world's axes. Following is the code for the `BoxIntersects` method of the `TerrainUnit` class, used to test the collision between a ray and the unit's AABB:

```
public float? BoxIntersects(Ray ray)
{
    Matrix inverseTransform = Matrix.Invert(Transformation.Matrix);
    ray.Position = Vector3.Transform(ray.Position,
        inverseTransform);
    ray.Direction = Vector3.TransformNormal(ray.Direction,
        inverseTransform);

    return animatedModel.BoundingBox.Intersects(ray);
}
```

In the `BoxIntersects` method you first calculate the inverse transformation matrix of the unit and then transform the position and the direction of the ray by this matrix. You need to use the `Transform` method of the XNA's `Vector3` class to transform the ray's start position because it is a 3-D point, and the `TransformNormal` method to transform the ray's direction because it is a vector. After that you can do the normal collision test between the box and the ray.

Now, to verify if a unit is found inside the camera's frustum you use the unit's bounding sphere. In this case, a collision test with the unit's bounding sphere is simpler and the precision is not very important. To test the collision between the unit's bounding sphere and the camera's frustum, you only need to use the `Intersects` method of the XNA's `BoundingSphere` class:

```
boundingSphere.Intersects(activeCamera.Frustum);
```

Finally, whenever the unit moves you must update its bounding sphere. To update the unit's bounding sphere you just need to translate it, because the bounding sphere is not oriented. Following is the code for the UpdateCollision method used to update the collision solids:

```
private void UpdateCollision()
{
    // Update bounding sphere
    boundingSphere = animatedModel.BoundingSphere;
    boundingSphere.Center += Transformation.Translate;

    needUpdateCollision = false;
}
```

Receiving Damage

To allow the unit to receive damage, you'll create the ReceiveDamage method, which receives the damage intensity as a parameter. The code for the ReceiveDamage method follows:

```
public virtual void ReceiveDamage(int damageValue)
{
    life = Math.Max(0, life - damageValue);
    if (life == 0)
        isDead = true;
}
```

When the unit's hit points reach zero, the isDead flag is marked as true. In this case, you can avoid updating this unit. The ReceiveDamage method should be virtual, allowing the units that extend the TerrainUnit class to overwrite this method and, for example, play a death animation for the unit.

Changing Animations

During the game, every time a unit changes its current action (or state) you need to change its animation. For example, the animation used when the unit is idle is different from the animation used when the unit is running. The unit's animated model (AnimatedModel class) has an array that stores all the unit's animations. You can change the unit's animation manually, but to do that, you need to go over all its animations, searching for the desired animation. This is needed because you don't know which animations the unit has, or in which order they were stored.

To ease the swap between animations, you can create an enumeration for the unit's animations inside each class that extends the `TerrainUnit`, where each enumeration lists the available animations of the unit's animated model in the order they were stored. For example, the `Player` class has an enumeration called `PlayerAnimations` and the `Enemy` class has an enumeration called `EnemyAnimations`, as shown in the following code:

```
public enum PlayerAnimations
{
    Idle = 0,
    Run,
    Aim,
    Shoot
}

public enum EnemyAnimations
{
    Idle = 0,
    Run,
    Bite,
    TakeDamage,
    Die
}
```

You use these enumerations to change the current animation of the model. To change the unit's animation you create the `SetAnimation` method in the `TerrainUnit` class. In the `SetAnimation` method, you set the model's animation using an integer value, which is the index of the animation inside the animation's array in the `AnimatedModel` class. However, because you don't know the index of the animations, this method is protected and only the classes that extend the `TerrainUnit` class (`Player` and `Enemy`) use it. Then, in the `Player` and `Enemy` classes you can change the model animation using the `PlayerAnimations` and `EnemyAnimations` enumerations. Following is the code for the `SetAnimation` method of the `TerrainUnit` class:

```
protected void SetAnimation(int animationId,
    bool reset, bool enableLoop, bool waitFinish)
{
    if (reset || currentAnimationId != animationId)
    {
        if (waitFinish && !AnimatedModel.IsAnimationFinished)
            return;

        AnimatedModel.ActiveAnimation =
            AnimatedModel.Animations[animationId];
```

```
        AnimatedModel.EnableAnimationLoop = enableLoop;
        currentAnimationId = animationId;
    }
}
```

The other parameters of the SetAnimation method allow the animation to be reset, looped, or prevent it from being changed before it has finished. Whenever an animation is set, its identifier is stored in the currentAnimationId variable and is used to prevent the current animation from being reset, unless you desire that, by setting the reset parameter as true. Following is the code for the SetAnimation method of the Player class:

```
// Player class
public class Player : TerrainUnit
{
    ... ... ...

    public void SetAnimation(PlayerAnimations animation,
        bool reset, bool enableLoop, bool waitFinish)
    {
        SetAnimation((int)animation, reset, enableLoop, waitFinish);
    }
}
```

And following is the code for the SetAnimation method of the Enemy class:

```
// Enemy class
public class Enemy : TerrainUnit
{
    ... ... ...

    public void SetAnimation(EnemyAnimations animation,
        bool reset, bool enableLoop, bool waitFinish)
    {
        SetAnimation((int)animation, reset, enableLoop, waitFinish);
    }
}
```

The SetAnimation methods created on the Player and Enemy classes allow the unit's animation to be easily switched and guarantee that a valid animation will always be set. The following code illustrates how to change the animation in the Player and Enemy classes:

```
player.SetAnimation(PlayerAnimations.Idle, false, true, false);
enemy.SetAnimation(EnemyAnimations.Run, false, true, false);
```

Drawing the Unit

To draw the unit you just need to call the `Draw` method of the unit's animated model. Because all the unit transformations are stored directly in its animated model, you don't need to configure anything else. Following is the code for the `Draw` method of the `TerrainUnit` class:

```
public override void Draw(GameTime time)
{
    animatedModel.Draw(time);
}
```

Unit Types

The next classes you'll create are `Player`, `Enemy`, and `PlayerWeapon`. You'll use each of these classes to create (or instantiate) different types of units. For example, your game may have many types of enemies (created using the `Enemy` class), where each enemy may have specific attributes such as velocity, hit points, and so on. To tackle this you can create a class that stores the available types of units in the game and the attributes of each unit type.

To store the available types of a unit and its attributes, create a static class named `UnitTypes`. Although you only have one type of each unit in your game—one type of player (a soldier), one type of enemy (an alien spider), and one type of weapon—the `UnitTypes` class allows you to add new unit types to the game easily.

In the `UnitTypes` class, first create an enumeration with all the types of players. For each type of player, you need to store its animated model file name, hit points, and velocity, as shown in the following code:

```
// Player
// ----------------------------------------------------------------
public enum PlayerType
{
    Marine
}

public static string[] PlayerModelFileName = { "PlayerMarine" };
public static int[] PlayerLife = { 100 };
public static float[] PlayerSpeed = { 1.0f };
```

Next, create an enumeration with all the types of player weapons. For each player weapon, you need to store its animated model file name, its maximum amount of ammunition, and the damage of its shot:

```
// Player Weapons
// ----------------------------------------------------------------
public enum PlayerWeaponType
{
    MachineGun
}

public static string[] PlayerWeaponModelFileName =
  {"WeaponMachineGun"};
public static int[] BulletDamage = { 12 };
public static int[] BulletsCount = { 250 };
```

Finally, you create an enumeration with all the types of enemies, where for each enemy you should store the name of its animated model, hit points, velocity, distance of perception, distance of attack, and damage. The distance of perception is the distance in which the enemy perceives the player and starts to chase him, while the distance of attack is the distance in which the enemy is near enough to attack the player.

```
// Enemies
// ----------------------------------------------------------------
public enum EnemyType
{
    Beast
}

public static string[] EnemyModelFileName = { "EnemyBeast" };
public static int[] EnemyLife = { 300 };
public static float[] EnemySpeed = { 1.0f };
public static int[] EnemyPerceptionDistance = { 140 };
public static int[] EnemyAttackDistance = { 25 };
public static int[] EnemyAttackDamage = { 13 };
```

Player Weapon

Now you'll create the PlayerWeapon class, which is one of the simplest logic classes in your game. The player's weapon, just as in the TerrainUnit class, is drawn as an animated model. Although the weapon doesn't have any animation, it does have some bones. Each weapon in the game has three bones. The first one is the root bone, which doesn't have any transformation. The second bone is the weapon's butt bone, used to attach the weapon to the player's hand. Last, the third bone is placed at the weapon's muzzle and is used as the start point for the bullet shot. Figure 12-6 illustrates the player's weapon and the weapon's bones.

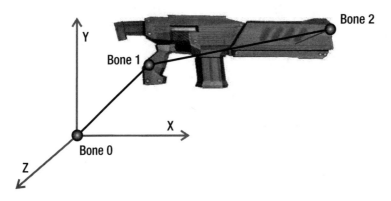

Figure 12-6. *Player's weapon and its bones*

You begin constructing the PlayerWeapon class by declaring its attributes. The PlayerWeapon class needs to store its weapon type, because you might have some different types of weapons in the game. You'll use the PlayerWeaponType enumeration of the UnitsType class to store the weapon type. The PlayerWeapon also stores other attributes, such as the current and maximum number of bullets, and the bullet damage:

```
UnitsType.PlayerWeaponType weaponType;
int maxBullets;
int bulletsCount;
int bulletDamage;
```

In the PlayerWeapon class, you need to store the position and direction in which a bullet exits the weapon (the fire position and direction). You use the fire position and direction to trace the shot ray, used to check whether the bullet hits an object. Finally, you need to declare an AnimatedModel for the weapon:

```
AnimatedModel weaponModel;
Vector3 firePosition;
Vector3 targetDirection;
```

Creating the Player Weapon

The PlayerWeapon class extends the DrawableGameComponent class. So, the PlayerWeapon constructor receives a Game (needed by its base class constructor) and a PlayerWeaponType as the constructor parameters. You use the PlayerWeaponType parameter to define which type of weapon you want to create. Inside the class constructor, the weapon's attributes are queried from the UnitTypes class, according to its weapon type. Following is the constructor code for the PlayerWeapon class:

```
public PlayerWeapon(Game game, UnitTypes.PlayerWeaponType weaponType)
    : base(game)
{
    this.weaponType = weaponType;

    // Weapon configuration
    bulletDamage = UnitTypes.BulletDamage[(int)weaponType];
    bulletsCount = UnitTypes.BulletsCount[(int)weaponType];
    maxBullets = bulletsCount;
}
```

Loading the Player Weapon

You can override the LoadContent method of the PlayerWeapon base class to load the weapon's animated model. You get the file name of the weapon's animated model from the UnitTypes class. Following is the code for the LoadContent method:

```
protected override void LoadContent()
{
    // Load weapon model
    weaponModel = new AnimatedModel(Game);
    weaponModel.Initialize();
    weaponModel.Load(PlayerWeaponModelFileName[(int)weaponType]);

    base.LoadContent();
}
```

Updating the Weapon

To update the weapon, you create a new Update method, which receives a GameTime and a Matrix. You use the GameTime to retrieve the elapsed time since the last update, and the Matrix class to update the weapon model according to a parent bone. The weapon's parent bone is the player's hand bone. In this case, the weapon is translated and rotated to the player's hand. You update the weapon by calling the Update method of its animated model and passing the received GameTime and parent Matrix.

After updating the weapon's animated model, the weapon's fire position—which is the position of its third bone, shown in Figure 12-6—is stored in the firePosition attribute. Following is the code for the Update method:

```
public void Update(GameTime time, Matrix parentBone)
{
    weaponModel.Update(time, parentBone);
```

```
    firePosition = BonesAbsolute[WEAPON_AIM_BONE].Translation;
}
```

Finally, to draw the weapon you just need to call the `Draw` method of its `AnimatedModel`.

Player

In this section you'll create the `Player` class, which has the player's attributes and logic. The `Player` class extends and adds some functionalities to the `TerrainUnit` class. Figure 12-7 shows the marine model used as the game player.

Figure 12-7. *A marine model. Courtesy of Carlos Augusto (http://www.floatbox.com.br).*

In the `Player` class, you first store the type of player you're creating, because you might have some different types of players in the game. You also store the player's weapon, because it is updated according to the player. For example, the player's weapon is always positioned in the player's right hand.

```
// Player type
UnitTypes.PlayerType playerType;
// Player weapon
PlayerWeapon playerWeapon;
```

Next, declare two attributes to store and control the transformations made over the waist bone of the player's animated model. You can use this transformation to rotate the player's torso around his waist:

```
// Waist bone
float rotateWaistBone;
float rotateWaistBoneVelocity;
```

Updating the Camera's Chase Position

The camera's default chase position is the center of the unit's bounding sphere. In this way, the camera is always focusing on the center of the player's model. You can make the camera focus on other parts of the player, such as his upper body, by changing the camera's chase position through an offset vector. Figure 12-8 illustrates the offset vectors used to modify the camera's chase position.

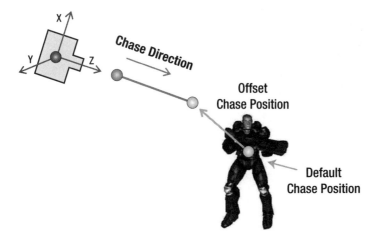

Figure 12-8. *Changing the camera's default chase position using the player's chase vector*

To change the camera's chase position, add a new attribute of type Vector3[] to the Player class, and name it chaseOffsetPosition. This attribute stores an offset vector for each camera in the scene:

```
// Camera chase position
Vector3[] chaseOffsetPosition;
```

Note that you need to manually set the camera offset vectors for the player when he is created. When the player is updated, he needs to update the position and direction in which the camera chases him. To do that, create the UpdateChasePosition method inside the Player class. You can update the camera's chase position by setting it to the center of the player's bounding sphere summed to the camera's offset, which is stored in the player's chaseOffsetPosition attribute. And you can update the camera's chase direction by setting it as the player's heading vector. Note that the camera offset vector is oriented according to the player's orientation vectors (headingVec, strafeVec, and upVec vectors), not the world axes. Following is the code for the UpdateChasePosition method:

```
private void UpdateChasePosition()
{
    ThirdPersonCamera camera = cameraManager.ActiveCamera
        as ThirdPersonCamera;
    if (camera != null)
    {
        // Get camera offset position for the active camera
        Vector3 cameraOffset =
            chaseOffsetPosition[cameraManager.ActiveCameraIndex];
        // Get the model center
        Vector3 center = BoundingSphere.Center;

        // Calculate chase position and direction
        camera.ChasePosition = center +
            cameraOffset.X * StrafeVector +
            cameraOffset.Y * UpVector +
            cameraOffset.Z * HeadingVector;
        camera.ChaseDirection = HeadingVector;
    }
}
```

Attaching a Weapon to the Player

To be able to attach a weapon to the player, create the AttachWeapon method. This method receives the type of weapon to be attached as a parameter. Inside the AttachWeapon method, create and initialize a new PlayerWeapon for the player. Following is the code for the AttachWeapon method:

```
public void AttachWeapon(EntityTypes.PlayerWeaponType weaponType)
{
    playerWeapon = new PlayerWeapon(Game, weaponType);
    playerWeapon.Initialize();
}
```

Aiming Objects

Since the player can aim anywhere in the scenery, he must be able to move his weapon's aim to the sides and also up and down. The player's weapon is connected to the player through a bone in the weapon and a bone in the player's right hand. You can make the player aim to the sides by rotating him around his Y axis, but you can't make the player aim up and down by rotating him around his X axis, because that would make him be off the floor. To solve this, instead of rotating the entire player model, you rotate the player model's upper body around his waist bone. Figure 12-9 illustrates the rotation being applied over the waist bone of the player.

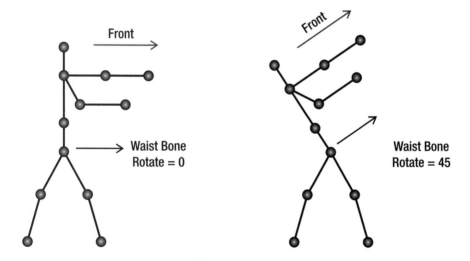

Figure 12-9. *Rotating the waist bone of the player's model*

You use the `rotateWaistBone` and `rotateWaistBoneVelocity` attributes of the `Player` class to apply a rotation over the player's waist bone. The `rotateWaistBone` attribute stores the current waist bone rotation, and the `rotateWaistBoneVelocity` attribute stores the velocity in which the waist bone is being rotated. You can modify the `rotateWaistBoneVelocity` through the player's `RotateWaistVelocity` property. To update the player's waist bone you create the `UpdateWaistBone` method with the following code:

```
static float MAX_WAIST_BONE_ROTATE = 0.50f;
static int WAIST_BONE_ID = 2;

public float RotateWaistVelocity
{
    get { return rotateWaistBoneVelocity; }
    set { rotateWaistBoneVelocity = value; }
}

private void UpdateWaistBone(float elapsedTimeSeconds)
{
    if (rotateWaistBoneVelocity != 0.0f)
    {
        rotateWaistBone += rotateWaistBoneVelocity *
            elapsedTimeSeconds;
        rotateWaistBone = MathHelper.Clamp(rotateWaistBone,
            -MAX_WAIST_BONE_ROTATE, MAX_WAIST_BONE_ROTATE);

        // Rotate waist bone
        Matrix rotate = Matrix.CreateRotationZ(rotateWaistBone);
        AnimatedModel.BonesTransform[WAIST_BONE_ID] = rotate;
    }
}
```

Note that you're clamping the `rotateWaistBone` value, defining a valid rotation range between `-MAX_WAIST_BONE_ROTATE` and `MAX_WAIST_BONE_ROTATE`. The index of the player's waist bone is stored in the `WAIST_BONE_ID` attribute and the waist bone is rotated around its Z axis.

Updating the Player

To update the player, you'll overwrite the `Update` method of the player's base class (`TerrainUnit`). In the `Update` method you first update the transformation of the player's waist bone. Then, you can call the `Update` method of its base class, which updates the player's position and animated model. You must call the `Update` method of the player's base class after the player's waist bone has been transformed, considering the new waist bone configuration when the player's animated model is updated. After that, you need to call the `UpdateChasePosition` method to update the camera's chase position and direction, and finally update the player's weapon.

You update the player's weapon by calling the weapon's Update method and passing the player's right hand bone as the weapon's parent bone. In this way, the weapon is updated according to the player's right hand. You also need to set the weapon's target direction as the player's front direction (as illustrated in Figure 12-9). Note that you need to transform the player's right hand bone by the player's transformation matrix before using it to update the player's weapon. Following is the code for the player's Update methods:

```
public override void Update(GameTime time)
{
    // Update the player's waist bone
    float elapsedTimeSeconds = (float)time.ElapsedGameTime.TotalSeconds;
    UpdateWaistBone(elapsedTimeSeconds);

    // Update player's base class
    // It's where the player's position and animated model are updated
    base.Update(time);
    // Update camera chase position
    UpdateChasePosition();

    // Update player weapon
    Matrix transformedHand = AnimatedModel.BonesAnimation[RIGHT_HAND_BONE_ID] *
        Transformation.Matrix;
    playerWeapon.Update(time, transformedHand);
    playerWeapon.TargetDirection = HeadingVector + UpVector * rotateWaistBone;
}
```

Enemy

The Enemy class is the one that has the enemy NPC's logic and attributes. Figure 12-10 exhibits a spider model used as an enemy in the game.

Figure 12-10. *An alien spider model. Courtesy of Psionic (http://www.psionic3d.co.uk).*

Differently from the player, the enemy is computer controlled, so you need to implement its AI. The enemy's AI is simple, having only four different states: Wandering, Chasing Player, Attacking Player, and Dead. Figure 12-11 shows the diagram of the AI built for the enemies.

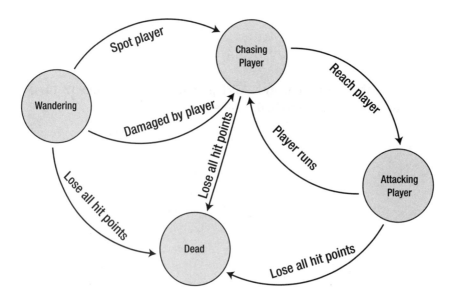

Figure 12-11. *Enemy AI diagram*

In the AI diagram in Figure 12-11, each circle represents a different enemy state, and the arrows represent the actions that make an enemy change its state. The enemy's AI starts in the Wandering state. In this state, the enemy keeps moving around the map randomly looking for the player. Whenever the enemy sees the player or gets shot by the player, he changes his state to Chasing Player. In the Chasing Player state, the enemy moves closer to the player until he is near enough to attack the player. When that happens, the enemy state is altered to Attacking Player. In this state, the enemy attacks the player successively until the player dies or the player runs. If the player tries to run from the enemy, the enemy's state is changed back to Chasing Player. Notice that once the enemy starts to chase the player, the enemy stays in a cycle between the states Chasing Player and Attacking Player, not returning to the Wandering state.

Each enemy has an attribute to store his current state, among an enumeration of possible states.

```
// Possible enemy states
public enum EnemyState
{
    Wander = 0,
    ChasePlayer,
    AttackPlayer,
    Dead
}

// Current enemy state (default = Wander)
EnemyState state;
```

For each one of the possible enemy states you'll declare some attributes and create a method to execute this state. To control the transitions between the enemy states, you'll overwrite the Update method of its base class.

Updating the Enemy

The enemy's Update method manages the transition between the enemy states. For every arrow in the AI state diagram, shown in Figure 12-11, there must be a condition in the Update method.

In the beginning of the Update method you calculate the enemy's chaseVector, which contains the direction from the enemy's position to the player's position. You use the length of this vector to check the distance between the enemy and the player. Then, for each player's state you check if you can execute this state or need to change it to a new state. Notice that all enemies have a reference to the Player class, which is used to obtain the player's current position. Following is the Update method's code:

```
public override void Update(GameTime time)
{
    // Calculate chase vector every time
    chaseVector = player.Transformation.Translate -
        Transformation.Translate;
    float distanceToPlayer = chaseVector.Length();

    switch (state)
    {
        case EnemyState.Wander:
            // Enemy perceives the player - Change state
            if (isHited || distanceToPlayer < perceptionDistance)
                state = EnemyState.ChasePlayer;
            else
                Wander(time);
            break;

        case EnemyState.ChasePlayer:
            // Enemy is near enough to attack - Change state
            if (distanceToPlayer <= attackDistance)
            {
                state = EnemyState.AttackPlayer;
                nextActionTime = 0;
            }
            else
                ChasePlayer(time);
            break;

        case EnemyState.AttackPlayer:
            // Player flees - Change state
            if (distanceToPlayer > attackDistance * 2.0f)
                state = EnemyState.ChasePlayer;
            else
                AttackPlayer(time);
            break;
```

```
        default:
            break;
    }

    base.Update(time);
}
```

Wandering

In the Wandering state, the enemy walks randomly through the map, without a specific goal. To execute this action, you need to generate random positions over the map within a radius from the enemy's actual position and make the enemy move to these positions. Following are the attributes of the Enemy class used by the Wandering state:

```
static int WANDER_MAX_MOVES = 3;
static int WANDER_DISTANCE = 70;
static float WANDER_DELAY_SECONDS = 4.0f;

static float MOVE_CONSTANT = 35.0f;
static float ROTATE_CONSTANT = 100.0f;

// Wander
int wanderMovesCount;
Vector3 wanderStartPosition;
Vector3 wanderPosition;
```

The WANDER_MAX_MOVES variable defines the number of random movements that the enemy makes until he returns to his initial position, and the wanderMovesCount variable stores the number of movements that the unit has already made. You can use these variables to restrict the distance that the enemy could reach from his initial position, forcing him to return to his start position after a fixed number of random movements. Besides that, the WANDER_DELAY_SECONDS variable stores the delay time between each movement of the unit. The WANDER_DISTANCE variable stores the minimum distance that the unit walks in each movement, and the variables wanderStartPosition and wanderPosition store, respectively, the enemy's initial position and destination while in the Wandering state. Finally, MOVE_CONSTANT and ROTATE_CONSTANT store a constant value used to move and rotate the enemy.

To execute the enemy's Wandering state you'll create the Wander method. In the Wander method, you first check if the enemy has already reached his destination position, which is stored in the wanderPosition attribute. To do that, you create a vector from the enemy's position to his destination and use the length of this vector to check the distance between them. If the distance is below a defined epsilon value (for example, 10.0), the enemy has reached his destination and a new destination must be generated:

```
// Calculate wander vector on X, Z axis
Vector3 wanderVector = wanderPosition - Transformation.Translate;
wanderVector.Y = 0.0f;
float wanderLength = wanderVector.Length();

// Reached the destination position
if (wanderVector.Length() < DISTANCE_EPSILON)
{
    // Generate a new wander position
}
```

Note that when the enemy is created, his first destination position is equal to his start position.

If the number of random movements the enemy makes is lower than the maximum number of consecutive random movements that he could make, his new destination position will be a random generated position. Otherwise, the next enemy destination will be his start position.

```
// Generate a new random position
if (wanderMovesCount < WANDER_MAX_MOVES)
{
    wanderPosition = Transformation.Translate +
        RandomHelper.GeneratePositionXZ(WANDER_DISTANCE);
    wanderMovesCount++;
}
// Go back to the start position
else
{
    wanderPosition = wanderStartPosition;
    wanderMovesCount = 0;
}

// Next time wander
nextActionTime = (float)time.TotalGameTime.TotalSeconds +
    WANDER_DELAY_SECONDS + WANDER_DELAY_SECONDS *
    (float)RandomHelper.RandomGenerator.NextDouble();
```

The enemy's random destination position is generated through the GeneratePositionXZ method of your RandomHelper class. After generating the enemy's destination, you also generate a random time used to start moving the enemy to his new destination. Following is the complete code for the Wander method of the Enemy class:

```
private void Wander(GameTime time)
{
    // Calculate wander vector on X, Z axis
    Vector3 wanderVector = wanderPosition - Transformation.Translate;
    wanderVector.Y = 0.0f;
    float wanderLength = wanderVector.Length();

    // Reached the destination position
    if (wanderLength < DISTANCE_EPSILON)
    {
        SetAnimation(EnemyAnimations.Idle, false, true, false);

        // Generate a new random position
        if (wanderMovesCount < WANDER_MAX_MOVES)
        {
            wanderPosition =  Transformation.Translate +
                RandomHelper.GeneratePositionXZ(WANDER_DISTANCE);
            wanderMovesCount++;
        }
        // Go back to the start position
        else
        {
            wanderPosition = wanderStartPosition;
            wanderMovesCount = 0;
        }

        // Next time wander
        nextActionTime = (float)time.TotalGameTime.TotalSeconds +
            WANDER_DELAY_SECONDS + WANDER_DELAY_SECONDS *
            (float)RandomHelper.RandomGenerator.NextDouble();
    }

    // Wait for the next action time
    if ((float)time.TotalGameTime.TotalSeconds > nextActionTime)
    {
        wanderVector *= (1.0f / wanderLength);
        Move(wanderVector);
    }
}
```

At the end of the Wander method, you check if the time for the next wander action has arrived. In this case, you normalize the wanderVector, which contains the direction from the enemy to his destination, and makes the enemy move in this direction through the Move method.

You'll create the Move method to move the enemy from his original position using an arbitrary direction vector. You can move the enemy by setting his linear velocity as the desired direction vector, inside the Move method. Remember that the enemy's position is updated according to his linear velocity by the Update method's base class (TerrainUnit). While moving the unit, you also need to set its angular velocity, heading the unit in the same direction it is moving. Following is the code for the Move method:

```
private void Move(Vector3 direction)
{
    // Change enemy's animation
    SetAnimation(EnemyAnimations.Run, false, true,
        (CurrentAnimation == EnemyAnimations.TakeDamage));
    // Set the new linear velocity
    LinearVelocity = direction * MOVE_CONSTANT;

    // Angle between heading and move direction
    float radianAngle = (float)Math.Acos(
        Vector3.Dot(HeadingVector, direction));
    if (radianAngle >= 0.1f)
    {
        // Find short side to rotate
        // Clockwise (CW) or CCW (Counterclockwise)
        float sideToRotate = Vector3.Dot(StrafeVector, direction);

        Vector3 rotationVector = new Vector3(0, ROTATE_CONSTANT *
            radianAngle, 0);

        if (sideToRotate > 0)
            AngularVelocity = -rotationVector;
        else
            AngularVelocity = rotationVector;
    }
}
```

In the Move method, you first set the linear velocity of the enemy as its direction parameter multiplied by the MOVE_CONSTANT variable. Next, you calculate the angle between the enemy's heading vector and its direction vector. You need this angle to rotate the unit and head it in the same direction it is moving. You can use the Dot method of XNA's Vector3 class to get the cosine of the angle between the enemy's heading vector and its direction vector, and the Acos method of the Math class to get the angle between these vectors from its cosine. After calculating the angle between the enemy's heading and direction, you still need to know from which side to rotate the unit—clockwise (CW) or counterclockwise (CCW). For example, you can find that the angle between the enemy's heading and direction is 90 degrees, but you still don't know from which side to rotate him.

You can find the correct side to rotate the enemy, calculating the cosine of the angle between the enemy's strafe vector—which is perpendicular to the heading vector—and its direction vector. If the cosine is positive, you need to apply a negative rotation on the enemy, making him rotate clockwise; otherwise, you need to apply a positive rotation, making him rotate counterclockwise. The rotation is set as the enemy's AngularVelocity and is multiplied by the ROTATE_CONSTANT variable.

Chasing Player

In the Chasing Player state, the enemy needs to move to the player's current position. You can do this by making the enemy move through the chaseVector vector, which is the direction from the enemy to the player, and is calculated in the enemy's Update method. Following is the code for the ChasePlayer method:

```
private void ChasePlayer(GameTime time)
{
    Vector3 direction = chaseVector;
    direction.Normalize();
    Move(direction);
}
```

Attacking Player

In the Attacking Player state, the enemy keeps attacking the player successively, causing damage to him. To do that, you can simply execute the ReceiveDamage method of the Player instance and wait for the next time to attack. The attributes that you need to create to handle the Attacking Player state is the delay time in seconds between each attack and the time the enemy could execute a new attack action:

```
float nextActionTime;
```

Following is the code for the AttackPlayer method:

```
private void AttackPlayer(GameTime time)
{
    float elapsedTimeSeconds = (float)time.TotalGameTime.TotalSeconds;
    if (elapsedTimeSeconds > nextActionTime)
```

```
    {
        // Set attacking animation
        SetAnimation(EnemyAnimations.Bite, false, true, false);

        // Next attack time
        player.ReceiveDamage(attackDamage);
        nextActionTime = elapsedTimeSeconds + ATTACK_DELAY_SECONDS;
    }
}
```

Finishing the Game Engine

By now you have already created all the game engine classes, helper classes, and almost all the game logic classes. What you have to do now is create a class to control the main game logic, and some classes to store and create the game levels. Besides that, you also need to create the main game class that extends the XNA's Game class. You'll create all these classes in the following sections.

Game Level

Each game level is composed of a fixed set of objects: cameras, lights, a terrain, a sky-dome, a player, and enemies. For the game levels, create a structure named GameLevel inside the GameLogic namespace. Following is the code for the GameLevel struct:

```
public struct GameLevel
{
    // Cameras, Lights, Terrain, and Sky
    public CameraManager CameraManager;
    public LightManager LightManager;
    public Terrain Terrain;
    public SkyDome SkyDome;

    // Player and Enemies
    public Player Player;
    public List<Enemy> EnemyList;
}
```

Creating the Game Levels

In the XNA TPS game, you create the game levels inside the game code, instead of loading them from a file. To do that, create a static class named LevelCreator in the GameLogic namespace. The LevelCreator class is responsible for constructing the game levels and returning a GameLevel structure with the constructed level.

First, create an enumeration inside the LevelCreator class enumerating all the available game levels. You'll use this enumeration further to select the game level to be constructed. Initially, this enumeration has only one entry, as follows:

```
public enum Levels
{
    AlienPlanet
}
```

Next, create a static method named CreateLevel to create the game levels. This method needs to receive an instance of the Game class, because it uses the Game's ContentManager to load the game assets and the Game's ServicesContainer to share some game objects. When the level is created, you add the CameraManager, LightManager, and Terrain to the ServiceContainer of the Game class, sharing these objects with all the scene objects. The CreateLevel method also receives a Levels enumeration containing the desired level to be created. Following is the code for the CreateLevel method:

```
public static GameLevel CreateLevel(Game game, Levels level)
{
    // Remove all services from the last level
    game.Services.RemoveService(typeof(CameraManager));
    game.Services.RemoveService(typeof(LightManager));
    game.Services.RemoveService(typeof(Terrain));

    switch (level)
    {
        case Levels.AlienPlanet:
            return CreateAlienPlanetLevel(game);
            break;

        default:
            throw new ArgumentException("Invalid game level");
            break;
    }
}
```

In the beginning of the CreateLevel method you must try to remove any CameraManager, LightManager, or Terrain objects from the game services container, avoiding adding two instances of these objects to the service container. Then, you use a switch to select the desired level to be created.

The first level of the XNA TPS game is called AlienPlanet. Create the CreateAlienPlanetLevel method to construct this level. Inside the CreateAlienPlanetLevel method, first create the game cameras:

```
float aspectRate = (float)game.GraphicsDevice.Viewport.Width /
    game.GraphicsDevice.Viewport.Height;

// Create the game cameras
ThirdPersonCamera followCamera = new ThirdPersonCamera();
followCamera.SetPerspectiveFov(60.0f, aspectRate, 0.1f, 2000);
followCamera.SetChaseParameters(3.0f, 9.0f, 7.0f, 14.0f);
ThirdPersonCamera fpsCamera = new ThirdPersonCamera();
fpsCamera.SetPerspectiveFov(45.0f, aspectRate, 0.1f, 2000);
fpsCamera.SetChaseParameters(5.0f, 6.0f, 6.0f, 6.0f);

// Create the camera manager and add the game cameras
gameLevel.CameraManager = new CameraManager();
gameLevel.CameraManager.Add("FollowCamera", followCamera);
gameLevel.CameraManager.Add("FPSCamera", fpsCamera);

// Add the camera manager to the service container
game.Services.AddService(typeof(CameraManager),
    gameLevel.CameraManager);
```

You need to create two different game cameras, where each camera is of the type ThirdPersonCamera. The first camera, named FollowPlayer, is used to follow the player, and the second camera, named FPSCamera, is used while the player is in the "aim mode." You need to add both cameras to the CameraManager of the GameLevel structure, and the CameraManager needs to be added to the Game's ServiceContainer. Next, create the game lights:

```
// Create the light manager
gameLevel.LightManager = new LightManager();
gameLevel.LightManager.AmbientLightColor = new Vector3(0.1f);

// Create the game lights and add them to the light manager
gameLevel.LightManager.Add("MainLight",
    new PointLight(new Vector3(10000, 10000, 10000),
    new Vector3(0.2f)));
gameLevel.LightManager.Add("CameraLight",
    new PointLight(Vector3.Zero, Vector3.One));
```

```
// Add the light manager to the service container
game.Services.AddService(typeof(LightManager),
    gameLevel.LightManager);
```

The game level has two lights: a main light positioned at (10000, 10000, 10000), which barely illuminates the scene, and a camera light positioned at the camera position, which highly illuminates the scene. You add these lights to the LightManager, which is also added to the game services container. After creating the camera and lights, you should now create the game's terrain and its material:

```
// Create the terrain
gameLevel.Terrain = new Terrain(game);
gameLevel.Terrain.Initialize();
gameLevel.Terrain.Load("Terrain1", 128, 128, 12.0f, 1.0f);


// Create the terrain material and add it to the terrain
TerrainMaterial terrainMaterial = new TerrainMaterial();
terrainMaterial.LightMaterial = new LightMaterial(
    new Vector3(0.8f), new Vector3(0.3f), 32.0f);
terrainMaterial.DiffuseTexture1 = GetTextureMaterial(
    game, "Terrain1", new Vector2(40, 40));
terrainMaterial.DiffuseTexture2 = GetTextureMaterial(
    game, "Terrain2", new Vector2(25, 25));
terrainMaterial.DiffuseTexture3 = GetTextureMaterial(
    game, "Terrain3", new Vector2(15, 15));
terrainMaterial.DiffuseTexture4 = GetTextureMaterial(
    game, "Terrain4", Vector2.One);
terrainMaterial.AlphaMapTexture = GetTextureMaterial(
    game, "AlphaMap", Vector2.One);
terrainMaterial.NormalMapTexture = GetTextureMaterial(
    game, "Rockbump", new Vector2(128, 128));
gameLevel.Terrain.Material = terrainMaterial;


// Add the terrain to the service container
game.Services.AddService(typeof(Terrain), gameLevel.Terrain);
```

The terrain material is composed of a LightMaterial and some TextureMaterial. After creating the terrain material, you need to set it into the terrain, and you also need to add the terrain to the game services container. In the preceding code you're using the GetTextureMaterial method to ease the creation of the TextureMaterial. The code for the GetTextureMaterial follows:

```
private static TextureMaterial GetTextureMaterial(Game game,
    string textureFilename, Vector2 tile)
{
    Texture2D texture = game.Content.Load<Texture2D>(
        GameAssetsPath.TEXTURES_PATH + textureFilename);
    return new TextureMaterial(texture, tile);
}
```

Now, you create the game's sky:

```
// Create the sky
gameLevel.SkyDome = new SkyDome(game);
gameLevel.SkyDome.Initialize();
gameLevel.SkyDome.Load("SkyDome");
gameLevel.SkyDome.TextureMaterial = GetTextureMaterial(
    game, "SkyDome", Vector2.One);
```

The game's sky also has a `TextureMaterial` that you can create through the `GetTextureMaterial` method. Last, you need to create the game's logic objects, which are the player and the enemies. The code used to create the player follows:

```
// Create the player
gameLevel.Player = new Player(game, UnitTypes.PlayerType.Marine);
gameLevel.Player.Initialize();
gameLevel.Player.Transformation = new Transformation(
    new Vector3(-210, 0, 10), new Vector3(0, 70, 0), Vector3.One);
gameLevel.Player.AttachWeapon(UnitTypes.PlayerWeaponType.MachineGun);

// Player chase camera offsets
gameLevel.Player.ChaseOffsetPosition = new Vector3[2];
gameLevel.Player.ChaseOffsetPosition[0] =
    new Vector3(3.0f, 5.0f, 0.0f);
gameLevel.Player.ChaseOffsetPosition[1] =
    new Vector3(3.0f, 4.0f, 0.0f);
```

After creating the player, you can set his initial position and rotation, modifying his transformation. To add a weapon to the player, you use `AttachWeapon` method. You can also change the default camera's chase position, creating an offset vector in the player for each game camera.

Now it's time to create the game's enemies. Because the game level usually has many enemies, create a method named `ScatterEnemies`, to create the enemies and scatter them through the map:

```
private static List<Enemy> ScatterEnemies(Game game, int numEnemies,
    float minDistance, int distance, Player player)
{
    List<Enemy> enemyList = new List<Enemy>();
    for (int i = 0; i < numEnemies; i++)
    {
        Enemy enemy = new Enemy(game, UnitTypes.EnemyType.Beast);
        enemy.Initialize();

        // Generate a random position with a minimum distance
        Vector3 offset = RandomHelper.GeneratePositionXZ(distance);
        while (Math.Abs(offset.X) < minDistance &&
            Math.Abs(offset.Z) < minDistance)
            offset = RandomHelper.GeneratePositionXZ(distance);

        // Position the enemies around the player
        enemy.Transformation = new Transformation(
            player.Transformation.Translate + offset,
            Vector3.Zero, Vector3.One);

        enemy.Player = player;
        enemyList.Add(enemy);
    }

    return enemyList;
}
```

The ScatterEnemies method receives as its parameter the number of enemies to be
created, the minimum distance from the player that an enemy can be created, the distance used to randomly position the enemies, and an instance of the Player. Inside the
ScatterEnemies method, you generate all the enemies in a loop. For each enemy, you first
generate a random offset vector using the distance parameter, and then check if each
component of this offset vector is bigger than the minDistance parameter. In this case, you
set the enemy's position as the player's position summed to the generated offset vector.
You also need to set a reference to the player in each enemy created. At the end, the
ScatterEnemies method returns a list containing all the enemies created.

You should call the ScatterEnemies method at the end of the CreateAlienPlanet
method, as follows:

```
// Enemies
gameLevel.EnemyList = ScatterEnemies(game, 20, 150, 800,
    gameLevel.Player);
```

Now that you've created all the game level objects, your level is ready to be played.

GameScreen Class

Now it's time to put all the game objects and logic together in a new class named GameScreen. The GameScreen is the main game class, where you define which game map should be loaded, how the player is controlled, and how the scene objects are updated and drawn. In sum, the GameScreen class contains the main update and drawing logic.

You should create the GameScreen class in the main namespace of your game project, the XNA_TPS namespace. The GameScreen class extends the DrawableGameComponent class, allowing it to be added to the GameComponents collection of the Game class. Start the GameScreen class by declaring its attributes:

```
// Game level
LevelCreator.Levels currentLevel;
GameLevel gameLevel;

// Necessary services
InputHelper inputHelper;

// Text
SpriteBatch spriteBatch;
SpriteFont spriteFont;

// Weapon target sprite
Texture2D weaponTargetTexture;
Vector3 weaponTargetPosition;

// Aimed enemy
Enemy aimEnemy;
int numEnemiesAlive;
```

The gameLevel stores the game level that is currently being played, while the currentLevel stores an identifier for the current game level. The inputHelper attribute, of type InputHelper, handles the game inputs. Next, the spriteBatch handles the drawing of the game's UI components, which are sprites; the spriteFont stores a font used to write on the game screen; the weaponTargetTexture stores the sprite of the weapon target; and the weaponTargetPosition stores the position, in world coordinates, that the weapon is aiming at. Finally, aimEnemy stores a reference for the enemy, if any, that the weapon is targeting, and numEnemiesAlive stores the number of enemies alive. After declaring the attributes of the GameScreen class, create its constructor:

```
public GameScreen(Game game, LevelCreator.Levels currentLevel)
    : base(game)
{
    this.currentLevel = currentLevel;
}
```

The constructor for the GameScreen class is simple: it receives an instance of the Game class and an enumeration with the name of the level to be played, which is stored in the class's currentLevel attribute.

Initializing and Loading Content

You can overwrite the Initialize method of the DrawableGameObject class to initialize the game objects and get all the necessary game services:

```
public override void Initialize()
{
    // Get services
    inputHelper = Game.Services.GetService(typeof(InputHelper)) as InputHelper;
    if (inputHelper == null)
        throw new InvalidOperationException("Cannot find an input service");

    base.Initialize();
}
```

In the preceding Initialize method, you're getting a service of type InputHelper from the service container of the Game class, and if the InputHelper service is not present in the service container, you throw an exception. Next, overwrite the LoadContent method to load all the necessary game assets:

```
protected override void LoadContent()
{
    // Create SpriteBatch and add services
    spriteBatch = new SpriteBatch(GraphicsDevice);

    // Font 2D
    spriteFont = Game.Content.Load<SpriteFont>(
        GameAssetsPath.FONTS_PATH + "BerlinSans");

    // Weapon target
    weaponTargetTexture = Game.Content.Load<Texture2D>(
        GameAssetsPath.TEXTURES_PATH + "weaponTarget");
```

```
    // Load game level
    gameLevel = LevelCreator.CreateLevel(Game, currentLevel);

    base.LoadContent();
}
```

In the LoadContent method, you first create the SpriteBatch used to draw the game UI. Then, you load the SpriteFont used to write on the screen and the texture for the weapon's target sprite. Finally, you call the CreateLevel method of the LevelCreator class to generate the game level, which you store in the class's gameLevel attribute.

Game Update

The game update logic is divided into three methods: Update, UpdateInput, and UpdateWeaponTarget, where the main method called to update the game is the Update method. You use the UpdateInput method to handle the user input, and the UpdateWeaponTarget method to check which enemy the player's weapon is targeting.

You create the main update method by overwriting the Update method of the DrawableGameComponent class. In the Update method, you first need to call the UpdateInput method to handle the user input. Then, you call the Update method of all the scene objects that need to be updated. Following is the code for the Update method:

```
public override void Update(GameTime gameTime)
{
    // Restart game if the player dies or kill all enemies
    if (gameLevel.Player.IsDead || numEnemiesAlive == 0)
        gameLevel = LevelCreator.CreateLevel(Game, currentLevel);

    UpdateInput();

    // Update player
    gameLevel.Player.Update(gameTime);
    UpdateWeaponTarget();

    // Update camera
    BaseCamera activeCamera = gameLevel.CameraManager.ActiveCamera;
    activeCamera.Update(gameTime);

    // Update light position
    PointLight cameraLight = gameLevel.LightManager["CameraLight"]
        as PointLight;
    cameraLight.Position = activeCamera.Position;
```

```
    // Update scene objects
    gameLevel.SkyDome.Update(gameTime);
    gameLevel.Terrain.Update(gameTime);

    // Update enemies
    foreach (Enemy enemy in gameLevel.EnemyList)
    {
        if (enemy.BoundingSphere.Intersects(activeCamera.Frustum) ||
            enemy.State == Enemy.EnemyState.ChasePlayer ||
            enemy.State == Enemy.EnemyState.AttackPlayer)

            enemy.Update(gameTime);

    }

    base.Update(gameTime);
}
```

Note that the order in which you update the objects is important. After reading the user input, you need to update the game's player. The player updates his position, the position that the camera uses to chase him, and the position of his weapon. So, after the player has been updated, you can call the UpdateWeaponTarget method to update the enemy that the player's weapon is targeting, and you can also update the camera. After updating the camera, you can update the position of the point light that is placed in the same position as the camera. To do that, you just need to set the light position as the new camera position. Last, you should update the game terrain, sky, and enemies. Note that you don't need to update all the enemies in the scene; you can update only the visible enemies or the ones that are chasing or attacking the player.

Controlling the Player

To handle the user input and the player controls, you create a separate method named UpdateInput. Inside the UpdateInput method, you handle each player action as described in the section "Gameplay" in the beginning of this chapter. The player has two different types of controls: the normal player controls, and the "aim mode" controls.

While the user holds the left shoulder button of the gamepad, the player is in the aim mode and cannot move. In the aim mode, the left analog stick of the gamepad is used to move the player's weapon target and the A button is used to fire. The following code handles the player controls while in the aim mode:

```
ThirdPersonCamera fpsCamera = gameLevel.CameraManager[
    "FPSCamera"] as ThirdPersonCamera;
ThirdPersonCamera followCamera = gameLevel.CameraManager[
    "FollowCamera"] as ThirdPersonCamera;

Player player = gameLevel.Player;
Vector2 leftThumb = inputHelper.GetLeftThumbStick();

// Aim Mode
if (inputHelper.IsKeyPressed(Buttons.LeftShoulder)&&
    player.IsOnTerrain)
{
    // Change active camera if needed
    if (gameLevel.CameraManager.ActiveCamera != fpsCamera)
    {
        gameLevel.CameraManager.SetActiveCamera("FPSCamera");
        fpsCamera.IsFirstTimeChase = true;
        player.SetAnimation(Player.PlayerAnimations.Aim,
            false, false, false);
    }

    // Rotate the camera and move the player's weapon target
    fpsCamera.EyeRotateVelocity = new Vector3(leftThumb.Y * 50, 0, 0);
    player.LinearVelocity = Vector3.Zero;
    player.AngularVelocity = new Vector3(0, -leftThumb.X * 70, 0);
    player.RotateWaistVelocity = leftThumb.Y * 0.8f;

    // Fire
    if (inputHelper.IsKeyJustPressed(Buttons.A) &&
        player.Weapon.BulletsCount > 0)
    {
        // Wait for the last shoot animation to finish
        if (player.AnimatedModel.IsAnimationFinished)
        {
            player.SetAnimation(Player.PlayerAnimations.Shoot,
                true, false, false);

            // Damage the enemy
            player.Weapon.BulletsCount--;
            if (aimEnemy != null)
                aimEnemy.ReceiveDamage(
                player.Weapon.BulletDamage);
```

```
        }
    }
}
```

Every time the player mode is changed, you change the camera used to view him, and when the camera is changed you need to set its IsFirstTimeChase property as true. Next, you use the left analog stick to control the player's angular velocity, the player's waist bone rotation velocity, and the camera's rotation velocity. When the player aims up and down you rotate the camera and the player's waist bone, and when the player aims to the sides (left and right) you rotate the camera and the player. Finally, when the fire button is pressed you first check if the player's weapon has any bullets. In this case, he fires a bullet at the aimed object. Here, you're using the duration time of the fire animation as a delay for the fire action. So, the player can only fire again after the last fire animation has finished.

If the player is not in the aim mode, he is in the normal mode. In the normal mode the left analog stick of the gamepad is used to rotate the player to the sides and the camera up and down, while the A and B buttons move the player forward and backward. Also, clicking the left analog stick makes the player jump, as shown in the following code:

```
// Normal Mode
else
{
    bool isPlayerIdle = true;

    // Change active camera if needed
    if (gameLevel.CameraManager.ActiveCamera != followCamera)
    {
        // Reset fps camera
        gameLevel.CameraManager.SetActiveCamera("FollowCamera");
        followCamera.IsFirstTimeChase = true;
        player.RotateWaist = 0.0f;
        player.RotateWaistVelocity = 0.0f;
    }

    followCamera.EyeRotateVelocity = new Vector3(leftThumb.Y * 50, 0, 0);
    player.AngularVelocity = new Vector3(0, -leftThumb.X * 70, 0);

    // Run foward
    if (inputHelper.IsKeyPressed(Buttons.X))
    {
        player.SetAnimation(Player.PlayerAnimations.Run, false, true, false);
        player.LinearVelocity = player.HeadingVector * 30;
        isPlayerIdle = false;
```

```
    }
    // Run backward
    else if (inputHelper.IsKeyPressed(Buttons.A))
    {
        player.SetAnimation(Player.PlayerAnimations.Run,
            false, true, false);
        player.LinearVelocity = -player.HeadingVector * 20;
        isPlayerIdle = false;
    }
    else
        player.LinearVelocity = Vector3.Zero;

    // Jump
    if (inputHelper.IsKeyJustPressed(Buttons.LeftStick))
    {
        player.Jump(2.5f);
        isPlayerIdle = false;
    }

    if (isPlayerIdle)
        player.SetAnimation(Player.PlayerAnimations.Idle,
            false, true, false);
}
```

Updating the Weapon Target

The last method used to update the game is the UpdateWeaponTarget method. In this method you need to check the nearest enemy that the player's weapon is targeting. To do that, you trace a ray starting at the muzzle of the player's weapon, with the same direction as the heading vector of the player's weapon. Then, you check the collision between this ray and the bounding box of each enemy, and store the enemy that is nearest to the player's weapon. Finally, you calculate the position, in world coordinates, that is used to draw the sprite of the weapon's target and store it in the weaponTargetPosition variable. Following is the code for the UpdateWeaponTarget method:

```
private void UpdateWeaponTarget()
{
    aimEnemy = null;
    numEnemiesAlive = 0;
```

```
    // Fire ray
    Ray ray = new Ray(gameLevel.Player.Weapon.FirePosition,
        gameLevel.Player.Weapon.TargetDirection);

    // Distance from the ray start position to the terrain
    float? distance = gameLevel.Terrain.Intersects(ray);

    // Test intersection with enemies
    foreach (Enemy enemy in gameLevel.EnemyList)
    {
        if (!enemy.IsDead)
        {
            numEnemiesAlive++;

            float? enemyDistance = enemy.BoxIntersects(ray);
            if (enemyDistance != null &&
                (distance == null || enemyDistance < distance))
            {
                distance = enemyDistance;
                aimEnemy = enemy;
            }
        }
    }

    // Weapon target position
    weaponTargetPosition = gameLevel.Player.Weapon.FirePosition +
        gameLevel.Player.Weapon.TargetDirection * 300;
}
```

Drawing the Scene

You overwrite the Draw method of the GameScreen base class to add your drawing code. You can separate the drawing code in two parts, where you first draw the 3-D scene objects, and then the 2-D objects (such as text and sprites). Following is the code to draw the 3-D scene objects:

```
GraphicsDevice.Clear(Color.Black);
BaseCamera activeCamera = gameLevel.CameraManager.ActiveCamera;

gameLevel.SkyDome.Draw(gameTime);
gameLevel.Terrain.Draw(gameTime);
gameLevel.Player.Draw(gameTime);
```

```
// Draw enemies
foreach (Enemy enemy in gameLevel.EnemyList)
{
    if (enemy.BoundingSphere.Intersects(activeCamera.Frustum))
        enemy.Draw(gameTime);
}
```

First, you clear the screen before drawing anything on it, and then you call the Draw method of all the scene objects to draw them. Note that the order in which you draw the scene objects here is not important. Next, you need to draw the 2-D objects, which are the UI objects. You draw all these objects using the XNA's SpriteBatch class. Following is the code to draw the game's UI:

```
spriteBatch.Begin(SpriteBlendMode.AlphaBlend,
    SpriteSortMode.Deferred, SaveStateMode.SaveState);

// Project weapon target
weaponTargetPosition = GraphicsDevice.Viewport.Project(weaponTargetPosition,
    activeCamera.Projection, activeCamera.View, Matrix.Identity);

// Draw weapon target
int weaponRectangleSize = GraphicsDevice.Viewport.Width / 40;
if (activeCamera == gameLevel.CameraManager["FPSCamera"])
    spriteBatch.Draw(weaponTargetTexture, new Rectangle(
        (int)(weaponTargetPosition.X - weaponRectangleSize * 0.5f),
        (int)(weaponTargetPosition.Y - weaponRectangleSize * 0.5f),
        weaponRectangleSize, weaponRectangleSize),
        (aimEnemy == null)? Color.White : Color.Red);

// Draw text
Player player = gameLevel.Player;
spriteBatch.DrawString(spriteFont, "Health: " + player.Life + "/" +
    player.MaxLife, new Vector2(10, 5), Color.Green);
spriteBatch.DrawString(spriteFont, "Weapon bullets: " +
    player.Weapon.BulletsCount + "/" + player.Weapon.MaxBullets,
    new Vector2(10, 25), Color.Green);
spriteBatch.DrawString(spriteFont, "Enemies Alive: " +
    numEnemiesAlive + "/" + gameLevel.EnemyList.Count,
    new Vector2(10, 45), Color.Green);

spriteBatch.End();

base.Draw(gameTime);
```

You should place all the code used to draw the 2-D objects between the Begin and End methods of the SpriteBatch class. The SpriteBatch changes some render states before drawing the 2-D objects. Because you don't want to care about the changed states, you can make the SpriteBatch restore them for you after the objects have been drawn. To do that, you need to call the Begin method of the SpriteBatch, passing its third parameter as the SaveStateMode.SaveState. The first and second parameters passed to the SpriteBatch's Begin method are the default parameters.

Next, you need to draw the weapon's target sprite. However, before you can draw it, you need to transform its position from world coordinates to screen coordinates. To do that, you can project the weapon's target position on the screen using the Project method of the Viewport class. In this case, you need to call this method from the Viewport property of the current GraphicsDevice. After that, you just need to scale the sprite, turning it independently from the screen resolution. Finally, you use the DrawString method of the SpriteBatch class and the SpriteFont that you have loaded to draw the player's health, number of weapon bullets, and number of remaining enemies in the map.

TPSGame Class

The last class you create is the TPSGame class, which extends the Game class and is the main game class. Start the TPSGame class, declaring its attributes:

```
GraphicsDeviceManager graphics;
InputHelper inputHelper;
```

The GraphicsDeviceManager attribute is responsible for creating and managing the GraphicsDevice for the game. Also, you use the InputHelper attribute to handle the user input. Now, create the constructor for the TPSGame class:

```
public TPSGame()
{
    Window.Title = "XNA TPS v1.0";
    Content.RootDirectory = "Content";

    // Creating and configuring graphics device
    GameSettings gameSettings = SettingsManager.Read(
        Content.RootDirectory + "/" + GameAssetsPath.SETTINGS_PATH +
        "GameSettings.xml");
    graphics = new GraphicsDeviceManager(this);
    ConfigureGraphicsManager(gameSettings);

    // Input helper
    inputHelper = new InputHelper(PlayerIndex.One,
        SettingsManager.GetKeyboardDictionary(
```

```
        gameSettings.KeyboardSettings[0]));
    Services.AddService(typeof(InputHelper), inputHelper);

    // Game Screen
    Components.Add(new GameScreen(this,
        LevelCreator.Levels.AlienPlanet));
}
```

In the class constructor, you first set the game screen title and the root directory of the content manager. Next, you read the game settings from an XML file, using the SettingsManager class, and use the game settings to configure the GraphicsDeviceManager and the InputHelper. After reading the game settings, you create the GraphicsDeviceManager and call the ConfigureGraphicsManager method, passing a struct with the GameSettings that have been read, to configure it. After that, you create the InputHelper, and use the KeyboardSettings of the GameSettings to configure it. Last, you create a GameScreen and add it to the Components of the Game class. After you've added the GameScreen to the Components of the Game class, it will be updated and drawn automatically when needed. Following is the code for the ConfigureGraphicsManager method that you used to configure the GraphicsDeviceManager:

```
private void ConfigureGraphicsManager(GameSettings gameSettings)
{
#if XBOX360
    graphics.PreferredBackBufferWidth =
        GraphicsAdapter.DefaultAdapter.CurrentDisplayMode.Width;
    graphics.PreferredBackBufferHeight =
        GraphicsAdapter.DefaultAdapter.CurrentDisplayMode.Height;
    graphics.IsFullScreen = true;
#else
    graphics.PreferredBackBufferWidth =
        gameSettings.PreferredWindowWidth;
    graphics.PreferredBackBufferHeight =
        gameSettings.PreferredWindowHeight;
    graphics.IsFullScreen = gameSettings.PreferredFullScreen;
#endif

    // Minimum shader profile required
    graphics.MinimumVertexShaderProfile = ShaderProfile.VS_2_0;
    graphics.MinimumPixelShaderProfile = ShaderProfile.PS_2_A;
}
```

In the ConfigureGraphicsManager method, if the current platform is the Xbox 360 you set the width and height of the screen's buffer as the width and height of the current display adapter. Otherwise, you set the width and height of the screen's buffer according to the GameSettings parameter. Last, you check if the current video card supports the shader model 2.0.

Summary

In this chapter you learned how to create a simple but complete TPS game. In the beginning of the chapter we quickly reviewed some examples of commercial FPS and TPS games. Then, based on this review, you created a basic design for your game, divided into defining the game, gameplay, and technical design parts. After that, you started to develop the game code, which was divided into three main namespaces: GameBase, GameLogic, and Helpers. In the GameBase namespace, you created all the classes for the game engine, some of which you created in the previous chapters. Then, you created all the helper classes in the Helpers namespace and all the game logic classes in the GameLogic namespace. After that, you created a LevelCreator class to create your game levels, and finally, you put it all together by creating a GameScreen class that handles the main game update and drawing logic.

■ ■ ■

CHAPTER 13

Closing Words

If you've reached this page, you've probably read the entire book, and now are probably wondering what the next steps are: what to do to sharpen your XNA knowledge further to create the next generation of games. That's the purpose of these last pages: to give you some insights and tips on where to go from here.

Before we do so, we'd like to thank you for your confidence in buying our book, and we hope that you had as much fun playing around with the samples and games as we did writing them.

If you didn't have fun, please get in touch with Apress and tell us what we can do better, so our next books can better suit your expectations and needs. You can find our contact information at http://www.apress.com.

Where You Are Now . . .

At this point, you should have (at least) two games: one simple 2-D game with some network features, and a simple 3-D game. Most importantly, by this time you should be familiar with game programming terms and have a basic knowledge of the XNA framework.

Creating neat game samples is good, but the games in this book are solely meant to provide you with practical examples of how to apply the basic knowledge you have about XNA to a real game. You'll find an improved version of the 3-D shooter at Bruno's site, at http://www.brunoevangelista.com; you can find some tutorials, news, and samples at José Leal's site, http://www.sharpgames.net (this last one only in Portuguese).

We do recommend that you go back and have a quick look at each chapter's summary, so you can refresh your memory about everything you saw, and note topics that you didn't understand well or want to revise.

Remember: you can always find the most recent code and any text or code errata in the Source Code/Download area of the Apress web site at http://www.apress.com. All you have to do is to look for the book's name.

When you're sure that you've gotten everything you could from this book, you can proceed further.

Where Do You Go from Here?

If you search for "XNA" in any common Internet search engine, you'll find (as of February, 2008) around two million hits. When you narrow down to an "XNA Tutorial" search, you get about half a million results, without quotation marks, and about ten thousand results when searching with quotation marks.

If you've ever tried to choose anything from among one thousand possibilities, you know that even one thousand is just too much information for a person to process—so forget about searching the Internet for your next steps, unless you know exactly what you need!

If you need good examples, `http://creators.XNA.com` is always your starting point; that site has samples for almost anything you'll need to create your 2-D or 3-D games. `http://www.codeplex.com` is also a good source for XNA projects, including some open source game engines and components.

But if there's a single piece of advice we can ask you to follow, it is that you don't start by analyzing samples or by trying to collect code on the Internet to create your own game engine, including everything you might need for a game. Too many people out there are creating samples, components, and game engines with XNA, and too few are creating real games, even simple ones.

So if you really want to learn XNA, start by creating a game on your own. Of course you can—and are encouraged to—write original games, but as a start we'd recommend a simple but fairly interesting game: Tetris.

If you start from the ground up and create your own version of Tetris, you'll exercise many concepts you'll use in every one of your future games: using the `Update` method of the `Game` class to detect collisions and update the game state (make the blocks fall); creating a set of classes with different behaviors (each block turns in a different way) but which share a common ground (every block falls), allowing you to create a hierarchy with a base and derived classes; dealing with user input; coding for game end and game scoring; and so on.

Besides exercising many common basic concepts, creating an XNA Tetris clone is also a good choice because you can create it within a couple weeks, so you can stay motivated for your next challenge. It also allows you to get a whole new insight about the difficulty of creating a game from the ground up, so you can have a proper feeling about the complexity of such a task and how each of the game components fits together.

After creating your Tetris clone, the next step could be a game that uses the same concepts, but includes some extra challenges, such as creating a breakout clone or a pinball game. In such games, you'd be using the concepts from Tetris, plus sound, some advanced-mode collision detection algorithms, and including some animated sprites.

An interesting variant of this second step should be creating a simple 3-D game, such as a 3-D version of Tetris, breakout, or pinball. Such games are interesting because although they use 3-D objects, you can still use simplified, 2-D–like versions of the collision detection algorithm.

After that, we suggest you create a network-enabled version of the Pong game: the game logic and graphics are simple, so you can concentrate on the networking details.

All these games are simple, and creating them will keep you motivated while you learn how to apply game concepts to real examples.

The next step is to create a game that involves some artificial intelligence concepts, such as a Pac-Man clone. Look for "A-Star path finding algorithm" on the Internet and you'll find many implementations of this algorithm, which guides the ghosts through the labyrinth right to the player character.

When you finish this . . . well, you get the idea. Start by defining your goal—a simple but complete game—and stick with it until you're done. Don't choose too bold an objective, or you might get tired of programming before your game is done. If you can't think about an original game at this point, don't worry—simply create a clone for a well-known game.

After your first game, keep on choosing new simple games, so each new one explores new concepts.

And keep on creating new games, looking for bright new ideas, looking for new concepts in game creation. But never forget the golden rule for any game: a game, no matter how simple or how sophisticated it is, must be fun. So keep on playing, keep on coding, and you'll be on the right track!

Happy XNA coding!

Index

You Need the Companion eBook

Your purchase of this book entitles you to buy the companion PDF-version eBook for only $10. Take the weightless companion with you anywhere.

We believe this Apress title will prove so indispensable that you'll want to carry it with you everywhere, which is why we are offering the companion eBook (in PDF format) for $10 to customers who purchase this book now. Convenient and fully searchable, the PDF version of any content-rich, page-heavy Apress book makes a valuable addition to your programming library. You can easily find and copy code—or perform examples by quickly toggling between instructions and the application. Even simultaneously tackling a donut, diet soda, and complex code becomes simplified with hands-free eBooks!

Once you purchase your book, getting the $10 companion eBook is simple:

1. Visit

2. Co
   ge

3. A
   r   ok.

ookshop

Offer valid through 10/08.